THE PRIMACY OF PERSONS
AND THE LANGUAGE OF CULTURE

THE PRIMACY OF PERSONS AND THE LANGUAGE OF CULTURE

Essays by
William H. Poteat

Edited and with an Introduction by
James M. Nickell and James W. Stines

University of Missouri Press   Columbia and London

Library of Congress Cataloging-in-Publication Data

Poteat, William H.
    The primacy of persons and the language of culture : essays / by
William H. Poteat ; edited and with an introduction by James M.
Nickell and James W. Stines.
        p.   cm.
    Includes index.
    ISBN 0–8262–0919–X
    1. Personalism.   2. Language and languages—Philosophy.
3. Knowledge, Theory of.   4. Philosophy and religion.   I. Nickell,
James M., 1930–   . II. Stines, James W., 1934–   . III. Title.
B945.P69   1993
191—dc20   93–14356
                                                            CIP

Designer: Kristie Lee
Typesetter: Connell-Zeko Type & Graphics
Printer and Binder: Thomson-Shore, Inc.
Typefaces: Galliard, Avant Garde and Avant Garde Condensed

To the convivial order of the friends and students of W. H. P. who have been inspired by his teaching and writing in the pursuit of their own visions of the primacy of persons

CONTENTS

PART THREE   The Ambivalent Language of Culture

PART FOUR   Freedom, Faith, and the House of Intellect

ACKNOWLEDGMENTS

We wish to express our appreciation to the following persons and agencies without whose aid and support this effort could not have come to fruition: St. Mary's College in St. Mary's City, Maryland, where James M. Nickell is Professor of Political Science; Appalachian State University (ASU) in Boone, North Carolina, where James W. Stines is Professor of Philosophy and Religion; Delores Ellis, for long hours of work in the transcription of the articles onto disks; Gail Dean, of St. Mary's College, who typed and retyped the manuscript several times; Tim Fox, of the University of Missouri Press, who copyedited the manuscript; the Cratis Williams Graduate School at ASU, for supplying stenographic assistance; the ASU College of Arts and Sciences, for twice awarding release time for work on this project; the many journals and publishers who have generously granted permission to reprint these essays (specific bibliographic information appears on the first page of each essay); and, of course, William H. Poteat, for his cooperation in the preparation of the manuscript and for his permission to reprint the essays "Psychoanalytic Theory and Theistic Belief," "Notes on Ricoeur on Freud" (previously unpublished), and "Moustakas within His Ambience."

OTHER MAJOR WORKS
OF WILLIAM H. POTEAT

Books

Intellect and Hope: Essays in the Thought of Michael Polanyi. Edited with Thomas A. Langford. (Durham: Duke University Press, 1968).

A Philosophical Daybook: Post-Critical Investigations (Columbia: University of Missouri Press, 1990).

Polanyian Meditations: In Search of a Post-Critical Logic (Durham: Duke University Press, 1985).

Recovering the Ground: A Philosophical Essay in Recollection (Albany: State University of New York Press, forthcoming)

Essays

"The Banality of Evil: The Darkness at the Center." Loy H. Witherspoon Lectures in Religious Studies, November 1988. (University of North Carolina at Charlotte Department of Religious Studies)

"For Whom Is the Real Existence of Values a Problem: Or, An Attempt to Show that the Obvious Is Plausible." In *Mind, Values, and Culture: Essays in Honor of E. M. Adams,* edited by David Wiessbord (Atascadero, CA: Ridgeview Publishing Co., 1989).

"Memory and Imagination." *Listening: Journal of Religion and Culture* (forthcoming).

"The Supreme Court of Iowa vs. Wild Oats." Maine Law Review 18.2 (1966): 173–85.

"The University and the Unknown God." In *The Christian Student and the University,* edited by J. Robert Nelson (New York: Association Press, 1952).

THE PRIMACY OF PERSONS
AND THE LANGUAGE OF CULTURE

INTRODUCTION

I

The following essays represent the first part of an intellectual adventure by William Poteat, which, we the editors believe, is relevant to everyone interested in the circumstances and conditions of our times. We emphasize at the outset that the adventure does not end with these pages; it has been carried forward in Poteat's later books, *Polanyian Meditations* (1985) and *A Philosophical Daybook* (1990), written long after some of these essays were completed, in which he undertakes the development of a post-critical logic. The former was greeted by Professor Richard Gelwick as fittingly placed "alongside the most seminal works of this century." Future works by Poteat will further develop issues and problems that he first adumbrated in the essays making up this collection.[1] This collection of essays, then, should be understood as in some sense a kind of prolegomenon for anyone wishing to study his more recent work.

At the same time, we believe that this collection, part of which is previously unpublished, is valuable in its own right. Our hope is that it will enable readers to enter empathically into Poteat's effort to cut through the layers of the Western philosophic tradition, particularly its Enlightenment accretions, to find a place on which we can stand and from which it is possible for us to apprehend the foundation on which to assert the value, validity, and worth of

---

1. Poteat has recently completed another work, entitled *Recovering the Ground: A Philosophical Essay in Recollection*, which is awaiting publication. In addition, there are new articles scheduled for publication.

the human person. It is the belief and concern of the editors that the rich, provocative, and highly relevant culture-critique and constructive reflection that the present collection represents should become more widely and readily available.

These essays should be of interest not only to the generations of professors and other professionals who received key inspiration as Poteat's students, but in turn, to their students and, more importantly, to all who take the tasks of theological and philosophical reflection seriously as these relate to each other and to: foundational cultural assumptions about language and the sources of knowledge, some of the basic verificationist puzzles that have haunted more than a few of theology's most cherished concepts, an educational philosophy centrally informed by the reality of persons, and the background of Poteat's subsequent works.

However, we would be less than candid if we did not warn the reader here at the beginning that the journey that he or she will undertake in these pages is not an easy one. And that for several reasons. In the first place, these essays, even when taken together, do not constitute a systematic and detailed exposition of Poteat's "formative ideas" that could easily be placed alongside the ideas of other thinkers (or even his later ideas) for purposes of comparison and contrast. The temptation is almost overwhelming to seek for an explicit and ordered formulation of a thinker's ideas. For how else can we be expected to evaluate the relevance and import of those ideas? But these essays do not yield themselves to this pressure for reasons that we hope to show later in this introduction. Suffice it to say that the critique of modernity that is at issue here is too radical, too encompassing, to fit into traditional modes of approach. Attempts to do so are almost bound to distort the significance of these pieces. Hence patience is required for that vision of the whole which unites the parts.

A second reason why the enterprise may be difficult for some readers is the wide range of topics that are covered and the degrees of difficulty that the reader will encounter in reading the essays. We understand that different readers will approach the readings with different interests and concerns. Some will be accomplished scholars with a sophisticated understanding of the language used, as well as the issues and concerns involved in the most apparently simple and straightforward of the essays as well as the most technical ones found here. Some readers may be more interested, for example, in the content of the explicitly theological essays. Still others may be more concerned with the articles focusing on some basic ambiguities that lie at the heart of our modern Western culture. And we hope that students relatively new to the issues raised here will also find these writings rewarding and revealing. Later in this introduction we will suggest some ways in which various readers may wish to approach the collection. However the essays are appropriated, however difficult some selections may be for the average reader, we believe that the effort to enter into them will yield new and important insights into what it means to be a human being in our time.

One reason for our issuing this warning of difficulties ahead is to enter our own disclaimer of having provided in this introduction a comprehensive overview of the variety of issues contained in the selected essays. Our intention is the somewhat more modest one of attempting to focus and give context to some of the central topics and concerns that animate them. A number of other important though less pivotal theses and themes than the ones we discuss here reverberate throughout the essays; but their mood and motivation remain informed by those at the center.

However difficult they are to articulate in a way at once brief and intelligible, these theses have occupied Poteat's intellectual commitment from the earliest to the most recent days of his teaching and writing. The energy and penetration and the deeply personal and global relevance of his pursuits have electrified and energized a host of undergraduate and graduate students who have taken those pursuits into the center of their own reflections, lives, and careers. Having issued our caveat and circumscribed our task, we turn our attention to the venture of elucidation.

II

First, a word needs to be said about Poteat himself. From 1960 to his retirement in 1987, William Poteat taught in the religion department of Duke University. Although he held several titles while he was there, his last was professor of religion and comparative studies. For the three years before 1960, he taught at the Episcopal Theological Seminary of the Southwest in Austin, Texas; and for ten years before going to Austin he served his academic apprenticeship in the philosophy department of the University of North Carolina at Chapel Hill. He earned his A.B. at Oberlin in 1941, his B.D. at Yale in 1944, and his Ph.D. at Duke in 1951. He has also held visiting professorships at Stanford University and the University of Texas, served for a number of years on the editorial board of the *Christian Scholar,* received numerous academic honors, and participated in the usual complement of lectureships, colloquia, consultations, and conferences that one expects of a widely known and active professional scholar.

The recitation of these bare facts, however, runs the risk of hiding the diversity of his interests, his standing as a teacher, and the devotion that many of his students came to have for him. Indicative of this devotion is the fact that for ten years many of his students, from both the academic and nonacademic world and from across the entire country, came together for an annual three-day symposium in the mountains of North Carolina in order to continue the dialogue into which they had entered with Poteat. Poteat was a particularly dynamic teacher who was able to engage generations of students with issues that were at once deeply personal and universally relevant.

Perhaps the reason for Poteat's impact on his students was most cogently expressed by Poteat himself. Early in his teaching career, he noted that

> my evolving personal style of pedagogy came to be dialectical. In introductory courses, I was increasingly struck in the midst of philosophical give and take by the incongruity between, on the one hand, the most radical conceptual commitments of my students, and, on the other, their express beliefs. I found, for example, that while tacitly, by an acritically received cultural inheritance, they were Marxists, Freudians, Darwinians, neo-behaviorists, or what have you, their explicit professions were different from and incompatible with these views, even though this was almost never recognized by them. Indeed, on the contrary, when these radical commitments were expressly presented to them as their own, most students initially rejected most of them out of hand—until they were rendered mute by the dialetically disclosed fact that they *were*.[2]

In this context one of the motifs of Poteat's pedagogy in writing, as in the classroom, was to elicit clarification of what sort of acts of personal subscription are required for the consistent holding of such explicitly attested beliefs and, indirectly, to create pressure, in the absence of the student's will or ability to provide such underwriting, to track down alternatives and their implications. Hence there was throughout his classes and there is throughout

2. "Religion and Culture as I See It: Being a Small Down-Payment on Collegiality" (Unpublished paper).

these essays a pervasive ironic mood exposing the contradiction between explicitly claimed theory or belief and de facto existential entanglement. The comprehension of such contradictions, of course, as the world has known since Socrates, is an exercise in therapy in the best sense of that word.

Within recent years Poteat's work has begun to be more widely known professionally. The North Carolina Religious Studies Association dedicated its 1985 program to a consideration of Poteat's work; there was a special session on his *Polanyian Meditations* at the 1986 national meeting of the American Academy of Religion; in 1987, the Southeastern Regional Meeting of the American Academy of Religion made "William H. Poteat's Philosophy of Religion" a theme of the section on philosophy of religion and theology, and the Central States Regional Meeting of 1988 also had a section on his work.

For many years Poteat was most widely known, for good reason, as one of the foremost American expositors of the work of Michael Polanyi. Poteat has been a student of Polanyi since the early fifties, having found in him a scholar who was making a radical critique that was profoundly correlated to the one that he himself was seeking to make.[3] With the publication of *Polanyian Meditations* and *A Philosophical Daybook*, it is now widely recognized that Poteat has emerged on his own as an important and seminal post-critical thinker. And it is the hope of the editors that this collection of his essays will help in making his work more readily available to the American public.

---

3. In the introduction to *Polanyian Meditations* Poteat describes how the discovery in 1952 of some early writings of Polanyi "accredited and greatly enriched the context within which initially to obey my own intimations." He then goes on to say that his meeting with Polanyi in Manchester in 1955 was full of excitement for them both and that following the meeting he took a typescript of Polanyi's *Personal Knowledge: Towards a Post-Critical Philosophy* (Chicago: University of Chicago Press, 1958) with him on the train to Sheffield and read it with mounting excitement. The chapter on "Connoisseurship" in particular proved to be "rich nourishment for my post-critical instincts."

Explaining why he had chosen to call his book *Polanyian Meditations,* he wrote: "I have called it *Polanyian Meditations* . . . because there is a sense in which it begins where my essay in *Intellect and Hope,* 'Myths, Stories, History, Eschatology and Action: Some Polanyian Meditations' [included in this volume], ends. I wanted to claim this continuity." But his choice of title, by its evocation of Husserl's *Cartesian Meditations,* was also meant to suggest that the book was not a contribution to Polanyian scholarship and interpretation. "It was rather an attempt to think *out of myself,* under the influence of now deeply interiorized Polanyian motifs, about matters nowhere dealt with as such in *Personal Knowledge*" (*Polanyian Meditations,* 6ff.).

III

We chose the title *The Primacy of Persons and the Language of Culture* for this collection of Poteat's essays because we believe that it represents two of the principle concerns found in them. On the one hand, Poteat pertinaciously seeks to affirm the primacy of persons, and, on the other, he perceives one of the basic occasions of the obscuring of this primacy to lie in certain profound ambiguities in the language, derived from our modern culture, that we use to refer to ourselves, to others, and to the world.

That such ambiguities exist appears to be unproblematic, but to notice them raises at the same time, *eo ipso,* the historical question as to whether the problem that issued in the present serious ambiguities of language came about as the result of some sort of "lapse" in the Western tradition, a crucial turning-point where the tradition went "wrong," or whether this "lapse," if there were one, was simply the result of a working-out of problems inherent in the whole of the Western philosophic inheritance. That is, did the Western tradition "go wrong" at some particular point, or was it vitiated with potentially lethal ambiguities from the beginning?

While the answer to this question is basically irrelevant for understanding the essays included here, given that the problem that these essays present for our concern is *modern* Western culture whatever its origins, it may be helpful nonetheless to recall that the formation of modern sensibility did occur in a particular historical period. Beginning as early as the fourteenth century, perhaps, and culminating in the seventeenth century certainly, there occurred something of a sea change in Western sensibility, a change with profound consequences for how we think about ourselves and the world.

Without trying to define the change too narrowly, we may say that the change involved the shift from understanding human beings as preeminently theonomous personalities engaged as participants in a great drama played out before God to an understanding of human beings as primarily autonomous individuals who were separable and ultimately self-contained, pursuing their individual development and private goals substantially in isolation from one another. Reality, too, came to be seen as paradigmatically external self-subsisting reality "out there," instead of a reality that was grounded in God's providential governance. It was as if, with apologies to Hegel, the whole of Western sensibility had undergone an *Entäusserung,* an externalization of the spirit, thus fulfilling the conditions that would make possible the reduction of the spirit to a systematic dialectics of consciousness. This external reality then ultimately appeared as primarily a spatial reality, deployed infinitely in three dimensions, in which objects stood out from one another in discrete existence. Such a reality was, by its very nature, primarily to be appropriated by means of the visual mechanism; hence sight became the dominant and most valuable of the senses. (We are still tempted to respond, "I *see* what you mean," to the verbal efforts of our conversational partner who has been *speaking* to us about what he wants us to know.) To the theonomous personality, truth was understood as coming through the Word of God, which the believer *heard* and to which he or she responded; for a theonomous personality, hearing must be the most important of the senses. In the new sensibility, at a less explicit level, sight provided the model for knowledge. In the world of the new sensibility, theory (*theoreo* in the Greek, meaning "I see") became the dominant concern of intellectuals. Yet, for a spatially deployed external world of separable and discrete objects, it was bound to be mathematics, that most external and least personal of sciences, that was to bring that world under the intellectual and, perhaps, the actual control of human beings. As Galileo wrote in *The Dialogue on the Great World Systems,* "The book of nature is written in mathematics, and he who would read her must learn that language." Without prejudging claims of historical continuity, it seems safe to say that the type of sensibility that culminated in the seventeenth century and bore fruit in the Enlightenment claims of the eighteenth was radically different from the sensibility that preceded it.

In his article "Moustakas within His Ambience," reprinted below, Poteat describes the historical situation as follows:

> Our history begins with Enlightenment, with the Renaissance, with Reformation. For good and for ill, we are creatures of modernity, of criticism, of revolution. Not only have we turned our backs upon the past, tradition, inherited ways, the harmonious balance between man and nature. We have been tempted, as we have de-divinized nature, following our Biblical inheritance, to divinize ourselves and there has ensued a ripening flirtation with godhood, with infinity, restlessness, tumult and madness.
>
> Descartes in his *Discourse on Method* consolidated the emerging hopes of his predecessors and drafted a program for our consciousness, saying: "By them (new principles of method) I perceived it to be possible to arrive at knowledge highly useful in life . . . and thus render ourselves

the lords and possessors of nature." . . . Under the impetus of these hopes, which have become at times a "sweet dream" of the heaven on earth, we have subjugated nature. And for three centuries we have found ourselves thrown back and forth in despair between the image of ourselves as a "useless freedom" in no way commensurate with the great, inane nature which is merely our subject and the image of a mere animal whose greater complexity only renders its existence within the bosom of a nature without grandeur the more meaningless. Our "humanism" is very often the diseased offspring of this impiety. Our discarnate freedom has no place in the universe, our visible form recapitulates no cosmos, no breath of God shines in our faces. We are alternately bewildered and ashamed of our own image. . . .

Our humanism keeps a mistress whose name is Nihilism.

We have quoted at some length because this passage reveals in language approaching poetry, and for that reason perhaps too vividly, the experiential setting and the deep anguish in which most of us as heirs of the Enlightenment, as heirs of modernity, find ourselves these days.

The great change in sensibility that occurred at the onset of the modern age has had dual consequences: on the one hand great advances in the "conquest" of nature, incredible progress in the areas of science, technology, medicine, and the genuine easing of the burdens of life through a productivity and an abundance unknown to previous ages. Yet, on the other hand, the "dark side of modernity" is undeniably present, producing at times social realities of unmitigated evil, such as totalitarianisms that resort to mass murder, calling it a "good for humanity." More frequently, of course, the "dark side" leaves us to wander aimlessly in a silent, nihilistic despair. Where do we stand and on what basis can we stand in this modern culture if we are to be able to assert a humane existence?

When considering the culmination of modernity's formative years in the seventeenth century, it is impossible to avoid Descartes, often called the father of modern philosophy. Descartes is probably most famous for his assertion *Cogito, ergo sum* (I think, therefore I am), which he propounded as the indubitable proof of his own existence. Equally important is his methodological axiom *De omnibus dubitandum est* (everything must be doubted), the alleged rubric guiding scholarly efforts in natural science, social science, history, and other disciplines, if they are to qualify for respectability according to the canons of the modern academy. Ontologically and epistemologically the most significant of Descartes's contributions was his bifurcation of the human being into two irreducible substances—*res extensa*, the body that each of us is and which is extended in space, and *res cogitans*, the thinking thing, an individual's mind, which separates each of us from the extended world, because it is a separate and distinct kind of thing—since it is not extended in space—from those things that go to make up the world. This Cartesian dichotomy, then, not only bifurcated human beings into mind and matter (in a sense, we really did not have minds before Descartes), but it removed human beings from the world as well, thereby depriving them of both a place in the world of nature and a history that was uniquely theirs. Additionally, of course, it created all sorts of epistemological problems that have bedeviled thought since his time.

In a profound sense, the malady of the modern world is a Cartesian malady. Milic Capek, in his book *The Philosophical Impact of Contemporary Physics,* indicates that the binding hold that classical physics exercised over our imaginations for so long was due to the fact that a "picture" held us captive. He wrote, "Classical physics simply cannot be forgotten . . . because its principles are embodied in the present structure of the average human intellect or in what is usually called 'common sense.'" Further, "Euclidean geometry and Newtonian mechanics are both based on deeply ingrained habits of imagination and thought whose strength is far greater than we are generally willing to concede."[4] We would argue in a similar vein that Cartesianism cannot be ignored because it is cognate to the Newtonian imagery and "its principles are embodied in the present structure of the average human intellect or in what is usually called 'common sense,'" and its "commonness" is historically conditioned.

From the very beginning, of course, intellectuals have attempted to refute the Cartesian dichotomy, and within recent years nearly everyone is prepared to admit the limitations of the Cartesian formulations. But the disturbing truth is these formulations have never lost their power over the modern mind. Capek also observed, "Even within physics, notwithstanding our declarations to the contrary, the classical habits of thought persist and the fact that they are driven into subconsciousness by being consciously rejected makes their influence only less easily detectable and far more insidious."[5] The conscious rejection of Cartesianism does not mean its disappearance. It has,

---

4. *The Philosophical Impact of Contemporary Physics* (Princeton, N.J.: D. Van Nostrand Co., 1961), xii, xiii.
    5. Ibid., xv.

perhaps, been driven only further underground, where it is more difficult to perceive, and therefore it remains more insidious than ever.

Another quote from Capek is worth our consideration: "The task of an epistemologist in contemporary physics is therefore a little like that of the psychoanalyst: to detect the remnants of classical thought beneath the verbal denials and conscious rejections."[6] Taking our cue from Capek, we can say that Cartesianism is still exerting its influence in less obvious ways but with perhaps more pernicious and insidious effects, just because having become a part of our tacit structure it continues to wield its influence apart from our explicit recognition. What is needed then is the exposure of Cartesianism in its tacit as well as its explicit dimensions in such a way that it can be recognized for what it is. It is one of the great merits of these essays that they undertake this task, revealing in an unavoidable and comprehensible fashion the hidden Cartesian commitments and their implications, which lie buried in some of even the most seemingly innocuous positions.

IV

Poteat's critical dialectic, then, has the widely varied and subtle manifestations of the Cartesian philosophical tradition as its chief target. Cartesian objectivism and its correlated mathematicism are seen as anything but benign in import. Poteat takes this mental set to correspond, at the least, to an utterly unself-suspecting and therefore highly imperialistic naïveté, and at worst, to a profound and growing cultural insanity.

But this latter judgment is nowhere given as though, self-contradictorily, from some Cartesian culture-neutral perspective. In the overview of Poteat's work it is clear that the concept of "personhood," packed as it is with the meaning bestowed upon it by the Judeo-Christian legacies, is primary. However, knowing what persons are, partially as a corollary to indwelling Judeo-Christian stories, does not bespeak something like a peculiar "religious" way of knowing. The presumption to uncultured knowing is a Cartesian abstraction; however, it is clear that for Poteat the alternative does not reduce to any simple, everyday, garden variety cultural relativism.

Poteat has thought of culture

---

6. Ibid., xv.

not as a certain form of social order or a system of practice or as physical artifacts, but as a repertoire of concepts, models, metaphors, analogies, images, picturings, myths, and stories shaping the life of a people. I assumed and do assume that these are somewhat susceptible of expostulation by dialectical means. In any pluralistic culture, of course, plural repertoires are intimately and often incoherently mixed. But the origins of all of them are religious: they are primitive—in the sense of radical— prereflective; numinously grounded and constitutive of reality. Religion and culture *thus conceived* are, therefore, bonded, even though unstably so—both synchronically and diachronically—by the inherent logic of the repertoires. I have believed that it is both possible and heuristically potent to explore the logic of these conceptual matrices, to establish their provenance where possible and draw out their implications.[7]

This statement draws into focus some of the major burdens of Poteat's work. On the one hand, it is a radical culture-critique centering particularly upon epistemology and philosophy of language. On the other hand, it is (1) a constructive apologia, which takes the form of conceptual mapmaking displaying the mutual affiliation of the central experience and concept of personhood and its cognates (such as "speaking," "agent," etc.) in the Western world with the Christian mythos of creation and incarnation, and it is (2) a continuing attempt to redescribe the knowing process in a way that is commensurate with the experience of the inalienability of the person and which points the way beyond the perils of subjectivism and objectivism.

That the tasks which Poteat set himself continue to be relevant is suggested not only by the plethora of writings that under his (and Polanyi's) tutelage continue to be produced, but also, as already noted, by the continued and apparently increasing power of that Cartesian paradigm of the human situation vis-à-vis knowledge and its pursuit, whether in the domain of theology and the humanities or in the domain of the natural and social sciences. Notwithstanding the apparent radicality of contemporary quantum physics or of deconstructionist themes in philosophy and literary criticism, Cartesian imagery, often explicitly disavowed, continues effectively to enchant, or, more appropriately, to disenchant, the culture of Western consciousness wherever it or its artifacts appear in the world. It is another aspect of Poteat's work that in the face of the disinherited and disembodied mind—or, rather, the presumption to that—it poses the task of confirmation in the widest and

7. "Religion and Culture as I See It."

most profound sense. It broaches the irony of the culture's self-imposed infirmity and seeks to remind it of its inheritance.

V

For Eric Heller, "the disinherited mind" was the mind of Europe dispossessed of all spiritual certainties. It was the mind of "disinherited children, to whom no longer what's been, and not yet what's coming, belongs."[8] It was a condition of such "banal experiential prosody" that

> its mere contemplation paralyzes the poetic imagination. It was the situation that Hegel had in mind when in his *Aesthetics* he wrote: If the mode of prose has absorbed all the concepts of the mind and impressed them with its prosaic stamp, then poetry has to take on the business of so thorough a recasting and remodeling that, faced with the unyielding mass of the prosaic, it finds itself involved everywhere in manifold difficulties. . . .[9]

For Poteat the loss of spiritual certainty and the immense difficulty of *saying*—in any eminent sense of the word—anything in the face of the "unyielding mass of the prosaic" is clearly correlated to the disinherited mind. But in him the deep roots of the disinheritance and disenchantment are one with a kind of illusion at the heart of Enlightenment tradition, and perpetuated by it, in terms of which objectivity is opposed to and excludes subjectivity; mind is opposed to body; doubt is more primitive than belief; ethos presumes to transcend mythos.

In summary, the modern flight of the imagination and of its prose expresses a fascination with the abstract that became hypertrophied to such an extent that language itself came to be seen ideally as a wholly deracinate system, living a life of its own, responsible only to a grammatical and syntactical coherence. While such a vision left language bereft of any but the most attenuated semantic anchorage or force, it, nevertheless, persisted in overwhelming Western modes of reflecting and speaking, extending even into present-day "postmodernity."

8. Heller's quotation is from R. M. Rilke's "Seventh Elegy" of the *Duino Elegies, The Disinherited Mind* (New York: Meridian Books, 1959), 157.
   9. Ibid., 153–54.

Consciousness, through its own projects, displaced itself, and in its own imagining became in the profoundest way lost in space, "spaced-out" as it were. Instead of the *place* (placedness) of a real and inalienable presence and vital orientation—the "mindbodily" person who, for Poteat, is a kind of prereflective "Garden of Eden" from which the reflective act inherits its primary endowments—we have the Cartesian ideal of total lucidity with its cognate disembodied mind and an assumed alienation of presence. Reflection had presumed to convert its inheritance into its achievement whether by transforming it into a thing for its objective gaze or, in the mood of alienated freedom, by observation and description of its deconstruction.

We may well describe this movement as a "loss of soul," whereby we mean to say, following St. Augustine, loss of contact by reflection with the intentionality within the body, with vital orientation. A "disensouled" eye, on these terms, would not see away from itself just as these (present) words, disensouled by withdrawal of all personal subscription or project by speaker or reader, lose their directedness and hence their semantic dimension and become less even than ink on paper—less insofar as the latter ("ink on paper") are taken to be words, tokens at once sensible and intelligible for someone. For Poteat it is clear that only a language radically impoverished compared to the one amid which we actually live could follow from this movement of abstraction, of personal withdrawal: a language without demonstratives; without egocentric particulars or personal pronouns; without verbs, tenses, or moods. It is demonstrative, egocentric particulars and tenses that *incorporate* language, with its marvelous powers of abstraction, into existence. Only because of them is it at once saved *from* being an empty but coherent tautology, such as a mathematical notational system, and saved *for* its work of mediating otherwise mute immediacy.

Even so, the mere presence of demonstratives in language, as tokens, does not alone suffice to accomplish this necessary *incorporation,* thereby avoiding the empty tautology. The demonstrative *this* is a blind surd, except for its ubiquitous and irreducible reflexive reference to an extralingual entity, itself no part of language: a reminder of language's late arrival upon the scene of existence and of its continuing parasitical dependence upon the prelingual givens of existence. Let language, as it can, increase our power by mediating immediacy; and let it do this by grasping in the network of words the "essence" of things. It still remains the case that its abstracting power is, in the end, bound by, e.g., its demonstratives, to existence, and that even *this* bond is not *essential*—not a function, that is, of the formal relations that some grammarians or linguists might imagine obtain *essentially* among its component particulars. (We leave aside here the question of whether, in terms of a *quite different model* than the one suggested here, one might argue that there is an "essential" connection between language and the prelingual. Indeed, Poteat himself has made such an argument in *Polanyian Meditations*.) For, even if this highly dubious view of language in general might be conceded, it still would remain the case that the essentially inassimilable reflexive reference to existence appears whenever *this* is taken to be more than a blind surd.

Now, it is precisely the absence, in the sense suggested above, of an essential connection between the abstracting powers undeniably possessed by language on one hand, and its concrete embodiment in existence on the other, which makes it possible for language to become meaningless, to "go on holiday," to cease to express reality. For it is the "unessential" bond that has to be periodically reestablished in the face of the momentum toward abstraction.

When a culture as a whole loosens its grip upon existence by a kind of vast sabbatical underwritten by increasingly empty abstractions, it is no longer possible to find ground that does not give way to the pressure of its own weight. The hallucinogenic properties of linguistic abstractions blur the boundary between reality and dream. The truth can no longer be spoken because the flaccidity of speech permits anything. Existence dissolves; passion can have no object, subjectivity vanishes in the manifold.

A rather strange but instructive current reification of this movement of reflection—in its polar relation to what is designated in the title of the present collection as "the primacy of persons"—comes, not from the right wing of linguistic essentialism or "fundamentalism," but from the left, where what is celebrated is the radical contingency of words as signification: that is, from various appropriations of the deconstructionist strategies of Jacques Derrida. Mark Taylor has applied these strategies to the theological and personalistic legacies of traditional Western culture. He describes "where we are" as a time that must be prepared to enter postmodernity by accepting not just the death of God, as has modern humanistic atheism, but also to accept the demise of the other outstanding landmarks in the same contiguous conceptual and ontological landscape—the self, history, and book (and, we might add, of course, such other cognates as agent, action, play, speech, author, vocation, natality, freedom, dignity, violence, etc.). Hence, fully to adopt the death of God is also, to go beyond humanistic atheism, to accept the death of the humanistic human or the person. Taylor notes that in fulfillment of Nietzsche's proclamation, the tremendous event of the death of God is still on its way to reaching the ears of man. Since the "difference" or "grammar" of God-talk and person-talk "trace" each other, "theological self" becomes a kind of redundancy; and with the absence of God we get also the "absence of presence" in person and word. It is clear that, for Poteat also, there is a kind of symmetry in waxing and waning among the concepts of God, person, word, speech.

But Taylor continues to inscribe, even while celebrating a presumable Cartesian disembodiment, a "time between times and a place which is no place." He seems at once both to see and not to see the irony of subsequently celebrating what amounts to alienated freedom—the absence of presence in the word and of the persistence of "difference." He speaks of the language of deconstruction as liminal and as possessing "no final or proper meaning" but seems to reckon as unimportant the question of what sort of intelligibility this disclaimer is to have if, in the absence of linguistic essentialism and the a priori, no actual embodied speaker/reader takes charge here. If the "erring" that Taylor celebrates is "missing the mark," then it, of course, traces the mark and, in turn, the forethrow of an embodied human consciousness.[10] That is, in the reader's very act of accrediting the conceptual landscape—in terms of which concepts may be said to "trace," to give rise to "difference," and to "deconstruct,"—he or she (the reader) is led back to that beginning which Kierkegaard insisted against Hegel. That is, he or she is re-minded by return from the linguistic ecstasy, the purely aesthetic mood that obscured his or her own existence, to existence—which alone, as Kierkegaard maintained, distinguishes being. Or, in Heideggerian terms, one is reminded by that being which is proximal and "not-to-be outstripped" even by deconstruction.

It is instructive to note here that Derrida has said that "I sometimes have the feeling that the Heideggerian problematic is the most 'profound' and 'powerful' defense of what I attempt to put into question under the rubric *the thought of presence*." That claim in *Positions* (1972) was reaffirmed at the International Colloquium on "Reading Heidegger" (May 1986). Derrida, being asked whether he would reaffirm the statement, said, "I should have

10. See Taylor, *Erring: A Postmodern A/Theology* (Chicago: University of Chicago Press, 1984), 15, 10, 12.

said that *something* in Heidegger, *something* in Heidegger's moves, or in the pages of his text, gives me this impression, and today I would say the same thing."[11] Our own reading of Heidegger supports Derrida's suspicion on this point. For all that deconstructionist thinking has taken from Heidegger, it may well be at the farthest possible remove from him on this most crucial issue. (Albeit it must be said that much in Heidegger's writing as well as his infamous affiliation with Nazism may well attest to his own existential equivocation with, and abstractedness from, this presence).

These brief allusions to some themes of contemporary deconstructionist thinking have been undertaken as a way of suggesting to the reader Poteat's position in terms of his sharing a preoccupation with a number of issues central to current debate while, at the same time, representing, perhaps, the starkest possible contrast as regards the directions he takes in addressing them. Taylor's deconstructionist work has been called—clearly in an ironic mood—"a victory of disembodied thinking." It might also be thought of as a remarkable sort of exemplification of what Kierkegaard called "unmastered irony," which, of course, as position, self-destructs. The mind-set that wishes to suggest that all texts and all presence deconstructs, including even the presence of absence, is certainly arguably due to a reflection that system-atically in advance gives "presence" away to a darkness that closes-off rather than discloses—that is, gives it away to a substantialistic ontology in terms of which presence would have to be a "fact" rather than that from which a fact *is possible*—i.e., that inalienable presence which is coincident with temporality and with speech itself. Or to put the matter in a slightly different, though co-extensive resounding, it is to sacrifice presence and being upon the altar of a subtle and even disavowed, but pervasive, visualist metaphor in which it (presence) is a "thing" that deconstructs much as an old disinherited and uninhabited house (a sort of cadaver) deconstructs and disappears from, or merges with, the visual landscape. If the presence and presencing of these current words is exhausted by this same sense of presence (implicit in any reduction of phoneme to grapheme or any phoneme-grapheme dichotomy), then the distendedness, hanging-togetherness, and remembering in time requisite to the production of an intelligible sentence and to the intelligibility of time and its ecstasies itself cannot obtain. In this way words would be

11. Quoted in David Wood, "Heidegger after Derrida," *Research in Phenomenology* 17 (1987): 114.

corpses as would, regarded under the same visual metaphor, each note of a musical composition. The last word uttered or written or the last note played would cease to be present once articulated in visually discrete spaces. "Tracing" as a temporal phenomenon is rendered unintelligible. Kierkegaard might focus the irony here by noting that a disembodied mind will always be eternal before its time.

That nothing possesses "own being" is, of course, a central observation of the Madhyamika tradition in Buddhism, and it correlates to the doctrines of no-self, of emptiness and of identity in nonidentity. The affinity of this perspective with the sort of deconstructionist parlance exemplified in Taylor's work has been noted by him and others.[12] But it is astonishing to see the suggestion by Taylor that his claimless claims, and claimed and reified claimlessness, are somehow to be affiliated with Kierkegaard, unless one assumes, ironically, the aesthetic modality of pure passivity before deconstructive mediation. For Kierkegaard, of course, a positive relation to the Christian Paradox would prevent us from despairingly objectifying ourselves into incidental flotsam in the midst of the eternal play of the void; and the relation to that paradox is not by way of metaphysics but, quite the contrary, it is by way of paying attention to the pathos of existence and by faith.

Now, for Poteat, it is clear that language enormously extends our power of conception and imagination beyond any we had in our prelingual past; however, it is equally the case that the prelingual past is still, though differently, present in our silences before and after the explicit apparatus of speech. Neither we nor our world are exhausted by language. Language is always at hand; and we may take it or leave it alone. Furthermore, if we take it, or take it up, we may do so diffidently, abstractedly, without passion; or we may do so carefully, soberly, with personal seriousness. If the "unessential" bond between language and existence and meaning has become attenuated by the (quite literally) absentmindedness of the age, then it is precisely myself who is this bond that has become so attenuated. This language, an asset when it has internal fiber and tone, and a firm semantic rootage, becomes a liability when it has become abstract, flaccid, and remote from existence. Uttering the truth becomes impossible, because language bends or breaks or "goes on holiday"; subscribing to the truth becomes impossible, because subjective

12. See "On Deconstructionist Theology: A Symposium on *Erring: A Postmodern A/Theology*," *Journal of the American Academy of Religion* 4.3 (Fall 1986).

seriousness is indistinguishable from absentmindedness; existence loses all resonance because reality and illusion have become one.

In such a situation, one has to rehabilitate language in order to be able to speak at all. To do this one has to rediscover that radical relation to our ambient language which permits us to take it up with seriousness, with subjective passion; which enables us to rehabilitate that "unessential" bond between language and existence which is our own subjectivity, our own mindbodily indwelling.

How does one manifest oneself in speech when the language one would use cannot support seriousness, when it has become corrupted by the linguistic ecstasies that are the corollaries just as much of the alienated freedom that characterizes current deconstructionist discourse as of the kind of essentialism epitomized by Wittgenstein's *Tractatus*?

This is Poteat's problematic and his polemical situation—strikingly reminiscent of that of Søren Kierkegaard in the ambience of Christendom's disinheritance of its own mind by way of surrender to the seductions of idealism; but it is also reminiscent of the situation of Michael Polanyi, who, in *Personal Knowledge,* set out to re-mind a culture abstracted and disinherited by way of enthrallment to the objectivist-positivist self-understanding of a seemingly omnipotent scientism. But, while Poteat owes much to these thinkers, his own approach to what he considers these suicidal tendencies of modern and postmodern thought represents a distinctive development issuing in the truly radical work of *Polanyian Meditations* and, currently, to further adumbrations on the "post-critical logic" that he propounded there.

Hence the essays of this present volume represent a kind of pilgrimage. They represent a rich theologically and philosophically informed culture-criticism in their own right; but they also represent a (not unequivocal) development toward the systematic reconsideration of the very foundations of reasoning that is found in *Polanyian Meditations.* This should indicate that Poteat's current relation to some of the materials of this present collection is, while by no means one of disavowal, clearly critical. In his own words:

> From "Faith and Existence" to *Polanyian Meditations* I am struggling to found, formulate and argue my thesis within the first person singular. Of course, the whole philosophic tradition militates against this, preferring as it does the third person. Therefore my efforts—never wittingly made (until *Polanyian Meditations*)—are compromised over and over again as I try to follow my instincts and stay in the first person at the

same time that I try to speak *to* the tradition. "Incarnate . . ." is an interesting stage. There at the heart of the argument I have the courage of my convictions; but then capitulate to Immanuel Kant, that (in the first *Critique*) third person thinker par excellence. I'm getting there in the series—all done in the 50's—"I Will Die," "God and the Private I" and "Death, Suicide. . . ." Only in *Polanyian Meditations* do I with some clarity embrace the first person as the only standpoint that can accurately represent the actualities of our knowing. In "For Whom Is the Existence of Values a Problem?" I explicitly operate out of the standpoint articulated in *Polanyian Meditations* and very cheekily conduct a post *Polanyian Meditations* argument by frontally assaulting the tradition. I really am a hopeless Yahwist. For me the world is creature; and in our knowings we respond as persons to it as to its creator. Our adventure of 2500 years in conceiving of ourselves as gods in relation to the *objects* of our knowledge is over. We did not become gods, we only became objects to ourselves.[13]

Clearly, then, the following essays should be read with that developmental background in mind.

VI

We said above that we would suggest alternative ways for the reader to approach his or her reading of these essays. First of all we should say that the essays are not arranged in chronological order, which would have been appropriate if the purpose of the collection had been to allow the reader to trace the development of Poteat's thought. Instead we have arranged the essays by four major groups, which, we believe, provide unifying themes for the essays placed in each group. Within each group, however, the placement of the essays is largely arbitrary, albeit the second group does follow a chronological order.

In the first group, entitled "Programmatic Essays," we have placed those essays that appear to us to give an overall view of the Poteatian enterprise and which indicate his position in relation to very basic and complex philosophical issues such as those related to the theory of knowledge and philosophy of language. The second group, entitled "Personal Language and the Language

13. From an unpublished letter to J. Stines, January 1988.

of Belief," includes those writings that are more narrowly focused on theological issues, but with the later ones employing the methods of linguistic and conceptual analysis. The third group, "The Ambivalent Language of Culture," contains essays that are primarily concerned with critiquing the ambivalent impact of language on our thought about the world of our culture, including language itself. Finally, in the fourth group, entitled "Freedom, Faith, and the House of Intellect," we include a number of works that represent theological and educational essays, which by the same methods show the range and diversity of Poteat's concerns but which do not fit easily within the other categories.

We believe that the preferred way of reading the essays is to proceed from group one through group four in the order they are presented; again, the order within each group is a matter of personal preference. However, those readers who bring a more straightforward interest in and familiarity with traditional theological themes may wish to begin with the essays in groups two and four, and then proceed to group one and group three. For those principally interested in the ambiguities of language in our culture, start with group three, proceed to groups one, two and four.

Finally, we note that the footnotes and references throughout this collection have been standardized and obvious errors corrected. Poteat has rewritten three paragraphs in "The Incarnate Word and the Language of Culture" for this volume.

In any case, our hope is that the readers of these essays will approach them as an opportunity to enter into an intellectual adventure that, like all adventures, summons us to existential participation, and perhaps, as for so many of Poteat's students, to emotions of recognition in a homecoming to a place never really left.

PART ONE

Programmatic Essays

PERSONS AND PLACES

Paradigms in Communication

We in the Western world have for a very long time commonsensically and primordially taken space to be that within which objects are enabled to be the particular objects which they are and, what is correlative to this, the medium within which these objects are distinctly separate—and indeed separable—from one another. Space, as we say, along with time, is one of the two fundamental coordinates by means of which we can make an identifying reference to any particular as *this* particular and also to make a *later* reference to a particular as *the same particular* (as one to which reference has hitherto been made).[1]

This has meant, of course, philosophical sophistications aside, that space as a field of action is the medium within which I *orient* my own body, whether in motion or at rest, to other bodies—be they animate or inanimate ones. I especially remark the words *later* and *orient* above because their very inexpungible presence in the text presents the theoretically sophisticated view that underlies our modern common sense with some paralyzing incoherences.

Since on its face it would be difficult to imagine, let alone prove, that our apprehension of the world of objects could be different from this commonsense view, as Kant seems definitively to have shown our tradition in arguing to space and time as necessary forms of sensibility for the appearance of any object

F. W. Dillistone and James Waddell, eds., *Art and Religion as Communication* (Atlanta: John Knox Press, 1974), 175–95.

1. This has been argued, I believe definitively, by P. F. Strawson, *Individuals: An Essay in Descriptive Metaphysics* (London: Methuen and Co., 1959), passim.

whatsoever, we must suspect that any incoherences, if such there be, must have a profound rather than a superficial source in the paradigms underlying the structure of our imagination. Such is in fact the case, as I shall argue.

It has been observed often that Western sensibility in general and the Western epistemological tradition in particular have been peculiarly in bondage to models fashioned upon the characteristic quality of visual perception in their discourse about *all* perception as such and even for discourse about knowledge. The history of this bondage lies quite beyond the scope of the present essay, but the manifold instances in our tradition of exceptions to such a generalization should not persuade us that there is not a telling truth in this claim.

Let us observe. The Greek verb *aisthanomai* means "to perceive, apprehend by the senses, to see, hear, feel." The Greek ancestor of *perception* is not by itself overcommitted to vision as a paradigm. And even when this radical sense is given over to a derived metaphorical use, there is no obvious prejudice favoring visual experience, for Liddell and Scott give as their second meaning for *aisthanomai* "to perceive by the mind, understand, hear, learn." There is as little comfort for this view in an analysis of the Greek verb *epistamai*, which is clearly affiliated with a *skillful doing*, with, in contemporary philosophical idiom, a *knowing how* quite as much as with the perhaps more statically conceived and less obviously "embodied" *knowing that*.

To be sure, when we come to the compound of *episteme* and *logia* from which the term *epistemology* is derived, we recognize that a new affiliation has been made. *Epistemology*, for which the *Oxford English Dictionary* gives "the theory or science of the method or grounds of knowledge," is a late coinage that singles out that branch of philosophy concerned with the theory or grounds of knowledge, and has thereby affiliated *logia*, as it appears in the ending—"logy" in many English compounds designating theories of or inquiries into sundry matters—with the term *theory*, from the Greek, *theoreo*, "to look at, view, behold; to inspect" and to "know (that)." Thus, beholding (as spectation), perceiving, and knowing form a real, even if not wholly stable, alliance. Perception, knowing, and spectation are, in short, etymologically linked.[2]

---

2. In all honesty it is improper to tax Plato with this misguidance. The richness and equivocacy of his "true" meanings need not detour us, since they are for the Platonic scholars. It surely is a fact, however, that the Plato of the Renaissance—the Plato uprooted from Pythagorean mysticism and from the Neoplatonism of Augustine and

It would be ludicrous of course to place too much weight upon this far too cryptic characterization of the valences that connect "perception," "skillful doing," "knowing that," "theory," and "theory of knowledge," as if they might be strung together like beads, leading straight to the alliance of models of *perception as such* with visual perception. Yet let us not be misled from a true insight by demanding a meaninglessly rigorous test of what will be allowed to induce such an insight!

The complex interrelations among these tokens and their changing uses and linguistic affiliations are quite beyond a detailed explication, even perhaps by historical philologists. But our perspective upon these questions must be clear: these affiliations are surely the result of something more than mere coincidence and something less than explicit convivial consent. The logical resources conveyed by the linguistic elements in our tradition have surely conspired to make these matchings seem "right" as we have moved along. And as they have seemed "right," they have seduced us into certain ways of beholding the world when other ways were once still possible, and insofar have committed us to talking about what we behold and what constitutes the act of beholding in certain ways rather than in others.

Even if it is not true without qualification, therefore, that Western sensibility in general and the Western epistemological tradition in particular have been peculiarly in bondage to a reliance upon the characteristic quality of visual perception as a source of models for discourse about all perception as such and even for discourse about knowledge, it must be admitted that a very strong bias in this direction does exist; and that even when tactile, aural, and visual experience are examined as distinct, there is seldom an inclination to distinguish *tactile* space from *aural* space and to distinguish both in turn from *visual* space. The inclination is rather to assimilate the former two to the latter.[3]

One thing is quite clear: even without a detailed collation of the ingredient models functioning at the most radical level in the analyses of perception and of knowledge in, say, the writings of Locke, Hume, Kant, even Berkeley, one

---

Plotinus—is the thinker who has most deeply impregnated the imagination of the West. It is this which matters here.

3. See especially Erwin W. Straus, "Forms of Spatiality," in *Phenomenological Psychology: The Selected Papers of Erwin W. Straus,* trans. Erling Eng. (New York: Basic Books, 1966).

can become intuitively aware of the superordination of a certain view of the characteristics of visual perception as a paradigm for solving puzzles of perception as such. Who can read Hume's analyses "Of Self-Identity" or "Of Causality" without recognizing the extent to which the problematics and the solutions are a function of Hume's having defined the conceptual limits of these discourses in terms of a particular model of some characteristics of visual experience?

It is not then a case of our commonsensical belief that space is that within which objects are enabled to be the particular objects which they are and the medium or form within which these objects are distinctly separate being false or even dubitable. It is rather that we have taken this (as I shall say) *derivative* notion of space and made it *primordial*. And the bias toward using the characteristics of visual experience as an epistemological model has had its part to play in this development. It has, if you will, provided an epistemological sanction for an uncriticized and therefore increasingly uncriticizable ontological presupposition concerning the radical nature of space and hence of the nature of those entities that "occupy" space, namely, bodies. The consequences of this bias, as I shall undertake to show, have not been trivial by having a merely theoretical bearing, but are on the contrary malign, indeed fateful, because they have shaped contemporary man's common sense. If this fateful issue is not as yet clear, it is nevertheless not premature to suggest that, with other influences, it has conduced to substitute in our commonsense conceptual repertoire the notion of this same "space" for that of "place." And when more has been said, I shall be able to contend that where the concept "place" becomes problematic, that of "person" becomes so too.

The model of spectation, statically, impersonally, and discarnately conceived, has had, however equivocal it may have been, a peculiar hold upon our imaginations.

Yet further preliminary observations remain to be made.

It is not enough merely to remark the extent to which a commonsensically unexceptionable conception of space has been allowed to become the ontologically radical conception; or even to observe the ways in which the visual models often finding their way into determinative roles in our epistemologies have interacted with this ontological bias so as to make them mutually reinforcing with this bias. One must go further and risk the simplification that the "subject" of the visual experiences from which these models are drawn is not only curiously passive—a *mere* spectator, as we might say—but a mere eye; in fact, a disembodied eye, which is oriented from no body of its own.[4] Indeed, it is a general characteristic of modern theories of knowledge, Kant's first *Critique* being a suitable example here, to take knowing as an accomplished fact and then undertake a "transcendental analysis" of its necessary conditions, rather than to observe particular feats of the acquisition of knowledge to determine the processes that in fact enter into them. I have written elsewhere concerning the wider implications of this motif.[5] But it is only necessary for present purposes to say that a preoccupation with knowledge as an accomplished fact instead of concern with the processes of its skillful achievement, however useful and just the preoccupation may be in itself, disposes the imagination toward a static rather than a dynamic picture of the noetic situation and therefore toward a passive rather than an active image of the "subject" of knowledge, the knower. And it is just this disposition that in due time makes us able not merely to tolerate but even to take as quite natural, because we take it quite unreflectively, the absurdity of the "visual experiences" of a disembodied eye.

I am not at all suggesting that in our epistemology and ontology we have consciously decided to operate with these absurdities. The fact, on the contrary, is that they inhabit our imaginations at so primitive a level and in such an equivocal fashion that, even when the presuppositions of these inquiries are quite explicitly under review, such factors are almost never even vaguely sensed, and even when sensed are not recognized as being significant.

If, across a conceptual landscape dominated by models drawn from visual experiences—visual experiences, in effect, imputed to the disembodied eye— we find ourselves in due course arriving at the paradigm of a knower that is a god, this should in no way surprise us. On the contrary, it is any alternative issue that would be surprising.

However, in this piece of intellectual, historical, detective fiction, let us double back once again.

What we take to be *our* commonsense view of space—and I am far from proposing that we abandon it—seems to have its roots in two special forms of

4. I shall not undertake to document this sweeping suggestion here, but will only bid the skeptical reader to examine the major epistemologists of our tradition with this question in the forefront.

5. See appendix to Langford and Poteat, eds., *Intellect and Hope: Essays in the Thought of Michael Polanyi*, 449–55.

spectation: that of those Renaissance painters and architects to whom we credit the recovery (more likely it is a *dis*covery) of linear or geometrical perspective (etymologically, "clear seeing"); and that of the Platonically oriented—that is, geometrizing and, later, mathematicizing— physical theorists. The relations between these that must have existed, even if only tacitly, in the ethos of Florence and then Pisa and finally of Padua cannot be detailed, since any important mutual influence would necessarily be unspecifiable. So much at least can be said: Italian artists of the fifteenth century were struggling experimentally to represent (i.e., cause to be *clearly* seen) three dimensions upon a two-dimensional surface as their own eyes beheld Roman copies of Greek sculpture (often as bas-relief on sarcophagi), and to do this in terms of some formalized principles; Italian Platonists—chiefly Galileo— were undertaking, initially through reflection alone (i.e., intellectual spectation), to comprehend the motion of bodies in terms of number. While painters were trying to produce a visually homogeneous pictorial-space—a space into which "movement" guided by a clear and visualizable prospect could be imagined—the Platonic physical theorists were trying to evolve an intellectually homogeneous universe-space for which number would provide a formalized scheme for conceiving the motions of bodies.

Whether these enterprises had any significant explicit relation to each other at the level of reflection, it surely must have incited and confirmed the imagination of Galileo to behold the buildings of Brunelleschi and Michelangelo, the paintings of Masaccio and Piero della Francesca, all about him. The sensibility that conceived and the skill that executed Masaccio's *Trinity,* its incredible barrel vault forcing the surface of the walls of the Church of Santa Maria Novella in Florence, cannot be imagined as having no affinity with the intelligence that, relying upon mathematics, authored Galileo's *Dialogue on the Great World Systems* while he was lecturing on mathematics at Padua.[6] And even if the connections are so subtle as to defy explication, can we imagine as unrelated the fact that Marsilio Ficino's translations of Plato should begin to appear in Florence in the generation after Masaccio mysteriously disap-

6. It surely is true, as Sigfried Giedion says, that "perspective was not the discovery of any one person; it was the expression of the whole era. . . . The significant thing is the mixture of art with science. . . . The two worked together . . . in the development of perspective. Indeed, one rarely sees so complete a unity of thinking and feeling—art and science—as is to be found in the early fifteenth century" (*Space, Time, and Architecture,* 4th rev. ed. [Cambridge: Harvard University Press, 1962], 31).

peared from that city forever; or can we put down to mere coincidence the growing influence of a logician such as Zabarella at Padua, who was so to stimulate Galileo? Nor can we lay it to mere chance that by the seventeenth century the ideas, however modified, of a philosopher like Plato, whose paradigm of true knowledge was that which is alone vouchsafed to a soul raised above history, *genesis* and *aisthesis* in pure, godlike epistemic vision of the very forms of things as they are, should nurture a revolutionary of the magnitude of Descartes, methodologically conceiving himself to be a discarnate intelligence, viewing and accrediting the clear and distinct ideas made known only through such as ascesis; and enjoining all true science with him to embrace such an ideal and such a method.

And so here is our irony: our "commonsense" conception of space, which has become our primordial conception of it, has its inception in artistic and mathematical spectation and achieves its consolidation in the model of a "discarnate," godlike knower for whom, it would seem, all knowledge must be an accomplished fact. And thus it happens that we, in the tradition, in the subtlest of ways, imagine ourselves as (at *least* in principle, we are careful to say, thereby begging the most staggering question of modern sensibility) godlike knowers viewing the homogeneous universe from which has been eliminated the heterogeneity of qualitative differentiation, which as mere incarnate knowers we find forever obscuring the view.[7]

Let me now turn from these altogether too fragmentary observations to state quite boldly my principal thesis. It is this: When the notion of *place* is assimilated to that of space—in that sense I have been delineating above—or when *place* is preempted by *space,* in this sense the concept of a person falls

7. Cf. Alexandre Koyre: "It is . . . sufficient to describe [the spiritual revolution of the sixteenth century], to describe the mental or intellectual attitude of modern science by two [connected] characteristics. They are: (1) the destruction of the cosmos . . . ; (2) the geometrization of space—that is, the substitution of the homogeneous and abstract space of Euclidian geometry for the qualitatively differentiated and concrete world-space conception of the pre-galilean physics" (*Metaphysics and Measurement* [Cambridge: Harvard University Press, 1968], 19–20). A reader who supposes there is an anomaly in my concern with a return to the heterogeneity of qualitative differentiation in concrete world-space at the same time that I appear to trace the triumph of the abstract, in part, to the glories of illusionistic naturalism in Renaissance perspectival painting, should be aware that it is solely the invitation of the eye to lead the imagination as a whole toward its self-abstraction into infinity, reinforced by the other elements I mention, that concerns me.

into grave jeopardy. It is my contention that precisely this inversion is a creature of modern sensibility, and that an intellectual enterprise undertaking to propagate a new personalism that does not conjure with this grim fact can accomplish nothing more than its own self-deception. It is no part of an anti-Copernican obscurantism to say categorically that persons live in "the qualitatively differentiated and concrete world-space"; and if their conception of the world, even down to what they regard as the world of everyday spatiality, is deeply infected by a profoundly inimical view, such as that of geometry, then they are on the way to cultural insanity.

As against the view that I began by calling the commonsense view, the conception that space is primordially that within which objects are enabled to be the particular objects which they are and the medium within which these objects are distinctly separate, I shall maintain that it is primordially that by means of which I orient myself, or, more exactly, by means of which I am oriented from within my body.[8] To such a view my orientation to my body as an object or from my body as an object among objects to others is derivative. Space is primordially a prereflective vectorial orientation, and this precisely is my body in its prereflective integration into a world. My body is a "system of anonymous functions," to use a happy phrase of Merleau-Ponty. It is within an oriented *whence* that primordial spatiality lies, and it is from within this *whence* that all orientation derives. If there is no such orientation from within a prereflective *whence,* then there is and can be no reflective orientation. In short, our so-called commonsense conception of spatiality presupposes as its *conditio sine qua non* this prereflective uncommon sense.

In contrast to this, let us examine Cartesianism. First, my self as a thinking being is absolutely distinct from (though it remains equivocally joined to) the body. "Thus extension in length, breadth and depth, constitutes the nature of corporeal substances; and thought the nature of thinking."[9] And again: "We clearly perceive that neither extension, nor figure, nor local motion, nor anything similar that can be attributed to body, pertains to our nature, and

---

8. It should go without saying that the logical force of the word *body* as it appears in the statement of the commonsense view is derivative and importantly different even as this formula as a whole is derivative; and similarly that *body* as the ground of the primordial sense of space has, as well, a primordial sense not to be assimilated to any derived sense.

9. René Descartes, *The Principles of Philosophy* 1.53.

nothing save thought alone; and consequently, *that the notion we have of our mind precedes that of any corporeal thing,* and is more certain."[10]

Thus we have a thinking mind, in every particular different from body or extended things, and of which we have both an indubitable and antecedent notion to any we have of corporeal things. Since mind is in every particular different from corporeal things, and since our notion of mind *precedes* our notion of body and is indubitable, it follows that our notion of *our* mind as ours has no reference to or dependence upon any *particular* body (which must render the genitive pronoun *our* incoherent!) and also has no reference to or dependence upon the one and only body that is the entire universe or alternately the *notion* of body as such. And even though, rather embarrassingly, Descartes takes it for granted that there is some way in which these radically disjunct entities are joined, we have here in fact a discarnate mind and an insensate body.

But there is yet in store an at once more primitive and less explicit embarrassment to the whole Cartesian enterprise. He says, "In this way we shall ascertain that the nature of matter or of body in its universal aspect, does not consist in its being hard, or heavy, or coloured, or one that affects our senses in some other way, but *solely* in the fact that it is a *substance extended in length, breadth and depth*."[11]

It is here that the paralyzing incoherence appears. For the concept of homogeneous quanta of space by means of which an extended "substance" is defined does not of itself provide us with the grounds for imputing *substantiality* to it; and in the repertoire for the mensuration of mere quanta of spatiality, there are no resources by means of which to specify that the spatiality has within it vectors, is inherently vectorial—having length, breadth, and depth as radii from some point of orientation. The price of defining mind in such a way as to deprive it of any incarnate existence is to deprive it of the very powers required for it to establish that extended things are *substantial* and that their spatiality is vectored—having length and breadth and depth; it is, in short, to deprive the mind of orientation. In a Cartesian world of extended objects, strictly speaking (and Descartes is often surprisingly lax with himself), not only do "length," "breadth," and "depth" have no meaning; neither, strictly speaking, have "extended" and "object." The lack of a primordial

---

10. Ibid., 1.8. Italics added.
11. Ibid., 2.4. Italics added.

whence of orientation that is anonymously *in* Descartes's world antecedent to his reflections upon the two kinds of substance open to reflection deprives the "substance," "length," "breadth," and "depth" of the *conditio sine qua non* of their having a meaning.

Now before such an incoherence as this, an imagination not already debauched beyond recovery would founder. Instead, faced with such an affront, the sensibility of the last three hundred years has been acquiescent and complacent. It is surely as Koyre has said: "It is a revolution so profound and so far-reaching that mankind . . . for centuries did not grasp its bearing and its meaning; which even now, is often misvalued and misunderstood."[12]

These three hundred years have not been without their dissenters, to be sure, as Hiram Haydn has documented in detail.[13] But no one saw so early or with a comprehension equal to the import of these events as Descartes's younger contemporary Pascal. Descartes's *Principia Philosophiae* was published in Amsterdam in 1644. It appeared in French in Paris in 1647. Sometime between 1656 and 1662 Pascal jotted down what we now know as Fragment 72 of his *Pensées,* and in it he set down the first and the definitive statement upon the radical incommensurability of *space* and *place.* He writes:

> Man's disproportion. . . . Let man then contemplate majesty, and turn his vision from the low objects which surround him. Let him gaze on that brilliant light, set like an eternal lamp to illumine the universe; let the earth appear to him a point in comparison with that described by the stars in their revolution round the firmament. But if our view be arrested there, let our imagination pass beyond; it will sooner exhaust the power of conception than nature that of supplying material for conception. The whole visible world is only an imperceptible atom in the ample bosom of nature. No idea approaches it. We may enlarge our conceptions beyond all imaginable space; we only produce atoms in comparison with the reality of things. It is an infinite sphere, the centre of which is everywhere, the circumference nowhere. . . . What is a man in the infinite? . . . Who will not be astounded at the fact that our body, which a little while ago was imperceptible in the bosom of the whole, is now a colossus, a world, or rather a whole, in respect of the nothingness which we cannot reach? He who regards himself in this light will be afraid of himself, and observing himself sustained in the body given him by

12. *Metaphysics and Measurement,* 20.
13. See *The Counter-Renaissance* (Gloucester, Mass.: Peter Smith, 1950), passim.

nature between those two abysses of the Infinite and Nothing, will tremble at the sight of these marvels. . . . For what in fact is man in nature? A Nothing in comparison with the Infinite, an All in comparison with the Nothing, a mean between nothing and every thing.[14]

If the foregoing observations have substance, then, let me repeat, the commonsense view of spatiality that has come down to us from the fifteenth through the seventeenth centuries, and which has tacitly become for us the ontologically *primordial* view, is radically incoherent. What is worse, its incoherence is humanly intolerable. Persons have *places*. The conception of space under review systematically preempts the notion of *place*.

I have argued that "extensions" or the perception of "extended" things presupposes a prereflective oriented *whence* from which radiating vectors distinguish length, breadth, and depth, which is to say that "extended" things are derivative, while the prereflective oriented *whence*—what we may now call *extension*—is radical.[15]

All this then means that for me, existentially, as the concrete person I am, *extension* is not first of all space, but rather is *place*, even as *extension* and *place* are the very ground of my being-in-the-world through my body as I move toward its many horizons of thought-action.

What then is *place*? *Place*, one must say, the original place, is the *extension* that is the *conditio sine qua non* of my ever coming to have my own and very particular somatic existence. Place is the *where* of my body in order that there may be a "where" of my "body," to which I have the most fundamental of all relations, and is the condition of my having any "relations" whatsoever. The "where" of everything else, which more or less determinately inhabits the ambience of my being-in-the-world, is secondary: that is, it has its "meaning" in the "where" of my "body" with *their* meaning in the where of my being-in-the-world. Even my "body" as *my* "body" is not in space. For in space every "extension" is interchangeable with any other of equal magnitude. But even with my "body" I have a relation that is privileged and inalienable—privileged and inalienable, that is, providing I do in fact *have* a

---

14. *Pensées*, trans. W. F. Trotter (London, 1932), Fragments 16–21.

15. Henceforth I shall distinguish the derived from the radical by placing double quotes around the derived. This will mean, though specific articulations of their relations may be opaque, that "extension" will stand to extension as "space" (in our developed sense) stands to space, "place" stands to place, and "body" stands to body.

"body"; providing, in other words, I have not abdicated it through pathology of some sort, such as catatonia. My relation to my "body" is, you might say, *logically* inalienable. Such, indeed, is the condition of calling catatonia a form of pathology. It is quite ordinary to say, "I seem to have mislaid my hat." "I seem to have mislaid my 'body'" requires some elaborate exegesis.

My body is a *place* and therefore it is possible for my "body" to have a "place"—a "place" which is privileged and inalienable in the same way that my "body" is so; and that by reason of the fact that my "body" and its "place" are logically correlative. As "I seem to have mislaid my 'body'" sounds queer, so "I seem to have lost my 'place'" sounds so.

The space occupied by my "body" is a "place," and this is so because my body is prereflectively a *place*. Indeed, the "place" which is my "body" is *the* "place" par excellence; and the "extended" world which is arranged around my "body" is not spaces but "places."

In all these "places" are the familiar satisfactions of my "body," all the goals I seek, all the objects of my personal fulfillment, all the ends of my very personal moral action.

A "place" is where I feel at home, full of objects and of relations upon which I have left my very personal stamp, expressed my own idiosyncrasy, part of my unique history. It is a domicile for the love that issues from the very center of my own person.

Space can never belong to me, nor I to it; but "places" can belong to me and I to them. It is out of the deep pathos of the inalienable relation between a person and a "place" that there issued from Pascal, facing a universe of mere spatial magnitudes, "the centre of which is everywhere, the circumference nowhere," his best remembered words: "The eternal silence of these infinite spaces frightens me."[16] It is out of this same pathos of our human identity with a "place" in the heterogeneity of concrete world-space that the author of Job speaks when he says, "He who goes down to Sheol does not come up; he returns no more to his house, nor does his place know him any more."

To be of no *place* is therefore to lack the ground of becoming a person; and to have no "place" is to lack the minimum conditions for remaining a person: a "place" that is the where of my "body."

This is not the only way in which we may understand "place," however—

16. *Pensées*, Fragments 16, 61.

though in making these next moves we shall be trading (quite legitimately and surely with exact phenomenological accuracy) upon the multiple meta-phorical or derived ways in which we unself-consciously use the word *place* in ordinary speech.[17]

"Place" may be the where of my "body" and to such an extent a necessary condition of my remaining a person. But a where for my "body" is not the sufficient condition of my remaining a person. Place is also to be understood as *status*. My place is a *whereon to stand,* a platform from which an action may be launched. A body that cannot be the medium through which intentional actions become progressively determinate is not the where of a person.

Thus place is the where of my body and the whereon to stand of my will; it is status. But place is also more than these: it is *room*. To be and remain persons it is necessary that we be able to carry at least some of our intentions to completion, to be, in short, the authors of actual and not merely of possible acts. If we cannot exercise a genuine moral will through having full sover-eignty over some of our acts, we cannot be fully personal. Now, in fact, we are *not* fully personal, and this is in part because we cannot command this full sovereignty. Yet it remains so that the extent to which we approach to per-sonhood is a function of an exercise of such sovereignty. For such an exercise we require *room*.

There is a particularly important and interesting elaboration on this theme that is more substantial than the pun upon which it appears to turn. In an important sense *room* is required no less for our making the world intelligible to ourselves—and here room means both time and distance and all variations upon these in their literal and derived meanings and the points at which these literal and derived meanings intersect. Time, room, distance, are necessary if we are to comprehend, to order, to hierarchize, and to integrate the imme-diacies of our fugitive affective lives and of our no less fleeting perception. Our contemporary obsession with immediacy causes us to overlook how genuinely unedifying sheer ecstasy or the blank stare of the shock of horror are. We cannot be persons when we have no room within which to compre-hend our experience. Indeed, we cannot, lacking time and distance, properly

17. I wish to make clear, in short, that the precision that I have undertaken to achieve up to this point by using conventions like place, "place," space, body, and "body," imprecise though even they are, will be abandoned in favor of a reliance upon the reader to read the shifting analogies off the contexts of their use.

have experience. We are condemned rather to the mere suffering of whatever happens to us. Existence becomes one undifferentiated happening. The liturgical shaping of a humane perception through art and ritual in order that we may comprehend love and death are to be replaced by the "real things"—as we now are taught to fancy it.[18]

Status and room have always been secured by ritual, which mediates the world, others, and ourselves even, to ourselves. The contraction within modern sensibility of place, status, and room have naturally been accompanied by the substitution of sheer spontaneity for the time and distance that is given in ritual—as Robert Coles so eloquently says:

> Ritualization among men, which has had a certain stability, even through all the changes in history, may well be breaking down now in a very critical way. . . . Psychoanalysis is a ritualized form of behavior. I hear people say to me now . . . we haven't got time, time for long analyses; we must confront one another at the moment, immediately, in an overwhelming way. And I find myself feeling old-fashioned, and saying, but we *have* to have time—time to get to know one another, slowly, tentatively, suspiciously, gratefully, surely, confidently. It *takes* time. . . . Wars can take a moment, and the world can be destroyed. And what do we get in art? . . . We get Brillo ads on canvas. . . . Maybe we can connect all this through that word "ritualization"; and wonder whether there isn't a breakdown affecting the artist, the writer, the warrior, the political leader, the psychiatrist, anyone, affecting the educator with his computer, which he's told he must use, and affecting some essential aspects of humanity, having to do with words and experiences like "distance" and "respect" and "sensibility," and a sense of carefulness. And the word "craft," which means *time* and thought and leisure—whether that, too, isn't so fatally collapsing that there is a breakdown in what you call ritualization.[19]

Surely it is obvious then that, the inalienable relation between persons and places being what I have claimed, the Cartesian image of extended things,

---

18. Events will almost certainly outrun the publication of these words, but now that the distinction between the actor and his role has virtually disappeared, and that between audience and cast along with it, there seems no reason why we should not carry immediacy, audience, and cast participation to the ultimate. Why not mount a drama (in the round) in which a different actor is put to death on stage each night of the run; even one in which the holder of the lucky ticket is allowed to choose the victim. Dissertations can be arranged on "The Head-on Collision at Eighty M.P.H. as a Work of Art."

19. "Symposium: Violence in Literature," *American Scholar* 27.3 (1968): 491–92.

which has come increasingly to dominate even our view of everyday spatiality, is profoundly inimical to personalism. For it is evident that place as the where of my body, as status and as room, is very far from being congenial with the abstract notion of infinite and homogeneous spaces that has so dominated the modern imagination—whose eternal silence Pascal found a weight hardly to be borne.

Let us here make the important concession. It may be appropriate and heuristically productive—who, observing the theoretical and technological prodigies of the sciences of the past three centuries could, short of being mad, deny this—to abstract ourselves from the heterogeneous aural, tactile, proprioceptive spatiality of the concrete world by means of the feats of spectation already described—whether this be the contemplation of the orbital paths of the planets as if from the sun rather than from the earth, as with Copernicus, or the contemplation of the nature of finite substances as if from the skeptically induced discarnate ascesis, as with Descartes. That is to say, it is appropriate to do so when we recognize what we are doing, that it cannot be both strictly and coherently done and, therefore, that it cannot be allowed to become the ground for the subversion of our unsophisticated confidence that the world is just as we know it to be. In such terms it is safe enough to concern ourselves with mere *things* that occupy space.

But a person has to be able to feel that the nature of things confers on him a place, a room to become what he is, a "whereon" to stand that is commensurable with his imagination and with the power of his moral will. To be deprived of a place is to become disincarnated, to be driven mad, to become an alien—to have no home or not to be at home. To think of oneself as a thing in space is to take oneself to be a *mere* thing—an observation that will seem not worth making only to those unacquainted with the scholarly literature in which there abound feats of intellectual ingenuity devoted to reducing man to an animal and animals to mere biochemical and physical integrations of varying complexity, all in the service of these "Cartesian" absurdities. To be deprived of a place is to become depersonalized, as Kafka represents it to us with both poignancy and terror in his story of Gregor Samsa, awakening one morning to find himself transformed into an enormous cockroach, his human mobility frozen by his crusty underbelly, his speech changed into the grotesque noises of a giant insect—which terrorizes his parents—but in whom there still remains the feeling for the pathos of his loss.

The man who has no place is first David Riesman's "outer-directed" man in a "lonely crowd"; then he falls into despair; and finally he disappears. J. D. Salinger's Holden Caulfield, shipped from "old Pencey Prep," the third private school to which he has been sent by parents who find his presence at home too demanding, wanders down Fifth Avenue, crowded with Christmas shoppers and Salvation Army Santa Clauses, and muses:

> I kept walking and walking . . . without any tie on or anything. Then all of a sudden, something very spooky started happening. Every time I came to the end of a block and stepped off the goddam curb, I had this feeling that I'd never get to the other side of the street. I thought I'd just go down, down, down, and nobody'd ever see me again. . . . Then I started doing something else. Every time I'd get to the end of a block I'd make believe I was talking to my [dead] brother Allie. I'd say to him, "Allie." And then when I'd reach the other side of the street without disappearing, I'd *thank* him.[20]

And so it is with us!

Whatever consolations Pascal may subsequently have found in Christianity, had he lived to complete the apology for which his *Pensées* were the notes, he was clairvoyant as to one matter: The human condition would have to find its ground and good in something capable of overcoming the human incommensurability of mere infinite space.[21]

More than a generation earlier, Donne, having heard of Galileo's telescope and imagined what its discoveries might imply, wrote in "An Anatomie of the World":

> And new Philosophy calls all in doubt,
> The Element of fire is quite put out;
> The Sun is lost, and the earth, and no man's wit
> Can well direct him where to looke for it.
> And freely men confesse that this world's spent,
> When in the Planets, and the Firmament
> They seeke so many new; they see that this
> Is crumbled out againe to his Atomies.

---

20. *The Catcher in the Rye* (New York: Grosset and Dunlap, 1951), 256–57.

21. Cf. Alexandre Koyre: "The dissolution of the cosmos means the destruction of the idea of a hierarchically ordered finite world-structure, of the idea of a qualitatively and antologically differentiated world, and its replacement by that of an open, indefinite and even infinite universe" (*Metaphysics and Measurement*, 20).

Kierkegaard knew with a lyricism all his own that Christianized man, no longer Christian, was caught in a demonic struggle with infinity, most powerfully expressed in the essentially musical idea of Don Giovanni, when he spoke of the overture of Mozart's opera:

> The overture begins with a single deep, earnest, uniform note that at first sounds infinitely far away, a hint which yet, as if it had come too early, is instantly recalled, until later one hears it again and again, bolder and bolder, louder and louder, that voice, which first subtly and coyly, and not without anxiety slipped in, but could not force its way through. . . . But soon it comes again, it grows stronger; for a moment it lights up the whole heaven with its flame, in the next the horizon seems darker than ever, but more swiftly, even more fiery it blazes up; it is as if the darkness itself had lost its tranquility and was coming into movement. . . . There is apprehension in that flash, it is as if it were born in anxiety in the deep darkness—such is Don Juan's life. There is dread in him, but this dread is his energy.[22]

We are not the first age in which man has felt that he has lost his place. The disintegration of the polis launched a flood of deracinate men upon the Aegean and Mediterranean world. But we are the first age in which man has felt the radical *contingency* of every place, felt, indeed, that the very notion of place has lost its meaning.

In fact, as we can now begin to see, the whole of modern culture could be described as an assault upon place, status, and room for personal action by the abstracting intellect. Before these developments reached their climax in Descartes's program, this assault was the source of great exhilaration and joy. Giovanni Pico, Count of Mirandola, wrote in 1486, in his "Oration on the Dignity of Man," putting these words into the mouth of God: "Neither a fixed abode nor a form that is thine alone nor any function peculiar to thyself have we given thee, Adam, to the end that according to thy longing and according to thy judgments thou mayest have and possess what abode, what form, and what functions thou thyself shall desire."[23]

The spiritual impulse behind these reflections is easy to find: it is

---

22. *Either/Or,* trans. David F. and Lillian M. Swenson, vol. 1 (Princeton: Princeton University Press, 1944), 105.

23. In Ernst Cassirer et al., eds., *The Renaissance Philosophy of Man* (Chicago: University of Chicago Press, 1948), 224–25.

angelism—the aspiration toward a deliverance from every particular place, every particular status, and the ambiguity of every particular moral action. The necessary and therefore fateful character of my *actual* place and time, of my *actual* status, and of my *always* ambiguous moral action is neutralized by abstract thought and becomes wholly contingent.

Classical thought did not really have a developed idea of contingency. Only in a universe that is viewed not as an eternal cosmos but as a created world that God might have chosen not to create is there a place for a conception of contingency.

It is clearly with such an idea that Pico wrote, believing that God had created the whole world and every particular in it. Thus one's station was not conferred by an eternal cosmos but by a providential God, who marks the fall even of a single sparrow.

What then began as a belief that my place is contingent in the sense that God might have called me to any of a number of other places (than the one to which I was in fact called) becomes the belief that my place is contingent in the sense that I might *choose* any other place—indeed, any place at all—and ends in the belief that my place is contingent in the sense that one place is just like every other, and that therefore none is any more *mine* than any other. Heterogeneous places have been transformed conceptually into homogeneous spaces.

Almost overnight the fifteenth-century joy of Pico turns to the mordant seventeenth-century anxiety of Pascal. He writes:

> When I consider the short duration of my life, swallowed up in the eternity before and after, the little space which I fill, and even can see, engulfed in the infinite immensity of spaces of which I am ignorant and which know me not, I am frightened, and am astonished at being here rather than there; for there is no reason why here rather than there, why now rather than then. . . . Man has fallen from his true place without being able to find it again.[24]

This attrition in the conception of contingency introduced into our sensibility through the Christian doctrine of creation reaches the point of exhaustion, and it is Jean-Paul Sartre who articulates the mood of the twentieth century when his Orestes, in *The Flies,* answers Zeus's threat that his words

24. *Pensées,* Fragments 205–427.

and actions are insubordinate by saying: "Foreign to myself—I know it. Outside nature, against nature, without excuse, beyond remedy. . . . Nature abhors man, and you too, God of Gods, abhor mankind."[25]

Lest any reader be seduced by my argument into a nostalgia for a pre-Cartesian world, or alternatively—what is more likely, if I am right in imputing these views to him—becomes irate at what he may take as a hankering archaism in me, let me be quite clear: I do not propose that we return to the fifteenth century, merely that we come to ourselves.

For it is important to recognize the extent to which this displacing of man from the world is a correlate of the proclamation in the Western world of the incarnation faith. We have already seen the relation between the propagation of this faith and the emergence of the conception of contingency. The motif of displacement is, however, ubiquitous in the images of both the Old and the New Testaments. Abraham was called out of his place in tribal life, which always remains in intimate alliance with the fertility of what is believed to be the cycles of nature, tied to its rhythms of birth, death, and regeneration. From this tribal life Abraham left Ur of the Chaldeans and set out for the land of promise, thereby becoming not only the patriarch of Israel, but a paradigm deep in the Western imagination.

Though birds have nests and foxes have holes, we are told the Son of man has no place to lay his head. Jesus, a Jewish bastard, an apprentice carpenter, and a companion of harlots, was without status. In death, even the tomb was no *place* for him. For each of us who would meet the Lord, there is no place where this must or even will more probably occur, for the Lord's place is wherever he chooses to manifest himself—which means it is no more *here* than *there*.

The incarnation faith deprives a man of his place in nature, in the city, in historical memory, in order to give him a place before the Lord. This means, of course, that my *place* before the Creator, whom I always meet at particular times and in particular places in nature, in the city, and in history, *displaces* me from these particular times and places. This is to say all become contingent for me because God, who acts as he will, might have chosen to meet me in any of many others. Nevertheless, the call is one always issued to my very particular life in a particular place in nature, in the city, and in history. This is my own

25. In *Two Plays,* trans. Stuart Gilbert (London, 1946), 96–97.

vocation. My *place* is now no longer necessary, but *neither is it like every other place*. It is the one particular place to which *I* have been called.

Henceforth, neither nature nor the city can be a place for me unless I have been called to it; unless, that is to say, I find myself placed before the Lord.

It also means that when the God who calls men to their particular vocations, who *places* them before himself, is no longer heard, then every place becomes for each man just like every other. Place has become radically contingent. The world becomes "de-placed," and each of us is displaced.

And this, I suggest, is where we find ourselves: Not knowing or having a place in nature, in the city, or in history, and finding our "vocation" at least ambiguous, we are a rootless, restless, placeless people—seeking with increasing desperation a place that, however tentatively, shall be ours.

This essay is not the place, nor do I feel an obligation, to undertake an answer to the state of affairs I have described. It is perhaps possible to say that what I have described is nothing less than the progress of a massive cultural psychopathology, and that the place to begin is with the admission that this is so.

The cure of insanity is sometimes achieved just by the retracing of one's inner history in order to re-perceive the world at those fateful junctions in that history where one came first to mis-perceive it. Whether this is so for us, I cannot say.

But this at least can be said. However moved we may legitimately be by the pathos behind the Sartrean Orestes' romantically and despairingly "willing to be himself"; however touched by the earnestness of the equally romantic "death of God" theology or "man's coming of age" or the "new hermeneutics" or whatever new variation upon the old theme there yet remains unexplored within the essentially fixed Cartesian terms, and is therefore currently chic or is just on the point of becoming so among all the theologians and savants, there is really, in the end, no alternative to calling these affecting laments by their right name: absurdities—absurdities borne of a fateful reliance upon a misconceived model of human knowing, human doing, and human being, for which the only cure is the disclosure that the model is both plainly wrong and lethal; absurdities to which we need not remain in bondage forever.

But this self-liberation will require a disciplined, arduous, relentless, painful, and patient process of seeking a post-Cartesian intellectual equilibrium, working at every point against the grain of our entire culture, denying ourselves the respite—and the sweet pleasures—of rushing into the streets every fortnight with some new messianic word.

MYTHS, STORIES, HISTORY, ESCHATOLOGY, AND ACTION

Some Polanyian Meditations

I

In this essay I shall talk about man and language from a perspective opened up for me by the writings of Michael Polanyi.[1] I am concerned first to show some modalities of my relation to my spoken and written words; how these issue in more or less tacit forms—among them: myths, stories, and histories; how each form may afford different ways of indwelling the ambience of my world (or of participating in the many different levels of Reality). Then I shall suggest that displaying these helps us to see something of the many forms of personal existence open to me. I shall conclude by suggesting the bearing of this new perspective upon some of the notorious perplexities over the meaning of myths, stories, and history; and of the language of theology and of religious performances generated by the lingering ethos of positivism.

A

Being-in-the-world and moving from within my own body toward its many horizons of thought-action goes on most of the time without my

Thomas A. Langford and William H. Poteat, eds., *Intellect and Hope: Essays in the Thought of Michael Polanyi* **(Durham: Duke University Press, 1968), 198–231.**

1. It is impossible to give specific references in the Polanyi corpus that, thus examined out of context, could yield the views I am here developing. It is the impact of the corpus as a whole that has educed these meditations.

having explicitly to attend to the process of integration that, taken globally, *is* my being-in-the-world. Some of the modalities of my being-in-the-world are the differing relations I may have to the more or less tacit articulate systems of language. In general, most of the time, integration among *these* occurs in a fashion analogous to that in which somatic particulars are tacitly integrated into even the simplest bodily movement. Indeed, movement, expressive gesture, ritual, speech, reflection, and wonder are all modes of my being-in-the-world.

No formal or explicit—or at least exhaustively explicit—specification of the integration among the varying logical neighborhoods of articulate speech or among the strata of Being within which, as a person, I quite unproblematically live most of the time is possible. Yet my existence is on the whole more or less personal and most of the time moderately integral because an integration is constantly going on in tacit ways.

First, I take it for granted that we all use words, that once upon a time each of us did not, and therefore that we all at some time had to learn to do so. Giving an account of how we do and how we did, I believe, would take us to the very prelingual ground of human intelligence. The wonder of it all is obscured by the fact that this initiation into speech and its skillful use is always going on all about us; and also by the fact that if we do start wondering about it, the closer we draw to the prelingual ground of human intelligence, the more difficult it becomes to say what it is we see, until finally it becomes impossible to say.

When I am speaking more or less skillfully and unself-consciously, my words are in my body somewhat as a musician's performance is in his before he has performed it, making their way toward the tip of my tongue, each bearing its still indeterminate intimations of its own propriety, which only become somewhat more determinate at that moment when, letting it loose into the world, I discern and acknowledge this propriety, however tacitly. This active-passive quality of my relation to my own utterances is, I believe, primitive and irreducible. It parallels Polanyi's tacit-explicit, subsidiary-focal, proximal-distal, attending-from–attending-to dichotomies and suggests as well the vectorial relation of the terms of the dichotomy: *given—the received*.

Paul Cézanne said, "I wait until the landscape thinks itself in me." And when I see his landscapes, I believe he very often did and that *it* very often did. To believe this is of course not at all to believe that Paul Cézanne was somehow disingenuous to sign "P. Cézanne" in the corner of *The Quarry at Bibemus* instead of signing it, say, *Q. at Bibemus*! Speaking too is like this.

Learning to speak is perhaps also like this. The word speaks itself in me, and having spoken itself in me, I speak it; having intimated its propriety to me, I greet it as my own—often with a feeling of surprise, occasionally with something stronger.

It is for this reason, no doubt, that each word, the propriety of which I come tacitly to acknowledge as I launch it into the world after its companions, already there, and just ahead of those waiting in their time to be noticed, seems at once both absolutely new and preexistent: absolutely new as a unique doing in a recognizably unique but indeterminate context; preexistent as an indeterminate intimation of its own propriety; preexistent also in the legacy of my native tongue.

Second, I shall assume, what seems to me not only consistent with but actually entailed by my first assumption, that each of us emerges from a prereflective, anonymous background into the increasingly personal existence of bearing a proper name and reflexively using the pronoun in the first person. We move out of a prepersonal, prehistorical background that is an indeterminate ground-meaning and ground-being from which we are projected into history and a more fully personal existence, while nevertheless always bearing within ourselves roots that reach into this anonymous background—even as Cézanne's landscapes bear within them their rootage in his body in its landscape.[2]

Every significant configuration—whether the mere orderly motility of my body, a spontaneous expressive gesture, an impromptu dance, 'choreographed'[3]

2. One might put the matter so: When I notice what it is like to be a person and try to say, among the many possible things I might say are: (1) "I exist as a person because I have emerged from a prereflective background into the reflective existence of having been given a proper name and of having been enabled to answer to it and of having been given my native language with the pronominal resources in it for making reflexive references to myself." When I talk this way, if I attend to what I say, I will be inclined to notice the sense in which personhood is a gift, that I am not my own author. It is this I think that issues in the many forms of the ontological "argument"! (2) On the other hand, I may say, "I exist as a person because I have received this gift, appropriated it as my own, thereby becoming the author of deeds [if asked, 'Who did this?,' I reply, 'I did!'], the agent of very particular acts, the integration of many intentions."

3. Throughout I shall use single quotation marks to call attention to an odd, equivocal, or, in context, logically heterogeneous use of a word or concept; and I shall use double quotation marks where I mean to be directing attention to the word or concept rather than using it to another end.

by nothing more reflective than the affects that inspire it and the body's limits that embody it, a religious rite, a declaration of love, a Petrarchan sonnet, a general theory of the universe as it is for macrophysics—all these are importantly alike (they are rooted in my body) and importantly different (the last in the series seems abstract and distanced from its somatic origins as the first does not.) The last therefore may seem equivocal and dubitable as to its vectorial relation to my world as the first does not.

I do not in fact hold the view that as we move over the range from the first case to the last we move from what is immediate and indubitable (some people have a most equivocal and tentative relation to their own motility) toward what is mediated and hence inherently dubitable. It serves my purpose here, however, to pretend that this is so invariably in order to suggest that to the many significant configurations that comprise my world I bear very different relations ranging from some that are immediate, unequivocal, and manifestly and indubitably bound into that world, to others that are mediated (through, e.g., reflection), equivocal, and having a dubitable vectorial thrust toward and anchorage in something other than the configuration itself.

This brings me to the third and final presupposition to which it seems important to call particular attention: that, namely, having to do with the relation between language (or articulate speech) and reality. Obviously, the making of it is already clearly foreshadowed in the foregoing.

When we have achieved that modality of being-in-the-world which is articulate personal utterance, we also are reflective in the highest degree—given thereby at once our highest powers of articulate affirmation and our most sophisticated forms of equivocation. Only highly developed languages have the explicit grammatical resources for distinguishing among moods—or modes: indicative, subjunctive, optative, vocative, etc. Don Giovanni hesitates not at all—"purche porti la gonella voi sapete quel che fa!" Faust's and Hamlet's inner life in their world is not to be compared with his; reflection—especially in its subjunctive mood—forces its way in upon them.

How then can we always be sure? The answer of course is that we cannot be. But if we *never* were, if there were no prelingual, prereflective Eden in which we confidently moved outward toward the limits of the world, the memory of which, be it ever so tacit, we bear within us at every moment, then there would be no reflection and we could not reflectively entertain our hesitations.[4] The subjunctive mood is, ontologically, parasitical upon a primordial indicative.

In all our personal acts of articulate assertion, whether of propositions concerning particular matters of fact, of general theories, of a comprehensive view of the universe, or even in more tentative heuristic explorations of the as

4. This is really to say that if the self were ever a wholly deracinate and absolutely lucid for-itself then, paradoxically, the conditions for the existence of such an entity would not be fulfilled and there could therefore equally be neither a self nor another. The import of this for the existence of an articulate framework such as one's natural language is that only on condition that *it* has its roots in an inarticulable and, to that language, opaque somatic intimation of itself in prepersonal configurations (upon which we tacitly rely) can there be such natural languages. The notorious history of our doubts about the bearing of language upon something other than itself (which perhaps extends as far back at least as Occam) results from the insistent belief that language is *not* prefigured in prelingual somatic intimations of itself. This has its significance for moral philosophy as well. Even those human acts which are entered upon with utmost lucidity have their origin in and retain their relation to my prereflective presence in the world (upon which I tacitly rely) and issue in consequences that I not only cannot foresee, but that in fact remain forever opaque. Whatever it is that bears my name therefore cannot be affiliated *only* with or exhaustively assimilated to these *lucid* volitions. (This insight I owe to Professor John Silber). Also cf. M. Merleau-Ponty, *The Phenomenology of Perception*, trans. Colin Smith (London: Routledge and Kegan Paul, 1962): "The other person is never quite a personal being, if I myself am totally one" (352, et passim). Finally this means that I cannot explicitly say what it is to be a self (person) because it is always an integration of the particulars of my body-in-the-world with (from the natural standpoint) its many different levels of reality and the principles governing the integration of each level through the determination of the boundary conditions left open by the principles governing the particulars in themselves at the next lower level. Also it is an integration of all my skills—motor and intellectual—of my formalized, reversible, and articulate as well as my unformalized and largely unformalizable intellectual, moral, and aesthetic powers of discrimination to a firmament of values and obligations. And finally, it is an integration of all these to anticipatory, heuristic powers. This integration is paradigmatically achieved in the act of comprehendingly using, with its always reflexive force, the pronoun in the first-person singular—within the context of our language and all its personal pronominal resources.

Any attempt to specify the nature of this comprehensive entity (to which reflexive reference is made) through the detailing of the particulars by relying upon which I perform this feat of integration must result in its destruction, in some measure; on the other hand, any attempt to assimilate the self to the mere act of uttering the first-person pronoun, be it ever so lucid, is to make the self less than an integration of the particulars of my being-in-the-world with its past, present, and future.

However, I must recognize both that, on one hand (from the natural standpoint), there is a stratification of organismic structures, skills, and formalized intellectual powers

yet unarticulated, we are relying proximally upon our inarticulate, tacit, and always incorrigible commitment to the privileged and paradigmatic reality for each of us of our own bodies in a world. This commitment, which we hold acritically, inarticulately, and tacitly, operates proximally as the token of the bearing upon Reality of our distal assertions of particular propositions that, if we do indeed *assert* them, we hold to be true.

Now, since assertions of particular facts are explicit and are made within an articulate framework, we do not hold either them or their bearing upon Reality (which is a question of a logically different order) acritically. Even so, because of our tacit, acritical commitment to Reality in our being-in-our-own-bodies-in-a-world, we cannot in good faith *assert* as true a particular articulate proposition concerning a matter of fact without *in the very same* act tacitly asserting its bearing upon Reality. The tacit-explicit poles are primitively, acritically given.[5]

---

that provides the ground conditions for some measure of continuity through time or for personal identity; and, on the other, that each new feat of integration is unique, an achievement, liable to failure.

I cannot explicitly say, then, what the self is, because when I am performing that feat which is the ultimate mark and norm of its reality, namely, reflexive self-reference, I am dwelling in an integration by relying upon largely unspecifiable particulars. To *attend from* the integration in which I dwell in order to *attend to* the particulars that jointly constitute it is to lose the ultimate focus that enables me to avoid identifying myself either with my body *simpliciter* or alternatively with the mere act of lucid choice or reflexive self-reference.

The making of promises, the putting of my personal seal upon a decision by saying, "I promise," "I have decided," is merely the final and highest act of integration in a hierarchy of integrations and, as such, may be called my subscription to myself. Through this subscription, at once tacit and explicit, I lay claim and come to have a relation to the particulars of my-body-and-its-past-in-the-world that is a *personal* one. (See n. 20 below for the bearing of these observations upon some Christian theological claims.)

5. Cf. Gabriel Marcel: "We are dealing with an urge towards an affirmation—yet an affirmation which it seems impossible to make, since it is not until it has been made that I can regard myself as qualified to make it. It should be noted that this difficulty never arises at a time when I am actually faced with a problem to be solved. In such a case I work on the data, but everything leads me to believe that I need not take into account the *I* who is at work—it is a factor which is presupposed and nothing more. Here, on the contrary, what I would call the ontological status of the investigator assumes a decisive importance. Yet so long as I am concerned with thought itself I seem to follow an endless regression. But by the very fact of recognizing it as endless I transcend it in a certain way: I see that this process takes place within an affirmation of being—an affirmation which I

How is it plausible to make such a claim?

All propositions that are asserted can be noncommittally *stated*—formulated, if you like, in a subjunctive modality. The bearing of such a noncommittally stated proposition upon Reality *can be*—one is tempted to say, in the light of the philosophic tradition since Descartes, *more than likely will be*—noncommittally evaluated. When, however, a proposition is *asserted*, its bearing upon Reality can only be committally evaluated; which is to say, in the light of our precritical and proximal reliance upon our own bodies as the primordial and indubitable token and paradigm of Reality, with the consequent conviction that all propositions held by ourselves to be true are disclosures of that Reality.[6]

Such are some of the relations among personal acts of assertion, the claims of truth for them, and claims of their bearing upon Reality.

B

But before going further with these words about words, I wish to enter a general caveat concerning concern with words. In a way, once the subject is brought up, it almost immediately becomes a dangerous and profoundly misleading preoccupation. We find ourselves trying to talk our way into and out of different ways of being in the taken-for-granted world of our existence. And this easily leads to our coming to believe that our ways of being-in-the-world are primitively and primarily formed and maintained by various tissues of words—words sighed, words asserted, declaimed, invoked, performed,

---

am rather than an affirmation which I *utter:* by uttering it I break it, I divide it, I am on the point of betraying it" (*The Philosophy of Existentialism*, trans. Manya Harari [New York: The Citadel Press, 1963], 17–18). There are striking parallels between Polanyi's tacit-explicit, proximal-distal dichotomies and Marcel's problem-mystery dichotomy, especially in their use for ontological analysis.

The reader is also referred to the very different but cognate findings of the student of human development Erik Erikson, whose "psychological" reflections upon our ways of being-in-the-world are of great import. See his *Childhood and Society*, 2d ed. (New York: W. W. Norton and Co., 1963), 247ff.

6. This elucidation must strike nonphilosophers as at best an ingenious feat devised to triumph over a difficulty that common sense would never allow to arise. This is in fact the case. But philosophy in the modern period and the sciences and even theory-laden common sense that get their own theories about knowing and doing *from* this philosophic tradition are so ubiquitously infected by this "subjunctivitis" that only a more radical form of reflection can overcome it!

and uttered straight, or uttered in quotes, or with exclamation marks and question marks—whether written out or implied in our inflection, in our raised eyebrows, or whatnot. And while I do not wish to say that this may not be so, or so often, or so sometimes, I want to insist that many things that are not in any sense words or tissues of words and that bear very few analogies with them are nonetheless bearers of meanings and significances and hence are conveyors of order by means of which or 'in' which we have our several ways of being-in-the-world: things like colors—alone or in combination; sounds, alone or combined, either simultaneously or successively—or both—with a tempo-relation varying variously with our pulse rate and hence with our stride, our gait, and our gestures; linear configurations that reproduce or vary from the archetypal horizontal or vertical axes of that radical locus in the world for each of us, our own body, or which are the actual traces of the gestures of that body or those of some other like it; things, too, like masses, large in relation to the primitive mass that is our own body, or small; or hard, powerful, overwhelming, like Stonehenge or St. Peter's; or grand, intricate, rational, humane, but numinous, like Chartres; or soft, minute, delicate, rare.

All these have an integrity of their own as presences in the world we are in, like Cézanne's shapes—apples and pears or Mont St. Victoire we call them—independent of the universe of words. And no less than with the words we depend upon for our meanings, they usher us into ways of being-in-the-world.

C

Novelists, critics, poets, theologians, and ordinary human beings are pretty well out of business, in their critical moments, if "person" and "action" come under a cloud. Ayer's *Language Truth and Logic* was a cloud that nearly everyone saw. The need for common cause was clear. But too much of the counterattack has been bemused by an idée fixe that the terms of the discussion about language had been definitively set for all time by A. J. Ayer or the logical positivists. It is merely a curiosity that in spite of all that has been written in this area by "ordinary language analysts" in and out of Oxford for nearly twenty years one still encounters in some of the things they write—especially about literary meaning and religious meaning—the ghost of A. J. Ayer. It is scandalous, however, how often he turns up in a quite unghostly fashion in the discussion of these questions by critics and theologians.

The special proprietary interest of both theology and of the language of religious performances in the concept "person" in literature, while obviously taken quite for granted by critics, has been singled out for attention by at least two latter-day so-called linguistic analysts, themselves by no means logical positivists nor by any means of the same persuasion between them. For both, "person" has a logically primitive role to play in works of literary art.

John Wisdom observes: "Novels which I have mentioned could be called studies of acts, but clearly they are better called studies of persons. A person is an exceedingly complex pattern in time."[7]

Gilbert Ryle, in a different context, in, that is to say, his widely read and widely misunderstood *The Concept of Mind,* which has been called, wrongly I believe, an exercise in linguistic behaviorism, says, "Where logical candour is required from us, we ought to follow the example set by novelists, biographers and diarists, who speak only of persons doing and undergoing things." And he goes on to add: "Men are not machines, not even ghost-ridden machines. They are men—a tautology which is sometimes worth remembering."[8]

But if Ayer's empirical verificationist view of meaningful language took a single form of discourse and made it paradigmatic for all speech to which we could give a cash value, perhaps Wittgenstein's alternative view of the realm of speech being comprised of a variety of language games, governed by constantly changing and seldom specified, sometimes unspecifiable rules, played with ever-evolving counters, and among which the only relation that obtained was that of a "family-resemblance," has led those who took the notion from Wittgenstein either to concern themselves narrowly with what

7. *Philosophy and Psychoanalysis* (Oxford: Blackwell, 1953), 225.

8. *The Concept of Mind* (London: Hutchinson University Library, 1949), 168, 81. Though they have not made explicit reference to the bearing of their findings upon the elucidation of the peculiar logical requirements of literary-artistic discourse, theological argumentation, and exposition of religious performances, two other Oxford philosophers—again of very different persuasion as between them—have reckoned with the peculiar logical status of person-words. P. F. Strawson, in *Individuals: An Essay in Descriptive Metaphysics* (London: Methuen and Co., 1959), argues to the logical unanalyzability and hence, in his terms, the metaphysical indispensability of "person." In a quite different form of argument, but still largely in terms of the linguistic method, Stuart Hampshire, in *Thought and Action* (New York: The Viking Press, 1960), makes out a similar case; one that is doubly interesting for being closer than hailing distance to the sort of thing one hears so-called existentialists saying.

they have called ordinary language; or, alternatively, to fail to notice the special proprietary interest—at least the presumption of it—in certain concepts or in certain tokens for certain language games—and also to fail to notice the inescapability of certain games. When Laplace said of God, "I have no need of that hypothesis," he was in a way making an important Wittgensteinian remark. The language games "physics" and "chemistry" have no use for the concept "God."

The token "God" is not the peculiar property of theological discourse or of religious performances, nor is even the token "Thou." Nor need it be so that the token "molecule" be copyrighted for exclusive use by chemists. Logicians have made excellent use of it. And obviously "hearts" no more belongs to poker than to bridge; nor does it belong exclusively to cardiology.

But even so, the token "God," having that use it has when governed by the logical context of theological argument or religious performances—which is to say when its meaning is a function of a particular and specifiable conceptual environment—*does* belong, as a concept, peculiarly to theology or religious performance; just as "molecule," in a yet similar case, is a proprietary interest of chemistry; just as also "hearts" in a game when it is "trumps" is a purely bridge-like concept.

There are many tokens in our speech that may have a use in many different games, just as many different ball games may be played with a ball designed primarily for tennis. But if we possessed no token of a certain sort and no special way of using it in a special conceptual environment, then there would be one game less to be played.

And of course I am suggesting that both theological discourse and the language of religious performances on one hand and that of literary art on the other are impossible without the common token "person," and the analogous *use* of that token, and that in this sense they both have a proprietary interest in this token and in this concept.

What we have been calling language games, after Wittgenstein, and sometimes call universes of discourse, if they have no tenses and no demonstratives, can be *distinguished* from one another. For example, we can easily start out playing bridge and end up with a very new game we have improvised as we play without having planned it and without having codified its rules as we went along. It would be odd to suggest in such a case that we should not come to entertain a number of important different beliefs and expectations about the world that usually result from such improvisations upon familiar universes of discourse when we are talking about the world. Poets perform such feats; metaphysicians do. They bewilder us and themselves. Often they edify us.[9]

Unlike an exercise in mathematics in which, lacking demonstratives, no references to the world and therefore to the many different language regions in our speech about the world are made, in a treatise on sociology or psycho-analysis or history or theology, however given any of these latter may be to the use of special sociological, psychoanalytical, historical, or other tokens, inevitably a reference to the world and hence to the many different language regions in our speech *about* the world will soon or late be made. This being so, we cannot think of these language games or universes of discourse as hermetically sealed off from one another. Even if we can spot with ease the other side of the *linguistic* tracks, rarely do we have to pass through any explicit border checkpoint.

In all languages by means of which, at some point, it is possible to make an extranotational semantic reference to the world, one inevitably, at some point also converges upon the contingent helter-skelter of our ingenious and bewildering improvisations with the 'other' languages we find being used by others and by ourselves to make that same or similar or analogous kinds of extranotational reference.

It may be useful to speak here of logical neighborhoods, of linguistic topographies, of certain conceptual sets that normally seem quite familiar but which can easily be altered beyond all recognition, or can be recognizably altered in such a way as to induce laughter—say, by leaving out, misusing, or using in an odd way tokens or concepts that have hitherto been quite familiar features of the landscape—misuses like puns or malapropisms, like *Alice in Wonderland,* or like a child's drawing or a painting by Cézanne or one by Georges Mathieu. Our first impulse is to say, "Oh no, that won't do at all! That's not the way it goes." But then, if we only look again we may want to say, "Well, by George, I never noticed!"

Freud took a concept like "sexuality"—and then "repression," "uncon-scious," "neurosis"—and shifted them about on the landscape of our talk

---

9. Cf. Wisdom, *Philosophy and Psychoanalysis:* "To gain a new apprehension of any part of reality we have to shake off old habits of apprehension crystallized probably in a well-known mode of presentation" (263). And: "So does it come about that new facts give us a new apprehension of old ones and a new apprehension of old facts new freedom in looking for new ones. The metaphysician doesn't even remind us of things we had forgotten" (270).

about minds and suddenly we felt confused, even a little alarmed—but also often pleasantly surprised—about "reasons," "causes," "responsible."

What I am trying to suggest by this is just that while in a given generation "physics," "psychology," "history," "theology" or whatnot may be quite recognizable logical neighborhoods because of their proprietary interest in certain concepts, they still can all become very strange to us overnight.

So much, for the moment, for languages, language games, universes of discourse—and hence for theological language, the language of religious performances, and the language of literary art. Unfortunately there are still other preliminary warnings to make—and this next is to be a most important one. There may be a Wittgensteinian fly-bottle waiting behind his own illuminating injunction, "Don't look for the meaning of a word, look for its use," into which we may heedlessly fly.

        D

So far we have had a few words about words. Let us now say something about saying.

In all our preoccupation with words as tokens or tools, as having this or that "use" according to the rules—specified or only implicit—like balls, rackets, bats, cue sticks, or chessmen, playing cards or kernels of corn in an improvised game or bingo—or as occupying this logical neighborhood, having this or that place in a conceptual topography, we are in danger of being misled by the notion of meaning as use—*when this is taken exclusively in conjunction with the language-game model*—misled, that is, into overlooking the user, a *conditio sine qua non* of something's having a use! The kinds of relations I may have to the words I may use cannot be exhaustively displayed in terms of the language-game analogy, or any other single analogy.

Perhaps the point is more concretely displayed if I observe that when we begin to think of "saying" we begin to see that flirting is not only different from lovemaking as poker is different from twenty-one; it is different in at least one importantly different way: with regard to flirting and lovemaking, my ways of abiding in my words and acts, the degree and nature of my personal backing they receive, the question of "good faith"—all these are important in contemplating the differences between *them* as they are *not* in contemplating those between poker and twenty-one. And seduction is, of course, yet *another* case—as Kierkegaard saw! Even to the point, I think, of implying that seduction is not merely a more advanced case of flirtatious advances.

In short, if we speak of logical neighborhoods, conceptual topographies, we must remark the most important fact about them: They are *inhabited*—and through them sayers—to keep to the metaphor—stride, dance, sneak, stalk, march, hide, jump out to surprise, and even pronounce benedictions, maledictions, interdictions, and sing the Nunc Dimittis. And these things they do joyfully, soberly, seriously, mockingly, absentmindedly, entreatingly, hopefully, prayerfully, lovingly, deceitfully, dogmatically, diffidently, performatively, and mindlessly—like a recorded announcement.

Our personal backing is behind our acts and our uttered words in many different ways. Sometimes we mean what we do and say, and saying is what we have done; sometimes we mean them, but not quite; sometimes we believe we mean them and are taken to mean them, but if we are asked, we are not sure; sometimes we don't mean them at all—and say so, with our eyes; sometimes we don't mean and don't by any means say. And it is difficult, now that you think about it, to say what exactly it is to say.

One might quite unproblematically say, "He played his ace rather absentmindedly, indeed, almost irresponsibly." We might even say, "There was something equivocal about his last stroke," though this surely begins to sound more like literary criticism than sports writing, more like Cleanth Brooks than even the elegant Allison Danzig, or at most like W. H. Auden sending a dispatch from Wimbledon! But the game analogy begins to show strain when we try to imagine saying, "On the fairways his game is open and straightforward, but on his approaches to the green his irons become hopelessly ironical." It becomes almost but never quite bankrupt when we try to imagine wondering to ourselves, "It is true, he has moved his bishop, but is he serious or is he just pretending?"

The environment of words, as we all know quite well, is not only other words, and the uses to which their resourcefulness permits them to be put. It is also the many different kinds of personal backing they may receive, the various ways of saying that there are—including hardly saying at all, and even not saying at all.

Making sense out of what has been said is, we all know quite well, a function not only of the sorts of things we find in dictionaries, grammars, logic books; nor is it a function only of pointing, gestures, facial expressions, and tones of voice; nor yet is it a function only of speech habits and usages. It depends also upon the skills of speakers and hearers; upon the confidence of each in the other, upon the bona fides of both. Above all, it depends upon concrete elements of which we are not even aware, even less have codified, including elements of which we *could* not become aware, hence *could* not codify.

To realize the extent to which this is the case, one need only contemplate the many ways we *fail* to make sense, and how amusing, because how surprising we find (when we do find them) the causes of these failures to be. If some of the causes of our failures are a surprise, then some of the causes of our successes go unnoticed. Indeed, the surest way to frustrate every attempt to "make sense" would be to keep our attention ever alert to the ways in which we *do*.

Speech, let us not forget, is something done with words (which suffer themselves thus to be used); and every action not only can be modified adverbially, but speech as action is a saying, a backing by someone of the words he uses in some one or another way.[10] Along with seeing the logical environment of words, that is to say, their ways of being used, we have also to attend to the kind of personal backing they receive from their users.

Merely sounding words is not 'uttering' them; mere uttering is not 'saying'; and saying is not one but many things.

Now, we all know this quite well—that is why I feel obliged to enlarge upon it still further.

There are not only "Stages on Life's Way"—aesthetic, ethical, and religious ways of being-in-the-world. There are ways, too, of *saying:* aesthetic, ethical—perhaps religious.

We are likely to know quite well what we mean when we observe, "He *says* he loves her, but does he really?" It seems like a different case, however, to reflect to oneself, "I say I love her, but do I really?" Different, but not absurd.

When we are "joking" are we saying what we have uttered? And what of "teasing?"

Suppose you are Walter Mitty, acting out a fantasy in imagination in which

---

10. The most acute and imaginative analysis of language in the analytic tradition of Wittgenstein (II) that takes seriously the notion of speech as an action, while focusing upon the "performative" and later what he comes to call the "illocutionary" force of language, is found in J. L. Austin's *How to Do Things with Words,* ed. J. O. Urmson (Oxford: Oxford University Press, 1962). E.g., "The more we consider a statement not as a sentence (or a proposition) but as an act of speech (out of which the others are logical constructions) the more we are studying the whole thing as an act" (20, et passim).

you depict yourself telling a story to an audience of one—to yourself—and suddenly you hear yourself say in imagination, voice full of reassurance, "The Captain will get us through; the Old Man will see us through." What kind of personal backing have the words you silently tell yourself; what kind have the bits of dialogue you hear? Would the case be different if you were to blurt them out, so as to be heard by a passerby?

Imagine you are an actor playing Hamlet in the classic style, as written in a definitive text of Shakespeare—what kind of *saying* would "Hamlet's" words be, what kind of personal backing would you be giving them? How would it be different if you played a "method" Hamlet?

When we flirt, we use words, and other things. And I think we would be inclined to say that it is a game, and a delightful one at that, even though it sometimes leads to much gamier stuff and hence stops being a game altogether—or becomes a very different sort of game. But if we use words when we flirt, are we saying them, and if so how? It's true that we can raise the question of "good faith" about flirtation. But it does seem very queer to wonder whether X's flirtations are serious or whether he is "only playing at it." Though many a woman must have half-wondered, "Is he flirting seriously, or merely putting me on?"

Courting, of course is a different case, as when we use a rhetoric of either a high or a low style to win the heart—or at least the favors—of a woman. To say, "I am courting in earnest," tells you nothing as to whether I am courting her favors or her heart. And, if I wonder myself whether it is her favors or her heart I am courting, a tape recording of what I have uttered to the lady won't tell me what I've *said*, where my heart is, where my personal backing stands, or 'lies'.[11]

---

11. W. H. Auden has raised some of these questions with characteristic wit in "Dichtung und Wahrheit (an unwritten poem)," in *Homage to Clio* (New York: Random House, 1960), 35ff. How can I say "I love you," Auden wonders, and then he imagines: "'My Love,' says the poet, 'is more wonderful, more beautiful, more to be desired than . . .'—there follows a list of admirable natural objects and human artifacts—(*more wonderful,* I should like to say, *than Swaledale or the coast of North-West Iceland, more beautiful than a badger, a sea-horse or a turbine built by Gilkes & Co. of Kendal, more to be desired than cold toast for breakfast or unlimited hot water* . . .). What do such comparisons provide? Certainly not a description by which *you* could be distinguished from a hundred possible rivals of a similiar type" (47–48). And again: "'I will love you whatever happens, *even though* . . .'—there follows a list of catastrophic miracles—(*even though,* I should like to

Or take the case of my recounting a dream to my analyst. Where is the personal backing here? It is not like recounting barely remembered past events where we are inclined to be equivocal in our backing because of our uncertainties. It is rather that giving a backing to the saying of our dreams is a queer kind of backing because the dreamworld is a queer kind of world. And while we're on the subject, why is it supposed that 'saying' my fantasies to another has a kind of therapeutic value for me? Discoveries may be made. But is not the different kind of 'saying' than that of my merely saying them to myself quite as important?

Or what of my describing my childhood to my analyst? What of my personal backing here? Am I misremembering or inventing the story? I may not know. My analyst will not care at first about the difference—though he may suspect. But the judge and jury? They will care.

We can remark, too, the kinds—different kinds—of saying involved in barefaced, sophisticated, and premeditated lying; unpremeditated, perhaps, in a way, 'unintentional' lying—as when I give myself a dramatically more interesting role in a narration of events in which I have been involved; or "making a good story better."

Or again, let us compare telling stories, bearing witness, testifying under oath.

Or let us imagine my signing my name to a confession exacted of me under extreme duress of an old-fashioned sort; 'signing my name' to a confession after being brainwashed; 'forging' my signature to a draft of 'my' bank account, while suffering from amnesia.

What does it mean to say, "X says he believes in the Creed, but does he really?"

What is it to be "as good as one's word(s)"?

All these questions point to different ways of formulating a general phenomenology of saying, an enterprise that would, I fear, prove both boring and unedifying.

What has been concerning me in all this is the curious relation of man to

---

say, *all the stones of Balbek split into exact quarters, the rooks of Repton utter dire prophecies in Greek and the Windrush bellow imprecations in Hebrew, Time run boustrophedon and Paris and Vienna thrice be lit by gas . . .*). Do I believe that these events might conceivably occur during my life-time? If not, what have I promised? *I will love you whatever happens, even though you put on twenty pounds or become afflicted with a mustache: dare I promise that?*" (48).

words; how through some poignant mystery we have occasionally the courage just to say something; and yet how even then—indeed especially then—it comes to us—this courage—unbidden, as a gift, but a gift that paradoxically, it may seem, if faithfully received, puts us into bondage: as if giving ourselves out of our prehuman silence into the realm of speech and saying is an act first of hope, then of love and thanksgiving for the world, but also an act by which everything becomes forever ambiguous and equivocal.

II

So far I have sought to view the phenomena of speech in terms of new possibilities afforded by Polanyi's work. I now wish to show the bearing of these general facts upon literary artistic languages on one hand and the languages of theology and of religious performances on the other; and to do this by attending particularly to the concepts "myth," "story," "history," "act," and "person."

A

In his *Empiricist's View of the Nature of Religious Belief,* R. B. Braithwaite, accepting the empirical verification theory of meaning, goes on to remark the analogies between certain religious statements and certain ethical ones. "The kernel for an empiricist of the problem of the nature of religious belief," he says, "is to explain, in empirical terms, how a religious statement is used by a man who asserts it in order to express his religious conviction."[12]

He goes on to suggest that the primary element in this use is that the religious assertion is used as a moral assertion. For him, a religious assertion is, then, an assertion of a general policy for action, of an intention to live a life of a certain sort.

Now, this suggestion is so patently simpleminded, in view of my earlier warnings as to the actual logical heterogeneity of languages, that you may well wonder why I have taken it seriously at all. And the answer is that it is an interesting and, as we shall see, revealing bit of simplemindedness—because, without explicitly saying so, even Braithwaite doesn't believe it.

12. *An Empiricist's View of the Nature of Religious Belief* (Cambridge: Cambridge University Press, 1956), 11.

First, he says: "The difference between religious and purely moral principles is that, in the higher religions at least, the conduct preached by the religion concerns not only *external* but also *internal* behavior. The conversion involved in accepting a religion is a conversion, not only of the *will*, but of the *heart*."[13] Now, the distinctions between *external* and *internal* and between *will* and *heart* have a great deal of analogy with different ways of saying and doing, of giving my personal backing to my words and deeds, of investing myself in what I do and what I say.

Of much greater interest is Braithwaite's tacit admission that there is an element in religious discourse that is not at all just declarations of policies for living a certain kind of life. He says, "The intentions to pursue the behaviour policies, which may be the same for different religions, are associated with thinking of different *stories* (or sets of stories)."[14]

Again, let us overlook the simplemindedness in order to take note of two things: (1) Braithwaite suggests here that, even if one need not have "stories" in order to complete the meaning of merely *ethical* policy statements, one *does* need them or at least one does in fact *have* them as parts of religious discourse; and that, if we did not have them as parts of religious discourse, it would be difficult to tell one religion from another. (2) Perhaps we shall discover that Braithwaite's important distinction between the "external" and the "internal," between the "will" and the "heart" (and my distinction between different kinds of personal backing) are themselves functions of the particular stories such that without *these* stories not only would the distinction between one religion and another disappear, but that between religion and ethics would disappear as well.

For all his attempts to assimilate religious utterances to declarations of life policies, Braithwaite very much believes in stories. Indeed, he believes, it turns out, in Christian stories, in a far more logically primitive sense, with a far greater range of logical efficacy than even he has realized. He believes in these stories *necessarily,* in a way; for even just as a moral philosopher, "action," "person," etc., have their meaning in their locus, for him, in a logical topography that is supplied by these stories. Like all of us, he is, if only in a cultural sense, a de facto Christian.

He believes in these stories and we may well ask, "Why?"

13. Ibid., 21. Italics added.
14. Ibid., 23. Italics in the original.

And I think the answer is just that policy-statements of a very general sort—like "I have decided to live an agapeistic life"—though *story-neutral* in appearance, when viewed and elucidated by a moral philosopher of a verificationist turn of mind, are seen in fact to be nothing of the sort. Such statements, when they are responsibly analyzed macrologically, are intelligibly interpretable at all only if their implicit "stories" are explicated. The need of stories (and I deliberately use the term vaguely at this point) then lies precisely in the fact that policy-statements are about intentions to act in certain ways, and action is inconceivable apart from stories. It is stories that display how the concepts "action," "person," "will," "heart," "inner," "outer" are used. The precise meaning of and hence the differences between Confucian policy-statements and Christian policy-statements are entirely a function of their differing stories.

Anyone who makes a declaration of a general policy for action in good faith has at the same time committed himself to some story or set of stories apart from which such a declaration would be unintelligible, even though the subscription to the stories be only tacit and becomes explicit only when someone ingenuously asks, "Whatever do you mean?" And this is so whether one is a Christian declaring an agapeistic policy, a Marxist declaring a socialistic policy, or a moral philosopher of a Kantian persuasion declaring a rational deontological policy.

"Action," hence a "policy for action," is logically incomplete without "stories." A universe in which the "saying of stories" is logically impossible is a universe in which the concepts "action," "person," "decision," "choose" have no use; and is therefore also a universe in which "right," "wrong," and "good" have no use.

But if I have made sport with Briathwaite's verificationist simplemindedness, it has been done by using the concept "stories" in so vague a way as to subsume under it concepts having as heterogeneous uses as do the concepts "myth," "folktale," "autobiography," "biography," "story" (in the sense of a narrative of events), "story" (in the sense of a conscious work of the art of fiction), "drama" (in the sense of a conscious imitation of an action), "ritual" (in the sense of a paradigmatic enactment), and "history."

The time has come for some sorting out among these—and since my concern here is mainly with that of "person" (as a concept that literary art, theological discourse, and the language of religious performance have in common and without which none of them would be possible), I shall consider mainly "myth," "history," "story," "person," "action."

In what follows I shall try to do three things.

First, I shall suggest that there are at least two conceptions of "myth": one I associate with its origin in primitive ritual, primitive cosmology, and with its fulfillment and near destruction in the great conscious works of tragic poetry of Greek antiquity; and in which there are, from our point of view, no persons—but only gods, heroes and "proto-persons," and in which there are, in consequence, no actions, in our sense, a sense yet to be displayed. The other view of "myth" is one that is clearly associated with "stories," in which, risking oversimplifications, I am tempted to say, there are "persons" and "heroes," but no "gods"; and with "history" in which there are certainly "persons" and perhaps some "heroes." To remark a second use for the concept "myth," as I shall be developing it, in no way diminishes its importance for us; but I shall hope to show that its meaning and use are dramatically altered in the new logical affiliations I wish to establish for it.

While "myth" in this second sense is neither "story" nor "history," it is a necessary extension of them that has to do with the beginnings and especially with the endings of actions and therefore shares with "stories" and "histories" references to persons. Indeed, it is myth, in this sense, that refers me to the logically heterogeneous "events" attending my emergence from my prelingual, prepersonal, prehistorical, anonymous background into which reach roots from my present personal existence and which therefore do in this irreducibly equivocal way make references to a person insofar as I see myself personally in their light. By means of them I grasp myself as both *given* and as *the receiver.* Further, not only do myths in our second sense *make references to persons,* in the full sense; insofar as the concept "action" is a necessary affiliate of "person," and, insofar as an action that cannot be regarded from the standpoint of its completion is not an action, in the full sense in which our tradition has for a very long time understood it; and finally, insofar as it is myth (in our second sense) alone that permits such a view of action, "myth" is a necessary affiliate of "person."

Secondly, I shall try to display the peculiar way of 'saying' one has in the art of fiction—in stories, in other words—hoping to underscore their differences from both myth, in both of our senses, and from history.

Finally, I shall suggest something about some overlooked aspects of the notion "history."

Before I can embark upon these perilous seas I must distinguish between mere "narrative" on the one hand and "history" and "story" on the other;

and I shall have in turn to distinguish between "history" and "story"—where in the latter case we have in mind chiefly a conscious product of the art of fiction.

It is obvious that "myths," "histories," "stories," and "narratives" are not and could not be conveyed in mathematical notations or in logical calculi—because (though not only because) there are no tenses or tense surrogates as parts of their logical grammar, as there are in all our natural languages.

However, though the suggestion, I know, ignores some common usage, there is, among the above cases, one form of discourse that takes place quite normally in our natural languages and therefore makes frequent use of the tense distinctions that are found there, but for which tenses have a different use, or at least, a different value from that they have in "myth," "story," and "history." I mean, of course, "narrative."

I do not wish to make a great play with this point. I only suspect that an important contrasting feature of the role of tenses and other time-words when affiliated with "myth," "story," and "history" can be elucidated by remarking their characteristic uses in "narrative"—though I shall also want to suggest that their use is not identical among the former three.

It is clear from the *Oxford English Dictionary* that the word *narration* has an intimate historical connection with courts of law; that to narrate is to give a recital of facts (not of events—which, when we tell of them, have an organic connection); that a narrative is such a recital. Reciting a set of facts seems to be a temporal affair in a way different both from deducing conclusions from premises and from giving an historical account—although they both consume time in the doing, and though the latter very much depends upon tense distinction.

But a narrative as *mere narrative* (and not as an important part of "history," which is a concept without use apart from that of "the facts") simply recites a list of facts. Think, for example, of the prosecution narrating the facts of his case, even if only by means of examining a witness; "On or about August 25, Poteat was proceeding down West Franklin Street . . . ," etc.

Now, in due course, no doubt it becomes the function of the prosecution to show beyond a reasonable doubt to reasonable men, that temporal and therefore perhaps causal connections (or the presumption of them) do obtain among the recited facts. But as a mere recital of facts—though this takes time and times are fixed within the words in which the recital is given and so on—this narration (though to claim this may require a rather esoteric distinction) is not a "story" nor is it "history"—as *mere narration*. It is the job of the prosecution, having done this much, then to show that the stuff composing what has been recited in the narrative as the facts can be so construed as to be seen as having 'organic' connections of the sort that would lead reasonable men to say, "These facts, if that is indeed what they are, do seem to add up to the crime cited in the indictment." In short, it leads reasonable men to construe the components of a narrative as so 'organically' related as to deserve to be called history.

Notice, we can quite coherently say: "Yes! No doubt about it! X happened. Y happened and so did Z. But did the crime claimed in the indictment happen?" If we can sometimes wonder whether the crime did occur, while having no doubts about X, Y, and Z, then sometimes concluding that the crime did happen is not logically on all fours with accepting X, Y, and Z, as narrated, for facts. And, if they are not on logical all fours, a simple narrative need not, indeed, cannot be equivalent to what we ordinarily mean by "history."

In a court of law, testimony is designed not only to establish what did or did not happen, but also to discover if all these things taken together have an 'organic' connection entitling them to be relevantly and meaningfully connected in such a fashion as will enable reasonable men to say: "Yes, this is a reliable history; the crime, as claimed in the indictment, *was* committed."

And when opposing counsel rises to object during direct examination that a question is *argumentative,* one thing he often means to claim is that (in the terms of my analysis) 'historical connections' are being prematurely made.

That which distinguishes a mere narrative of facts from what adds up to a crime, and that also which distinguishes one type of crime from another— first-degree murder, manslaughter—is precisely questions about there being *intent* and about the nature of the *intent*—often notoriously difficult to establish and certainly established, if at all, in a logically very different way from establishing 'the facts'. A narration of the facts becomes judicially material only when intent, that is, a *person* personally *behind* 'the facts', an agent, an actor more or less giving his acts a personal backing, enters the account of events. For it is only then that the narrative becomes more; it is then that it may add up to a crime.

Recitals of facts then—in the above sense—though they are, in two different senses of fact, necessary conditions of both stories and of histories, are not the same as stories and histories.

Let me now drop this overrefined distinction, since I trust that it has by now done its work.

The most distinctive characteristic of myth in the classical sense to remark for present purposes is that though, like a story it unfolds in time, so that in one perfectly good sense we may say there are 'events' recounted (though I warn you, they are of a logically most peculiar sort) and we may say that these 'events' are laid out in time, so that, in one sense, we want to claim that Y was *after* X and *before* Z (as we are not tempted to say of the relations stated in a tenseless mathematical notation), it is not a report of unique events, and, in *our* senses of these notions, has neither a beginning nor an end—as a circle has neither beginning nor end. Myths, in this classical sense, look very like stories and histories because the notation in which they are presented has tense distinctions, and because something seems to *happen* in them—in our sense of "happen." But in fact they are at least as much like what is given in tenseless mathematical notations, since what is given in them is eternal, or given eternally.

Their origin seems to have been associated with the ritual enactment of the passage of the cosmos through the course of its finite order. Being finite, as is, say, a circle, one could say both that from any given point in this course one could view the entire course as already given, eternally given, eternally repeated (if it were not absurd, one is tempted, for the sake of logical accuracy, to say "eternally 'peated'") and that therefore nothing (new) ever happened or nothing (really) new ever happened; and also say from that same given point that there were things-familiar, eternally repeated things yet to happen.[15]

15. When I awkwardly characterized as finite the order of the cosmos, as ritually and mythically conceived, and when I speak of the passage of the cosmos through this course as one in which, in our own quite uncontroversial sense, nothing (new) happens, some of what I mean may perhaps be elucidated by aspects of the following model. With a pair of ordinary gaming dice, it is possible to compute with mathematical exactness the finite number of possible combinations and permutations of turned-up die sides. One could specify, if one wished, each single possible combination of such turned-up sides; and one could also specify the finite number of such possibilities. Let this case now stand for the cosmos as classically conceived. If one knows of it what one would know as the result of the computations and know it quite apart from actually observing any exhaustive run-through of its possibilities *all* that is logically possible in that cosmos (one could say, *all* that eternally is in it), then *from that standpoint,* one would regard the contingent possibility of actually making an exhaustive run-through as "time" in which, in a way, nothing happens.

In myth construed in this way, the first of the two ways I wish to display, there are no events, no novelties, no decisions, and therefore no actions and no persons—in our sense of these notions (yet to be deployed).

It is in the great conscious works of tragic poetry by Sophocles, Aeschylus, and Euripides, which in fact presuppose the elements of these myths as they have come down to them from ritual, the oral traditions of folklore, and finally the epic, that the peculiar logic of these myths is best seen, for it is precisely in these works of conscious art that the ultimate pressure upon the logical limits of the ancient myths is brought to bear.

In these plays, ancient myth, even with its now attenuated hold upon the notion of a finite course for the cosmos, survives, as is well attested by the great sigh of ritual-magic relief that one hears from the final chorus at the end of *Oedipus Tyrannus:*

> . . . see him now and see the breakers of
> misfortune swallow him![16]

But in them we do begin to see heroes and guilt and salvation and therefore intimations of acts and persons; therefore intimations too of stories and of histories.

Now, the strain under which myth, in the first of our senses, is put is related to the fact that tragic poetry, as is not the case with ritual, folk-myth, and even the oral antecedents of epic, is a conscious work of art.

Saying myth and saying tragic poetry are importantly different kinds of saying. The kind of personal backing we find in one is crucially different from that we give the other. The extent to which we abide in the words of one is not the same as in the other. We are serious in the one as we are not serious in the other. The Eucharist may be dramatic, but for the true believer it is not a play. To say that art gains some kind of autonomous life of its own is to say it loses the seriousness of ritual and the seriousness too of myth. It becomes *play* when it becomes conscious of itself.

W. H. Auden has said, "There is a game called Cops and Robbers, but none called Saints and Sinners."[17]

16. Sophocles, *Oedipus Tyrannus,* trans. David Greene (Chicago: University of Chicago Press, 1954).

17. *Poets at Work,* ed. Charles D. Abbot (New York: Harcourt, Brace and Co., 1948), 170.

Art, and hence the art of the story (as I wish to understand it) are absolutely necessary to our life as persons, but not merely because they are serious, but rather because they are, at the same time, play.

I must now briefly discuss art as play.

St. Augustine, in his reflections upon his youthful willful act of stealing pears, which he did not want, expresses one of the profoundest impulses of the human spirit—the impulse to author an absolutely gratuitous act, decisively, and with impunity, to assert man's independence of all necessity. The act whereby one willfully disobeys the law is seen by Augustine as a perverted image of God's transcendence of the world. He says: "And wherein did I, even corruptedly and pervertedly, imitate my Lord? Did I wish, if only by artifice, to act contrary to Thy law . . . so that . . . I might imitate an imperfect liberty by doing with impunity things which I was not allowed to do, in obscured likeness of Thy omnipotence?"[18]

It was the nineteenth century that particularly explored the interesting logical alliances among "art," "crime," "play," "sanctity," the "acts gratuite," and "personhood."

A successful ultimate transcension of necessity such as was sought by Kirilov was unimaginable in terms of Greek myth alone. But in their great conscious works of tragic poetry, the Greeks depicted the penultimate transcension by man of necessity. This contributed importantly to their view of man as distinct from everything else there is. Since the tragedy was a play, that is, a conscious work of art, the spectator could indwell the action being imitated with less than ritual or mythic seriousness, and thereby vicariously depict and enjoy the freedom of the hero, the while retaining amnesty from the retribution that befalls him. He could both dwell in and not dwell in the imitated action.

Literary art, precisely because it is play, a let's pretend, enables us to have a certain detachment, to come into some sense of what is reflexively named by the pronoun first-person singular. By being fictive, literature divorces us from the world of what, in any given age, we soberly choose to call reality. It is precisely by this means that we discover what it is to transcend the world as a self. In saying, "Let's pretend," we perform an act of freedom from the world of necessity.

Now, it is only when art and existence are so distinguished as to enable us

18. *On the Trinity*, book 11, chapter 5.

to *pretend* that we achieve this freedom from the world of necessity. At the same time, it is only when, having made the distinction, we do not go on to mistake art for existence that we can remain human. Existence is serious and dreams are not; existence can fully engage our personal wills and art cannot; history we are fully engaged in, by fiction we are not.

Those for whom this distinction has not yet become clear are either primitives or children; those for whom it has vanished are madmen.

Even, however, when one has said all this, one must concede that if we achieve an attitude of irony toward what is serious by our aesthetic indwelling of a story, we also achieve some substantive view of our own personhood because even an aesthetic indwelling is nevertheless a *genuine indwelling*. Even stories are things in which I after all do, in a sense, believe. The fiction I read of which I want to say, "That is *my* story, in a way," is a form of words to which I may be said to give a high degree of personal backing. And insofar as this is true, it is appropriate to say that it is in terms of such a story that I understand who I am and what I am doing when I act.[19]

B

It remains now to suggest some differences among uses of the concepts "story," "history," "myth" (in our first sense), and "myth" (in what I shall henceforth call the eschatological sense).

The best way to round off this already overprotracted analysis is to consider the above concepts in the light of the concept "action."

A *story* is a temporal deployment of events that differs from myth, in the

19. Hannah Arendt has commented with great beauty upon this. She says: "The scene where Ulysses listens to the story [at the court of the King of the Phaeacians] of his own life is paradigmatic for both history and poetry; the 'reconciliation with reality' . . . came about through the tears of remembrance. The deepest human motive for history and poetry appears here in unparalleled purity: since listener, actor, and sufferer are the same person, all motives of sheer curiosity and lust for new information . . . are naturally absent in Ulysses himself, who would have been bored rather than moved if history were only news and poetry only entertainment" ("The Concept of History," in *Between Past and Future* [New York: The Viking Press, 1961]). Though Miss Arendt's way of sorting out the concepts "history" and "poetry" (or "story," as I say) is far from precisely congruent with my own in this essay, I find her way illuminating and congenial, and elucidatory of matters that are not here at the center of my concern, but which in another setting might well be.

classical sense, in that it requires the concept "happen" in a logical environment other than that afforded by ritual reenactment, the passage of the cosmos through its finite course and eternal return; it requires the concept "person"; and it requires that of "action." In a sense that can be made clear only at the very end of this inquiry, it requires "beginnings" and "endings"—but "beginnings" and "endings" such as are appropriate to a conscious work of art to which our relation is aesthetic, in the 'saying' of which our personal backing is at least equivocal, in which the indwelling of our words is not confused with a commitment to existence as such.

History is a similar temporal deployment of events, bound to what we question-beggingly, but unproblematically, and, I think for present purposes, benignly call 'facts'. It too requires the concepts "happen," "person," and "action"—as well as many others that are of small concern here. It too speaks of "beginnings" and "endings." But, since our 'saying' of history is serious as our 'saying' of stories is not; since we make history our own as with a mere story we do not; since our personal backing of it is not equivocal, and our indwelling of our words is precisely a commitment to existence; our saying of the 'beginnings' and 'endings' of our own history are serious in the way appropriate to a person, and yet, these 'beginnings' and 'endings' of my history, about which I am serious, are not themselves parts of that history—except as logical extensions of it that are *mythical*, in the eschatological sense.

I may be the agent of my own acts, or at least of some of them—including the 'act' whereby I claim a particular deployment of events clearly rooted in facts, as being my very own story, even if perchance some or even much of this 'act' of claiming and indwelling my own story occurs on the psychiatric couch. I may, indeed I must, be also the agent of the tacit 'act' of claiming the logically problematic mythical account of 'beginnings' and 'endings', without which the history that I claim as my very own would be incomplete. Without these 'accounts' of radical beginnings and radical endings, the concepts "person," "action," and "happen" will not function as they must if history is not to become either a mere *story* or a mere *myth*, in the classical as opposed to the eschatological sense.

In the nature of the case, I cannot be both the agent of particular acts that make up my history and also the 'agent' of its logically heterogeneous 'beginnings' and 'endings'—not, anyhow, agent in the same sense. To do so would require that I should be a God, an "author and finisher"; it requires me to be both unproblematically *in* my history and also *outside* of it. If I were such a being as this, I could not also be an agent and a person in history, in those senses of these notions we have developed.

Let me now briefly analyze certain aspects of the concept "action."

What is an action? I want to say in the first place that the universe of action is necessarily *dramatic*. But then this does not get us very far.

What do I mean? I mean that such a universe is one in which the concepts "person" and "moral discrimination" have logical autonomy. Neither "person" nor "moral discrimination" can be regarded as assimilable to or analyzable into other concepts without remainder. "Person" cannot be analyzed as "dynamic biochemical system" or as "animal"; "moral discrimination" cannot be reduced to "instinct," "desire," "organic" or "biochemical system seeking to remain in homeostasis" or to their sum.

No concept is logical-topography-neutral. In some sense, it would be appropriate to use the concept "agent" of Oedipus, Orestes, Hamlet, Job, and William H. Poteat. It would be misleading in the extreme to suppose that "agent" as a concept could have the same use in all five cases—or, indeed, in any two. Let me bring this out by using a somewhat outlandish analogy. Imagine at one extreme a victim of schizophrenia in a state of complete catatonia. At the other, conceive an electronic computer more sophisticated than any now in existence.

In the one, we have a case of a recognizable member of our own species of whom we might hesitate to use the concept "person." In the other, an electronic machine of which we seem increasingly willing to say that it "solves problems," "makes decisions"—even perhaps that it "acts."

I think most of us recognize that in the latter case we are using a rather extended analogy.

In the former, however, our hesitations over using the concept "person" are more real and certainly more poignant. (Why, by the way, is that?) I think we are inclined to hesitate over the use of "person" because it is unimaginable that any 'intentions' will ever be made 'public'. We may even wonder over the propriety of using "intentions" in such a setting.

A member of species Homo sapiens who never says anything or does anything verges toward the limits of the applicability of "person." We recognize this even in the most ordinary ways. We say things like, "He is very much of a person"; "He really doesn't seem human."

Now, remembering all the warnings already issued, I will define an action as a public occurrence that is intended by a person. Someone who bears a proper name and has a unique spatiotemporal existence and of whom, if it is asked, "Why did X happen?" can answer, "I was trying to Y," is properly called the agent of an action.

Another way to put this would be: An action is an occurrence that we have good reason to believe derives its meaning from the fact that the occurrence was opted by Jones *as Jones*. This means of course that an actor (in the sense of one who professionally plays parts on a stage) is not *as actor* the agent of actions except those required by his profession.

I am aware of difficulties here, and aware that what I have just said runs counter to a good deal of common usage. Yet it is precisely these divergencies I need to bring out.

The actor in a play is not, in the presently relevant sense, the agent of actions, because what occurs on the stage derives its meaning (comes to be acts at all) not from *his* intentions, *his* story, but from the text of the play.

Hamlet intends to kill the king. If asked, "Why did Hamlet kill Polonius?" we do not answer, "Because Sir John Gielgud intended to kill the king and made a mistake." Even less are we likely to say, "Because Sir John Gielgud intended to kill Sir Ralph Richardson."

Now, this yields the distinction between an occurrence that derives its meaning from a play and one that derives its meaning from a personal intention. It also underscores one of the differences between art and history; between play actions and 'serious actions'.

But even this does not take us far enough.

Everyone who says of me, "Poteat is reading in order to pass his exams," has in mind a particular story—the story of Poteat.

Not only so. When I say of myself, "I am reading because I intend to pass my exams," I have in mind a story—or more properly, a minute tract within a story—that I would call *my* story. This again yields the distinction between a play-story and a serious-story. A serious-story is the story of at least one bearer of a proper name, having a unique spatiotemporal existence, who sees his own action as deriving from this story; and who, if asked, "What are you doing?" would answer by recounting some tract of that story. Or to put the matter less awkwardly but more vaguely: What is for a person a serious-story is history.

There can be no action without a story; there can be no history without the serious and unique intendings of existent persons.

C

A story becomes a history because the deployment in time of events which we see to be the products of "actions" or "persons" in the light of this story is claimed by someone as his very own.

I suggested above that "history" in this sense, with which "person," "action," and "intention" function unproblematically, remains incomplete unless it is possible for me to *say, indwell, give my personal backing* to references to radical beginnings and endings which cannot be on logical all fours with the story I have made my very own. I cannot claim to be both the "author and the finisher" of my own history.

I want to conclude now by saying that those references to radical beginnings and endings comprise the substance of eschatological myth (a usage which has no hint of the pejorative in it); and that far from being mere adornments of history, as we understand it, they are absolutely essential conceptual conditions for "action," "person," and "history" having that use which we by now are incapable of abandoning.[20]

III

What then are we to make of all of this?

We may say, I think, (1) that eschatological myths, stories, and histories, though they constitute a small fraction of the many articulate forms in use among men, though they are logically heterogeneous in their uses and are variously indwelt by their users, are peculiarly and irreducibly affiliated with the articulation of personal existence, intention, and action, as we have for a

20. A Christian theologian might well say at this point: "The self to which I subscribe but cannot know [see n. 4 above] is to be known only in hope and through faith, whereby I see myself as one already known." Cf. Kierkegaard: "'By relating itself to its own self and by willing to be itself, the self is grounded transparently in the Power which constituted it.' And this formula again, as has often been noted, is the definition of faith" (*The Sickness unto Death,* trans. Walter Lowrie [Princeton: Princeton University Press, 1941], 216). And, he might continue: "In the present time we do indeed see only through a glass darkly, yet in terms of eschatological myth, as St. Paul has put it definitively for the Christian, even now in hope by faith we know ourselves as creatures who also always have been known." Of this I should be inclined to say: it is this claim which has often given such intensity and depth to the view of personal existence within the history of our own sensibility.

very long time understood these; (2) that they all enjoy, their heterogeneity notwithstanding, the same kind of legitimacy in relation to that understanding; and (3) that they are only upheld and integrated into a complex though stratified logical topography through the personal backing and subscription 'from within' of those persons whose modalities (among others) of being-in-the-world they are.

All this means, finally, that uses of, or references to, eschatological myths in theological argument or in religious performances—myths like the creation, the fall, the resurrection—are not *in principle* more problematical than each and every articulate form in use—though each and every such form is not problematical in the same way; nor, indeed, is any given form in the same way differently problematical from all others at every time.

Every such form depends upon and has no stronger legitimation than its grounding in its living use among men. If the use of any language requires justification, then the use of each and every language requires it—an absurd and impossible program, since at least *one* language will always have to be acritically used. All that can be reasonably required is the disclosure of analogies and disanalogies obtaining among the heterogeneous forms actually in use.

Such a fiduciary grounding cannot be explicitly prescribed; nor is there any sure protection against its eventual erosion.

After three centuries of a quest for, if not an assurance of, certainty we must contritely confess that we in the Western world have lived by nothing more substantial than hope, recognizing nevertheless that hope has always been rewarded by unexpected knowledge and that speech, made bold by hope, has always disclosed to us more than we could explicitly anticipate and than we can ever fully say.

> What the dead had no speech for, when living,
> They can tell you, being dead: the communication
> Of the dead is tongued with fire beyond the
>   language of the living.[21]

---

21. T. S. Eliot, "Little Gidding," in *Four Quartets* (New York: Harcourt, Brace and Co., 1943).

FURTHER POLANYIAN MEDITATIONS

Michael Polanyi begins his consideration of whether the premises of science can be known by posing the following question: Can science be said to rest on specifiable presuppositions, be it on rules of correct procedure or on substantial beliefs about the nature of things?[1]

Pre/Text: An Interdisciplinary Journal of Rhetoric (Fall 1981): 173–87.

The following has been excised by a radical surgical procedure from a four-hundred-page manuscript, *Polanyian Meditations: In Search of a Post-Critical Logic.*

The motifs that form the armature of these more protracted reflections are my claim that rationality, that is, the "hanging togetherness" of things for us, and logic, that is, the explicit form of the "making sense" of things for us, is more deeply and ubiquitously—though inexplicitly—embedded in our ordinary thinking and doing than we are likely to notice. We fail to remark this because when called upon to reflect on these facts we are likely to do so in the light of models—"a picture held us captive" (L. Wittgenstein)—formed by critical philosophy, beginning with Descartes, which increasingly took mathematics and formal logic to be the preeminent paradigms of the form of the "hanging togetherness" of things and of the "making sense" of things. Against these implicit assumptions of these second-order accounts of rationality in our philosophic tradition I argue that mathematics and formal logic derive from and remain parasitical upon the "hanging togetherness" and "sense-making" that we archaically know within our integral mindbodily rootedness in the as yet unreflected world and in our unreflected thinkings and doings in that world. For it is my thesis that language—our first formal system—has the sinews of our bodies, which has them first; that grammar, syntax, the ingenuous choreography of our rhetorical engagement with the world, the meaning, semantic and metaphorical intensionality of our language are preformed in that of our pre-lingual mindbodily being in the world, which is the condition of their possibility. And I contend that, while this is not the thesis of Polanyi's *Personal Knowledge,* it is the unavoidable implicate of the rhetoric—the language, images, and conceptual repertoire—of that book.

The form of the question taken in context clearly implies that a scientist, alive, sentient, oriented in the world, and engaged in the activity of inquiry, is governed by a *practice,* a way of *doing* that may or may not be exhaustively reflected and identified. The very formulation of this implication suggests yet another puzzlement: when and to the extent that the elements of such a way of doing come to be reflected, yielding thereby *explicit* rules of procedure, what is it to which reflection has attended in doing so? Which is really to ask a bedrock epistemological question: What is reflection; how and by what means is it accomplished; what are our reflective instruments?

Polanyi's question also implies that this same scientist's inquiry is shaped, as he says, by "substantial beliefs about the nature of things," which equally may or may not be exhaustively reflected and identified; and this formulation suggests again the puzzlement over what it is to which reflection attends when it reflects and identifies these beliefs. In other words, we are led to ask, how are we to identify our substantial beliefs about the nature of things?—on its face, an odd-appearing question in the ethos of the Enlightenment where the answer usually would be self-evidently: either one approaches inquiry free of any such beliefs; or one approaches it only in a state of lucidity about them! No third view seems to be afforded by our philosophic tradition.

The "picture"[2] we seem invited by Polanyi's questions to contemplate is

---

As radical in relation to the tradition of critical philosophy as is *Personal Knowledge,* taken on its face, I believe the "argument" that is implicated with its rhetoric—in the "logic" of its language, the vectors of the intentionalities of its metaphors—is even more archaic and therefore yet more potent. The only thing I find surprising about these claims is that they seem to me at once quite outrageous and self-evident.

1. *Personal Knowledge: Towards a Post-Critical Philosophy* (Chicago: University of Chicago Press, 1958), 160.

2. I have used this vague word *picture* quite deliberately but with some trepidation. I want, if possible, to induce you by means of this usage to attend reflectively from time to time, as you read, to the way you find yourself being mindbodily in the world with the words of this text and their meaning. Ask yourself: "What is the gestalt of which I perceive myself to be a part, how would I depict that gestalt, what is the picture in the midst of which I find myself?" For of course it will be part of my argument that one's way of being mindbodily present in the world with the written or printed words of a text, no less than with our second-order, reflected *account* of our activity of existing in the world, including our activity of knowing, is a function of the "logic" of this picture. Since the picture has a "logic" it must then have "implications": it will include and exclude possible ways in which meaning might appear and be embodied. Furthermore, I

that of an inquirer whose very being is, in any ultimate sense, inextricably trammeled within the world's body in the very musculature of his activity in inquiring, the activity *itself* shaped among many other things: by "rules of procedure" of at least *some* of which he is, perhaps, unaware and, what's more, of which it may be logically impossible for him to become aware; and by "substantial beliefs about the nature of things," which may be equally elusive.

It is of course not being claimed that there are *never* any "rules of procedure" or "substantial beliefs about the nature of things" of which we are or at least can become explicitly aware—aware antecedent to and as the explicit directives for inquiry. The supposition is rather that there are some "rules of procedure" and "substantial beliefs" of which we are not and may not be able to become explicitly aware; yet that *these* "rules" and "beliefs" actually guide inquiry; and finally that, even if we have become aware of them, this awareness was arche-genetically achieved only "after" unreflected but productive *inquiry* and then only by our noticing, in reflection, after the fact, what

---

have used "picture" rather than "image," "concept," "model," "metaphor," "analogy," and, indeed, many other words signifying a gestalt of meaning, a "shape" of sense, each of which possesses a certain felicity, because I believe "picture" can comprehend all these other notions while still inviting the most concrete kind of reflection on your part. There are indeed perils for me in this. The obvious affiliation of the word *picture* with the word *see* may be a seduction. Perhaps a tactile, proprioceptive or audial "picturing" would serve better, if such could be embodied in the medium of a printed text such as is just now before you. But since I am asking you to *reflect,* to "turn back upon" the way in which you and I are in the world, the use of a *form*—that is, a reflected shaping—of our experience of seeing, is inevitable, it being the sense by means of which we are able most fully to draw away from the primordial fact of our being prereflectively in the world. I would willingly, for reasons which will gradually appear, dissever the word *picture* from its familiar affiliation with the words *see* and *draw* in their everyday use: for example, by speaking of Mozart's G Minor Quintet, K 516, as audial picture; by speaking of my possession of a motor skill like the game of tennis or the art of glassblowing, as my having and being in the midst of a proprioceptive or haptic picture; by speaking of my orientation to the environment of smells as possessing and dwelling in an olfactory picture—an "ordorscape," as W. H. Auden has wittily called it—or by identifying my "knowing how to go on" when given the series 1–3–5–7 . . . as my "having a picture"—as when we say: "Ah, I've got the picture." (See Wittgenstein, *Philosophical Investigations* [New York: The Macmillan Company, 1955], paragraphs 151, 179). Clearly, there are important disanalogies among even the above cases. I invite the reader, even so, to remark, then to dwell in and, finally, as he reflects, to rely upon these analogies in order to begin to sense the "logic" of the picture of his own being in the world that he at once *has* and is *in the midst of.*

"rules" and what "beliefs" we recognize to have been implied in our actual *doing* of the inquiry. The very notion of unknowable rules of procedure is largely alien to our philosophic tradition regarding such matters. The introduction of such a conception into the interpretation of our feats of scientific knowing not only raises questions about methodology, especially about second-order accounts thereof; but it raises questions, too, about the nature of logic, i.e., the form of the connectedness of things in the processes of thought, hence about the nature of mind—and by implication, about the nature of the body and its relation to the mind.

If then, there are "rules of procedure" and "substantial beliefs about the nature of things" of which we cannot or at least do not know and, in any case, may not/cannot/need not know prior to the beginning of inquiry, then two striking inferences may be drawn. First, the concepts "rule" and "belief" are doing duty largely unfamiliar in our philosophic tradition. Second, the "picture" of an inquirer's way of being-in-the-world in his activity of inquiry, classically formulated for the Enlightenment by Descartes's *Discours de la Méthode,* is implicitly under drastic revision. For that picture, taken strictly in terms of its own logic, is the paradoxical one of an inquirer divested of all previous beliefs, speaking and writing no language—hence without a culture—and armed before the fact with explicit rules of procedure(!), therefore disentangled from his own being-in-the-world in his inquiring activity.

As I appear to myself moiling amid the words you have just read, embrangled here in my own inquiry, immured it seems by the intractable stuff of my native language, with its complex history, its dense plaiting of verbal roots and its rich plexuses of metaphorical intentionalities, dragging me this way and that, and not suffering itself to be more than provisionally, tentatively, and partially unpacked, in order that I might reflect upon knowing, being, and reflection, *while I am in the very midst of my activity of knowing, being, and reflecting,* the Polanyian picture strikes me as much closer to the mark than does the Cartesian one.

But there is another picture in view of which we may establish our relation to Polanyi's question. We may depict a speaker/writer using words and in using them giving form to concepts in the texture of their overlapping-intersecting nexuses. The "logic" of *this* picture will lead us to ask: How is Polanyi using concepts such as "assumption," "presupposition," "logic" ("logical"), "belief," "valuation," "rule," "method," "fact" ("factuality"), "procedure," and the like? We must, I think, assume that any attempt to construe their force in the terms laid down by the received philosophic tradition will confuse or mislead us.

Our interest in this question arises from the realization that Polanyi's *explicitly* stated attack upon the regnant view of the nature of scientific knowing—indeed all knowing—is less radical, less obviously "non-trivial" (in the received philosophical sense of this expression) and less broad in its general philosophical import than the "criticism" being accomplished in his often quite unwitting innovative use of the above concepts. It is in fact one of the achievements of *Personal Knowledge* that it intimates a different "logic," an alternative picture of our knowings and sayings, so that in its light we can appreciate how there can be this difference between what a writer *knows* he intends to say and what he "intends," but in a different sense, to say. And I do mean to claim that what *he knows* he intends and what he "intends" in a different sense are both his intentions, albeit the force of "his" and "intends" will vary in the two cases. Indeed, it is one of the goals of these meditations to show that the consistent tacit logic informing even Polanyi's unwitting feats of conceptual innovation is a function of the specific mode in which he is mindbodily made present to the world as he actively shapes and is shaped by the language that begins to form the text of *Personal Knowledge,* himself sinewed into and innervated by its metaphorical bonds and vectors, toward the text's peculiar comprehension of its own constituent particulars. For example, to take a crushingly obvious case, an author appears very differently in his text, if, say, "I have found" is substituted for "It is found."

This means that in *explicitly* examining the actual procedures of scientific inquiry and *doing so while using the above concepts in novel ways,* concepts such as "logic," "belief," "valuation," "rule," Polanyi is at the same time *tacitly* fashioning an alternative picture—albeit all unwitting—of the way a scientific inquirer, namely, himself, sees his relation to the world as he brings that relation into reflection; and at even a "deeper" tacit level, an alternative picture of the way the inquirer is *in* the world "behind" his acts of inquiry is being expressed in the very reflection whose medium is these concepts used in *this* way. From this will perhaps begin to emerge an importantly different view of the way in which knowing and being are implicated with each other in the actual knowing and being of Michael Polanyi as these appear in the text of his book. Now all this entails that Polanyi in writing the book *Personal Knowledge* is "borrowing," "putting on," "taking up," relying upon the grammatical, syntactical, and semantical resources of the English language together with much else; that insofar as he *relies* upon these, he assumes them, they are *assumptions* for him. Further, we may say that in a different but nontrivially analogous way he *relies* upon, he *assumes,* that is, *takes as his own,* the explicit arguments that he formulates and that he in turn, having taken them as his own, assumes, that is, takes for granted, relies upon these arguments as the ground of still others. And again, he states and in stating relies upon, that is, he assumes, takes for granted, lays claim to as his own the explicit premises on which these arguments are grounded. Finally, and most important for the argument at this juncture, he *assumes,* lays claim to, takes for granted, relies upon his own mindbodily being-in-the-world *in the particular way afforded him by the metaphorical intentionalities of the very language that is the instrument of his reflection and in which he is entangled as he writes.* Tacitly, at the deepest conceivable level, Polanyi takes for granted, relies upon, *assumes,* dwells in his own way of being mindbodily in the world as he is linguistically shaped and entangled in the very words he is in the act of writing down. This is the *ground* of his whole enterprise. This is where he could not help but "stand" as he first sat down to write, pen in hand, with a particular working repertoire of English words at his beck.

There ought to be nothing either unfamiliar or controversial in such a claim. You and I are not in the world in the way that a stone is. We are at once both distanced from and sinewed into the world as a stone is not. As we and our world are being reflected into being in us, we simultaneously both *have* and are *in the midst* of a picture. The structure of this picture is expressed in "language": in the style of our movement; in the bearing and mein, the timbre and mood of either our erect or of our recumbent bodies; in the pitch and the color of our voices; in the key, the tempo, and phrasing of our gaits; in the resonance and the hue of our glance; in the pace, the diction, weight, momentum, and metaphorical intentionalities of our speech.

If, then, a man at once invariably both *has* and is *in the midst of* such a picture—if, that is to say, he both *has* and is *in the midst of* an audial picture in hearing Mozart's G Minor Quintet, a proprioceptive or haptic picture in practicing a motor skill, an olfactory picture by virtue of an orientation to an odorscape, a praxis in "knowing how to go on"—then his knowing where and how he is and his being where and how he is are *radically* connected: opposing sides of a single coin. The one is a reduplication of the other. Upon this connection he relies; it is the bedrock "assumption" of his existence.

Polanyi's own *implicit* "assumptions," then, including that "assumption" which is his own mindbodily grounding in the world as he generates and reflects the question about the premises of science, suggest that the structure of his way of knowing is a reduplication of the structure of his way of being-in-the-world. For Polanyi then, a theory of knowing must be inextricably implicated with a theory of being. And this is so since knowing, hence coming to know, hence seeking to know, are all things we have been *doing* both before and after reflection because we are alive, sentient, and—usually—oriented in the world. Knowing (and this not one but many sorts of thing) is merely a special class of human activity subsumed under the larger class, viz., the complex repertoire of ways of humanly being-in-the-world. Our account of our knowings must therefore express and retain this bedrock, irreducible logico-ontological reality else it will generate all manner of dualisms that in practice we will find to be quite incredible. And yet because this reality is itself the very radix of knowing-being or of being-knowing, it is meta-problematic, to use Marcel's coinage: that is, the *ground* of reflection is finally opaque to reflection.

My acts of seeking, coming to know, accrediting, holding, and upholding my knowledge in the world, then reflect (indeed, quite exactly, they are reflections of, that is to say, they are "back-upon-bendings" or "inwardcurvings toward") my hitherto unreflected acts of living-in-the-world.

But before going ahead let me return to my reference above to Polanyi's implicit "assumptions"; some of which, I have claimed, are embodied in and therefore implied by what he *does,* and are therefore grounded in his mindbody; another of which is the very actuality of his mindbodily being as such. In taking these up he "lays claim to" what he *does* and to what is therein implied; in being and in persisting in being alive, he lays claim to his own actuality.[3]

---

3. Speaking in this way about a person's relation to his own being will appear odd to you only if you forget that the endorsement of our existence is not something that can be taken for granted. Various forms of psychopathology—the rejection of some aspect or other of our own sexuality, say—attest to the contingency of our relation to ourselves. Perhaps advanced schizophrenia attests to a refusal of one's own body and through this to a refusal of being in the world. Suicides of a more dramatic and eschatological sort surely suggest that we do *consent* to being, since it is always possible for us to *refuse* being absolutely. The burden of proof, therefore, would rather appear to be upon those who would wish to claim such data are without import for philosophical anthropology,

I have placed the word *assumption* between double quotation marks as a warning. Very often an assumption is taken strictly to be the sort of thing that is only "made" or "taken up" or "claimed" in the mind and therefore not in the mindbody; and what's more, it is taken, once made, to reside *in* the mind explicitly, that is, in the manner of a proposition that we could readily utter; in other words, as our picture often has it, an assumption is *in* the mind and even if not in fact reflected, at least readily reflectable. The picture also has it that the move from "reflectable" to "reflected" does not depend upon a mindbodily act.

This warning seems appropriate, since we shall find that Polanyi places the word *assumption* in such novel logical environments as to give it a logical force very different from that which it usually has in the received tradition.

Indeed, it is well that we early on draw a further inference from my suggestion. This claim about the "assumptions" grounded in Polanyi's mindbody as he is thinking-writing *Personal Knowledge* implies no less that *my* oriented mindbody in the world as I read it is simultaneously also making assumptions. As I am just now mindbodily oriented to my emerging argument, reflecting it into being by means of the medium of my words that are in my "memory," in my "mind," in my "ear," in my "hand," and in the tip of the ballpoint pen with which I am just now writing down words in full view of my "eyes," I am now, and was earlier when reading the words on page 160 of *Personal Knowledge,* mindbodily and therefore a fortiori in some sense *bodily,* making assumptions, by the very act of "taking up" existence in the world. In short, it implies that my own mindbody is an assumption that I take up and rely upon and is "present" even if only tacitly in my words, for me as I write and for you as you read.

This further means, of course, that one of the theses of these meditations bears reflexively upon its own formulation on these pages in these words. As I articulate it in my words, embrangled in their metaphorical intentionalities in virtue of which I both *have* and am *in the midst of* a picture, I at once make a comment upon this phenomenon and instantiate a particular case of it.

---

epistemology, and a theory of being. When therefore we *assume*—either in the passive sense of "taking for granted" or in the active sense of "taking up"—we are making an *affirmation,* either tacitly or explicitly, whether this be of a premise of thought, the "condition" of an act, or the "act" itself of persisting in being from one moment to the next.

To be more concrete, all this implies, for example, that it would certainly be legitimate and sometimes may be logically demanded that we say of the structure of a physical skill that some of its particulars, whether gross or fine-grained, stand to others of its particulars in a way analogous in certain respects to that in which assertions stand to assumptions when the latter are the logical ground of the former—whether these are tacitly held or explicit.

Doubtless it will be rejoined that this is a mere analogy and not an illuminating one at that, since one cannot literally say: "Muscles make assumptions." Indeed, so. Given the complacency that quite naturally attends our invocation of the too neat distinction between literal and figurative meanings in a presumably familiar and unproblematic language game, and taking the bare words *muscles make assumptions* in the context that, without alternative directives, they will have by default in the commonsense discourse of modernity, it is difficult not to acquiesce in this rejoinder.

However, if what is underway in Polanyi's thought is a large scale, even if rarely an explicit, rearrangement of concepts in order that we may think post-critically about our knowing and being, then we must discover how to fit the words *muscles make assumptions* into a new context, an alternative picture: one in which this conceptual rearrangement, hence this new way of thinking, will be allowed to occur.

Therefore I shall claim that as certainly as the component particulars of a motor skill do "hang together" and are perceived by us as "hanging together," and jointly mean that skill, they stand in "logical" relations with one another and with the skill as their comprehension. The elements of a skill are *integrated* in the skill. Their mode of hanging together and of meaning the motor skill that they jointly intend as their own comprehension is their logical relation; is indeed, their logic. Surely, if one remarks the marvelous disposition of the body's several parts to the totality that they jointly comprise, then to say, "There is a grand logic to the body," is not to say anything in the least problematic.

Finally, as such an integration this motor skill *supports,* can be the *ground* of the action that depends upon this comprehension. It can, in other words, be the "assumption" upon which the act is based. When therefore I rely upon my mindbodily being-in-the-world as the *conditio sine qua non* of my action, it is the assumption in which the act is grounded. My mindbodily being-in-the-world, itself finally opaque to reflection, is my bedrock assumption; nor is this something given once-for-all: static, fixated.

For example, when I am stroking a tennis ball whose flight across the net I have picked up as soon as possible after it has left the strings of my opponent's racket, my whole body from my feet on the ground up flows in one seamless, integral arc through my calves, thighs, buttocks, back, shoulders, arm and hand, and into the rackethead toward the point on the court where, as I follow these with my eyes, the flowing arc of the racket and the flight of the ball converge. What you will find immediately above, on this page, is not the *actuality:* "Poteat stroking a tennis ball." Rather (in relation to my act, just now, of stroking a tennis ball in fantasy, which fantasy depended upon words, if at all, in a most equivocal way) you will find the issue of a second-order act: viz., "a written down description of Poteat stroking a tennis ball."

When I stroke a tennis ball, my body and I are in the world, "behind" the seamless arc that ends in the impact of rackethead and ball and in the follow-through: "behind" the seamless arc as the ground of its integration. But I am able to stroke the ball at all only because I have *disattended* from the way I am in the world "behind" the seamless arc in order to *attend to* the flight of the ball that I may strike it.

The tennis professional from whom I am taking a lesson attends instead to the way in which I and my body are in the world "behind" the seamless arc and to the way I dwell in that arc as I execute the stroke and follow-through. He has disattended from his own being-in-the-world in order to attend to my being-in-the-world. This I can do, if at all, only marginally while stroking a ball. Yet if my mindbody were not able to integrate, quite seamlessly, to my own motor acts the tennis pro's explicit analysis of my stroke—*and, in time, to do so quite flawlessly,* without even vague maxims for how this is to be done—then tennis lessons would be impossible.

Now, in the light of this example, I want to make the perhaps extraordinary suggestion that between stroking a tennis ball, as just described, and formulating and asserting a theory or devising and stating a description of something in the world, there are important analogies that should be remarked. And I would ask you to note immediately that what I have *just* done in asserting the preceding sentence is *itself* the act of "proposing a description of something in the world"—namely, a description of the phenomenon of devising and stating a description of something in the world. What I have just done is to suggest that devising and stating a description, hence a fortiori any mindbodily act of speaking or writing down words, is like stroking a tennis ball. Indeed, in the very act of choosing the words I have *just* written down in order to shape the aforesaid description I am already coming to see the relation between the words I am in the very act of writing down and the world that they are being written down "about" in a way dictated by the words that are being written.

What are the implications of this proposal of mine? Had I suggested, for example, that devising and asserting a description of the world were like putting round pegs into round holes and square pegs into square—*and, in saying this, obviously had in mind that the pegs were like my words and the holes were like the world I was trying to describe*—you would be induced to think about the world and my (our) relation to it through language in a certain way; and to have one rather than another picture of my way of being-in-the-world "behind" my words, since I have preferred to any other *this* particular way of describing my (our) relation to the world through language.

Inasmuch as I have claimed instead that devising and stating a description is like stroking a tennis ball, it should be obvious that in the very course of saying this I am both *having* and being *in the midst* of a very different picture of the world "behind" my uttered words. You may also readily guess the kind of pictures I am likely to devise, if you were to say, "Tell me, Poteat, how do you see yourself in the world?"

As then I rely tacitly upon the several parts of my body and upon my integral mindbody as a whole in order to produce the impact of rackethead upon ball, so also do I rely tacitly upon the grammar, syntax, and semantics— the "logic," if you will—of what I have just said in our mutual native language, in order then to go on to say what *follows* from what I have said (follows in both a temporal and "logical" sense) in the setting of what I am *at the same time* in the course of "saying," viewed in some more global way; viewed, that is to say, from the standpoint of what the "whole" of our conversation is about. So also do I rely tacitly upon my mindbodily apprenticeship to and appropriation of the rules of a formalized system such as logic and mathematics in order then explicitly to deduce valid conclusions from their application. I know "how to go on" with them because I have been apprenticed to a practice: the practice, say, of construing the printed page of a book as a text to be read, not as a design—"Black on White," say,—to be contemplated.

The tacit component upon which relies any inquiry into our acts of knowing and an account thereof cannot itself be explicitly known *in* that inquiry. The dependence upon tacit components of a given feat of explicit knowing that has issued from a given skeptical inquiry cannot itself be known explicitly *in* that skeptical inquiry. The tacit all but systematically vanishes before explication. Obviously, this kind of complexity exists in *accounts* of knowing, not in *knowing itself,* since the complexity of the reflected exists at all only for reflection. This puzzlement of mine (itself fueled by the Enlightenment dissatisfaction with anything short of total lucidity) over the relation between the tacit and the explicit and over the way to *express the nature of this relation* (as well as my present choice of *this* way to express it) is implicated with our inherited model of what it means for there to be a "logical" relation both between the elements of a *given* discourse and a different relation between one order of discourse and another, "logically" heterogeneous, one. Here it is a question of the many ways in which we might express how it is that things "hang together": for example, to take but a few cases, we might say that "things" hang together and are perceived as hanging together in the way in which muscles do within the integration of our motor acts; they hang together and are perceived as hanging together in the way in which words in a sentence do; they hang together and are perceived as hanging together in the way that notes in a melody or movements in a dance do; they hang together in the way that ground and figure do for Gestalt psychology; they hang together, too, in the way that premises and conclusions do; and in many other ways as well. And when we undertake to express the way in which the elements in our feats of knowing hang together, it matters very much which of the above ways (or some other) is taken to be the paradigm for a second-order account for them. For example, the tension and intentionality embodied in the "hanging together" of ground and figure would seem a far better picture for reflectively expressing the structure of knowing, perceived as essentially an occurrence in time; whereas the kind of hanging together of premises and conclusions as embodied in a logical notation is, at least as this is depicted in the philosophic tradition, a model more suited to expressing the atemporal, "transcendentally deduced" relation among the elements of knowledge, which is being described as an already "accomplished fact."

I should then conclude epistemo-genetically (as indeed also *logically*) that when we view our mindbodily being as an integral totality, embrangled in the temporal thickness of the world, it is the logico-epistemological sense of "assumption," the sense, namely, of the philosophic tradition, which is *derivative,* while it is the mindbodily sense that is radical, the sense that my own mindbody is the ultimate "logical" ground and condition for me, the logical matrix in which the derived is rooted and from whose own intentional logic they have their meaning: that in other words our formal, reversible logic is reflected out of our mindbodies and that therefore concepts such as "cause" and "imply" could mean nothing to us, if we were not, anterior to their explicitation in our acts of reflection, both motile and oriented mindbodies in the world.

What I have just claimed is pregnant with my most archaic perplexities and with the most fundamental assumptions that have given rise to them; some buried so deep in the history of my own mindbody as to be quite beyond the reach of reflection, hence of articulation; indeed, some of which, e.g., the several particulars which can be integrated to a motor skill and it to an act, could not by definition achieve a standing in reflection. Yet how can I say this, for how can I "know" it? One of the root "assumptions" that lay buried until it achieved articulation—the assumption, namely, that what I have just said in the preceding sentence concerning my archaic perplexities and the assumptions that issue in them—is the assumption that what the sentence asserts is true. I have given articulate form to a "claim" to "know" things and to "know" of their "logical" connectedness, some of which I am, in this very sentence, suggesting cannot be known. Therefore, if what is being claimed in this sentence is true, then at least part of what is claimed in this sentence *cannot* be true—namely, the part claiming that there are unknowable archaic "perplexities" and the "assumptions" that give rise to them in the history of my mindbody of the existence and the unknowability of which I can claim to *know*. But how can this be? The "logic" of this self-referential sentence, thus disclosed, seems to reduce my claim to absurdity. And yet this disclosure, while deepening my perplexity, does not weaken the hold of the original claim upon my mindbodily being. It in no wise impeaches for me my mindbodily confidence in and sense of the "logical" decorum of my initial utterance of the sentence as I wrote it down at the beginning of this paragraph. Indeed, I want to say that the words of the uttered sentence, so inextricably trammeled with my mindbodily being as, relying upon it, I write it out from within the history and contemporary being of the very mindbody upon which these words "reflect"—the words of the sentence I say—address themselves to a more primitive appreciation of meaning for my mindbody than the lucid unpacking of the sentence's "logic." Its words satisfy a more radical, a more archaically ontological sense of meaning and decorum in me. And in so doing they express, embody, and bear in themselves the compelling sense of their own appositeness, a sense bordering upon necessity, which, as I read my own words, I find elicited from my mindbody, which is reading them.

This surdity hopelessly embrangled and implicated at the radix of speech and reflection will not suffer itself fully to be reflected; but nevertheless it "shows itself." It is this mute but eloquent oppugnancy which will always appear, soon or late, so long as I begin, finally end and, in the meantime, continuously vest my inquiry into meaning, sense, order, logic, and speech within my own lively and concretely actual mindbodily activities of shaping and discerning meaning, sense, order, and logic; and in speaking. However great may be the impetus in the practice of other methods for reflection to outstrip and disown its prereflective roots, to sublime itself and impute infinite flexibility and reflexivity to itself—subject to the *Gestalten* and "logic" of different pictures, in my above sense—unfailing fidelity to that method which initiates and grounds reflection upon the nature and *arche* of reflection from within my actual mindbodily activities, including reflection itself, will return again and again to this surdity which, while oppugnant to reflection, is reflection's ineffaceable source and antecedent.

The radical truth about our being-in-the-world is then simple, though it is not simply said, since it can be said at all only by means of a feat of estrangement from that simplicity. Only speech, our preeminent human power, which in second-order accounts of our doings and knowings can alienate us from ourselves, is powerful enough, this being done, to disenthrall us from these sometimes self-estranging pictures.

The "biography" of my mindbodily unity, no less than in the grammatical and syntactical hierarchies of language and speech, is rooted in a hierarchy of forms, structures, orders, systems, which are more ancient than my reflective intelligence. It is these forms in harmony that give to my archaic mindbody— even long before it has moved for the first time in my mother's womb, within which her beating heart rhythmically pumps the blood of life through my fetal body, forming itself toward my primal initiation into the very foundation of my first and most primitive cosmos—its growing toward wholeness destined to become a person who will have discerned the meaning in human speech, since even before this it will have indwelt the beating rhythm of patterned and hence meaningful sound. These forms are for me, even *still* for *conscious, reflective, critical* me, archetypically the forms of measured time: tempo, beat, strophe, pulse.

There is then an archaic prejudice far older than I in my prereflective and unreflecting mindbody to indwell *all* form, meaning, and order in the world as the kindred of the first order I have known, the order of my mother's beating heart. And this prejudice that is older than I is nevertheless always present, even at this very moment, as the measured beat of my own heart, the pulsing at my temples of my own blood.

Even though, therefore, these archaic forms, which give me a "body" before I am a knowing person, do not know themselves, it is only by virtue of them that I am a mindbody that in time becomes the instrument of speech and hence the embodiment of reflected intelligence.

When, therefore, I make the claim that it is by means of the blind, mindbodily, motoric rootedness of a sense of being myself an *agent*, hence of being myself a cause that, learning language, I am given the prelingual infrastructure for acquiring the competent use of the very word *cause*, I make it as the outcome of the practice of the phenomenology exhibited in the foregoing paragraphs.

If my claims about the assumptions underlying Polanyi's question concerning the specifiability of rules of procedure and of substantial beliefs about the nature of things are prima facie plausible, then we should not expect to be able to cash, in the text of *Personal Knowledge,* such concepts as "induction," "deduction," "logical anteriority," and the like at the familiar exchange rate long since established by the philosophic tradition.

In speaking or writing about the world, you and I—you, as you listen or read, I, as I speak or write—are inextricably embrangled in the intentional bonds of our mutual native language within the midst of which we meet each other and the world. This language has the sinews of our bodies, which had them first. Its grammar, syntax, meaning, metaphorical, and semantical intentionality are preformed in the "grammar," "syntax," "meaning," "metaphorical," and "semantical" intentionality of our prelingual mindbodily beings-in-the-world, which are the grounds of their possibility.

Now notice straight away that *embodied in the words you have just read* is a picture of the way you and I and the world are at once separated and sinewed together. My way of being-in-the-world in the act of writing is both expressed in and formed by the very words I am *just now* in the act of writing. The activity of composing what I come to write is a comprehensive feat of my existent ductile mindbody. What I am on the point of shaping into words—as much for myself as for you—is not arrayed before me in the way we imagine the visible world to be—as if, disembrangled and distanced from me, I have a perspective upon it, can command a view of the whole; as if I might exercise a sovereign gaze over a lucid transaction between the words by *means* of which I shape and the sense that their plaiting together *express*. Rather, it is only through the choreography of words I mindbodily *move into* and *dwell in* as I write that what I mean comes to stand in the world somewhat on its own, exactly as the movements and gestures to which I give myself over cease to be the latent energies and meanings of my mindbody at that fluent moment when they appear as the patent, worldly dance I dance. My lexicon, at once constrained and made potent by the connective tissues of its etymologies, tonic with plexuses of metaphorical tension, dwells in my mindbody as the performance dwells in that of the musician before he has performed it. For me to compose—whether as I speak or write—is *actively* to flow along the mindbodily lines of intention, which is this living, incarnate, carnal lexicon. When this is accomplished, I begin to have somewhat before me—we begin to have somewhat "between us"—the figure toward which I have all the while been fingering.

On the other hand, you, there, move forth from your linguistically shaped and embrangled mindbodily being-in-the-world in order to dwell in these my written words so as to understand them or to understand them more fully. And because *you* are entangled in *your own* linguistically shaped being, you are drawn *in a certain way, rather than in some other*, into the metaphorical shapings of my written words.

If you and I sculpted our motility in the world, each conforming himself to the other as in a dance, with music that we sang together as we moved, we should both be in the world in the way we were by virtue of the rhythmic and sonic *picture*—our song—which, as we sang and danced, we would at once both *have* and *be in the midst of*. There can be nothing controversial about this. As little can there be in the claim that as we speak and hear, write and read, our mutual way of being-in-the-world is shaped by the picture we *both* have and are *in the midst of*, embodied in the metaphorical intentionalities of our language.

The picture itself, then, is made of words. The reflection upon the picture, too, is made with words. And the etymological radicals of these words are indisseverably plaited into the roots of our carnal being-in-the-world, in fact, into our incarnation: in movement and flection, taction and traction, in tension and torsion, in pulling away and pulling together, in conjugation and conjunction, in action and proprioception. This is why language works. Our similar mindbodies conjointly in the world give it the necessary traction.

The torque and valency bonds of the words, with their complex root systems, used in the original picture above, then in the reflection upon that picture, once-removed, itself a picture, and finally in the paragraph immediately above, again, a picture, bind you and me and the world together in a very different way than any picture would whose language was mainly shaped by a fantasy of a discarnate experience of spectation. And it may well be wondered whether I have not seriously rigged the game against myself in having used the word *picture* to name the phenomenon I am here describing.

There are many, many words in both what we may call ordinary language, as well as in philosophic discourse, and indeed in the special vocabularies of many intellectual disciplines, that are fundamental: they variously serve to state or allude to the ubiquitous, rudimentary, and obvious fact and differing forms of the connectedness of things.

Some of these, to take a few as examples, are "form," "order," "whole," "integrity," "cause," "reason," "motive," "meaning," "gestalt." Not quite on logical all fours with these, but clearly consanguine with them are "logic," "logical," "necessary," and "contingent." Yet these latter and their uses will have to be considered alongside the former.

The suggestion that these words belong together in a single class is perhaps surprising. In the best of circumstances, since they are fundamental, and therefore the range of their logical efficacy must be conceded to be very extensive when we deal with them, as I shall, in a rather abstract, generalizing way, that is, without placing them in some actual logical matrices of their familiar uses, such a classification of these words, even if plausible, would seem to be so loose as to be capable of making no clear philosophical point. That, of course, remains to be seen. All I mean to be claiming at the outset is that all of these words—and many others as well—are usually used to express the connectedness of one thing with another, or the coherence of many things together.

If the deliberately vague expressions such as "the connectedness of things" and "hanging togetherness" be authorized, then we shall be able to consider "form," "order," "gestalt," as well as "logical," "necessary," and "contingent," in *relative* context-neutrality, thereby to explore the "logical" impact upon their uses as they are subject to the varying logical stresses implicit in the differing pictures operative in the archaeology of our imaginations. How, we will ask, do "form," "order," "logical," "meaning" function differently when we are given to hearing and reading their meaning (i.e., recognizing their uses) first in terms of a paradigm derived from an account of vision; and then in terms of one drawn from an account of audition. My assumption is that, if our uses of the aforementioned fundamental words were governed primarily by the logic of a picture abstracted into an account of seeing from the unreflected "phenomena" of seeing, the conception of the world that we should have would differ importantly from that we would have, if our uses were governed instead by the logic of a picture abstracted into an *account* of hearing from the unreflected "phenomena" of hearing. Furthermore, I conjecture that our imaginations in the West, increasingly in modernity, have superordinated the visual picture over the auditory one. Finally, I believe that these pictures, competing rather unevenly in our imaginations, have derived respectively primarily from Greek thought and Hebrew thought, and that much of the dissent in our tradition, though rarely wittingly so, has turned around the inclination somewhat to redress the imbalance and to arrest the hypertrophy in our imaginations of the visual picture.

Unpacking the import of these suggestions would, I think, provide us with potent heuristic devices for discerning the "argument" that is implicated with the rhetoric of *Personal Knowledge: Toward a Post-Critical Philosophy*.

THE INCARNATE WORD AND
THE LANGUAGE OF CULTURE

I

The "problem" of the relation of Christianity to culture is not, I think you will agree, a distinct set of issues occupying a separate cubbyhole within Christian apologetics. It is a more general way of positing the same sort of question as has engaged our attention under such other more specific headings as "The Logic of the Singular," "Philosophical and Christian Ethics," "Christian Faith and Metaphysics," and so on. As the problem is more generic, so it is more difficult to say something about it that avoids both empty generality and a falsifying specificity.

You will notice that the presupposition of the above set of topics—"Philosophical and Christian Ethics," "Christian Faith and Metaphysics"—has been the existence of two conflicting or at any rate differing sets of categories that it has seemed important to relate to one another because, we may assume, we are in some way committed to *both* of them, or at least recognize the claims of both. A clarification of these claims is desirable not merely in the interests of mental health; but in the interests of truth as well. To ask with Tertullian, "What has Athens to do with Jerusalem?" may be the short way with both the question and the answer. But it nevertheless both recognizes the existence of Athens and Jerusalem and declares their nonidentity. To do this much is to have created for all time a problem: How are Christian categories of various sorts properly related to other categories of a parallel sort?

Secondly, you have noticed that the enterprise of asking and answering this

The Christian Scholar **37.1 (March 1954): 113–30.**

kind of question not only entails someone who is perplexed by the conflicting claims of alternative ways of apprehending the world, but also entails that the conflict be recognized as a conflict, that the competing claims be articulated, and that the desire for a resolution of the conflict be formally expressed by the statement of alternative possible solutions and a prior definition of what a satisfactory resolution would be like, if obtained. Now, patently, one has these conditions fulfilled only when there is a philosopher about the place with a new set of categories, identical with neither set now in conflict, in terms of which a resolution is to be judged a success or failure. Or—to put it differently—if holding or using a set of categories is a first-order activity; and being aware of two different sets of categories to the use of both of which one is partially committed is a second-order activity; then proposing a resolution of their conflict and defining what sort of situation would constitute that resolution is a third-order activity. And, accordingly, there must be second-order and third-order categories operating before these activities can proceed. I will call the third-order activity category-analysis, although in principle any instance of it systematically places one set of categories beyond analysis. In short, you have *problems* like "Revelation and Reason," "Christianity and Culture," etc., only when a certain philosophical—I mean critical—disposition is abroad. It may be incipient or full-grown. The critical spirit may be naive and blundering or sophisticated and subtle. But if it is not present at all, this kind of problem will not arise. It may be true that whenever a closed society is broken open by the working in it of alien presuppositions, the critical spirit finds a fertile seedbed. In any case, it seems to me certainly true that the critical spirit must be present if this sociological fact is to produce questions, perplexities, and problems. You don't have a "problem of culture"— that is, a theory concerning its source, meaning, destiny and value—until you are aware you *have* a culture. You aren't aware that you have a culture until you begin to be vaguely apprehensive over the waning stability in your life that culture has hitherto imparted. You do not begin to experience this instability in life until you've ceased believing what you once believed—which is to say until you've started to believe other things instead, or at the same time. "The Owl of Minerva only begins her flight when it is already dark."

The most fundamental conflict of basic categories in our Western experience, as we all know, was that which occurred when the Gospel was preached to the Hellenized world. By the very nature of the Gospel, it is impossible for the Christian to write off the whole world of secular culture as meaningless, for his proclamation is precisely that Jesus Christ, begotten before all worlds, is not a tribal deity or a culture-hero but is *Lord of All*. At the same time, there are certain facts of life that have to be faced. The Christian is surrounded by—indeed helps to propagate—a vast amount of human activity, much of it most impressively organized, over which, in any obvious and straightforward sense, Jesus Christ is manifestly *not* Lord. On the contrary, he is "foolishness." When St. Paul said to the Athenians, "He whom ye ignorantly worship, I declare unto you," he accepted a challenge that Christianity *had* to accept, if it was to persist in believing that Jesus Christ was truly the Son and that His Father was truly maker of Heaven and earth. Any separation of the Father and the Son would have meant both that Jesus Christ was not related to the whole of human existence and that the one God had not been incarnate *in* that existence.

The "problem of culture," as we understand it, is, then, a product of Christianity. If, as a Christian, you occupy a standpoint that is in principle committed to relating itself positively to all other standpoints; if you are *systematically* under the obligation of finding a place in the scheme of things for all other systems of thought, standpoints, or categories because you believe that Jesus Christ is Lord of All, then you have philosophical perplexities that others do not have!

A college or university professor who is a Christian, like it or not, is faced with just such problems. What are the conceptual and personal claims of his Christian view of the world upon his profession, his discipline, and his public responsibility?

It is probably well before we become completely fogged-in by this use of the word *category* to try to offer some working definition of it. For the purposes presently at hand, I think it sufficient to say that a category is any a priori form, as with an isolate "sense-datum" (for those who suppose there are such things, or that it is helpful to pretend there are), or "space," "time," "causality," "atom," "valency-bond," "Social Contract," "hybris," "the end of history," "the withering away of the State" and "compulsive neurosis," that serves to give structure to the world, or—what comes to precisely the same thing—organizes and orders various segments of the world. I would want also to include here those basic analogies, key images, root-metaphors, together with the intentionality that inspires their persistent use.

I do not wish to enter the debate over the "source" of these categories. When I call them a priori, I mean only to be saying that they are the conditions of the possibility of the kind of experience that is the terminus of the particular activity of knowing, believing, imagining, and sensing in which they *do* play a part; and that if the categories were different, the character of what is known, believed, imagined, or sensed would be different, even if perhaps similar; and that, if there were no categories whatever, then there would be nothing that could be known, believed, imagined, or sensed.

Further, I am aware—indeed, I would remind you—that a category such as "sense-datum" is what it is in the context of a highly complex set of relations with *other* categories, which, taken together, comprise a language, or a language-stratum; and that the temptation to suppose otherwise while one is doing philosophical analysis is very great and certainly to be avoided. It need not be that language-strata are closed systems to one another. On the contrary, it is precisely one of my claims here that they are very much open to each other, that categories from one get used in another and so on. I am simply anxious to remind you that when this happens, the category changes and the language changes. To take a more obvious example: the word *history* means different things to Herodotus, Augustine, Ranke, Toynbee, and Niebuhr— though, as Wittgenstein would say, its meanings in these different categorial relations may have a family-resemblance to one another.

Finally, for my present purposes, I hope it will be sufficient to say that these categories are built-in to the various written and spoken languages that we actually use about a vast number of different sorts of things and therefore are, taken together, the bearers of our presuppositions; and that these languages are used in a bewilderingly varied number of ways, overlapping with one another to produce (when we are in our theoretical posture) puzzles that Professor Gilbert Ryle has called "category-mistakes," but also producing (in our practical activity) an enrichment of our possible experience.

If we wish to consider the relations between the Incarnate Word and the language of culture, there must be a frank facing of a prior question: What is meant by the assertion, "God was in Christ?" What sort of a claim is it? What is the "logic" of such a proposition—if it is a proposition? What is the relation between the language of theological discourse about the Person, the Work, and the personal appropriation of the saving activity of Jesus Christ to the languages in which we discourse upon the various human activities and goals that, taken together, are human culture? We cannot hope to get very far toward answering these questions here. But it is well to know what the questions are! And I shall try to suggest some lines of attack without presuming to do more.

It might appear quite possible to take any classic formulation of the doctrine of the Person and Work of Christ and proceed from there. However, I believe we must admit that it is these very formulations and the categories in which they are made that are thrown in question. Whatever one may believe about the final adequacy of Rudolph Bultmann's answer to the problem, no one, I think, can deny that his *New Testament and Mythology* raises the crucial question for Christian apologetics. It recognizes that everything is in flux; that we can no longer contrast Revelation and Reason, Christianity and Culture, Theology and Philosophy with any confidence because we can no longer be at all sure what we mean by any of these categories.

Given this state of flux, the approach of apologetics tends to assume: (1) That one of its major functions is category-analysis; to take a single popular example, that of distinguishing between the I-It relation and the I-Thou relation. (2) That the 'revealed'[1] truth is on logical all fours with truth having other credentials at least to the extent that it is apprehended in quite human categories, susceptible of logical analysis alongside other categories— even though this need not prejudge the question of *what* is revealed through these. And here arises a most interesting and perplexing reflection, namely: The category 'revelation' is not found, as such, in the Bible! It is a category that is the product of the critical spirit evoked by the collision of biblical and Greek modes of thought, devised to contrast truth of one sort with truth of another. But it is itself the product of philosophic curiosity—albeit one that is directed upon understanding the Bible as the "Word of God" in contrast with the "word of man." To say, "Thus saith the Lord . . ." is one thing—we might say, "doing prophecy." To talk about what it means to say this is quite another: "doing philosophical analysis." The category 'revelation' is the product of this latter kind of enterprise. (3) Finally, apologetics, as it is frequently practiced today, assumes that Christianity is a faith among others; that we all have our presuppositions; and that none has a stronger case than any other, since none has a "case" at all—in the sense of absolutely compelling reasons in support of it. This line has no doubt been very productive. It is the working out of the natural tendency of the critical philosophy since

---

1. The use of single quotes indicates that the word and not its referent is the object of attention; double quotes indicate that the word is being used in a slightly odd way.

Kant—a movement itself unintelligible apart from an appreciation of the impact of biblical categories of thought upon Western philosophy. But it has its defects both as a philosophic analysis and as an apologetic technique. As an analysis it too readily acquiesces to the view that our "faith" has no logical dependence upon our experience—I use the word here in the broad sense of whatever happens to us—a claim that is both difficult to refute and difficult to believe! And it also frequently obscures crucial logical differences among basic beliefs by the use of a generic term like "faith." As an apologetic technique it has the virtue that it paralyzes the enemy. Unfortunately, however, it also paralyzes the user.

Within the context of the general instability or irrelevance of our inherited categories of thought and of the present popularity of this kind of apologetic, I wish to make some suggestions concerning the relations of the Incarnate Word to the language of culture. To this end I shall try to be attentive to two major questions: (1) What is the Christian claim? (2) What categories does it introduce into Western thought?

II

Generation after generation, the Christian makes the bold claim, "God was in Christ . . . ," "The Word became flesh," to Jews a stumbling block, to Greeks foolishness, to a vast number of our contemporaries—not excluding ourselves—simply unintelligible! Can any sense be made of this?

I want to make it clear that I am not concerning myself with (1) psychological causes of peoples' believing this, if they do; or (2) logical reasons why they ought to believe it. I am, rather, concerned with what sort of thing they might be said to believe when they believe this claim; and what are the logical and categorial relations of what they are believing to the vast number of other quite different sorts of things that they believe. Now—this is not answerable once and for all! Either you mean: What did this man *think* he was believing when he believed the statement: "God was in Christ. . ."?—and you are engaged in some historical research; or you are asking: What does it mean when *I say,* "God was in Christ. . ."—which may involve you in some analysis of your own thought. But neither of these is the answer to the question: What does the expression "God was in Christ. . ." mean, as such? For it is precisely this question that every age seeks to answer for itself in terms of (1) its own reading of the Word of God within its own tradition, historical situation, and according to the light shed by the Holy Spirit, and (2) the categories of its own historical time, e.g., those of, say, Freud, Marx, Heidegger, or Carnap. And, paradoxically, what is just said can be said at all only because such categories as 'Word of God'—in relation to and in contrast with the 'words of the Bible'; 'Tradition'—in the special sense used in Christian theological discourse; 'historical situation'—with its built-in Christian interpretation of history; 'Holy Spirit', and so on, are used; and these categories are either historically undetermined themselves or are relative. If they are the former, then spurious is the vaunted claim of Christianity to rest upon 'events' (and the word *event* means, even in Christian usage, things that "happen" in myths, things that "happen" in nature, things that "happen" in history) that actually have a *date,* interpreted by faith. If the latter, then as every generation seeks to answer the question for itself, it has, at the same time to define in its own way the very categories in terms of which the questions shall be posed. The difficulty is nicely illustrated in the following passage from a recent article of Professor Tillich: "Religion," he says, "should . . . accept one of the most powerful criticisms of the intellectual, namely that the symbolic material is changing because the relationship to the ultimate is changing. . . . And when you ask, 'Is that valid also of the Christ?' then I would say, 'It is not, because the Christ in sacrificing His temporal and spatial existence did not bind us to any special forms of symbolism but transcended them and became the spirit on which the Church is based.'"[2] But, of course, we then have to ask: "Did the Christ who sacrificed his spatial and temporal existence, thereby refusing to bind us to any special forms of symbolism, *bind* us to the *symbol* of a Christ who sacrificed his spatial and temporal existence, in order to liberate us from any special forms of symbolism?"

Now, naturally, there will be a certain consternation with this sort of playing with words. We want to say, "Yes, but after all, the confrontation with the living Christ is an experience that is perennial. There must be a common core to all these experiences! Its meaning may be difficult to specify, but all men, of whatever generation, have seen *something* to accept or reject in the claim: 'The word became flesh.'" Well, I do not doubt there are confrontations with the living Christ; or that there may be family-resemblances among

---

2. Paul Tillich, "Religion and Its Intellectual Critics," *Christianity and Crisis* (March 7, 1955).

these instances. But I would also remind you, first, that words like 'confront'—as it is constantly appearing in theological discourse these days—'living', 'Christ', and 'experience' are categorially loaded words in the sense both that they have different *contemporary* uses and, certainly, different *historical* uses; and, secondly, even if there is something ineffable beyond all the overlappings of languages—something which shows through the cracks, as it were—something which all the talk is "about," which is nevertheless not exhausted *by* the talk—even, I say, if there is this something ineffable, is it not impossible to say *what* that common core is?

Let me emphasize that I am not concerned at present with the possible inexpressibility of that which all language is *about,* i.e., the "ground of Being" or the *Ding An Sich.* Nor, I think, am I ignoring the "problematic of truth" as it is set forth in the pre-Socratics, in Plato's *Republic,* in Augustine's *De Trinitate,* and elsewhere.

What is important for us is that Christianity seems to be making a quite *positive* claim that there is a *paradigmatic experience* (which, following my own philosophical commitments, means a paradigmatic set of categories—or language); that however different from other kinds of experience it may be (and we are now familiar with quite an array: aesthetic, moral, religious, scientific, sensuous, and so on) it bears a distinct resemblance to these other kinds of experience, and is, indeed, actually and *crucially* related to some of these. If I may borrow a Kantian distinction for non-Kantian purposes for the next few lines, I might say: The Christian claims that certain very peculiar sorts of "events," which are events in no sense familiar to us in the realm of necessity (because it seems inappropriate to use spatial and temporal words about them, and because they are not "caused"), occur in the realm of freedom where, for example, I use the personal pronoun *I* "about" myself; but not about myself as an "object," and where I experience profound changes "*in*" myself (which are peculiar in that they have no cause in the familiar sense, and are not processes in the familiar sense) which I call 'redemption' or 'reconciliation', or 'atonement'. At the same time the Christian seems to be claiming that the realm of freedom and what "happens" *there* is crucially connected with the realm of necessity and what has happened there; that redemption is inextricably related to the Jesus of history; that to be reconciled with God in the "confrontation" with Jesus of Nazareth "causes" us—in a peculiar, if not embarrassing, sense of the word *cause*—to confess Him as the Christ. This means further that the Christian holds not only that an event in the realm of necessity—Jesus of Nazareth[3]—known to us in a subject-object structure, is the "cause"—in a peculiar sense—of an "event" in the realm of freedom—which, if it stands before us within a subject-object structure at all does so only in an extremely odd way; but also that there is a third kind of "event," namely, *the Christ,* who is neither just the Jesus of history, nor yet just the "effects" in my life "wrought" in the realm of freedom, but a *new reality* who is known neither as an object in the *familiar* sense, nor as an "object" in the unfamiliar sense, i.e., in the way I am aware of my own I. He is neither an object to me as is the historical Jesus; nor is he just the same kind of thing as my experience of my own subjectivity. For He is a *reality* of whom it can be said that he is really present in the sacraments. It also means that for the Christian, God is *positively* known "within" what we now call the historical world; or more properly, His paradigmatic activity is encountered in relation to a paradigmatic experience *within* the historical world (in the familiar sense) thus constituting a *new* "history"—the history of the Church—where the Christ is known and, in any case, where the symbol 'Christ' is used. And this new history—the history of the Church—comes into being in and through the life—indeed, it is the life—of a living community who *enact* and *reenact* this paradigmatic unification of events in the realm of necessity and events in the realm of freedom, thereby experiencing a reality that is neither profanely historical nor eternal, but is precisely the *new* creation and hence requires a whole new language to express it! And, though we must not suppose that 'faith' means just one thing, I think we can say that when we hear the expression 'historical events as seen through the eyes of faith'—and the like—that an "experience" of the practical unification of the language of profane history and the language of "processes" in the realm of freedom has been had. *This* kind of experience is one of the things for which 'revelation' stands in the *new* language of Christian theological discourse!

Apart from Christianity, God is known only as "not this . . . not that. . . ." Augustine says, "There is in the mind no knowledge of God except the knowledge of how it does not know Him."[4] The God who is "known" as "not this . . . not that . . ." in our experience of alienation and sense of His

---

3. I do not forget that historical language is also quite different categorically from that of natural science. I think it safe however not to introduce the further qualification in the interest of preventing my analogy from becoming unnecessarily complicated.

4. *De Ordine,* II, 18, 44.

absence, becomes known as the Christ in our experience of reconciliation and sense of his presence. And the Christ event is this peculiar kind of "event," which can be spoken of neither in the language of ordinary subject-object discourse, nor in the strained language with which we try to speak of the realm of freedom; but—if I may persist in my linguistic analogy—requires a *new* language occasioned by the *practical* unification of these two other levels of discourse. The word *Christ* refers to just this "experience" of reconciliation in confrontation with the Jesus of history. To know God in Christ is to have this "experience," which is neither identical with ordinary subject-object experience nor yet wholly different from it so as to be quite beyond the subject-object dichotomy! As W. H. Auden has put it memorably:

> Because in Him the Flesh is united to the Word without magical
>   transformation,
> Imagination is redeemed from promiscuous
> fornication with her own images . . .
> . . . .
> Because in Him the Word is united to the
> Flesh without loss of perfection, Reason is
> redeemed from incestuous fixation on her own
> Logic . . .[5]

No doubt the line of my argument, which has been trailing along through some fairly dense undergrowth, seems suddenly to have disappeared altogether. And it is very probably the obscurity surrounding the ambiguous, if not equivocal use of words like *experience* and phrases like *practical unification* that are to be held to account. Therefore, allow me to backtrack myself briefly.

W. T. Stace, in dealing with some of the same questions as those before us, has said of the mystical experience, which for him is quite beyond the subject-object dichotomy: ". . . in that experience time drops away and is no more seen . . . it is eternal, that is to say timeless . . . there are in it no divisions and relations of 'before' and 'after.' . . . From within it is God. For it is not a consciousness *of* God, a divided consciousness wherein the mystic as subject stands over against Deity as object. It is the immanence of God Himself in the soul."[6]

---

5. "For the Time Being," in *The Collected Poetry of W. H. Auden* (New York: Random House, 1945), 452–53.

6. *Time and Eternity* (Princeton: Princeton University Press, 1952), 76, 77. Italics in the original.

Now, I have no intention whatever of exploiting Stace's embarrassment at having to call what the mystic has "an experience" while at the same time insisting that it does not have a subject-object structure. (It is relevant to notice here that 'experience' is used both as verb and noun, but that it has a built-in subject-object meaning. When I say, "I am experiencing pleasure," this state of affairs clearly has a subject-object structure. 'Pleasure' is the object of the verb *to experience*. When I say: "I have an experience of pleasure," 'experience of pleasure' is *here* the object of the verb *to have*; and 'pleasure' is the object of 'experience', though in the epistemological rather than the grammatical sense. Here we have, if you please, a subject-object structure—'experience of pleasure'—within a subject-object structure—'I *have* an experience of pleasure'.) But there is something important here for us. If it were the case that the mystic "experience" absolutely transcended the subject-object dichotomy, and if the distinction between the experience and that of which it is an experience were wholly absent, then (1) there would be no way in which it could even be alluded to in subject-object language, and (2) we couldn't be aware of the experience of being God or of being identical *with* (a relation-word) Him. Strictly speaking we could not be aware at all. We could have no awareness during the "experience," nor a fortiori any recollection of it after the "experience." It would be a mere lapse of consciousness of which we could not in principle have any awareness. The mystic experience then *must* bear *some* analogy to ordinary experience if it is (1) to be an "experience" (and here I'm not at all quibbling over the use of the word), and (2) if it is to have some relation, *other than mere resemblance,* to ordinary experience. We may, then, admit that it is an "experience" of a very peculiar sort; but if there is no analogy whatever between it and ordinary experience, then it is not an *experience* of *any* sort, and it is difficult to say *what* it is, if anything.

Now, this means that when we use expressions such as the 'experience of the numinous', 'the mystic experience', 'the immediate awareness of God', we have to exhibit their logical peculiarity. Generally, the Eastern religions do so by focusing upon the *differences* between these and our experiences of tables and chairs and then devising a limiting-concept of what lies beyond the subject-object distinction. It qualifies this kind of awareness, in other words, by describing it as though it were *non*awareness. The goal of religion for them then becomes in principle the achievement of a "knowledge" which is not a *knowing*. Biblical religions on the other hand are informed by the basic analogy of the I-Thou relation. Accordingly they qualify this odd kind of use of 'experience' by describing it as essentially dialogical rather than monological, as like the dialogue which the self has with itself and others. This analogy was inherited by Christianity as it changed from that of a dialogue between a Thou and a Covenanted Nation to one between a Thou and a faithful remnant and finally between a Thou and a faithful suffering servant and Messiah. The symbol, 'the Christ', is, you might say, logically possible when a single faithful Messiah has as its correlate the individual who now has a vivid sense of his personal, active I, since salvation comes to and through the historical *person* rather than through and to the nation. The practical experience of personal reconciliation with God in confrontation with the Jesus of history is the experience of the Christ! The fact that the language of ordinary historical discourse about the Jesus of history has been unified in the practical—if you like, existential—experience of the apostles with the quite different language for discourse about profound changes that take place within ourselves—the realm of freedom—is symbolized by the words, *The Christ.* When I myself *have* this experience in relation to the symbol, I am not dealing with anything symbolic, but directly know the very reality symbolized! If I may put it awkwardly, I am no longer *referring to* a reality; I am *in* that reality.[7] As it is said, "If any man be in Christ. . . ." Yet I am *in* that reality not as a molecule of water is in the ocean, but as a person is *in* a personal relation.

Now: I must develop further the meaning of the expression 'Practical unification of languages'. Let me emphasize that what follows in no way makes pretensions to dealing with all the issues. I am only suggesting a kind of model or map that would guide a more ambitious analysis. Earlier on, I spoke of different ways in which we use event-words such as 'happen', 'occurrences', 'occasion', 'event' and so on. I also used the Kantian distinction between the realm of necessity where categories like 'cause', 'time', and 'space' are appropriately and, I shall say, *literally,* used (albeit I think that what constitutes the literal use of a word is a matter for "decision"), and the realm of freedom, where, if they are used at all, and it appears inescapable that they should be, then they are "inappropriately" used (and here I use 'inappropriately' inappropriately). I suggested that when I say, "X happened

---

7. This is, of course, very awkward, since 'in' is no less a relation-word than 'to', and if all relations disappear, on my own accounting, then so also must all discourse!

in history"—however different historical language may be from natural-scientific language—I was referring to an event that had a cause and of which time-words—such as are presupposed by dating—would be appropriate; and that when I say, "I was reconciled to God"—I am also speaking of an "event," but one that is different from the other: an "event" of which my use of event-words to refer to it is peculiar and, further, one where cause-words and time-words are not appropriate. (I am, of course, taking my stand alongside Kant, for the sake of my analogy, in according the privileged use of cause-words and time-words to their role in *Naturwissenschaft*). Let me condense all this into a distinction between event in sense-one and event in sense-two.

Now: I went on to say that for the Christian the Jesus of history (*event in sense-one*) and the experience of reconciliation with God (*event in sense-two*) were related, not merely by a *logical resemblance,* but "causally"—in, as I said, a peculiar, if not embarrassing, sense of "causally." Perhaps it would be easier if we said "internally" rather than "causally" related. And I said the unification of the two different languages gave rise to the symbol 'Christ', and to a whole new language including the word *history*—now, however, understood as *heilsgeschichte*—and phrases like 'Holy Spirit', 'the Body of Christ', 'the real presence', etc. Here, on this level, the use of the word *event* in the expression, 'Christ-*event*', would be called *event in sense-three*. The problem with which we are faced is: How is such a unification of languages accomplished? We have had offered us in the last thirty years two solutions: (1) an ideal meta-language, which would unify languages and eliminate unnecessary ones and (2) a theoretically infinite hierarchy of languages or language-strata. The chief exponent of the first, Wittgenstein, completely abandoned the project as hopelessly misguided. The second is faced with the fact that an appeal to language-strata leaves unsolved the problem of how the strata are related to each other; and further leaves out of account the manifest fact that the world of naive experience—which is not so innocent as it seems—is not discontinuous but a whole of a sort.

I believe, their dogmatic tone aside, that the "ordinary-language philosophers" are moved by a sound instinct at this point. They seem to sense that a clue to this puzzle is to be found in *practice*—in the actual *using* of language. If we could get them to focus on the *user* of language with the same eagerness as they examine language's *use*, they might help us.

Let me pursue this a step further. Let us suppose that *Me* is a word that appears in the language in which we customarily speak of the Jesus of history and is therefore correlative to *event in sense-one;* and that *I* is a word that appears in the language in which we would speak of profound "events" that have occurred "in" ourselves and is therefore correlative to *event in sense-two*.[8] When I speak of this distinction between 'Me-language'—the sort used when I deal with "myself" as an object—and 'I-language'—the sort used to refer to my own subjectivity—the 'I' in the expression 'When I speak . . .' has a different logic from 'I' in the expression 'I-language'. In the first case, 'I' is *being used in a very concrete way as subject of the verb, 'speak'*. In the second case, 'I' refers to the peculiar kind of 'awareness' I have of myself as user of the personal pronoun in the nominative case—in contradistinction to that of which 'Me' is used. Let me then say that 'I' is in one case being used. In the other case *that* it is used and that there is "something" of which it is used is a fact that is being talked about. In other words, language is being used to talk about the *user* of language and *that* language—has a *user.* 'I' is used both as the subject of the language and as the object of the talk about the user of language. Let me call these respectively '*I in sense-three*' and '*I in sense-two*'— whose correlative, you will remember, is '*event in sense-two*'. I would suggest that 'I' in sense-three'—what we frequently call the existential self—is the correlative of the "living Christ." It is this that helps us make sense of St. Paul's words: "It is no longer I who live, but Christ who lives in me."

How then do we unify these various strata of language? I think we must say that their connection is not *logical* but *practical*. They have their sole connection in the experience and activity of the *user* of language, who "stands behind" every particular language that he may find it expedient to *use* about the world, even the metalanguage that he uses about *other* languages. This user of language is peculiar in that he can never become an *object* of experience—or, as we might wish now to say—never be objectified *in* language because he is the presupposition of all language use, the subject of every instance of discourse, and therefore, systematically eludes languages and

---

8. For this distinction, as well as for many other of the features of this argument, I am indebted to an extended correspondence and later face-to-face conversations with Ian Ramsey, Nolloth Professor of Christian Philosophy at Oxford, and Fellow of Oriel College. I should further call attention to an excellent article by Professor Ramsey, "The Systematic Elusiveness of 'I,'" *Philosophical Quarterly* 5.20 (July 1955): 193ff., which bears upon this issue. Finally, since writing this, I have seen the manuscript of a lecture given before the Oxford Socratic Club by Professor Ramsey in which this same sort of analysis is applied to the language of the Creeds.

metalanguages ad infinitum. Or if we wanted to say that he *must* in some sense be an object, he is so in a very odd way. He is only found "behind" the language *just now being used*. Yet language and its *ever* having been used is inconceivable apart from him.

If the unification of languages occurs in *practice* through the *user,* then metalinguistic *theory* ("spectation") can *never,* as a matter of principle, locate the connection. When these languages are the subject of inquiry from a metalinguistic standpoint, there *is* no connection whatever, for the *user* is now 'behind' the metalanguage and the *languages* themselves are not now being used. It is only the metalanguage that is *now* being used! The "mind-body problem" is theoretical, not practical. It becomes a problem for theory because *theory* ("spectation") systematically removes the solution in advance.

Notwithstanding all this, and of course inevitably, as is shown by my own present efforts to talk about the way in which different levels of reality or different languages may be unified, theoretical statements or formulations *have* been given. The classical formulations of the relations of the two natures of Christ, of historical event and response, of nature and grace, and so on, are efforts, within the demands of their historic times and the categories then in use, to characterize the kind of relation existing between two or more levels of discourse. The current debate revolving around Bultmann is another such. What I have been saying here is yet another. If I am, in this present theoretical account, embarrassed by the difficulty of sorting out the levels of discourse that are involved, keeping them related to one another, and at the same time *saying* all this about them, it is because I am doing theology and a kind of linguistic analysis and not encountering Christ in the practical activity (and here I would include the act of praying) of faithful response. Yet, if what I have said above is true, it is *only* here that the unification can occur. And of course we now see the most striking motif of biblical religion exhibited: "Be ye not *hearers of the Word only,* but doers"; "Not every man who *sayeth,* 'Lord! Lord!' shall enter into the Kingdom of heaven"; "Let your light so shine before men, that they may see your good works and glorify your Father which is in heaven." This irreconcilable difference between spectation and action, between the aesthetic and religious attitudes, between imagination and will, between contemplation and enactment, between potentiality and act, between the eternal logos and the Word made flesh stands between every other view of reality and Christianity. I am not saying here that it is only the Christian faith that emphasizes *doing* the will of God once it is known. I am saying that there can be no *knowing* of God and His will apart from enactment. The *knowledge* of God depends upon a doing; the doing is a *knowing*. God is not known by "faith"—as though it were some special "God-knowing" faculty. He is known *in* the act of faithfulness. When the expression, 'the Christ' is used as a symbol, it refers just to this knowledge of God that we have in this "experience." For Christianity believes that God is Act par excellence, and is known paradigmatically in the intersection of "event-in-sense-one" and "event-in-sense-two," which gives rise to the "event-in-sense-three" through and within that very act whereby I am myself. The divine is crucially known in *Christ*—that experience which includes the practical unification of components that are susceptible of description in terms of "Jesus of history language" and "reconciliation-redemption language." And Christ is known only in my own existence—in my enactment of myself, since for me to exist is not to be a possibility, but to *act*!

At this point, there is an inclination, no doubt, to suspect that all the sleight-of-language ingenuity of the foregoing adds up to a practical denial of the Incarnation, that the Jesus Christ here set forth is not only patently not the Christ of the Creeds and classical formulations, but also that he is not *real* in any sense! I agree that one cannot bypass this issue. I can only reply that it seems to me quite possible at once to accept this analysis as sound in principle and still to confess the Creeds, with no reservations that would not apply equally to this analysis itself; and to counterattack with some more sleight-of-language. For instance, if you say, "But *this* Christ is not a 'reality,' the Incarnation did not, in your view, 'really' happen, the Word did not 'really' become flesh," I should then have to ask, "What does the word *real* mean?" and then go on to suggest part of the answer. It may be that, among other things, what we mean when we say, "X is real," X can be cashed in *this* language (i.e., any language that one has chosen to be *the* language par excellence)—and that therefore when we ask, "But is this really real, though?" we are implying that it is not cashable in the language that we hold, at that moment, to be the privileged one. Now, if this is the case, one can always require that the language in question show its certificate of special consideration!

Having said this, I would then conclude by saying, "God *really* was in Christ, Very God of Very God!"

Now I want to say something hopelessly cryptic on what seem to me to be some of the implications of this interpretation of the language of Christian discourse and its reliance upon the notion of the "practical unification of languages." To this end I want to take a text from W. H. Auden's Christmas Oratorio, "For the Time Being," and, through an exegesis of it, try to make my point. He says, speaking of the Christ Child:

> By the existence of this Child, the
> proper value of all other existences is
> given, for of every other creature it can be
> said that it has extrinsic importance but of
> this Child it is the case that He is in no
> sense a symbol.[9]

I want to attend especially to the phrase: "He is in no / sense a symbol."

I have been saying that the expression 'the Christ' is the symbol of the occurrence of a practical unification of the language in which we speak of the Jesus of History and the language in which we speak of the "inner" experience of being reconciled to God; and that 'Christ-event'—which I designated 'event-in-sense-three'—refers, in the primary sense, to that actual experience of reconciliation with God in *practical relation* to the life, teachings, crucifixion, and death of the Jesus of History, which the Apostles had; and, in a secondary sense, to the same experience that I have whenever I have it. When therefore we say that the "Word Became Flesh," we mean first this, for us, paradigmatic practical unification, which became the *Kerygma* of the Church, which is an "event" in-sense-three, and has a "date" in "history"— albeit in peculiar senses of 'date' and 'history'; and also we mean that actual reenactment of this paradigmatic event, the incarnating of the "Word" in my existence (that is, the acts whereby I am myself), that "making present" of the living Christ in my own existence that is not a copy of the original, a mere recollection of the paradigm, or a contemplation of the *parousia* of the Apostles, but is the real thing, the *Incarnation itself,* just right here within the very act of existing which is myself! *This* Christ does not point beyond itself as a sign refers; He does not direct our attention to some other reality which is mediated to us by Him; He does not invite our attention to or contemplation of a reality beyond the subject-object dichotomy. He is our present life renewed, in all its existential concreteness. As St. Paul says: "For me to live is Christ. . . ." He is in no sense a symbol.

This means that in the central act of Christian faithfulness, the Holy

9. *The Collected Poetry,* 451–52.

Communion, we approach the paradigmatic unification of event-in-sense-one and event-in-sense-two as a symbol—the bread *refers* to the broken body; the wine *refers* to the shed blood. But in ways better understood by depth-psychology than rationalistic Protestantism, but ultimately not to be understood at all, we remain to be confronted in the very depth of our existence with a reality—the nonsymbolic Christ.

Yet it will be asked: What is distinctive about these Christian Symbols and realities? Is it not the case that signs and symbols may have both intrinsic and extrinsic interest for us? And in any case, does not every symbol in its semantic role direct our attention away from itself and toward a reality in which our interest is or may be intrinsic, and which we may then grasp immediately?

Obviously one does not enter into these troubled waters without being thoroughly outfitted with categorial commitments of a most elaborate sort that he would not only like to specify clearly, but to defend as well. However, the need for brevity breeds a certain daring. I would answer first that signs and symbols *in their semantic role* never have for us intrinsic interest—though, it does not follow from this that they may not be regarded apart from their referential function. Secondly, we are directly and immediately aware—in many subtly different senses of 'directly' and 'immediately'—of realities to which our attention has been drawn by signs and symbols functioning in their semantic role. I am even willing to say that there are different kinds and degrees or levels of participation in realities—albeit, I think an analysis, not possible here, would show that the kind of epistemological object is correlative to the kind and degree of participation of the epistemological subject—which is to say that subject and object are categorially correlative. All I need to say here is this sort of thing: I directly participate in the reality of a tree when I experience a tree; there is no word *tree* referring to sense-data of a certain sort, which have been in constant conjunction with other sense-data, and which therefore *refer* to these other sense-data, etc., ad infinitum. What I want to admit here, in other words, is that in the same sense in which 'the Christ', functioning as a symbol, brings us to a nonsymbolic reality in which we participate immediately, the sign 'tree' brings us to an analogous reality in which we participate immediately, in that sense of 'immediately' appropriate to its use with reference to trees. But now I want to draw a very difficult, perhaps precarious, distinction in order to call attention to something of greatest importance, if the peculiarities of the Christian claim are to be seen.

Let me suggest that you reflect upon the difference between what happens when the word *tree* is spoken, let us say, in some place where no tree is to be seen, and you have an image before your mind; and what is happening when, either with the curiosity of the artist or that of the botanist, you directly perceive a tree standing before you in all its concrete reality. Clearly, there are all sorts of important features involved in this difference, and it may be that we can alter what is before your minds to fit the varying demands of different epistemological problems, and that to this extent the analogy is not a compelling one. But nevertheless, I ask you to believe that we may say that *a possible* difference between the two situations sketched above is the following: The 'I' that is entertaining an image of the tree, upon hearing the word *tree*, is not very profoundly engaged in *personal activity*. The image is just there and, at most, my act of *imagining* correlative to it is there. And built-in to the image of the tree is the property of "being possible" rather than "being actual." Insofar, you might say, as I am engaged in reflecting upon a possible tree, I am, in some degree correlative to it, a possible self. But, by contrast, when I perceive the *existential* tree, the I that perceives it is engaged in considerable *personal activity* of responding to, being involved with, bound-up in the tree before it with its body, its senses, its movements, and so on. There is the real tree over there; over here is a correlative I engaged in the *activity* of responding to it. There is an "otherness" about the existential tree that makes vivid my own sense of my own *activity* in perceiving it. Of the former situation I want to say that it is more symbolic because it has reference to possible realities and possible acts of responding; of the latter, I suggest that it is less symbolic insofar as reality and activity of response are actual. That situation in which, by virtue of a total action of my total self, I became most vividly sensible of my *personal* I (e.g., in a situation of choice concerning my self in its final meaning as in the question, "To be or not to be . . .") would be the most concrete and actual and hence least symbolic situation possible.

If it is the case, then, that there is an analogy between the way the sign 'tree' brings us to a reality, immediately perceived, and the way the symbol "Christ" brings us to a nonsymbolic reality, wherein the distinctiveness of 'the Christ' as a symbol? (And I want to be perfectly clear that I am not at the moment asking about the nonsymbolic reality, but rather about any peculiar properties which the *symbol* may have when it functions semantically within Christian discourse. In short, I am concerned with the semantics and pragmatics of the symbol, 'Christ'.)

I think we can afford to be satisfied in the present context with this schematic answer. I have been saying that the expression, 'the Christ', is in its semantic role a product of the practical unification of the language of straightforward history and of personal crisis and decision in the experience of the apostles; that it therefore "refers" to that experience; and that, finally, it appears in the discourse of Christians who see a very special significance in that experience, stand in a special relation to it, and reenact it in their own lives. When we are enjoined in the Holy Communion to "Do this in remembrance of me . . ." the *remembered* Christ ceases to be remembered and becomes really present because of the *doing*! Elsewhere I called these, respectively, "event-in-sense-one," "event-in-sense-two," and "event-in-sense-three." Let us suppose then that the expression 'suffered under Pontius Pilate' is straightforward history—or "event-in-sense-one"—kind of language; that the expression 'one thing I know, that though I was blind, now I see' appears in the language of personal crisis and decision—is therefore 'event-in-sense-two' kind of talk; and that the expression 'He who has the Son has life; he who has not the Son has not life' appears in the discourse of the community of Christians where a new "history" has come to be.

Now what I want you to notice here is this: *First* the symbol 'the Christ' is used in a community as both the focus of its historical memory and as the center of its paradigmatic act—the act by which it is itself. As St. Augustine says of the Holy Communion: "Receive therefore and eat the Body of Christ, you who are already made members of Christ within the Body of Christ. Take and drink the Blood of Christ. Lest you should fall apart, drink that which binds you together." Therefore it is a device par excellence for recollection and enactment (and here we are concerned primarily with the pragmatics of the term). Secondly, the symbol is itself the product of a fusion of two other languages: that of actions (history in the familiar sense); that of decisions (history in the less familiar sense). The Christ points to *action, decision, and enactment*. The symbol systematically points away from itself toward the most concrete, most nonsymbolic, of all realities, an action of the total self, where there is no separation between means and ends, knowledge and will, subject and object (in the conventional epistemological or monological sense), intention and thing intended, possibility and actuality. But the surpassing or overcoming of all these dichotomies is one that, far from obliterating the personal I in some impersonal being or nonbeing, heightens the sense of personal activity and reality. 'The Christ' as a symbol is the correlative of the pronoun, *I*—when used to refer to that being "of which," as Hume said, "we have an intimate memory and consciousness," which stands behind all language, yet which, as *active,* systematically eludes all language. Christ, the reality, is the correlative of the existing, acting self. Therefore, when we experience the reality of the living Christ, it is a matter of indifference whether we say "I live" or "Christ lives in me." In place of the conventional subject-object dichotomy, we now have *I-Thou!*

The Christian claim is that here, in Christ, we encounter God paradigmatically. The nature of the symbol 'the Christ' is such that it brings us to the most concrete reality there is, that is, ourselves as actively in relation to God. As Augustine says, "He is nearer to us than we are to ourselves, even when we are far from Him." It is Jesus Christ who brings us to ourselves.

You may feel at the end of all this that what I have said has only a remote bearing upon the general problem of "Christianity and Culture"—as it is usually discussed—and with this I am of course forced to agree. Perhaps the best that can be said for this paper is that it seeks to provide a prolegomenon to certain aspects of the larger questions. I have already said that other ages approached the problem differently and formulated their answers differently. From this it follows that my analysis in no sense pretends to describe what men in other times using different categories were in fact doing while supposing they were doing something else. What I have tried chiefly to do is state the problem of Christianity and the problem of culture at what I take to be their deepest levels—the level of categories and language. And, after the fashion of the time, I have sought to describe their relation to each other in terms of that between Christian theological discourse and other forms of discourse about other things. The surface has only been scratched.

There are at least two major questions that belong to this inquiry, which time forces me to omit: First, how 'the Christ' is both a *yes* and a *no* to culture. What do we mean when we say this? How is this dialectical relation to culture built-in to the symbol itself? Second, what further categories and symbols does the symbol 'Christ' provide us with so that light is shed upon the logical (faith and reason), psychological, and sociological properties and relations of other categories actually in use; and upon the plight of man in human culture—alternating between a despairing relativism and a presumptuous absolutism. But that is for someone else to do.

One final word. Earlier on I said that a category is what it is in the context of a highly complex set of relations with other categories, which taken together, comprise a language.

So it is with 'the Christ'. In trying to specify what it is as a symbol, I was forced to employ a whole network of categories; and I was also forced to show some of the various relations in which these stand when used for this purpose. The symbol 'Christ' can equally well stand for a network of other symbols, together with the categories by which their meaning is to be specified. When understood in this way, it is possible for us to say that the Incarnate Word introduces into language as it is used—and thereby into thought and thus into action and hence finally into culture, which is itself a practical unification of languages—a new set of categories, which transforms its very fabric. Words, like *nature, to be, know, faith, freedom, tragedy*—to name but a few— can never be used again in quite the same way.

It is as Auden has said:

> Because in Him the flesh is united to the
> Word without magical transformation,
> Imagination is redeemed from promiscuous
> fornication with her own images. . . .
> . . . .
> Nor is
> there any situation which is essentially more
> or less interesting than another. . . .
> . . . .
> Because in Him all passions find a logical
> In-Order-that, by Him is the perpetual
> recurrence of Art assured. . . . Because in
> Him the Word is united to the flesh without
> loss of perfection, Reason is redeemed from
> incestuous fixation on her own logic . . . the
> possibilities of real knowledge are as many
> as are the creatures in the very real and
> most exciting universe that God creates with
> and for his love. . . . Because in Him
> abstraction finds a passionate For-the-Sake-
> of, by Him is the continuous development of
> Science assured.[10]

10. Ibid., 452, 453, 454.

The Christ relates all of the human activities, which taken together, comprise culture, to the most concrete of all realities, indeed, the only concrete one, the "existential" self realizing itself in active response to the God, who though He made heaven and earth, is yet so near to each of us that anyone so minded may call Him "Father." In so doing, He affirms its every gesture, the while redeeming it all from "incestuous fixation" upon itself.

PART TWO

Personal Language and the Language of Belief

FAITH AND EXISTENCE _____

"It is natural for the mind to believe, and for the will to love; so that, for want of true objects, they must attach themselves to false." Pascal, in this highly characteristic fragment, which, as others of his, contains implicitly a whole philosophy, seems to be saying that faith is inevitable. Is this true? And if it is true, does it matter?

It would be nice if we could simply say "yes" to the first question and then deal with the various ways in which it does matter. But with the word *faith* it is as with so many of the fundamental terms of philosophy and theology: it is the focus of always earnest, frequently heated partisanship until someone dares to propose an examination of the obvious, and it is discovered that no one is quite sure what it means and therefore what are its relations to the various terms with which it is most frequently coupled in debate. For example, we find faith and *reason* frequently contrasted. This is a kind of intellectualistic statement of the problem. But faith is also paired with *doubt,* with *skepticism,* with *despair.* Now, I suppose no one would seriously argue that despair and skepticism are synonymous in their meanings—however real may be a certain internal connection between them. And I think we should regard as absurd the suggestion that doubt and reason are equivalent—though Descartes thought he had found a certain methodological doubt that was serviceable to reason. I think even that we should be prepared to see distinct nuances in the words *doubt* and *skepticism.* But what is to the point of this discussion is the question: Does not the meaning of faith shift and reflect rather different light as it is paired with first one and then another of these

The Hibbert Journal 52 (1953–1954): 245–51.

notions? Though clearly we cannot explore the implications of all this in the present context, I believe we must answer our question in the affirmative—recognizing nevertheless that it is meaningful to use the word *faith* in all of these cases; that is, that there is some element in "faith" in each usage that is common to all. Further, I am prepared to risk the claim that a consideration of faith, whether in relation to reason, doubt, skepticism, or despair, will produce the conclusion that it is, indeed, inevitable; and that while this does not tell in favor of any particular faith (and you will notice that another usage for the word has entered the discussion, for I am now talking not about a certain disposition of the self, but about a certain "content" toward which one holds that disposition), it does reveal to us something of the greatest importance concerning the nature of man (even if to "know" this is itself dependent upon an acknowledgment of faith).

These various alternative ways of considering the nature and inevitability of faith are both exciting and basic. But there is one that really matters to us; one that renders all the others frivolous by comparison because it concerns—indeed, ultimately concerns—each one of us as an existing individual at the point where arises the question: "Who am I, what do I ultimately love, in what can I ultimately trust?" This might be called: Faith in relation to personal identity and existence. It is here that faith is most naturally contrasted with despair. The remainder of these reflections shall revolve about this relation.

The thesis that I wish to consider may briefly be stated thus: (1) *Without faith, defined as love and trust, I cannot exist as a person, nor can I have a personal identity*; (2) *I can ultimately love and trust only that which fulfills personal existence*; (3) *If there is no object of love and trust that does fulfill personal existence, or if I cannot respond to that in love and trust, then I am in despair.*

What does it mean to exist *personally*? What is it to be this particular existing person who I am? Apart from what would my *personal* existence be literally inconceivable to me? I certainly cannot imagine myself without *a* body—but, inspired no doubt by vanity, I frequently imagine myself with a more graceful or magnificent body than I in fact have. Indeed, I have actually seen some for which I should be glad to exchange my own. Nor can I imagine myself without *a* mind—though I can also wish that I had that of Einstein, Plato, or Pascal. (Of course, in my heart of hearts, I'm really quite attached to both my mind and my body and I am not at all sure that I would exchange them.) But I am certain that I would not exist personally without this particular will of mine and all the various acts—good and bad—that flow from my particular volitions. In a sense, I can have Pascal's mind by "thinking my way into" it; and having done so, I can actually look at the world with Pascal's mind. But one thing is clear: I can "think my way into" his mind only by willing to do so with my *own* will—and should I wish to will what he willed I can do so only by some willing of my own; and I certainly cannot will *his* acts, for the twofold reason that we are not contemporary in time and that they are *his* rather than mine. You and I may be able to love a common object, but each loves it with his own love—and that is highly personal.

Now, of course, the last observation betrays the weakness of our analogy— and we must not press it! Clearly, when we *know* a common object we each *know* it equally with our own mind. And this is really to say that as selves we are not very satisfactorily sundered into parts. Our bodies and minds are not really interchangeable with others' at all. They are just as *personal* as our wills. But we do rather feel that our wills are the *centers* of our persons, that our bodies and minds are at the service of our wills even if our wills are subject to limits imposed by them. Yet, though the analogy is at bottom precarious, even sophistical, it serves to call attention to what seems to be a fact: that for me to *exist personally* means that I am the agent of concrete intentions, directed toward particular ends or persons, through concrete acts in particular moments of time; and that we know one another and even ourselves as persons par excellence through these acts that express intentions. For it is here that my intentions, expressed in this particular act directed upon this particular objective, encounter yours, and what is most deeply personal in us meets.

To exist *as a person,* then, is *to will* and *to act.* But what does this mean? Let us note first that though it is legitimate, perhaps, to speak of "the will" and of "willing," etc., there is no such thing as an act of "willing-in-general." We may say that among men we observe a phenomenon known as willing. This is harmless enough. What we mean in actual fact is: we observe A willing X, B willing Y, and C willing Z. If I *will,* I always will something, not "everything-in-general" or "nothing-in-particular."

Secondly, to will is to desire. To desire is to possess *in anticipation.* To desire requires that there be a certain separation between "myself" in one state and "myself" in another state. And for this separation to exist requires a certain duration of time. *To will* therefore is to desire *now* what can only be in the *not-yet,* and *to act* to secure, that is, *to direct myself toward,* that which is *not-yet.* Now, the future, which is *not-yet,* cannot, on principle, be an object of *certainty.* What is *likely* to happen may be a matter of high probability—but this is still not certainty. If we are able to bet on high probabilities, then we are fortunate—and we are forced to *trust,* so far as the particular volition is concerned, only to a small degree. But even so there is *always* the element of *trust.* And we may observe parenthetically that no matter how high the probabilities in a given situation (for example, in the case of a decision to get married—where the sociologists assure us that "it is a good gamble"), if the threat of failure is one that we could countenance only with the greatest anguish, we do not undertake it lightly. In short, risk is not to be calculated in terms of statistics alone. It is all-important what is at stake for us on the throw. We *do* live by faith, every moment—even if this faith is something of which we are not made conscious in every moment. Indeed, that we are spared such consciousness is evidence of grace operating in our lives, for, apart from it, apart from the ability to "accept" the continuity of the world and of ourselves, we should be like the man of whom Kierkegaard spoke, "who went mad by being at every moment conscious that the world went round." In this sense we are *given* to ourselves, and it is this of which we are to be reminded by the Gospel injunction, "Be not anxious!"

Thirdly, to will and to act requires not only a *trust* concerning the *not-yet,* which cannot be an object of certainty, but toward which one is necessarily oriented if he is to "possess in anticipation"; it also requires *continuity of will.* If I do not persist in a certain inclination or affection from the *now* until the *not-yet;* if, in short, I want fidelity of purpose, then none of the individual acts that, taken together, are the expression of my intention, will ever be effectuated. In other words, every act of will necessitates both *love* and *trust,* because not only does the future bring unforeseen exigencies "in the objective state of the world"; but action respecting the future is frustrated as well by a failure of will, a breach in fidelity. Hence there is always a double risk involved. No one can act, or begin to act, or begin to begin to act, without faith. Therefore, *one cannot exist personally without faith, since to exist is to act.*

But now we must make another point—not altogether new, but an amplification of the above. It is this: *I can have no personal identity without faith,* i.e. *love and trust.* This is not new because to have a personal identity is the same as to exist personally. But this clarification will enable us to see that *a man's identity is given by that which he ultimately loves and trusts,* for it is this that imparts unity to all his purposes, volitions, and acts by defining *his existence,* as a whole; that as he is faithless to this he insomuch loses his identity; and that if he is absolutely faithless, he is in despair. We might say that what a man ultimately loves and trusts gives "shape" to his many particular acts of will; and since his existence is his activity, the "shape" of his activity is his personal identity. The Bible sums the matter up perfectly when it says, "As a man thinketh [a freer translation would permit "decideth"] in his heart, so is he." As a person I "decide" my loyalties in each of my choices. By this process I establish my own identity. As I commit myself for tomorrow by each decision today, so am I. Not only do I actually seek to respond to the object of my ultimate love and trust in every concrete act; it is in this process that I maintain my identity. I am not only *becoming* what or who I am; I *am* what I ultimately love and trust.

This means, you see, that in order to live from today till tomorrow I have to choose, decide, act, and plan not on certainties, but on uncertainties; not merely matters upon which I happen at the moment to be in doubt or concerning which I am in ignorance because of the limitations upon my present knowledge, but matters that on principle cannot become the objects of knowledge in a way relevant to my present exigent choice. Fate, chance, the irrational, the unpredictable, Providence—call it what you will—always enters my life in time. Of course, one can always say: "But this is not fate or chance or the irrational at all. Given infinite time and an infinite intelligence, one can discover that what seems fortuitous to a finite intelligence in finite time will be seen to have a reason and hence to be predictable." Quite! And this is precisely God's situation. Unfortunately I do not happen to be God— and what's more, I have to act right now—as W. H. Auden puts it:

> The sense of danger must not disappear:
> The way is certainly both short and steep,
> However gradual it looks from here;
> Look if you like, but you will have to leap.[1]

It means something else also. Time and existence in time are *decisive.* It is like an "ever-rolling stream" that "bears all its sons away." Time is decisive in a twofold sense: *first, what is past cannot be called back, what is done cannot be*

---

1. "Leap before You Look," in *The Collected Poetry of W. H. Auden* (New York: Random House, 1945), 123.

undone; second, by the same token, what is past is over and done. The one view remarks the decisiveness of time with a backward glance; the other remarks it with a forward glance. Because of the one we feel the pathos of time; because of the other we see its promise. Through the one we weep over our sins; through the other we look forward with a renewal of faith and in hope. In the act of repentance is combined both this backward and forward glance. Time also confronts us with a double possibility: *in us,* fidelity or infidelity to what we ultimately love and trust; *in the object,* trustworthiness or untrustworthiness. There is no escape from this. Every act in which we are faithful is threatened by the possibility of our infidelity in the next; but—every infidelity is followed by the possibility of love and trust. The same contingency that is the source of the threat is also the source of a promise. Yet even our "faithlessness" is just the substitution of one object of love and trust for another.

Since we always will in the direction of the uncertain future and therefore gamble on uncertainties; since time flows on and in a sense makes all our mistakes, bad risks, and failures "eternal" failures, as it were; we "can't go home again." As Leon Bloy once said, "Suffering passes, but the fact of having suffered never passes." When we have been fools or wicked; when we betray what we love or when what we have trusted fails us; we cannot start over with a fresh sheet. And from this derives the pathos of our personal existence. We are embarked and there is no escape from the risks and decisions that every day we must make in faith—unless we think to resort to suicide; and of course Hamlet remembered that we might better "bear those ills we have than fly to others that we know not of." The decisiveness of time presents me here with the question: How can I accept myself and my betrayals in the presence of the betrayed?

Yet, the decisiveness of time means not only that the past *cannot be annulled.* A different orientation is possible, one toward the future, which says, not looking bitterly toward yesterday, but responsively toward tomorrow: *The past is over and done.* Each new day is really new and brings with it new possibilities, new choices, ever new acts of commitment in love and trust, ever new possibilities of becoming a new creature, with a new faith and hence a new identity. The problem here is this: How can my love and trust be renewed? For the Christian Faith the double possibility with which we are perennially confronted is *sin* and *repentance.* Therefore, "choose ye this day whom ye will serve."

Is it not clear beyond a doubt that faith is, indeed, inevitable? And can there be anything that matters more? For now we see that the inescapable, ever-importunate and decisive question at the heart of *my personal existence* every day of my life is: Whom can I ultimately *love* and *trust*? Is it not also plain that it cannot remain unanswered—even when I do not ask it, for my very existence is itself the answer I am giving? Because of its firm grasp of this fact, the biblical-prophetic tradition recognizes that man always loves either the true God or idols, that between them there is no neutral ground. This means that he either loves the transcendent God who can smite him, or an image of himself. To live thus, not knowing who I am and not caring, is this not insanity? Pascal has mordantly characterized such a state of mind: "We run carelessly to the precipice," he says, "after we have put something before us to prevent us seeing it."

The ultimate exigency in my life is therefore to find and maintain *my identity* and *my existence* through faithfulness to an object capable of sustaining my ultimate love and trust. And if I have no such, I am in despair. It is a task that is both inescapable and fraught with terrors at every step—no matter what my faith. And I am always faced with contradictions that I have neither time nor capacity to resolve. There is, first, the problem of *finitude:* At every moment I am called upon to make an absolute commitment, to enact "eternity" into time, to express *my* "ultimate meaning" in an individual act; yet I do not know the ultimate meaning of human existence and cannot be sure that I have rightly calculated probabilities. I cannot *exist* without love and trust, yet I cannot remain faithful for ten consecutive minutes. I must risk all as though I knew the end of history when I do not even know what the next hour will bring—or what the one that is just passed has meant. I feel that life has a meaning, that it is no mere "tale told by an idiot," for in the very attempt to deny it I affirm it; yet I am always faced with that ultimate contradiction of life—death. Though I can try to love and trust myself, I find myself both unlovable and untrustworthy. And when I love what appears to be really other than myself—an ideal, whether that be the self I would become, my family as an abstraction, my race, my nation, my civilization—I realize that these are simply gigantic mirrors of myself—idols, in short, powerless to help because powerless to hurt—still without a true "other" that I can love and trust. I desire an absolute object of devotion capable of rousing a total response in me, of heart, soul, mind, and strength, and find such in an encounter with another existing person like myself; yet even here I find a being neither lovable nor truly trustworthy, for, like me, he or she too is faithless and will die.

The ultimate object of my love must be *truly* "other" than I; not the product of my form-discerning rationality, but someone who meets me, confronts me, not in some general category, but in a unique, free, and contingent act. I must be presented with the "irrational" otherness of his freedom vis-à-vis myself. This alone is capable of evoking my ultimate devotion as a person, since only thus does he bear to me the same relation that I bear to him; viz. the relation of freedom; and this is the condition of real love, since it is the condition of true reciprocity. As W. H. Auden says: "Love's possibilities of realization Require an Otherness that can say I."[2]

The ultimate object of my trust must overcome the contradictions of my existence and make this particular existing person who I am meaningful in spite of this resolution. Therefore, it must overcome the limits of finitude and death—not simply by transcending them and annulling the meaning of life and finite existence, for such cannot be the object of ultimate trust to an *existing* being *while he exists*. It must justify my acts even though they fail. It must overcome the meaninglessness occasioned by my betrayals and infidelity, which I am powerless to remove from the past.

If there is no such being for me to love and trust, then I am in despair. For what is despair? It is the declaration: "I do not exist, I have no identity because there is nothing I can love and trust." But, strangely, there is even faith in this despair. The self loves and trusts itself—and nothing else, in the moment that it gives expression to despair.

Whom then can we wholly love and trust but God? How can we wholly love and trust Him except as the Word made Flesh, the crucified and risen Lord; dwelling, as we, amid all the vicissitudes of history, taking on our mortality and sin, and encountering us here as a *Person*, thereby presenting us with that which can fully evoke our power to respond with heart, soul, mind, and strength; even as he overcomes the power of sin and of death, without annulling man's freedom or the meaning of finite existence? Is anything else sufficient? Apart from this are we not in despair?

---

2. "For the Time Being," ibid., 447.

_ ON THE MEANING OF GRACE _____

One of the most powerful parables of an existence without grace has come from the literature known as existentialist—so largely preoccupied with a clinical exploration of the tense and angular outlines of an only *human* world of wakefulness and effort. Jean-Paul Sartre, in his play *No Exit*, depicts three people in the hell of human existence, where they have nothing for which to hope except that which they can make; no justification save that which each can him- or herself secure in the presence of the others; no value except the courage they can go on exhibiting by affirming themselves. This is a sleepless world in which one cannot shut his eyes; where there is no giving and receiving and where "hell is other people." Over the entrance to this drawing room, which is the stage set of the play, the author has written, as it were, "No Exit."

St. Paul says: "I can will what is right, but I cannot do it. For I do not do the good I want, but the evil I do not want is what I do." Hell is *not just* "other people." It is also being oneself! And the Apostle cries, "Wretched man that I am! Who will deliver me from this body of death?" Human existence is the very opposite of graceful. It is awkward—which is to say, it is turning-the-wrong-way-ward! Our lives are brought to calamity because we try too hard to save them from calamity. We are always *careful* about ourselves—anxious to say and do and be the right kind of person, the person who will be accepted by "other people." It is "other people" who make us *careful*, and, being full of care, we cannot forget ourselves. We are the prisoners of the image of ourselves, which we are forever so anxiously creating and preserving in the

The Hibbert Journal 57 (1956): 156–60.

presence of "other people." Hence we never know the wonderful freedom of *carelessness*.[1] This is why "other people" is hell.

When this fact about our existence is brought powerfully to our attention, we look for an exit. We *try* to surrender ourselves. How odd a thing to do: to *try* not to try! We see how we are in fact the prisoners of an image of ourselves, which we hold up like a mask to other people—that the hell that is "other people" is a hell we make for ourselves—so we become resolute. Something must be done. What? Why, we must carefully extricate ourselves from the hell of care. This is why hell is being oneself!

Anyone who has ever lain awake at night has enacted a parable of the graceless world. Unable to sleep, we toss and turn. Then we decide to relax—giving our undivided attention to untensing of attention. And as our effort increases, so we move farther from our goal: the ceasing to give ourselves a goal. The deeper our anxiety over being awake, the wider awake we become. Insomnia is not just being awake. It is being full of care about being awake; and the insomniac *never* goes to sleep except by grace. As the first light of dawn is seen, he says, "Oh well, I'll not get any sleep *this* night"—and falls asleep.

In a very real sense, the fallen world, the world in which "other people" and being oneself are hell, the world in which we are forever careful of ourselves, and in which we can neither give nor receive gifts, is an insomniac world. And in it we cannot put ourselves to sleep. Occasionally we experience something that doesn't belong—a *reversal* of everything. We see the first light of dawn, and make a confession about ourselves: "Oh well, I'll not get any sleep this night"—and we discover what grace is.

In one sense, perhaps, we may say that the modern world is peculiarly insomniac. I do not merely mean insomniac in the sense suggested by the actual volume of sleeping pills consumed by modern men; or even merely that hinted at profoundly by a *New Yorker* cartoon some years ago that showed two working girls *en déshabille* in their small New York flat, one of whom says to the other, "I don't know whether to take a benzedrine and go to the party or a nembutal and go to bed." I rather mean that modern culture is insomniac in principle. Its gracelessness is perfectly illustrated in its assumption that all

---

1. Our ambivalent feelings about "care" are perfectly expressed in the ambiguous meaning of "careless." We say, "Fine careless rapture." But we also say, "Don't be so careless!"

problems will yield to human foresight. Its *care*fulness is perfectly symbolized by technology. And in Marxian Communism we have its perfect philosophic embodiment: namely, in the refusal to accept anything as "given." (Grace, "gift," "give," "given," are all cognate words). For the Marxian, nothing is "given," in the sense of "to be received and cherished just as it is." The human mind is not "given": if you don't like it as it is—brainwash it! Human nature is not *given:* if you want to make it over, produce a revolution.

Now I want to suggest that we look at the word *grace* and some of its cognates to see the many lights given off by them in their many uses. Only so, I think, can we begin to get some impression of the richness of the meaning of grace as we use it in the Christian community in an expression like, "The Grace of our Lord Jesus Christ. . . ."

Notice that the root appears in many different parts of speech: "grace" (used as a verb), "graceful," "gracious," "graciousness." Notice too that its Latin root, *gratia,* ties these words to "gratuity," "gratitude," and "gratis" (meaning "free"). Finally, observe that through *gratus,* "grace," etc., are linked to "beloved" or "dear" and through these in connection with gratitude to "gift," "give," "given"—as when we use it to express the difference between what we "find already there" and those things that are produced or contrived; between the something with which we start and which may therefore be taken for granted, and that which we must ourselves supply; between those things upon which we may depend, for which we need expend no effort, and whatever gets to be "there" only through our own exertions. A gift and "the given," however, are not only "there without effort," and hence need not to be seized, but only to be received. They are *free.* So that grace, gift, "the given," receive, gratitude, free, and freedom all have familial relations of different degrees of consanguinity. And is it not odd how "take for granted"—i.e., "receive as a gift" (with appropriate gratitude)—gets perverted into the notion of accepting as a due, as when we say, "You seem to take it for granted that . . ."?

Perhaps the most illuminating jobs done by this word and its cognates are in connection with actions and persons.

Of Nathan Milstein's violin playing or Margot Fonteyn's dancing we say, "How graceful!" We mean, of course, "How easy," "How effortless," "It seems to be done without trying." We could also say, "How completely free!" And we go on to see this means that the playing has grace not merely because it is effortless, but also because the effortlessness is connected with receiving and accepting—"a taking for granted": in the case of playing the violin, putting beyond the scope of attention and *care* the question of where the fingers must be put to sound the right notes and which notes come next. "Awkward" violin playing is effortful and unfree, because we cannot "take for granted" the habitual responses of the trained concert violinist and therefore we cannot free our attention from the rules—"the law"—in order to "give" ourselves—there is that word again—to Beethoven's music. This shows us a profound and important connection between being able to accept, receive, and take for granted, and being able to *give*. The frustration we feel in personal relations when, *care*ful and alert to seeking acceptance from others, we cannot take ourselves and our acceptance *by* others for granted and are therefore unable to give ourselves *to* others, is in every way analogous to the way most of us play the violin. This is what it means to be *self*-conscious.

And this brings us to another use. Frequently, we characterize a certain way of life as "gracious living." While this is sometimes taken to be saying something about the outward forms of living, I think it legitimately refers to the character of the way people are related to each other. I suspect that "gracious living" is free, effortless, interpersonal relations. People are able to give themselves to one another. And, in the light of the connection remarked above between being free, being able to give, and having something to take for granted, I suggest that part of the "gracious living" is the result of the fact that it is rubric- and ritual-governed living. In our rationalistic society, ritual tends to be despised—even though observed in practice. But in fact, ritual-governed behavior "gives" us something to take for granted. Internalizing the "rules" frees us for other things. Is not what we ordinarily call an "awkward situation" one in which one doesn't know what to do and one in which therefore everyone suddenly has consciously to "contrive" something? There are certainly many senses in which the Christian sacraments and Christian ritual are, as we say, "means of grace." But we must not ignore their role as that which is simply "given," something that we may take for granted, something that we need only accept in order to be liberated from our own ingenuity for something else.

When we say, "That was a very gracious thing to do," we generally mean it was gratuitous, not required—something for which we may feel gratitude. When we characterize a person as "gracious," do we not mean unself-conscious, free, able to take himself for granted and therefore one who is able because of accepting himself to give himself to others?

Having grace then seems to involve being able to *accept* and having something on which one may depend. Or put another way, it is being able to receive and acknowledge something that is "given." And when we say of actions or persons that they have grace, it generally seems to be appropriate to say that they are free—they exhibit some special kind of deliverance; in them there is a peculiar and very important kind of fulfillment.

Thus, through grace our being is fulfilled; we are delivered from carefulness—from "other people" who have become hell for us because we have forever to be watchful of the mask we hold before them; from the hell that is being oneself because we cannot "take ourself for granted"! The only exit we have into wholeness from the "awkwardness" of our present life is through the portal of grace.

What have these uses of grace and the connections among its cognates to do with the familiar Christian uses? We have observed that the characteristic human "awkwardness"—the turning-the-wrong-way-wardness—is feeling unlovable, unacceptable to others; needing this acceptance; and consequently being forever under the goad to make ourselves loved through our cleverness, ingenuity, and the "beauty" of the mask we hold up. It is this which puts us on the alert, animates our attentiveness, makes us *careful*. All this may be put in another way. Human life seems to be poisoned by the inability of each of us, by taking thought, to do what we want above all else to be able to do: to give and receive gifts.

Giving and receiving is a radically uneconomic transaction. To have a true relation of giving and receiving, it is required that there be a giver for whose gift no reason can be given and whose gift implies no claims upon him to whom it is given. No less, it requires a receiver who accepts the gift as implying no merit on his own part and who sees no concealed obligations attached to it. In truly free and fulfilled personal relations, the giving and receiving is of ourselves.

Now, life would be quite literally unbearable if there were not in it a modicum of what we might call *natural grace*. After all, we *do* fall asleep from sheer exhaustion!

But for the Christian, Jesus Christ is God's incarnate gift. He is grace par excellence. Through him God gives us as a gift to ourselves. In accepting the gift of ourselves we come to depend upon the giver. We may "take ourselves for granted." Being accepted, we may accept; accepting, we can then give.

From the "awkwardness" of our usual life we can, however briefly, live gracefully. When St. Paul has so mordantly characterized himself in the insomniac body of death, he cries, "Who shall deliver me?" In the next breath he says, "The law of the spirit of life in Christ Jesus hath made me free from the law of sin and death." Every Christian, when in the posture of faith, knows the reality of this hope and experiences the accomplishment of this deliverance.

THE ABSENCE OF GOD

Near is
The God, and hard to grasp.
And where there is danger,
The saving powers grow too.[1]

I will show them my back, not my face,
In the day of their calamity.[2]

I

Our own time and its interpreters have made us peculiarly aware of the precarious relation that exists between men and the "reality" that stands over against them and is mediated to them through myth, symbol, ritual, language, historical memory, technique, law, and all the other organs of culture that enable us to become and remain human. The roughly three decades between Spengler and Toynbee have produced a climate in which, even if he would prefer to forget the whole nasty business by Confident Living and Positive Thinking, the literate layman is vaguely aware that human existence, and the community and hence culture which it presupposes, are not simply to be had for the asking, and thus finds himself in the rather desperate and conservative state of mind about his own culture, shabby as it is, that is

The Hibbert Journal **55 (1956): 115–23.**
1. F. Hölderlin, "Patmos," in *Hölderlin Poems,* trans. Michael Hamburger (New York: Pantheon Books, 1952), 217.
2. Jer. 18:17, RSV.

reminiscent of Hilaire Belloc's unhappy youth, *Jim: Who Ran Away from His Nurse and Was Eaten by a Lion*, concerning whom the moral was pointed:

> And always keep a-hold of Nurse
> For fear of finding something worse.

And while it is certainly true that a man does not depart from a culture by the same door wherein he entered, the recollection of the disintegration of Hellenic culture, out of which arose our own, is relevantly called to our attention as an instructive paradigm. Whether we think in terms of "spiritual dead men abiding in autumnal cities" or "universal churches mounting upon the wreckage of universal states"—the problem, in short cycle or long, is apparent: men begin by having a vivid sense and firm grasp of the "reality" that is over against them, and end by asserting (an act presenting its own philosophical problems, to be sure) that "nothing is; even if anything were, it could not be known; even if it could be known, it could not be communicated." And even if an almost incalculable spiritual gulf separates Kirilov, to whom, since God is dead, "everything is permitted," from Gorgias the Sophist and Pyrrho of Elis, the alternation throughout history of belief and skepticism, of the presence and the absence of "Being," of the proximity and remoteness of God is a familiar pattern.

If we were frankly to start with certain biblical categories (making no attempt to justify doing so), how would the intellectual landscape of our time look? Do they shed any light upon the alternating presence and absence of "Reality"? Can we view some of the characteristic contemporary cultural phenomena as bearers of judgment and, therefore, in spite of themselves, of redemption and hence of hope?

W. H. Auden observed several years ago that "Christians and the Church today share with everyone else in our civilization the experience of 'alienation,' i.e., our dominant religious experience . . . is of our distance from God." Can the "absence of God" be biblically interpreted?

II

It was Nietzsche who, philosophizing with a hammer, scandalized the comfortable late Victorian age with his declaration, which he took to be both a personal confession and an historical judgment, "God is dead!" This was not the first intimation. Pascal in the seventeenth century had been over-whelmed by the God who hides himself, and Pascal seemed to believe he did so with singular guile in a universe the "centre of which is everywhere, the circumference nowhere." Contemporary, so-called atheist, existentialism is the most recent version of the same claim. And let it not be forgotten that the Christian Kierkegaard was in this respect closer to Nietzsche than to the average parish priest. Finally, in an overpowering succession of characters who were radical deniers, Dostoyevski left no doubt that the modern soul was sick to its very depths from the absence of God.

As the spokesman of this mood Nietzsche may be taken to be representative, and as such can be seen to be a modern prophet—not merely in the loose sense in which that title is carelessly conferred upon any man who attacks his time, but in a sense approximating the biblical use. Nietzsche, in a very profound way, was an enemy of idolatry and, we may say from a biblical perspective, the revealer of the God who becomes present in his holiness only when he seems completely to have disappeared.

Idolatry is a state of mind expressing itself in many different subtle ways. An idol may "hide" the God who is really present by "containing" him, by restricting his freedom, by "making him present" within the limits of human imagination. When Job presumed to arraign God for his injustice, he was proposing to confine him to a simple calculus of reward and merit, to an anthropocentric system of meaning. But idols—whether they be of stone and gold, or systems of meaning such as a scholastic theology—may equally well conceal from us the fact of God's withdrawal, his absence. Idols contain and limit the God who manifests himself by being present. They also veil from us the God who manifests himself by becoming absent.

The idol conceals God by "containing" his presence; it conceals him also by hiding his absence. Nietzsche is the prophet par excellence against the second form of idolatry. To the self-satisfied bourgeoisie, drowning their existence in routine godliness and pious secularity, Nietzsche says, "God has abandoned you!" What we have to ask is: What are the positive elements of this kind of radical nihilism as much in evidence in contemporary culture?

The other side of the protest against this second kind of idolatry—the proclamation of the disappearance of God—is the annunciation of absolute titanism or absolute evil incarnate. In the place of the now empty symbols of Christian transcendence we have a kind of negative transcendence: Nietzsche's transvaluer of all values, the anti-Christ; W. B. Yeats's beast which,

> . . . somewhere in sands of the desert
> A shape with lion body and a head of a man,
> A gaze blank and pitiless as the sun,
> . . . .
> . . . its hour come round at last,
> Slouches towards Bethlehem to be born[3]

or Goetz, in Sartre's play *Lucifer and the Lord*, who seeks above all else to perform an act of absolute evil.

Perhaps the most powerful recent image of this negative transcendence has been provided by Albert Camus in his novel *The Plague*, where the North African city of Oran, standing for our civilization, carefully and willfully insulated against mystery and transcendence, is suddenly invaded by bubonic plague. Of Oran, Camus says:

> Perhaps the easiest way of making a town's acquaintance is to ascertain how the people in it work, how they love, and how they die. In our little town . . . all three are done on much the same lines, with the same feverish yet casual air. The truth is that everyone is bored, and devotes himself to cultivating habits. . . . Certainly nothing is commoner nowadays than to see people working from morning till night and then proceeding to fritter away at card-tables, in cafes and in small talk what time is left for living. Nevertheless there still exist towns and countries where people have now and then an inkling of something different. In general it doesn't change their lives. Still they have had an intimation, and that's so much to the good. Oran, however, . . . seems to be a town without intimations; in other words, completely modern.[4]

Into such a self-contained existence comes the plague—and no one will believe it! "The usual taboo, of course; the public mustn't be alarmed, that wouldn't do at all. And then, as one of my colleagues said, 'It's unthinkable. Everyone knows it's ceased to appear in Western Europe.' Yes, everyone knew that—except the dead men."[5]

The only kind of transcendence possible in the world in which "God is

---

3. W. B. Yeats, "Second Coming," in *The Collected Poems of W. B. Yeats* (New York: The Macmillan Company, 1950), 215.

4. Albert Camus, *The Plague*, trans. Stuart Gilbert (New York: Alfred A. Knopf, 1948), 4.

5. Ibid., 33.

dead"—i.e., in which everything is tasteless and void of goodness because nothing is transcendently good—is transcendent evil—plague-carrying rats, coming up out of cellars to die in the streets. This alone can shake the equanimity of the "treeless, glamorless, soulless . . . town of Oran [which] ends by seeming restful and, after a while, you go complacently to sleep there."

Alongside the discovery of the death of God and of negative transcendence, much contemporary art, philosophy, and letters is overwhelmed by the sense of a "loss of ontological reference" and the relativization of all meaning. By the first of these I mean the sense that the relationship between men and a reality that stands over against them has been broken; that all the organs of culture are but more or less coherent tautological systems that do not refer to anything outside the systems themselves; that, to use Joad's vivid phrase, the "object has been dropped"; that reason is involved in "incestuous fixation upon its own logic."[6] In this connection it is interesting to reflect upon the changing conception of contingency. The contingent for the realist tradition is that which, having no cause within itself, requires a cause; for Kant, "cause" is not to be given this kind of metaphysical extension; in Sartre, the contingent is the absolutely "underived." The one says: there are contingent beings, hence there must be a cause per se; the other says: there *can be* no explanation. Contingent beings are absolutely underived, they are just "there," hence absurd!

Philosophers so antithetic to one another as Jean-Paul Sartre and Ludwig Wittgenstein are intrigued by the lack of any essential connection between the words we use and the "reality" to which they "refer."

Sartre has a character in one of his novels say: "I murmur: 'It's a seat,' as a sort of exorcism. But the word remains on my lips: it refuses to go and rest upon the thing. . . . Things are delivered from their names. They are *there*, grotesque, stubborn, huge, and it seems crazy to call them seats or to say anything whatever about them."[7]

Wittgenstein observes: "Every sign *by itself* seems dead. What *gives* it life? In use it is *alive*. Is life breathed into it there? Or is the *use* its life?"[8]

One can almost see the kind of linguistic hybris, the human impiety of

6. W. H. Auden, "For the Time Being," in *The Collected Poetry of W. H. Auden* (New York: Random House, 1945), 453.

7. *The Diary of Antoine Roquentin,* quoted by Iris Murdoch in *Sartre: Romantic Rationalist* (New Haven: Yale University Press, 1953), 12

8. *Philosophical Investigations* (New York: The Macmillan Company, 1955), paragraph 432. Italics in the original.

wanting to seize it by force, which causes "reality" to retreat and finally disappear. It seems to be true, as Hölderlin says,

> But the serving maids of Heaven
> Are miraculous
> Like all that's of heavenly birth.
> He who would grasp it by stealth
> Holds a dream in his hand, and him who attempts
> To grow like it by force, it punishes.
> Yet often it takes by surprise
> Him who has hardly begun to give it a thought.[9]

Observe, for example, the way in which the constant repetition of a word soon renders it an alien, grotesque, and meaningless sound. We say: Isn't that a "funny" word? This would seem to be the result of (1) stripping it out of its context of intersubjective use—where its referential function has been forced upon us by its actual employment, and where we have the sense of its belonging to an interpersonal universe of meaning that is "over-against" any one of us; (2) rendering it a "tool"—a "thing"—through simple technical manipulation, so that it becomes "familiar"; and (3) concentrating upon its mere sensuous presence, with the result that we lose sight of its reference. From this we see the wisdom of the commandment "take not the name of the Lord in vain," i.e., don't get familiar with his name, for then, among other things, it ceases to *mean*.

All of this is, I suggest, a kind of linguistic hybris. We take the word by violence rather than allow it to refer. We assault it rather than allow it to speak.

Now, it is precisely the familiar, banal, secular, common use of everyday language that is nonrevelatory. The mystery cannot break through. It is the poet, for example, who takes language and by doing "violence" to it, breaks through its secular use. Every great poem is a "judgment" upon language—showing its finiteness, its existential conditionedness, its contingency, and the idolatrous tendency of man to presume to seize, manipulate, and control with language a closed universe. Thus a poem "reveals" by "concealing"—it affirms "Reality" by negating familiar realities. Oddly enough, when we view the linguistic positivism of a Wittgenstein biblically, we can see him as a kind of prophet against man's presumption, against his self-enclosed, self-

9. "The Journey," in *Hölderlin Poems*, 189.

complacent, autonomous, verbal world in which he feels secure because he supposes it possible for him to grasp with his words "Reality" as it is. Here we see the word of man smashed by the Word of God. The "stability" of the rational, verbal world is revealed here in all its contingency. The real "Copernican Revolution" in "epistemology" began not with Immanuel Kant, but in the prophetic attack upon man's inveterate tendency to fashion idols—figments of imagination—that he takes to be the very structure of ultimate reality.

By the relativization of all meaning I mean that tendency to locate all order and structure not in something other than man, but in man's fluctuating historical consciousness. The earlier Wittgenstein says: "In the world everything is as it is and happens as it does happen. *In* it there is no value."[10] Speaking from an entirely different tradition, Sartre says: "The existentialist does not think that man is going to help himself by finding in the world some omen by which to orient himself. . . . Therefore he thinks that man, with no support and no aid, is condemned every moment to invent man."[11]

The whole weight of modern subjectivity and the sense of the loss of God was expressed earlier by Pascal: "We burn with desire to find solid ground and an ultimate sure foundation whereon to build a tower reaching to the infinite. But our whole groundwork cracks, and the earth opens to abysses." Perhaps nowhere has this abyss been so powerfully conveyed visually as in the eyes of Georges Rouault's painting *An English Clown.*

When we view these cultural phenomena—the absence of God, negative transcendence, the loss of ontological reference, and the relativization of meaning with all of their accompanying anguish, what—from the the standpoint of the Bible—can we make of it? Are there categories in biblical thought that enable us to understand both man's precarious relation to the reality that stands over against him and the periods in human history, like our own, when that which is mediated to man through culture becomes but a "dream in his hand"? Can our nihilism be seen as the bearer of judgment and hence of hope?

The problem of nihilism is no doubt susceptible of a dialectical treatment. But more relevant for us here are two familiar biblical images: the "face of God" and "God's back." I want to consider especially the phrase, "I will show them my back, not my face, in the day of their calamity."

10. *Tractatus Logico-Philosophicus* (London: Routledge and Kegan Paul, 1949), 6.41.
11. *Existentialism* (New York: Philosophical Library, 1947), 28.

We must begin by recalling that the root-metaphor underlying biblical categories is that of personal relation and encounter. This is the privileged language of biblical discourse, and any attempt to reduce it to something else or to begin at another point is illicit.

This being so, it follows that the God of Abraham, Isaac, and Jacob is known only when he reveals himself—even as other persons are known to us *as persons* only as they "reveal" themselves, speak, and address us.

Secondly, this means that the God whom we encounter as the "other" in the moments of our most vivid sense of our own personal existence (though we may see him subsequently as related to every moment of our existence as judge and redeemer) is known initially and paradigmatically in the personal ecstatic experience of supreme fulfillment or ultimate despair. It is when I am "beside myself" with hope or despair that the God of the Bible appears as the *Thou* who is correlative to myself when I am most vividly aware of myself as a person—as ultimately fulfilled or threatened.

Thirdly, this suggests that, though he may be seen as related to the regular, normal, routine, predictable, expected round of daily existence—in short, to the *saeculum*—he is neither known nor unknown here. God is known as present in the ecstasy of hope and fulfillment; he is known as absent in the ecstasy of despair. We either see his "face" and feel his nearness, or we see his "back" and experience his remoteness. We either know him by his love or encounter him as wrath.

If, biblically speaking, God reveals himself in all moments of existence when we stand "outside ourselves," what is the revelatory significance of the ecstasy of despair? What is the meaning of those occasions when a community or an individual is "beside itself" with a sense of God's absence? Why, in other words, does God withdraw?

Jeremiah's phrase is quite clear on this point: God confronts us with both his face and his back. He is present to us as near; he is also present to us as far. He is present as absent, no less than he is present as present. The *absence* of God itself testifies to his *presence as absent*. The God who is a *Deus absconditus* is discovered through his absence, through the forlornness of the world from which he has withdrawn, but which by this very fact, alludes to him. We know him negatively as the "something which is missing." To know that God is absent, to know that he is *not* here, is to know him negatively. And should the foregoing sound like empty rhetoric or willful paradox-making, let one simply ask what is involved when we, quite commonly, say, "We missed you."

Do we not mean that someone was seen to be absent and *through that very fact* was present?

But let us pursue the "logic" of this image further. When you are speaking to another person, you sometimes notice the lapse of attention: the wandering gaze, the whispered comment to another companion, the growing interest in something else. Your inclination is to say, "Leave the room, if you must, but don't remain here not paying attention to me!" In other words, to use the language of Jeremiah's image, we are much more offended by someone who turns his back upon us and remains in our presence, than by someone who simply walks away. For in the former case, they are present to us as absent. This shatters our self-confidence. We are *confronted* by a person but by his *back*. We discover that we are not the center of his attention, that the world doesn't revolve about ourselves. We become aware of a *personal center* other than ourselves. He "presents" or "presences" himself to us through his inattention, his "absence."

In Jeremiah's words God says in effect, "I will confront Israel with my inattention, in the day of their calamity." God becomes absent.

But, we may ask, Why does God do this? The short answer would appear to be, "Because Israel has forgotten me"—i.e., because she has not really been attentive to God. However, before we can fully appreciate what this means, we shall have to do some further unpacking of the image.

When I confront you face to face—an *I* before a *Thou*—when we look into one another's eyes and are completely absorbed in personal relation, each is the center of the other's gaze and attention. But suppose I begin to speak. I become more and more diverted from you: I am explaining something to you, I am struggling with the *problem* of articulating ideas, I am trying to communicate them to you. I say to myself: What words shall I use? What will he understand? What sort of a chap is he, anyway? Isn't there some way I can make him see this profound thing I have to tell him? And so on. I have had to *detach* myself in order to talk to you. You, as a person, are no longer the focus of my attention. I am now preoccupied with *my* thoughts, *my* words, *my* problem of communication and all the rest of it. I am now directing *words—noises*—at you. I am objectifying you, making of you a kind of *thing*.

And, of course, you sense this; and being yourself a center of personal freedom who stands in the same kind of relation to me as I stand to you, namely, a free relation of giving and receiving, you instinctively withdraw.

T. S. Eliot treats this kind of relationship very subtly in *The Cocktail Party*.

Lavinia Chamberlayne has abruptly left her husband, Edward, we may suppose in protest against having been made a thing by him. And Edward is shattered by her departure, not so much, it would appear, because he has lost face, but because of the profoundly disturbing discovery that Lavinia is an "otherness that can say, 'I.'" He says:

> Why, I thought we took each other for granted.
> I never thought I should be any happier
> With another person. Why speak of love?
> We were used to each other. So her going away
> At a moment's notice, without explanation,
> Only a note to say that she had gone
> And was not coming back—well,
> I can't understand it.
> Nobody likes to be left with a mystery:
> It's so . . . unfinished.[12]

Lavinia, who is better known by Edward than by anyone else in the world, can make herself "known" only by leaving him. Edward, who knows his wife so well that he can anticipate her every reaction, doesn't become aware of her until she is gone. Lavinia *absents* herself, and by so doing *presents* herself as an unfathomable *person*, with depths that have been forgotten or ignored by Edward. Edward, who is quite sure he knows her better than she knows herself, has his *image* of her, which is to say, his *idol*, shattered by Lavinia's departure.

Why then does God withdraw? He absents himself in order to become *present* in his *holiness*. He *conceals* himself in order to *reveal* himself as beyond every anthropocentric system of meaning. When we try to enclose him, to grasp him, to gain control of him so that we can manipulate him, he withdraws, turns his back upon us, revealing our dependence upon his unfathomable mystery. The positive content of God's withdrawal is his holiness, the mysterious depths of his being. The negative content is the emptiness, confusion, loss of identity, dread, alienation, and loss of meaning that results from the shattering of our idols. Our self-centeredness and illusion of self-sufficiency is breached from beyond us. We experience the ecstasy of despair.

12. *The Cocktail Party* (New York: Harcourt, Brace and Co., 1950), 29.

When we view through this biblical image the art, philosophy, and letters of our time with their emphasis upon the death of God, negative transcendence, the loss of ontological reference, and the relativization of meaning, we see them as profoundly revelatory. For they say, in effect, "In the day of our calamity God has shown us his back and not his face." This means to the Christian that he must receive the full force of judgment implied in contemporary culture, for he knows that God is very far from our expectations before he becomes the fulfillment of our life and the perfecter of our hope. But it also means to him that the God who appears as a judge in his absence, is known as redeemer when he becomes present.

FOREKNOWLEDGE
AND FOREORDINATION

A Critique of Models of Knowledge

I

Whether or not one needs to agree that all our philosophic perplexities are but the product of an absentminded or an ecstatic use of language and, therefore, require for their dissolution only some language therapy, there can be little doubt that of some of them this may be true. There are, for example, certain problems that are the product of our trying to employ logically incompatible analogies: The puzzle, that is to say, is actually produced by our slipping back and forth between two analogies which will not mix.

The traditional question as to whether God's foreknowledge entails foreordination seems in certain respects to be a case of this kind. While I am not of the opinion that we can settle by this kind of analysis alone all the vexatious problems tangled together in a bundle (which includes divine omnipotence in relation to human freedom, as well as theodicy), except, of course, by ruling all theological talk to be out of bounds in principle, it does seem to me that certain difficulties can be brought to light by showing the incompatible models of what it is to know (and therefore, by analogy, what it would be to foreknow) that are operative in certain formulations of this issue.

Journal of Religion 40 (January 1960): 18–26.

II

The problem of the relation between divine foreknowledge and fore-ordination—to be referred to henceforth as "the problem"—is, stated in its simplest terms, thus: If God knows the world in a fashion analogous to that in which we are thought to know it, but, as is appropriate to omnipotence, without the element of contingency that infects all *our* knowing of it, he must know all past and all the future as though they were present. From this it seems to follow that what will be for us in the future is, since already known in a present to God, what it *is*, for God, and is already what it *is to be*, for us. And this being so, these questions arise: Is it conceivable that the activity that we take to be one of freely choosing and deciding could really, under these circumstances, be what it seems to us to be? Even if we can answer this affirmatively, can the activity of freely choosing be thought to have an efficacy in the course of the world which it appears must be determined to be what it is to be, if God is to be thought of as knowing it in, for him, a present?

We may take Augustine's wrestlings with Cicero in regard to these questions to be typical of the history of the argument. He says:

> It is not the case, therefore, that because God foreknew what would be in the power of our wills, there is for that reason nothing in the power of our wills. For he who foreknew this did not foreknow nothing. More-over, if He who foreknew what would be in the power of our wills did not foreknow nothing, but something, assuredly, even though He did fore-know, there is something in the power of our wills. Therefore we are by no means compelled, either retaining the prescience of God, to take away the freedom of will, or, retaining the freedom of the will, to deny that He is prescient of future things, which is impious. But we embrace both.[1]

The seriousness of Augustine's efforts need not be doubted, even if the force of the argument really turns upon a play on words. But what is of interest here, beyond the form of the argument that Augustine tries to develop against Cicero, is the fact that the problem should have arisen in the first place. Cicero is willing to deny divine omnipotence for the sake of

---

1. *City of God,* trans. Marcus Dodd (New York: Hafner Publishing Co., 1948), 1.198, book 5.

human freedom. Augustine says, "we embrace both." How is it that this perplexity did not seriously arise for the two greatest philosophers of antiquity, Plato and Aristotle?

I should like to suggest that the problem is acute for Augustine because there are incompatible analogies at work in his thought; that a Greek model of knowing and a biblical model of knowing are in conflict. And though showing this to be so in no way settles the question as to which of the models is to be preferred; nor that we do not have to use both for discourse about God; nor even that we have to use either; it does enable us to see that the assumed conflict between believing in God's omnipotence and believing in the contingent character of the world's future is a product of conflicting analogies.

A modern, and one might call it a secularized, formulation of the same problem can, I think, be shown to be rooted in the same conflict in models of what it is to know—though it is best put now in terms of differing conceptions of the relation between logic or language and reality. This modern view has been called "logical predestinationism"[2] and may be characterized as follows: If I say, "X will occur tomorrow," what I have said must, by the law of excluded middle, be true or false. Therefore, even though I may not know *now* whether "X will occur tomorrow" is true, it is in fact now already true or false. Hence, though we do not *know* what the future will bring, what it will bring is already settled, and a god could know that what this is, is to be. What is to be already must include either the occurrence of X or the nonoccurrence of X, and while this either/or suggests a contingency in the future, it in fact only means that the future is still unknown *by us*. This is the view of logical predestinationism.

Logical predestinationism is a position from which escape is fairly simple, for we fall into it (however much impetus to believe it there may be in our experience as selves environed by forces over which we have no control and, therefore, however well this doctrine may serve as a powerful *symbol* of our general helplessness in the world) because of a confusion in language.

When we say a proposition *must be* either true or false, all we mean is that

2. See F. Waismann, "How I See Philosophy," in H. D. Lewis, ed., *Contemporary British Philosophy,* 3d ser. (London: George Allen and Unwin, 1956), 455ff. Gilbert Ryle has also treated this problem in a somewhat different way in his *Dilemmas* (Cambridge: Cambridge University Press, 1954).

under certain circumstances we would be willing to use that proposition, i.e., assert it; and that under different circumstances we would be willing to assert its negate; and that in our language these two possibilities are exhaustive. When we appeal to the law of excluded middle and say therefore that a given proposition must be (i.e., is right now) either true or false (thereby seeming to say that, though we may not *know* just now which it is, it *is* already one or the other), we are only saying that certain forms of words in our language are used by us in certain ways; that these ways are governed by rules; that the rules are such that you cannot in any given set of circumstances both assert and deny the same proposition; and that in this set of circumstances either the proposition or its negate is true.

When I assert "X will happen tomorrow," one may take me then to be expressing my belief that probabilities are such that a state of affairs will occur tomorrow, where I would be willing to assert "X is/has happening/ happened." And when we say "X will happen tomorrow" *must* be either true or false, we are saying something about the rules of our language. This is a *logical* "must be."

The confusion arises to begin with as the result of an ambiguity in the use of the term *true*. When we say that a proposition is true, we mean that it states what is the case, that there is some state of affairs in the world of which we are willing to use it. When, however, we say that a proposition *must be* true or false, we are making a statement not about any state of affairs in the world or the actual assertability of any proposition, but about the rules of our language. Therefore to say that "X will happen tomorrow" must be either true or false is not to say that something, X, is already destined either to happen or not to happen tomorrow; but only that "X will happen tomorrow" is the sort of expression in the English language that may have one or the other of two truth values and can never have both.

As the solution to the problem of logical predestinationism is easy to come by, so its value when we arrive at it is not great; and, in any case, it does little to illuminate for a serious Christian theist the problem of God's foreknowledge in relation to foreordination. For this formulation of the problem and its solution are entirely neutral as regards the theological questions. It merely shows that the future need not be supposed to be predetermined merely because of the logical fact that a proposition needs to be either true or false. Indeed, it might be held that this analysis shows us only (1) that our *knowledge* of the future is never more than probable; (2) that nothing as to whether the future is determined can be made to follow from the assertion of the logical law of excluded middle; and (3) that therefore the future may or may not be settled in advance, but we cannot know in advance that it is predetermined, and when what has been future becomes present and comes to be known, there is no characteristic of what is now known from which we might infer an answer to the question as to whether or not at any past time what now is was predetermined to become what now is. It is this neutrality concerning the theological questions which makes this a "secularized" formulation, and, being neutral, an analysis of it sheds little or no light for one who wishes to believe that in some sense God has a care for the future of the world and its history and yet is at the same time quite sure that this does not foreordain what the future will be—at least in a way and to an extent that renders the human activity of choosing and deciding inefficacious in the course of the world. As Augustine said, "We embrace both."

In terms of what model or models of knowledge, then, is it possible to "embrace both," and what analogy can be imagined to have produced Augustine's—and many another's—discomfiture?

If we operate with a broadly Platonic paradigm of what can be known and what it is to know, we find ourselves committed to the view that genuine knowledge is *episteme,* a grasp of the eternal forms by an act of intellection. Further, we are committed to denigrating *pistis* (which can only yield us true opinion of the historical world of coming into being and passing out of being) and *dianoia* (which operates discursively with the merely hypothetical) in comparison with the categorical certainty and immediacy of epistemic knowledge.

Suppose we take this to be the model of knowledge and derive from it a conception of God's knowing and therefore of what it is for him to foreknow. What would this yield?

If on this model God is to be thought of as knowing with certainty and immediacy, then it will have to be assumed that *what* he knows eternally *is* and has not become. What he knows eternally, and immediately, as is appropriate to omniscience, we know discursively in a temporal order and mediately. Suppose we take as an example my coming to know the conclusion of a three-term syllogism. From the two premises I can, obeying the rules of deduction, *draw* the conclusion. The conclusion is already *determined* to be what I will in due course deduce that it is because of what is given in the premises. God does not come to know the conclusion. He knows the conclusion at the very "moment" that he knows the premises. God can be said to "know" the conclusion only because it already *is* for him what it *will be* known by *us* to be; and, certainly on the Platonic model, its being so is in no way the product of his willing it so. Such things may be said to be what they are eternally known by God to be only because they always *are*; they do not *come to be*. For them to be knowable in any genuine sense of "know," they must be eternally what they are, which is to say, "foreknowable" because "foreordained." God may be thought to "foreknow" in this scheme only because what he is thought to know always is.

But this has little to do with the God who is the *creator* of the world of history and change, who is thought to have brought it into being out of nothing, and who providentially watches over every sparrow's fall. For that matter, the Platonic God cannot be thought of as knowing the historical world at all. He knows only the structure of eternal forms. Aristotle's introverted God is where we finally come out with this model. And with such a God, there can be no thought of his foreordaining, for neither does he ordain. Strictly speaking, with reference to the world of history and change, God neither knows nor foreknows, ordains nor foreordains.

If, however, you take God seriously as the maker of heaven and earth, you have quite a different problem.

Suppose, for the sake of brevity, we say that on the Platonic model God's knowledge is the immediate grasp of an analytic system. In that case the kind of knowledge of the world of history that the *creator* must be thought to have would be a knowledge of a system of synthetic propositions. Foreknowledge is no longer the immediate grasp of a system of analytic truths. It becomes knowledge of the "*future*" truth of certain synthetic propositions. If this is different from logical predestinationism, how is it so?

Using this model, calling God omniscient would seem to involve that all *true* synthetic propositions are for God in the present tense and are known by him to be true; that is, there is a state of affairs corresponding to each of these synthetic propositions in the present tense (for God). Further, it would seem to involve for us, by contrast, that there are some synthetic propositions in the past tense that are known or are capable of being known by us to be true; some in the present tense that are known or are capable of being known by us to be true; and some in the future tense concerning the truth or falsity of which we do not and cannot now know. I am of course perfectly well aware that we frequently—and quite legitimately—say that we "know" that "X will occur tomorrow." But I will take this to be a weak sense of "know" and, in any case, not on the same logical footing with "know" in the earlier use. We use "know" in this strong sense only of occurrences in the past or the present, for only what has happened or is happening for us can be known in this sense. And I take it to be part of the difference between a finite being whose life and knowledge unfold in time and an infinite being who is eternal and omniscient that for the latter there is no *weak* use of "know."

Now, though this is not *logical* predestinationism, even if analogous to it in certain respects, it certainly entails foreordination. We use "know" in the strong sense only of events that *have* transpired or are transpiring—that is, only of what *can have been* or *is* now a possible term in a cognitive relation. To use "know," in the strong sense, of some state of affairs which is *not* or has not been, is contradictory. Hence to speak of God's foreknowing by analogy with this strong sense of "know" entails that a state of affairs is, for him, hence has been, is, or *is to be,* a possible term in a cognitive relation for us. Therefore, for God to foreknow requires that there be something that now *is* for him, and therefore *is to be* for us; and this means that what *is to be* is fixed!

There is, then, no deliverance from the foreknowledge-foreordination relation by means of this model of knowledge and a fortiori no possibility of "embracing both" a belief in God's provident care over the world of nature and history and a belief in man's freedom.

Is there then an alternative model of what it is to know (or, to put the matter linguistically, does the concept "know" sometimes function in a different logical environment) that has been operative in the thought of theologians, which by its incompatibility with the model analyzed above has produced "the problem," and closer attention to which might enable us to clarify, if not fully to resolve, our difficulties?

I believe there is. It will be necessary first to distinguish two aspects of the way the model functions: that by virtue of which it is possible to think of God's relation to nature and history, and especially to their future; and that by means of which we are enabled to conceive God's relation to man as being of such a character that man's freedom is a reality, even though God remains omnipotent. At bottom, I believe only one basic model is dominant here, though I shall not be concerned to explore this in detail. Nor will I attempt to show how the two different aspects of the way the model functions are related. Finally, I will only point out two difficulties in this formulation of the question that I shall not here consider. The first of these is that the concepts with which we think about "nature" and those with which we think about "history" are sufficiently different as to cause us to wonder whether one analogy alone will serve to relate God to the future of both (in a way relevant to the clarification of "the problem"). Second, even if this difficulty is removable, can a single model do double-duty both for relating God to nature and to history, on the one hand, and to man, on the other?

III

Let us begin by considering the different model of what it is to know insofar as it functions to relate God to the world of nature and history and especially to their future in what has been called both providence and foreknowledge.

First, it must be pointed out that the God who is thought to have a relation to the world and man of the sort that produces "the problem" is the *Creator.* This means that he transcends the world in the way that an agent is thought to transcend his own acts. It also means that the creation has the character it has and exists at all only because God has willed it should be and that it should be in the way that it is, even as my acts may be said to have the character they have and to become actual only because I have willed them so (unless, of course, I bungle). To be sure, there are crucial disanalogies involved between man's and God's activity at both points. It would be absurd to think that man's acts are created by man ex nihilo as God's are thought to be; and the question as to how the analogy is to be appropriately qualified to fit God, and what right we have to use it at all, are real perplexities. Even so, it is clear that the existence of "the problem" presupposes the use of the Platonic model together with the analogies drawn from the discourse we use about human volition where concepts like "actor," "act," "intend," "plan," "anticipate," "choose," "steadfast," "faithful," "hope," and so on, function. The God who is supposed to know, foreknow, have a care for, predetermine the course of nature and history is, according to this analogy, the God who is their creator. Therefore, the character that the world has had for us at any given time in the past, has for us at any given present, or is to have for us in any given future, is the function of God's 'acts', 'plans', 'choice', 'hopes', and 'faithfulness'.[3] That is to say, the world has been, is, and will be a certain way because it was, is, and will be *willed* to be that way, by analogy with what might be said about my intentions, my

---

3. I have put these terms in single quotes to call attention to the fact that they function analogically here.

willing, and the actualization of my acts. The world is, in short, contingent in every detail; hence there can, on this analogy, be no question of God foreknowing the way the world is to be in the fashion that would be so, if the model of knowledge were one where he was thought to know the world, in our strong sense of "know," eternally and immediately (because it eternally *is*) what we only *come* to know in time and by the mediation of discursive reason. In other words, a God who is the creator of the world is imagined as standing in a relation to the world's *being* what it is/is to be; and must be supposed to *know* of its being what it is/is to be; in a quite different fashion from the way imagined in the case where he is *not* thought to be its creator.

Is there, then, some model of what it is to know operative within these volitional analogies? That is to say, does it make sense to use the concept "know" in a logical environment with "actor," "act," "intend," "choose," etc.? If God is thought to make the world to be (ordain that it shall be) in a certain way, and this is thought by means of analogies to our own volitional activity, what, in terms of these analogies, does it mean to think of God *knowing* and *foreknowing* his creation?

Obviously God can be thought of, in these terms, as knowing what he *had* done, just as I can be expected to give a report of what I have done.

Second, God can be thought of as knowing how, generally, he does things, again, just as I could report on my dispositions and tendencies to do or not to do certain things.

Third, God, can be thought of as knowing of his own intentions in a fashion analogous to that in which I can be expected to be able satisfactorily to answer questions about my plans and goals—providing I have some—whether it be short- or long-range ones about which I am asked. In the case of God, this knowing is not *now* knowing something about the way the world is to (must) be. It is rather a knowing now of what he plans now that the world *shall* be. But knowing this is not a knowing now of the way the world *must* be going to be; nor is it knowing anything about the way the world is now. It is a knowing *now* what his plans *now* are for what will be. And even presupposing an all powerful will to execute his designs, knowing what these designs are now does not "determine" or actualize them now. The designs only become actualized when they are no longer known merely as designs, but are known as acts, i.e., enacted designs. At any given "moment" of God's being thought to know his designs and intentions, his knowing these, in terms of this analogy and its built-in model of knowledge, makes no difference in the realm of the actual.

Finally, it may be said of God by analogy, as it would be said of me, that he knows whether and to what extent his intentions have been successfully realized.

In all this, it is clear that God's foreknowing in no way involves a foreordaining. To be sure, it might be rejoined that God's intentions, he being all powerful, never fail of fulfillment. It does not follow from this omnipotence, however, that his intentions cannot change, thereby introducing the notion of the contingency of the future, which is what is at issue.

But then it is replied that God's radical difference—his greatness vis-à-vis man—is his fidelity, the constancy of his purposes, his never failing love. Quite! But to say that God is always faithful is to speak (since "fidelity" is meaningless apart from the correlative notion of "infidelity") of him in terms that retain the element of contingency. Therefore, even if God's intentions never fail of fulfillment, he being all powerful; and even if his overall intention of love never changes, he being ever faithful; this testifies to the fact only that everything which God *intends* is realized, *not* that his knowing what his intentions are *entails* that they are always realized. The element of contingency is always built in with this analogy, even when it is qualified by the confession of the pious that God is always faithful.

When therefore we relate God the creator to the world of nature and history in terms of this analogy with its model for what it is to know, we can speak of his *knowing* the creature without being driven to thinking that the foreknowing of his own acts foreordains them (in any sense that would not comport with the notion that the future of nature and of history are contingent—with the notion, that is to say, that man in his own historical existence cannot be thought of as in interaction with the acts of a God whose acts are in some real sense contingent in a way analogous to that in which those of another person's acts, with whom I have to do, are thought to be). In this sense, at any rate, it is possible to "embrace both" God's foreknowledge and man's freedom.

IV

There remains a final question to be treated in this essay. Earlier, I suggested that a distinction must be drawn between the way in which God is conceived to be related to the world of nature and history and that by which

he is thought to be related to persons, since obviously resolving the putative difficulties for thinking of God's creation—the events of nature and
history—as being genuinely contingent while at the same time maintaining
the providence and sovereignty of God, is not the same thing as showing that
my relation to God in the full heights and depths of myself as a *person* is
compatible with God's being sovereign and providential—unless of course it
is to be argued that I can be exhaustively accommodated to the concepts by
which we think of nature and of history. The remaining issue is this: If the
model of what it is to know and therefore for God to *foreknow*—which avails
us of this analogy—can be made to function in such a way as to assure us, on
this analogy, that the future of nature and history are contingent, is there
some means of thinking of God's relation to persons that makes their "freedom" more than just a contingency, but makes it in some genuine way the
freedom and taking of responsibility for one's self that I believe we regard as
conditions of full personal existence? Earlier I suggested that the root analogy
of biblical thought can accommodate us in both ways. I shall not here attempt
to show how these two different aspects of its function are connected. I only
want to ask whether there is a way of using "know" of persons in our ordinary
language that is such that we can think of God as *fore*knowing by analogy
with this without on one hand qualifying his providence and sovereignty, nor
on the other limiting, in principle, man's full freedom as a person in a relation
of giving and receiving. Finally, it will be relevant to ask whether this use has
any support in biblical ways of thinking—the traditional source of the Christian and Jewish impulse to speak at once of God's sovereign care over the
world and of man's responsibility as person. The manifest fact that men
forfeit or pervert their freedom in this sense, or are deprived of it by other
men, does not tell against the functioning and usefulness of such a notion, if
it can be found, in our discourse about ourselves as persons and about God
as personal.

Perhaps we can bring out this different concept of "know" with the
following cases.

We might imagine someone saying, "He used to know me, but he has
forgotten me," where the opposite of "forget" is to "remember"—have
recollections of, noticing a familiar expression about the eyes, a characteristic
gait, a special laugh, etc. "To remember" here means to be able to call back to
mind, make certain intellectual associations, etc., that is, to know certain
things *about* a person. But we can also imagine a woman saying of her lover,

"He used to know me, but now he has forgotten me." And here she is not at all saying that he cannot re-*cognize* her. He can call her by her name, reminisce quite effectively upon their past love affair, remark upon her mannerisms, etc., which are quite familiar to him. Yet—he *has* forgotten her. He no longer knows her. The woman is quite right. He recognized her in every detail, but he no longer knows her.

Or think of someone obviously smitten by a beautiful but remote woman. He might say, "She doesn't even know I exist." And here what he is saying is not that the *belle dame sans merci* cannot call his name, has not seen him as he walks by, perhaps with a somewhat sick expression of longing on his face, etc. What he means is that he is no object of her *attention*.

Again, could not a wife say to her husband, "You know, I am beginning to feel that I do not know you any more." It would be a very bad joke were he to reply, "Why, remember, I'm your husband, the one that takes all the abuse. My name is George Jones. Yours is Mary Jones. *Jones,* can't you remember! I'm the man that lives at the same street address as you, and pays the bills." Not only does this not allay her feeling of pathos, but it has no logical relevance to the sentiment she has expressed. "Know" was not functioning here in any such way as to be met by what George said.

Suppose in a moment of great paternal solicitude I were to say to my daughter, "My dear, when you were still in your mother's womb, indeed, even before you were conceived, I knew you." How differently do we know someone whom we have "known" in their mother's womb from someone whom we casually encounter!

Finally, we are told in many parts of the Bible, as it is translated into English, that "he went into her and knew her." Indeed, this sexual use of the verb *to know* is the privileged use. And it is said, "Your heavenly Father marks [i.e., remarks, notices, *knows*] the sparrow's fall."

Now, what I wish to point out is only that variously in these cases, "to know" is to *acknow* (*agnitio*); it is to recognize (not re-cognize), to accept, care for, love, be faithful to, encounter in a fully personal way. For God to *know* me as a person in all my heights and depths is to acknowledge and be faithful to me as fully a person. And for God to *fore*know me, in terms of this model, is not to limit, qualify, or denigrate my being as free and responsible (although in fact this relation with him is always being perverted into something less than this). On the contrary, it is the necessary condition of my *being* a person. Finally, when, in English translations of the Bible, we read such words as *remember, forget, faithful, faithless,* etc., it is evident that it is in this logical environment that "know" and "acknow" function. What we find in our ordinary language for expressing our relations to one another as persons is given support in the biblical model of "to know." And it is in terms of this model that we think by analogy of God's providence over us as persons.

It is possible, then, as Augustine wished for it to be, that we may "embrace both" a belief in God's omniscience and a belief in man's freedom, providing we do not mix incompatible models of knowledge, or try to assimilate all uses of "know" to a single model and then draw our analogy for *fore*knowledge from it alone.

BIRTH, SUICIDE, AND
THE DOCTRINE OF CREATION

An Explanation of Analogies

I

Prima facie, nothing would seem to be more unlikely to clarify the peculiar nature of certain concepts in theological discourse than an analysis of the expression "I was born" and an examination of the nature of a decision to take one's own life. Nevertheless, I believe that such an inquiry will be of value in explicating certain features of the language of "beginnings" that is a familiar part of theological discussion, and one that has perhaps presented peculiar difficulty in the one hundred years since the publication of Darwin's *Origin of Species.*

One of the many things that Christians profess to believe about God is that he is "maker of heaven and earth"—where this is taken to mean that before the divine act, through the utterance of God's Word whereby the world with which we have to do is thought to have become what it is, there was nothing. Hence the so-called doctrine of *creatio ex nihilo.* This view, it is supposed, is a characteristic of both Christian and Jewish belief that sets them apart from the beliefs of all religions—such as Hinduism, Buddhism, etc.—that are either explicitly or implicitly a-theistic, and also against metaphysical systems where either there is no God, in the theistic sense, or where, if there is, he is thought to be no more than an artificer, working upon some antecedently given matter.

Mind 58 (1959): 309–21.

Along with this belief, it is also asserted that man is made in the image of God. Let me, as preliminary, take this to mean, so far as the present inquiry is concerned, that man, himself a creature, stands to the created world (understood as the subject of our public, common sense, or even our scientific curiosity) in a way analogous to that in which those who believe in *creatio ex nihilo* suppose God to stand to this world.

Now, it is notoriously difficult to assimilate logically what is thought to be meant by *creatio ex nihilo* to the many other things that we say about the world (whether we interpret the concept "world" here in the Kantian sense as a regulative principle for *cosmologia rationalis,* or merely as any given finite sum of synthetic propositions about phenomena that may be thought of as being "in" the world, taken in the Kantian sense). Theologians have declared the notion to be a mystery,[1] and philosophers, beginning in the modern period with Kant's antinomies, have generally regarded it as having no definite meaning.

I propose to show that though *creatio ex nihilo* is indeed a queer conception, which leads theologians to speak of mysteries and philosophers to speak of nonsense, in fact the notion is not so remote as has been supposed from certain demands within what is nowadays called our ordinary ways of speaking; and that within these ordinary ways of speaking where we are talking in a logically extended way about matters that are both meaningful and important to us as persons, there are displayed analogies with the sort of thing the theologian has in mind when he uses "creation" and "image of God." To anticipate later argument, I think it can be shown by an analysis of some of the things we normally say and think of ourselves as persons that what we mean when we say them is logically heterogeneous with certain other things we say about ourselves, and therefore they may be said to be both "queer" (if we take as our paradigm for what is "unqueer" these other things we say) and yet meaningful; and that in them some analogy with what one might mean by *creatio ex nihilo* is to be found.

While, of course, this does not necessarily accredit the use of analogies

---

1. "In the history of religion the ideal of real creation first appears when God, instead of being considered a merely natural force, becomes a transcendent Being. We do not know this God through experience or reason but through faith, and we know of the mystery of creation by the same means" (E. Frank, *Philosophical Understanding and Religious Truth* [New York: Oxford University Press, 1945], 58).

drawn from these tracts of our ordinary ways of speaking for describing God; and while it certainly does not authorize the use of theological language in general; it does give us some genuine insight into what it is that the Christian might mean when he uses them.

This, I propose to do by exploring suicide as in some sense an act of absolute and radical destruction; and by analyzing certain features of the expression "I was born."

II

The impulse to see man as in the image of God, and especially to see that image manifest paradigmatically in a dark and violent gesture of defiance, destructiveness, and nihilism, is of such antiquity that we cannot but wonder what kind of posture man is thought to achieve in relation to the world and to himself in these acts in which it seems so natural to see the image of God. Adam and Eve are promised that, if they will eat of the tree of the Knowledge of Good and Evil, they will become as God. While this is a calamitous act, it is nevertheless one in which man is felt to exhibit a real if perverted likeness to God. Man's act of rebellion is in certain respects logically like God's act of creation! The logical parallel between God's act of creation and man's act of destruction is clearly assumed. If this be so, it is necessary to explore some of the features of the way we think of ourselves that are built into our talk about ourselves as persons.

St. Augustine, in his *Confessions,* reflecting in later life upon a boyhood act of wantonly stealing pears that he did not want and could not possibly eat, and concluding that the only possible answer to the question "Why did I do it?" was "It was forbidden," goes on to make even more explicit the curious logical connection between God's creative activity and man's willful rebelliousness. He says: "And wherein did I, even, corruptedly and pervertedly, imitate my Lord? Did I wish, if only by artifice, to act contrary to Thy law . . . so that . . . I might imitate an imperfect liberty by doing with impunity things which I was not allowed to do, in obscured likeness of Thy omnipotency?"[2] And then, elsewhere, doubtless having the same case in mind, he says, "For

2. *Confessions,* book 2, chapter 6.

souls in their very sins strive after nothing else but some kind of likeness to God, in a proud, preposterous, and, so to speak, servile liberty."[3]

A similar tie between God the radical creator and man the radical destroyer is shown in Albert Camus's brilliant essay *The Rebel*. He says of modern revolt: "Metaphysical rebellion is the means by which a man protests against his condition and against the whole of creation. It is metaphysical because it disputes the ends of man and of creation. . . . When the throne of God is overthrown, the rebel realizes that it is now his own responsibility to create the justice, order and unity that he sought in vain within his own condition and, in this way, to justify the fall of God"—that is, to become God himself.[4]

Again, the American poet E. E. Cummings seems to suggest that man as a radical destroyer of the world is the most apt antithesis to and hence the best source of analogies for God as creator ex nihilo when he writes:

> when god decided to invent
> everything he took one
> breath bigger than a circus tent
> and everything began
>
> when man determined to destroy
> himself he picked the was
> of shall and finding only why
> smashed it into because.[5]

Finally, in Dostoyevski's novel *The Possessed*, we are confronted by Kirilov, who, believing that God does not exist, nevertheless so conceives of the God who does not exist and who therefore must be replaced, that only an act of suicide by him is a genuine earnest that he himself may be thought to have become his God. He says: "Full freedom will come only when it makes no difference whether to live or not to live. . . . A new man will come, happy and proud. To whom it won't matter whether he lives or not. . . . Everyone who desires supreme freedom must dare to kill himself."[6] In other words, the indifferent contemplation of suicide seems for Kirilov to exhibit a posture in

---

3. *On the Trinity*, book 11, chapter 5.
4. *The Rebel*, trans. Anthony Bower (London: Hamish Hamilton, 1953), 29–31.
5. *Poems: 1923–1954* (New York: Harcourt, Brace and Co., 1955), 404.
6. *The Possessed*, trans. David Magarshack (London: Penguin Classics, 1953), 125–26.

relation to oneself and the world that is in some way or other like that which God has been thought to have to the world that is his creature.

Preliminary to analyzing further the significance of these striking parallels, it is necessary to consider what can be meant by the concept "world," for it seems to me to be a very ambiguous one, and its ambiguity is the source of much confusion concerning what is meant by God as the creator of the world. Being perforce brief, this will be vague.

Doubtless there are many more uses of the concept "world," but let us consider here only three.

"World" can be used, as Kant seems to have thought, as an idea of the Transcendental Reason, and as such functions as a regulative principle for a *cosmologia rationalis*. The concept in this use has no content—in Kant's sense—but nevertheless provides us with guidelines in the pursuit of a goal that, though never to be achieved, nonetheless governs the progress of scientific understanding. This use of the concept is largely irrelevant to my present inquiry.

The world may also be thought of as that which can be exhaustively cataloged by a, practically speaking, infinite number of straightforward subject-predicate sentences in a language system that we will, in order to educe the distinction essential to my purposes, imagine as having no use of first-person singular pronouns. In fact, of course, if we eliminate first-person singular pronouns, it is difficult to imagine what pronouns like *we* and *you* could do in the language (where they are steadfastly held to be unanalyzable into demonstratives like *this, that, these,* and *those*); and therefore we may eliminate them as well. Now we have a language with only the demonstratives, and the third-person pronouns. But surely, a language that does not use the first-person pronoun would have to reduce even the third person to "it," i.e., "he," "she," and "they" could only mean what could be cataloged in reports of behavior (actually we should have to say "events") or dispositions to behavior. We now have a language in terms of which nothing can be said about persons.

In the language thus truncated, the world will be the sum of synthetic propositions that could conceivably be shown to be true or false. It would, in other words, be the world that could be known to us, and which is thought of in our scientifically dominated culture, as the world of common sense, and of all of the sciences themselves. Therefore it will be the world as it is "known by science." It will be objective, that is, it will be what can be cataloged exhaustively in a language having no personal pronouns. It will be in practice, a third-person world, remembering that the only pronoun in the third person that remains is *it*. It will be, in other words, the public world as it must be imagined to be apart from anyone actually experiencing it. It is the world as we would all agree it *must be;* all epistemological relativism aside, in the language of our model, it cannot be described as being experienced by anyone in particular.[7] It is a world in which there are no persons, because "I" and "my" cannot be used in the language that described it. Therefore, it cannot be the world *of* or *for* anyone. No doubt a description of the world in this way would be a tour de force, and would involve a language that is very awkward, when compared with our ordinary ways of speaking about the common sense world. Nevertheless, I think it an imaginable one, and is in fact the ideal goal of all objective scientific knowledge, albeit the concepts that may be meaningfully used varies among sciences.

In contrast with this, and as our third use of the concept "world," let us imagine what we could speak of a language in which there are first-person pronouns. What differences would immediately appear?

First the world would be *of* and *for* someone. What I would mean by the world would be *my* world—though, committed as I believe we usually are to using "world" in the second of our three senses, this may be obscured. What is meant by "world" in this sense would include all of those features that could be cataloged in "third person" language as in sense two. But by adding the first-person pronoun all of this would be radically transformed by the additional characteristic of the world being mine; not just the world as I experience it from a particular point of view in a third-person way like the third-person way in which you, from a different particular point of view, also experience it (in other words, the first-person pronoun does not merely introduce the possibility of epistemological relativism); but mine in the sense that I have a relation to the body, its behavior and the environment of its actions (which is the world for *me*), which is part of what I mean by "I," that can never be identical with the relation that *you* have, and that cannot be expressed in the language lacking the first-person singular pronoun. That

---

7. Given the purposes of my model, it is an irrelevant criticism to observe that modern physics has had to argue that an ideal observer or at least an observation point always has to be posited.

this statement would seem to be analytic does not weaken the force of the distinction.

Perhaps this can be illustrated in the following way. In the terms set forth above, the expression "I will die" when used by me cannot be exhaustively analyzed into a purely third-person reading of "This body will undergo a radical change, including ceasing to behave in certain ways," etc. References by me to the body and its behavior which is part at least of what I mean by "I" can never be made to be logically equivalent to references by me to bodies and their behavior which are not. "I will die" can never mean for me just the same thing as "There is a body in the world (in the second sense) which one day will cease to behave as it now does." What is being asserted is not just about an object in the world (in the second sense) in the way that "This body (as a component of the world in the second sense) will die" is about an object in the world. My body and its behavior is not in the world *for me* in the same way that your body (to avoid the possessive pronoun, we'll call it "Smith") and its behavior is in the world for me. For me to describe my death as the end of certain kinds of behavior in the world is not *for me* the description of an occurrence *in the world* at all like an account by me of Smith's death as an occurrence *in the world*. For myself, I am not *in* the world as Smith is in the world.

Now, taking as our paradigm Kirilov's suggestion that the act of suicide will be the earnest of his having achieved Godhead because it will exhibit a characteristic in himself that he conceives to be essential to Godlikeness, how may the posture of a man to himself and to his world as he contemplates suicide be likened in certain respects to the posture of God when he is thought to be the "maker of heaven and earth"?—and it must be remembered that the parallel we are here drawing is between God as radical creator and man, as in some sense, a radical destroyer.

If we take seriously our distinction between the use of the concept "world" in the second sense above, where what is meant in the nature of the case cannot be something that is *of* or *for* someone in particular; and its use in sense three, where it is always *my* world; then I think it is quite meaningful, using "world" in sense three, to say that my suicide is an act of destroying my world. If, that is, we keep in mind how "world" is functioning here, we may say that when I take my own life, I destroy the world! As destroyer of the world, in this sense, I stand to the world in my act of radical destruction, as God seems to be thought to stand in his act of radical creation. The posture I assume toward myself and the world (in sense three) as radical disposer is logically different from that I assume as disposer of this, that, or some other characteristic or feature of myself or the world. I am not destroying something or other in the world. I am destroying the world *as a whole*. I may be thought, in other words, speaking metaphorically, to take up a relation to myself and the world as a whole, to stand "outside" myself (in our ordinary uses of *myself*); and this bears some analogy to what the Christian seems to be believing about God's relation to the world when he declares him to be "maker of heaven and earth."

Or, to put the case in a slightly different way, in the act of suicide I am, with reference to what I name with the personal pronoun *I,* bringing something radically to an end. Just as Hamlet's question "To be or not to be . . ." is logically not like "To be or not to be a doctor, lawyer, or merchant chief . . .", so contemplating the ending of my life is logically not like ending a job or a marriage. It is an end of *all* possibilities for something, namely, for what I name with the personal pronoun *I,* and not just the ending of certain possibilities such as this or that. We can say "After his divorce he was re-married," or "he was sadder but wiser." To go with the expression "After he died . . ." there are no expressions logically like "he remarried" or "was sadder but wiser."

I want to say then that though the act of suicide may not be thought of as destroying the world insofar as it is taken as an object for thought in the third person, nevertheless, the world as *my* world, *in* which part of what I mean when I use the pronoun *I* of myself is to be found, which is the environment of the acts of the body that is part of what I mean by "I," and is accordingly the world in our third sense, *is* destroyed. And the posture that I have in relation to the world, thus construed, is analogous to that which God is thought to have to the world (in either of our first two senses) as its radical creator.[8] There are three equally important features of this analogy to be emphasized. First, as destroyer of the world (in sense three), I have a view of myself as what may be called a radical agent. In the act of suicide, I perform an act that makes nothing out of something. My act is the reverse of God's, which makes something out of nothing. A world that can be imagined, in terms of the

---

8. There is a dangerous pitfall in the analogy here, for we may be tempted to infer from it, at this stage, that God and his world are identical. But this would be an invalid inference for, as I shall show, I and *my* world are not identical either.

present analysis, to have an end can equally be thought to have a beginning. When I imagine the end of the world by imagining a state of affairs in which there is no longer the world *for me,* I am thinking of a situation logically no more nor less queer than when I think of the world as having been created.

Secondly, in thinking of suicide as an act of destroying the world, I am thinking of the world as coming to an end, that is, as being finite. There is in this the greatest possible contrast with the way that we, quite properly, think of the world when using the concept "world" in sense two. The world in the third person, the subject of our purely scientific curiosity, is in practice, and rightly so, open-ended, infinite, and therefore not a possible object of experience, as Kant seemed to imply in his refusal to make the concept either an empirical one or one of the understanding. Accordingly we can derive no analogy for God's relation to the world that is his creature, from our relation to the world in sense two, for nothing ever radically begins or ends in *this* world.

Thirdly, it is having this kind of relation to the world (in sense three) that I have as a radical agent, that constitutes, for the Christian, my being in the image of God.

III

It still remains for me to show that there are certain logical pressures within what we ordinarily say and think about ourselves as persons that are not less "queer" than, because logically analogous to, saying of God that he is "maker of heaven and earth." To do this I will undertake to analyze the expression "I was born."

Frequently we find ourselves answering questions such as "When were you born?" And we do not take these questions to be odd in any way. We answer by giving a date, such as "In April of 1919," or "Shortly after the First World War," or, if the context is appropriate, we may say, "In the year of the great earthquake," etc.; or we may be asked, "Where were you born?" and answer, "In Kaifeng, China," or "In the Presbyterian Hospital." If we are to take these questions as in some way mystifying we would probably be taken to be resorting to, perhaps suspicious, evasion, or to be mere troublemakers. For the questions obviously presuppose possible answers in terms of straightfor-wardly datable and locatable events, which occur in the objective world, which is spread out in time and space; and which, in practice, extends infinitely backward and forward from the event expressed by "I was born." As such, the event may be thought to have all the complexity that any of the events in this world has: one may, for example, consider it from the standpoint of historical chronicle, from the standpoint of biology and genetics, or from the standpoint of obstetrics. And saying that "I was born" is true will certainly entail that certain historical, biological and genetic, or obstetrical propositions will be true. One may even wish to go so far as to hold that the proposition "I was born" can be exhaustively analyzed into all the propositions of the same logical sort as those above, the truth of which would be entailed by the truth of "I was born."

We take "I was born" in this way most of the time, and quite rightly so, as evinced in our willingness to answer the question "When were you born?" by straightforwardly offering a date, and not precipitating any philosophical quarrels about it.

But if we take this legitimate because, in most cases, quite adequate interpretation to be the paradigmatic or only one, we are left with some serious puzzles. For this puts me in the curious position of *celebrating* a chronicle of events, or biological and genetic or obstetrical facts, and the like, when I celebrate my birthday! To honor and observe duly with solemn rites only certain obstetrical facts seems a very odd form of behavior. And in fact I do not think any of us is doing this when we celebrate our birthdays, however impossible it may be to conceive of there being something to celebrate unless there *were* or *had been* some obstetrical facts. If we analyze "I was born" into the sum of true propositions about obstetrical and other facts, and the like, that are entailed by the truth of the proposition "I was born," then there seems to be nothing left of the sort that as persons we celebrate—nothing, indeed, in which we could take other than a purely obstetrical interest.

Now, why is this so? I believe we can say that it is because concealed in the language in which we are asked "When were you born?" and in the answer "In April of 1919" is a subtle commitment to the objectivist language that possesses no personal pronouns or else does not take them seriously; and therefore a birthday can never be described as *my* birthday. Or to put it differently, if we take the question "When were you born?" to be like "When did you come into the world?" we answer the question in such a way as to predispose us to take the meaning of "into the *world*" in the second of the two senses above. It is obvious that in this view, my "coming into the world" is not a radical event. When do we start counting "being in the world"? At conception? At the moment I leave my mother's womb? Or do we start with the gleam in my father's eye? Birthdays are celebrated only by persons, for a birthday is not what we understand it to be unless it is *of* and *for* someone, unless there is only one person who uses the pronoun *mine* of it. Only what can be of and for someone can be celebrated; and nothing in a world described merely in a language lacking personal pronouns can be so described. The fact that we celebrate birthdays therefore suggests that "I was born" cannot be exhaustively analyzed into reports upon obstetrical events, etc., in our language having no personal pronouns.

If, however, "I was born" thus analyzed tells some of the story of my coming into the world because the proposition "I was born" entails that there will be certain obstetrical and other facts, what is left out? The answer is of course that the world into which I am described as having come, is the world in sense two above. And there is not *for me* any world in sense three until I use "I" and "mine." With this act, the world in sense three comes into being, the world which is *my* world. And it is an absolutely novel act, for only I can use "I" and "mine" *for* and *of me* and *my* world. The absolute discontinuity between there being no world in sense three for me and there suddenly being such a world because someone uses "I" and "mine" of it is the same as the logical discontinuity between language two having no personal pronouns and language three which does have them. And this is paralleled in the ontological discontinuity between there being nothing and there being something, which is involved in the doctrine of *creatio ex nihilo*. In the act of suicide I make nothing out of something, the reverse of God's act of creation. In using the first-person singular pronouns, I make something out of nothing. It is from this that our analogy for God as "maker of heaven and earth" must come. To speak of God as creator is not the same as saying "I was born," but it *is* in certain respects logically like this.

IV

Let us then ask in conclusion how some of the apparent conflicts between science and religion—with particular reference to the notion of creation—can be shown to be the result of a confusion concerning the logical status of their respective claims.

Earlier on, I suggested that the implicit ideal of all objective scientific inquiry is a catalog of everything there is in a language from which we might imagine all the personal pronouns to have been dropped out, for such a catalog yields a world that is as it is independent of its being known from any particular point of view or by anyone in particular. I also suggested that within limits imposed by the program itself this is a perfectly legitimate enterprise. Let me now anticipate what is to follow and suggest that the putative conflict between science and religion—between Fred Hoyle and Genesis—respecting creation is the result of failing to notice the subtle commitment in this program to the concept of "world" as I have defined it as sense two above; and further because of a failure to notice that many of the things we say and think quite ordinarily about ourselves as persons rather operates with the concept in sense three. Finally, if our analogy for creation is to be drawn from the kind of discourse in which I say of myself "I was born," where this expression is analyzed as inassimilable to a language having no personal pronouns and therefore must be understood as at once saying more than can be said in such a language while entailing all of the sorts of things that can, a compounding of the confusion is always possible. For this means that what is named by "I" and "world" in our language possessing personal pronouns is not entirely unrelated to the body and its environment that is described in the language that lacks them, because the concepts "I" and "world" (in sense three) could not be used were not the concepts "body" and "world" (in sense two) already in use, while the converse is not the case. Our language having personal pronouns says more than one lacking them, but not more in the sense of adding further information of the same logical sort as already known through the pronounless language. Adding personal pronouns changes *the whole* picture, but it is an already familiar picture that is *transformed,* seen in a different light. This means that, in speaking by means of our analogy, of the world as having been created, we run the risk of misconstruing the relation of religious claims about creation of the world to scientific claims about the world in either of two ways: (1) supposing there to be absolutely no connection between them;[9] (2) supposing the connection to be of the sort obtaining between two propositions within one of the language systems in our model. To say that the world is created, using our

9. Karl Barth and Rudolph Bultmann, in different ways, seem to me to come very close to suggesting this view.

analogy, is not to report an additional fact about it like saying that there are material objects in it. Saying of the world that it is created stands to the fact of its being extended in a way analogous to saying of a body that it is a person stands to its having three dimensions.

Now, perhaps the difficulties can be elucidated in the following way. Let my body—in so far as it is extended, an organism, and capable of what might be called directed activity—be the kind of being about which the physicist, biologist, and psychologist speak. Within their conceptual schemes the notion of creation as the emergence of absolute novelty does not appropriately operate. Why? Because of everything that may be conceived as being reported in the concepts of the aforementioned disciplines we can imagine asking "What was the cause of *that*?" (where "cause" functions in a straightforward explanatory way), and we would expect to be given an answer by reference to some antecedents on a common logical footing with the events or behavior reported by these disciplines, using a covering law that embodies the concepts of these disciplines. Each of them, in other words, takes any given event or piece of behavior reported by means of their concepts to be continuous with other events or behavior of logically the same order prior to the one reported and so on ad infinitum. While obviously the physicist, biologist and psychologist operate with differing concepts appropriate to their own modes of explanation; and even though one may wish to hold that for this reason there is logical discontinuity of a sort among these modes of explanation, since, e.g., no complex of *physical* facts qua physical logically entails any biological fact; there is an analogy among these modes in the respect that within the limits of their explanatory interest any fact, event, or piece of behavior is preceded by a theoretically infinite series of facts, events, or pieces of behavior of the same logical order. And their explanatory interests, far from requiring a notion of a radical discontinuation of these series, would in fact be frustrated by it.

The implicit ideal of these accounts of the world is a catalog in a language in which there are no personal pronouns.

When, however, we add the personal pronouns everything is changed. However much the use of this new and enriched language may imply the appropriateness, within the specified limits, of the truncated one, we are now speaking of the world as *my* world and *yours*. A body and its environment may be thought of as becoming *my* body in *my* world—which is to use "world" in the third of our senses—when someone, namely you or I, can use

of them the expression "*my* body in *my* world." Since nothing in the truncated language logically implies the new components of the richer one, we
may say that *my* body in *my* world is, as *mine,* radically discontinuous with *this*
body, a body, *the* body, etc., in the world (taken in the *second* sense). And it is
this fact that makes it possible to speak of *me* and *my* world as having come
into being *out* of nothing, i.e., as having been created.

To have shown the source of the analogies by means of which the Christian
speaks of God as "maker of heaven and earth" is not the same as showing that
these analogies ought to be used.

I have attempted here only to argue that the doctrine of *creatio ex nihilo* is a
logically queer notion; but that it is not as remote as is supposed from many
things we say and think about ourselves in quite ordinary ways, and that an
analysis of the kind of posture a man may be thought to assume to himself and
his world in contemplating suicide and of the expression "I was born" display
this fact. Persuading a man that he ought to think of the world as having been
created is not unlike persuading a man who speaks a language having no
personal pronouns that there are persons.

GOD AND THE "PRIVATE-I"

I want to show certain, I think, quite obvious but perhaps important peculiarities of the role in our language of the first-person singular pronoun in order to suggest an analogy between the logical role in certain forms of discourse of the concept "I" and of the concept of "God." In the course of doing this, I think the use of certain theological concepts may be displayed.

I

Ever since the time of Hume all talk by ourselves about ourselves has been regarded as being in some way problematical, if not embarrassing. And the unavoidable use of the first-person singular pronoun by each man of himself has tempted us into assuming that each one of us enjoys a unique cognitive relation to himself concerning which, at any rate, the broadly empirical tradition in philosophy has made us feel slightly sheepish.

The most recent, although certainly not the most unambiguous, assault upon what he himself has called the "privileged access" theory of self-knowledge is that of Gilbert Ryle in *The Concept of Mind*. I want to begin my analysis with a look at part of his ingenious argument. Ryle says: "John Doe's ways of finding out about John Doe are the same as John Doe's ways of finding out about Richard Roe. To drop the hope of Privileged Access is also

Philosophy and Phenomenological Research 20.3 (March 1960): 409–16.

to drop the fear of epistemological isolation: we lose the bitters with the sweets of Solipsism."[1]

Now, in fact, I believe Ryle is quite unsettled in his mind as to whether he wishes to stand on so bold a statement, as perhaps will be seen later on when we consider what he has to say about "the systematic elusiveness of 'I'" and the functioning of the first-person singular pronoun. That is a technical question in Rylean exegesis that does not interest me. What I do want to show, using Ryle's remark above, is that such an analysis of self-knowledge is quite obviously false, and that the impossibility of accepting it shows us something important regarding the peculiar status and function in our language of the first-person singular pronoun.

First, Ryle, in having adroitly done away with the bitters of solipsism by denying the hope of privileged access, has created a new problem. By making this move he has enabled us to overcome the haunting sense of being quite alone, and has shown us that we can after all know other minds. Alas he has done all this in such a way as to make everything about each of us something quite public, or at any rate in principle publicizable. Further, though we have on his terms an assured knowledge of other minds, there is now no longer the possibility of knowing of their *otherness*. If John Doe only comes to know or find out about John Doe as he comes to know or find out about Richard Roe, then John Doe would know of the differences between himself and Richard Roe only in the way he knows of the differences between Richard Roe and Mary Poe; and this would mean that he could never use the pronoun *I* of himself, *my* of his body or his past and his future in order to distinguish the things named by these from the things named by *his, hers, yours,* etc.

Let us make my point in a preliminary way by putting it quite vaguely: without a "feeling" of myself still left over, and logically beyond the reach of any kind of behavioral reports I may make about myself after having put questions to myself as I might be imagined putting them to Richard Roe, including even reports about the linguistic behavior of using the pronouns *I* and *my,* I cannot know of the *otherness* of other minds. It makes sense to talk about *other* minds only if "I" and "mine" mean something more for me than what can in principle be linguified in reports of actions, dispositions, thoughts, feelings, and so on. To say, "No one knows what it is like to be me," is not at all

---

1. *The Concept of Mind* (London: Hutchinson University Library, 1949), 156.

to say something like, "I am shut up in my own mind," interpreted in such a way as to imply that I do not know what you are thinking or that you cannot know what I am thinking, providing I am willing to say.

In reply to this Ryle would want to say—"Yes, but the something left over, the I that cannot be assimilated to these reports of behavior or dispositions to behavior is systematically elusive." Indeed he says just this: "To concern oneself about oneself in any way, theoretical or practical is to perform a higher order act. . . . To try, for example, to describe what one has just done, or is now doing, is to comment upon a step which is not itself—one of commenting. But the operation which is the commenting is not and cannot be, the step on which the commentary is being made."[2]

Now, this analysis seems to me to be quite unexceptionable, as far as it goes. By means of it, in conjunction with his analysis of the question of privileged access, Ryle has succeeded in recalling to our attention some important facts. First, he has shown that "I" functions in a definite logical relation to empirical propositions about behavior or dispositions to behavior so that even though John Doe may not know John Doe precisely in the way that he knows Richard Roe, he certainly never knows something named "I" that is *entirely* independent of his own behavior, thoughts, feelings, or dispositions; even if this does not entail that, what is named "I" is just the *sum* of such behavior, reportable thoughts, feelings, and dispositions. Secondly, he shows that this knowing of his *own* acts and dispositions to act is knowing something that is genuinely part of what he means by "I." But most important, he suggests that "I" is a logically extended concept since what it names over and above what may be stated in and hence known by means of reports upon behavior or dispositions to behavior systematically eludes, at any given level of reporting, incorporation into the reports of that level. What I am taking issue with is the inference drawn by him from these discoveries. Do I not have a genuinely cognitive relation (in an unusual but permissible sense of cognitive) to what is named by "I" when I use it, which you in principle *cannot* have to what is named by "I" when I use it? "I" when I use it of myself, does not refer to a *ghostly* thing because what it names for me over and above what it names for you is not a thing at all since a *thing* is just what can be exhausted by terms in the predicate position of a sentence on any *given* logical level. From this it

2. Ibid., 195.

need not follow that we may not by analogy use the concepts "know," "thing," etc., in correlation with the first personal pronoun, if we can show that it is a logically extended concept that requires such unusual couplings. The issue really is just this: Can *my* world be exhaustively described in straightforward "thing"-language, or is that "thing"-language brought under a peculiar kind of pressure when I try to describe my relation to myself and to my world *insofar as they are mine*? Is "person" a concept logically assimilable to "thing"-language without remainder?

Therefore, the statement "John Doe's ways of finding out about John Doe are the same as John Doe's ways of finding out about Richard Roe" is false. To see that it is false and in what way false is to see something of the peculiar role in our language of the first-person singular pronoun. If we take seriously the logically peculiar role of "I," then we can explain how on the one hand it seems that what "I" names is assimilable to reports of behavior or dispositions to behavior, thus getting rid of all ghostly entities, and yet how it is possible on the other hand for *me* to be "aware" of its naming something that is not assimilable in this way. However publicizable what is named by "I" may be, there is always *for me* something that cannot be put into public discourse. It is this private relation that I have to myself, displayed in the logical fact that only I can use "I" of me, which underlies the urge to solipsism, which cannot be "said," but as Wittgenstein remarked, "shows itself."

The meaning of "I" is, for my hearers, certain behavior, etc., which is quite public. But "I" also means *for me* something more than this, something that is in principle not negotiable in ordinary public discourse about what I have done, and am now doing, or am generally disposed to do, etc.; something that is, if you like, systematically elusive, but elusive of this kind of public discourse only, not completely elusive of my awareness. To put the matter metaphorically, when I use "I," I am talking both about what can be made public and what cannot; about what can be put into language and what cannot. "I" is a logically extended concept. It is about, I will now call them, *acts;* but it is, *for me,* also about something more, namely, *the actor.*

II

Suppose, however, that one wished to hold that this argument from experience is an inconclusive one; and that until this putative amphibious life of the term *I* has been exhibited by an analysis of its logical grammar nothing can be concluded. Is there support to be found for the view I am pressing against Ryle in the logical behavior of "I"? I think there is. Suppose for the present limited purposes I were to define a language simply as a syntactically ordered system of terms having transferability. By "transferability" I mean that the various terms in the system are more or less adaptable to use by anyone in a wide variety of existential situations for calling the attention of others to particular features in these situations. For example, we can use verbs to designate certain kinds of actions or events, nouns to denote particular things, adjectives to characterize these particulars, and so on. I will take it that proper names like "Julius Caesar" and "Albertus Magnus" are no part of language, since they lack the requisite transferability. Even so, if there were no surrogate names in language, it would be a wholly abstract analytic system like mathematics, with no existential reference. In English it is chiefly demonstratives and pronouns that serve to tie language to particulars. "This" and "that" are substitute names having maximum transferability. They may be used by anyone to make reference to any kind or any individual particular in any existential situation. "He" and "she" are also surrogate names having a high degree of transferability, but not so great as "this" and "that." Now, in terms of this admittedly simple-minded scheme, I want to look at some of the characteristic behavior of the first-person singular pronoun by comparing it with the pronoun *he* and with the proper name "William H. Poteat."

First, let us notice that, unlike the proper name "William H. Poteat," "he" and "I" may be used to refer to any number of different particulars, even if when they are actually so used, they are always equivalent to one and only one proper name. *Like* proper names "he" and "I" on the occasion of their being used name particular persons; in use they are equivalent to proper names. *Unlike* proper names however they share with other terms in language some degree of transferability. But while "he" and "I" are, unlike proper names, parts of our language, they do not possess the same degree of transferability. "He" may be used by an indefinite number of people of an indefinite number of people on different occasions; and when used by any given person may mean a different person on every single occasion. Whereas "I," though it may be used by an indefinite number of people, can, when used by any person, mean one and only one person on every single occasion. We must say, then, that "I," unlike "William H. Poteat," possesses transferability and therefore qualifies as a part of language; but that unlike "he" it possesses only minimum transferability, since whenever it is used by a given person, "I" means one and only one person on every occasion that it is used by that person. And this, of course, means that "I" always functions reflexively; that is, it does not just name a person, such as does "William H. Poteat." It names the *namer*. It recoils on language and its user. "I" is a part of language like "he" because of its transferability. It is a term like "he" or "the man next door" with which we can make reference to a particular of which we want our hearers to notice certain characteristics that will appear in the predicate position of our utterance. But at the same time "I" is *not* a part of language like "he" because its transferability is minimal. That is, in any given use, it always names its user, and hence always functions reflexively.

Now, I do not pretend that there is anything very surprising in this analysis. But I think we must not overlook the logical grammatical fact that "I" has this amphibious status in language. It behaves like any other subject term in a subject-predicate sentence; and therefore it seems plausible for us to suppose of it, what we would suppose of any other subject-term, that whatever the subject-term calls attention to can theoretically be exhausted by adding a perhaps infinite number of terms to the predicate position. "I" always functions reflexively. It not only calls the attention of the hearers to a particular about which something is being said, it refers reflexively for the speaker to his own activity of speaking, and this is not on logical all fours with *what* is being said. We might show this by means of the following case: I can theoretically give a complete report on Jones's activity; I can never give a complete report on my own activity, because after the last thing to be said, there would still remain one further thing to be said, namely, a report to the effect that I had just said the last thing.

This curious fact leads Ryle to speak, I think rightly, of the systematic elusiveness of "I"; rightly, that is to say, if one understands that what is being eluded is incorporation into the language found in the predicate position. What he ignores, or is at least unclear about, is the reflexive activity of "I," which activity refers both to the speaker and to the subject of what he says, which is himself. "I" catches me in the activity of using language. It not only picks out a subject for predication, it reflexively picks out for me the activity of picking out, since the subject of the predication is, in predicating, engaged in the activity of picking out.

"I" not only names what it is about which something is to be said, it acts reflexively to allude *for me* to my activity of saying; it means *for me* my activity of meaning; it intends *for me* my activity of intending; it points *for me* to my activity of pointing. The systematic elusiveness of "I" shows that though others (my hearers) may correlate what I mean by "I" with straightforward reports of behavior or dispositions to behavior, it is impossible for me to do so, for when I use "I" in order to say something about myself at one logical level, there is the fact of my activity of saying this about myself at another logical level yet to be reported. Thus we see that whether we appeal to our actual experience or to the logical behavior of the first-person singular pronoun the conclusion must be the same. I do have a privileged access to myself.

In light of this analysis, it may be possible to conclude with a suggestion as to certain analogies between the logical behavior of "I" and that of "God."

III

If it were true that the kind of relation that John Doe has to himself is precisely of the same sort that he has to Richard Roe; if, that is to say, the "I" when used by John Doe means nothing more for him than what can, at least in theory, be publicized in straightforward subject-object language; then everything there is is in some sense public or at least in principle publicizable. There is no "private-I." The impulse to solipsism is a mere product of linguistic confusion; it not only cannot be said, it does not even show itself. Or, to put the case linguistically; there are not any logically extended concepts "on the borders of language" that put it under peculiar pressure. I have argued that there is at least one such logically extended concept and that when I use it of myself, it always alludes to a reality that is logically beyond all possibility of incorporation into the public world of subject-object discourse; and that therefore I do have a private relation to myself. Or, to put the matter ontologically, I, *as I see myself,* am always both in the world and not in the world.

If we understand that the world is just that which can be successfully incorporated into the conceptual structure of ordinary subject-object discourse, we will see that it is intelligible precisely because it has a conceptual structure—it is a world of essences. At the same time, if we accept the logical amphibiousness of "I," we will see that the extent to which "I" cannot be wholly assimilated into the structure of language, i.e., the world of essences, is the extent to which we want to say that it precedes essence, that it is radically free, that it is irrational (systematically elusive, if you like), that it is a transcendent being, etc.

"I," as this logically extended concept, functions in theological discourse with such notions as "freedom," "fellowship," "grace," and "reconciliation"; and this by reason of the fact, among others, that these concepts allude to "experiences" that are on the borders of our linguistically limited experiences subject to the restrictions of this world, namely, the world where everything makes sense because it can be spoken of. Grace cannot be said, it shows itself.

In the Judeo-Christian tradition, we generally think of God as creator, that is, as actor par excellence, and therefore of the world of nature and history as his acts. Earlier on, I said that "I" when I use it, however well this may signify to my hearers what or who it is about which or whom something is being said, and consequently however plausible the assimilation of the meaning of "I" to reports on behavior or dispositions to behavior may seem *to them,* can never mean *to me* just this, and nothing more. "I" can mean to my hearers, and to me, the sum of my acts or dispositions to acts. To me it always means both the *acts* and *the actor,* i.e., myself, because it always functions reflexively.

In view of this parallel, I will say that the logical relation holding between the ordinary subject-object discourse by means of which we transact our ordinary public affairs and the concept "God" is analogous in certain ways to that which holds between that same form of discourse and the logically extended concept "I." Just as we can meaningfully speak of the acts, behavior, intentions, etc., of the self, and even see that there is some kind of correlation between acts and intentions, using our ordinary subject-object form of discourse, and can do this without assuming that the meaning of "I" is entirely exhausted in this discourse; so we can speak of God's acts, behavior and intentions, etc., in straightforward subject-object discourse about the events in the world without assuming that God is just the sum of these events. Yet to think of them as God's acts—i.e., to use "act" of them rather than "event," "occurrence," etc.—is logically like calling *my* behavior "acts." In both cases an actor who is not assimilable to his acts is the presupposition of the form of discourse. And even as we can speak of certain events in the world that on most occasions we would think of as the acts of persons by using physical, historical, psychological, or economic concepts in the place of the concepts actor-acts, so we can also speak of events in the world in a non-theological idiom. Just as saying, "Smith was killed when Jones's arm, holding a heavy club at the end, smashed down upon him," is compatible with saying, "Jones's act was one of willful homicide," so saying, "The Battle of Britain was the result of a concatenation of economic forces," is compatible with, "The Battle of Britain was the Judgment of God." Settling the question as to whether there is any reason for saying this sort of thing is, again, logically like wondering whether talk about persons and their intentions is licit. So too, the task of trying to infer the existence of God from certain characteristics of the world is analogous to trying to infer the existence of persons from the behavior of bodies. As to theological language and falsification: The problem of falsifying the proposition "God loves us," that is, showing what would have to be different about the world for one to stop believing the proposition to be true, is analogous to the problem of falsifying the proposition "She loves me." As Basil Mitchell has rightly shown, the logical relation between statements about God's love of man and statements about what happens in history, etc., is such that certain things that happen do seem to be evidence against this claim.[3] Yet, there can be no rule regarding when this would or should become decisive evidence against it. And furthermore, the difference between what is named by "God" and what is named by "she" is the difference between someone who is thought to be absolutely trustworthy and someone who is not.

None of this has shown any necessity for talking about God at all, and certainly not for talking about him in the ways traditional to the Jewish and Christian faiths. It has, however, shown that the Rylean attempt to fashion a flattened-out logical behaviorism will not do; that "I" is a logically extended concept that demands a structure of mythical discourse to give body and meaning to each man's experience of his private self; and, that finally, certain traditional elements of theological discourse have the same kind of use, hence the same kind of legitimation.

3. "Theology and Falsification," in *New Essays in Philosophical Theology*, ed. Anthony Flew and A. MacIntrye (London: S.C.M. Press, 1955), 103–5.

"I WILL DIE": AN ANALYSIS

I

The concept of death, as is well known, has been a central preoccupation of much of contemporary so-called existentialist thought—whether that is expressed through discursive philosophical analysis, or in the novels, plays, and other literary devices associated with this movement. Man is not only pictured as the creature who dies, perhaps the only creature who dies; and death is not only seen as the peculiar threat to all human meaning that it is. Man in the face of death is believed to reveal not merely the ultimate human value of courage, so that, for example, Sartre and Camus have chosen in their novels and plays to place their protagonists in the presence of death. When in the presence of its threat, the hero's actions are decisive: he is thought to become human or to fail his humanity in a paradigmatic way. All this may be caught in Heidegger's expression *Sein Zum Tode*—the mark of the human as such.

But if the existentialists are simply telling us what every man knows, even though he may be in flight from his knowledge, namely, that he will die; or even if they exhort us to see and to incarnate the moral value of courage; they can hardly be said to have performed any very striking philosophical service—though they may have done what all great literature does: make us *engage*.

But what is actually involved is, as it seems to me, something at once more radical and more definitive of their overall philosophic objective. The preoccupation with death is not merely an interest in reminding us of the most

The Philosophical Quarterly 9.34 (January 1959): 3–15.

unpleasant of all "empirical" facts; or of enjoining us, as Plato suggested it to be the philosophic task par excellence to enjoin, namely, to practice to die.

The interest is, in fact, at bottom a conceptual one, although the existentialists themselves have not explicitly acknowledged this and may not even have realized it.[1]

By this I mean that implicitly it is recognized that to understand what it is to be a self, a subject, *Dasein*, a *pour-soi*, authentic, radical freedom, is to understand what it is for me to die. Or, to put it in the idiom of the linguistic analytic branch of contemporary philosophy: to understand how the concept "death" functions is to understand more about how the concept "self" does; to observe how these two correlate with each other and how *they* in turn correlate differently with other (in relation to them) logically heterogeneous concepts is to understand the difference between being a man and being just a thing.

Finally, Bultmann's confused and naive proposal to substitute the Heideggerian myth for the New Testament myth implicitly recognizes at least that the difference between the modern scientific or even the modern common-sense view of the world and that of the Christian faith, whose central claim is that Jesus Christ has overcome sin and death, is a profound conceptual difference and that, by further implication, the difficulties can only be removed by a clearing away of conceptual underbrush.

But this interest, though certainly dominant here, is not limited to the so-called existentialists. In a quite different way, and within a context where conceptual analysis is an explicit program, there has been and perhaps is now a growing interest in the concept "death" among the Anglo-American analysts.

As long ago as 1921, when the German edition of his *Tractatus* appeared, Ludwig Wittgenstein, the father of the Vienna Circle positivists, at the end of his discussion of the philosophy of logic, made a brief but exciting remark upon the logical peculiarities of the concept of death: "As in death, too, the world does not change, but ceases. Death is not an event in life. Death is not lived through."[2] Subsequently in his classic article on "Meaning and Verification," Moritz Schlick indicates some of the logical issues involved in the

---

1. To be sure, Heidegger has sought to distinguish his own program from those of Kierkegaard, Jaspers, and Marcel, as he sees them, by the use of the categories "existential" and "existentiel," the one being soteriologically oriented, the other being primarily a "scientific" task—a step toward a fundamental ontology.

2. *Tractatus Logico-Philosophicus* (London: Routledge and Kegan Paul, 1949), 6.431, 6.4311.

concept of death in the course of investigating the general principle of verifiability, formulating them in terms of whether it is meaningful to wonder if "I can be a witness at my own funeral."[3]

More recently, A. G. N. Flew, asking "Can a man witness his own funeral?" is not primarily concerned with general questions of meaning but with the concept of death, and concludes that the suggestion that we survive death is self-contradictory.[4]

It is my conviction that the analyses so far made have failed to appreciate what is really significant about the logical puzzles surrounding the concept of death, and have not noticed what I believe to be implicit in Wittgenstein's dark saying and to be even more hidden in the quite different descriptions of the existentialists, namely, that important connections hold among the words *I, death, world, human,* and *last things, the end of history, the end of the world.* And not only so: that when we discern something of the logical behavior of these terms we shall see something of the role of theological language in general and of its legitimation—indeed of its inescapability. I propose therefore to analyze the expression "I will die." As I do so, I urge you to think of what I will be saying in the first person. That is, whenever I use the expression "I will die," think "*I* will die," not "He will die." I believe this to be essential to seeing what I hope to have you see.

Now then, what I want to argue is the following: (1) Flew, in holding that to think of the survival of death is to think a logical contradiction, is quite right, though trivially right, because analytically so, *if "death" is a concept that simply correlates with or is logically assimilable to reports or predictions of events,* (biochemical, social, physiological, auditory, etc.) and "acts" and behavior. Further, this correlation of "death" with more or less straightforward reports or predictions of events in the commonsense spatiotemporal world is, with *a certain amount of not very plausible forcing,* possible. I want to show, however, that in our ordinary use we do not force and that *then,* in certain circumstances, the concept "death" has an extension and hence an acceptable use beyond reports and predictions, about acts and ordinary events. (2) That this extension of the concept is not recognized when the verb *to die* is conjugated merely in the second or third persons, but is clearly to be

3. "Meaning and Verification," *The Philosophical Review* 45 (1936).
4. *Hibbert Journal* 54 (April 1956). Ian Ramsey has undertaken to meet Flew's argument in *Hibbert Journal* 54 (June 1956).

seen when I *use,* not just mention, "I will die" of myself. (3) That when I use the expression of myself what I am asserting is not assimilable to reports or predictions of events or behavior in the commonsense world, but is neverthe- less perfectly—though, no doubt, strangely—meaningful. (4) That even if Flew were to say, e.g., "After I have died, there will be nothing"—and to say it thoughtfully of himself—he is himself using the concept "death" in an equivocal and logically peculiar way, that is to say, in a way not assimilable to reports or predictions of events or behavior in the commonsense world, and, furthermore, in a way which is, *in respect of its unassimilability,* logically like "death" as it functions in what a Christian might say, for example: "When I die, I shall have fellowship with God." (5) Finally, that when we observe the peculiar behavior of "death" in the first-person singular, we shall be struck by the logical peculiarity of "I" itself—which is, I believe, one of the points that the existentialists try rather misleadingly to make.

If such an ambitious program can be made to "come off," it may be possible to suggest something about the meaning of eschatological concepts in general, such as "end of history," etc. I want to show, in short, what I believe to be the case, namely, that "death" in certain of its commonsensically acceptable uses is a logically extended use and is hence an, if you will, eschatological concept; and that "I" when it is coupled with death in this logically extended use is also logically extended, and hence may be thought of as a kind of metaconcept; and finally (without trying here to display its complicated logic) we may say that these logically extended concepts require and therefore legitimize and properly function within the structure of what I'll call myth.

II

Prima facie, the expression "I will die" is a possible candidate for classifica- tion only as a performatory proposition (where the saying of something is itself the doing of it) or as a straightforward empirical prediction.[5] A third view which would hold it has certain logical affinities with each of these seems hardly possible.

But it cannot be construed as performatory, for uttering the expression "I

---

5. J. L. Austin, "Other Minds," in A. G. N. Flew, ed., *Logic and Language,* 2d Series (Oxford: Basil Blackwell, 1953). See 143ff.

will die" is not the same thing as dying in the way that uttering the expression
"I promise to so and so" is the same thing as promising to so and so.

We must ask, then, whether it is possible to construe it, as the import of
Flew's analysis would seem to demand, as a statement to the effect that at a
certain time in the future some behavior now observable in the world will no
longer be observed, and nothing more.[6]

Let us first concede that my saying "I will die" entails certain quite ordinary
empirical propositions of a predictive sort—propositions about biochemical,
social, physiological, auditory, and other events or behavior in the experienceable world. It does not follow, however, from this entailment that "I will die" is
assimilable to a finite number of such propositions, in the sense that the
meaning of "I will die" as I use the expression of myself can be analyzed
without remainder into propositions of this sort. Neither does it follow that it
cannot be so analyzed. Flew, if I understand him, is holding that it can: that
when I say, "I am alive," I mean there is observable behavior of a certain sort,
and nothing more; and when I say, "I will die," I mean that a time will come
when there will not be any such behavior, and nothing more. We then must
determine on other grounds whether or not such as assimilation is licit.

How shall we proceed? Let us begin by assuming, even if it requires an
implausible forcing, that "self" or "I" may be exhaustively analyzed in terms
of a finite number of reports about behavior (in the ordinary sense). I use the
term *behavior* rather than *acts* because on the surface—though probably not
in the long run—"acts" is a more question-begging term, since a world in
which there are acts but no actors is a logical impossibility, and the question
we are facing here is just that of whether there are actors over and above acts
(behavior).[7] Further, let me assume that these reports about past and present
behavior are being given in the first-person singular. What are the characteristics of the verbs that I might be imagined as using, for example: to run, to
think, to wonder, to justify.[8] If I use any of these or even others to report upon

6. I take M. Schlick to be putting a similar case about the type of proposition we are to
take our example as being.

7. One may certainly wonder whether it really makes any better sense to speak of
behavior with no behavors—although our sense of linguistic propriety is not so obviously violated; and this may account in part for the fact that a reductionistic behaviorism
has a superficial plausibility.

8. I use some of these examples because Gilbert Ryle, in *The Concept of Mind,* has
given a logical behavioristic analysis of mental concepts so that to say "Jones thinks he is

myself or to predict about myself, I will find no difficulty whatever in conjugating these verbs in every possible tense, every possible person. I can with perfectly good sense say, "I wondered, I wonder, I will wonder." There is in the English language a vast number of verbs that I may use to report and predict in the first person in any tense, and which are like our examples above and like one another in the respect that they make perfectly good sense when conjugated in the first person in any tense. This suggests that the first-person singular can simply be accommodated to the verbs of our language in any tense and that my reporting "I wondered" is logically precisely like my reporting "Jones wondered"; and that if someone should ask what I meant in these two cases, I would submit further reports on Jones that I took to be evidence that "Jones wondered" is true, which would display what I took myself to be meaning when I said it; and that I would submit further reports, logically of the same sort, where the pronoun *I* would be substituted for "Jones" in order to show what I meant by "I wondered." In other words, the pronoun *I*, when it is actually put to use with the verbs with which we report or predict in the experienceable world, behaves in precisely the same way that the proper name "Jones" does: all the verbs are conjugable in all tenses, etc. When I use "I" to report on Poteat, the verbs I use are governed by the same rules as when I use "Jones" to report on Jones. Jones, being for me, no more than the sum of the things I can report on him, using these verbs, it follows, by parity of reasoning, that I am for me no more than the sum of things I can report on myself, using these verbs.

Is the case, though, really as impressive as this? No! Of the verb *to die* these things cannot be said. It makes perfectly good sense for me to say, "Jones is dying," "Jones has died," or "Jones will die." I cannot sensibly say, "I died." This verb cannot be meaningfully conjugated in the past tense, first-person singular—or, if it is, it cannot be *used*. The parallel between the case of I reporting or predicting about myself and I reporting or predicting about Jones breaks down here. This verb behaves quite differently in the two cases. There is no apparent difference when we look at "I will die" and "Jones will die." The role of "die" in these two expressions seems to be identical. When, however, we try to conjugate "to die" in all persons in the past tense its odd

---

God Almighty" is to say something that can be analyzed into reports on actions and dispositions of Jones, relieving us of having to posit "ghostly occurrences behind the scenes."

role becomes quite clear. It cannot be used in the past tense, first-person singular. Though it can be used in the future tense, first-person singular, its curious status and role in the language must not be overlooked. "To die" is not an activity on logical all fours with "to run," "to think," "to wonder," "to justify." Not only so. "I" is also logically peculiar. It does not behave consistently like the proper name "Jones" (unless "I" and "Jones" happen to be naming the same person). First, "Jones" is not a part of the English language as is "I"; "I" is not a proper name; yet "I" is never used without becoming exactly equivalent to someone's proper name. Secondly, there is at least one case where "I" cannot be meaningfully coupled with a verb in the English language in every tense, whereas there is *no* case where "Jones" (when "Jones" does not name the same person as "I") cannot be so coupled. In other words, it is significant that the odd behavior of "to die" occurs only in the first person. It points to the logical unassimilability of "I" to reports or predictions about behavior (in the ordinary sense).

Now we must ask whether this linguistic fact concerning the behavior of "I" and "to die" can be shown to have the significance which it must, if it is to bear the weight of my argument. Does this lack of symmetry here show that Flew's and Schlick's implied proposal to construe "I will die" as analyzable into reports or predictions about certain forms of behavior and nothing more not only fails, but fails in a way that permits me to conclude that "I" is what I have called a kind of metaconcept and that "to die" has in certain circumstances a logically extended though commonsensically meaningful use: that, in short, it means certain empirical predictions—and something more?

To begin with we may observe a further and perhaps trivial fact about these terms: that when we couple them in the present tense, first-person singular, "I die," "I am dying," the expression generally appears in a quite different kind of context from that in which "I will die" is uttered. If you will imagine hearing me say, "I will die," I think you will feel that I am saying something quite different—and not merely by reference to tense—from what you would feel that I would be saying if I were to say, "I am dying." I think you would not imagine me in the former case to be primarily making reference to certain future contingent empirical facts that might be expressed in propositions about biochemical and physiological events in the way you might imagine me to be if you heard me say "I am dying"—not even that there is now a body that emits the sound "I" which one day will not emit that sound. If you heard me say, "I am dying," I think you might be inclined to ask, "Have you received a mortal wound? Does your pulse grow weak? Is your sight getting dim?," etc. Whereas when I say, "I will die," you are not apt to think in these terms. You are perhaps more apt to reflect, "Yes, I will die, too."

Nevertheless, let us give this, as I have called it, somewhat forced analysis its full credit. Let us assume that "I will die" is just a statement about my body and its behavior in the future tense. Suppose we take it to mean that there is a certain organism which at some indefinite future time will undergo a radical change, including ceasing to behave in certain ways, etc., known as death. There seems to be nothing problematical about saying this, even though inevitably there will be an end at some point to my actually experiencing this process of change, even if an end that I do not experience, just as I do not experience the end of being awake.[9] There is nothing problematical about this, for there is no respect in which the occurrences predicted in my statement, so construed, are not about experience in a straightforward way. All of us have experienced occurrences *like* this all around us. All that I am saying is that *this* body (Poteat's) will one day cease to behave in certain ways, and that its ceasing to behave in these ways, including emitting the noises "I," "here," and "now," and also the noises "I will die" will be taken as signs that I am dead, and that when I say "I will die" I am only predicting that there will be a time when all this will be true. Is there any logical embarrassment in any of this that would lead one to resort to all this talk of "death" being a logically extended concept? I think there is and that it can be shown by taking a closer look at the expression "this body."

Usually *this* is a demonstrative pronoun which a speaker uses to make an identifying reference to a particular. My hearers understand the reference because "this" is tied to a particular place and time by relation to the body from which the word "this" is emitted. When I make a reference to a particular object in the world other than my body, let us say, by my pointing a finger at it, the identity of the particular being called "this" is established for my hearers because it has a certain spatiotemporal relation to my body, which emits the noise "this," and because they too have a spatiotemporal relation to my body. But I want to urge that "this," when used to pick out the body of the speaker, functions differently *for the speaker.* Of course, it is obvious that the

---

9. It is not an accident that we use the expression "He is asleep" as a euphemism for "He is dead," since there are real parallels between the relation of "going to sleep" and "experience" and "dying" and "experience."

object of my identifying reference has not the same kind of relation to my body when the object is my body as when it is not. What is important here is that, when I say, "*This* body will undergo a radical change, including ceasing to behave in certain ways, etc.," I am making a reference to something in the experienceable world that has the unique status among such objects of being at least part of what I mean by "I." There is only one "this" in the world of which W. H. Poteat can use "I": When one uses "this" to make reference to the body and its behavior to which he may also make reference by using "I," the term *this* functions in a unique way. Even if one wanted to say that there are other extended objects in the world besides the one called "my body" to which I could make reference either with "this" or "my"—any object belonging to me—I do not think that any other object may be said to be "mine" in the same way that my body may be said to be. The characteristic of qualifying as "this" (having a certain determinate *relation* to a body from which the sound "this" is heard to come) is not the same characteristic as that of being the body from which the sound "my body" is heard to come and to which the expression "*my* body" is recognized by myself as applying. One cannot assimilate "*my* body" to "*this* body." And I recognize that everyone else has a similarly unique relation to the object that is his body.

Therefore reference by me to the body and its behavior, which is part at least of what I mean by "I," can never be made to be logically equivalent to references by me to bodies and their behavior which are not. Hence, "I will die" can never mean for me the same thing as "There is a body in the world which one day will cease to behave as it now does." What is being asserted is not just about an object in the world in the way that "*This* body will die" (where the body in question is *not* mine) *is* about an object in the world. My body and its behavior is not in the world *for me* in the same way that Jones's body and its behavior is in the world for me. For me to describe my death as the end of certain kinds of behavior in the world is not *for me* the description of an occurrence *in the world* at all like an account by me of Jones's death as an occurrence *in the world*. For myself, I am not *in* the world as Jones is in the world. For me, therefore, to say of myself that I will no longer be in the world is to use logically extended concepts. Thus, again we see the asymmetry of the logical grammar of "I will die" when I use it of myself and "Jones will die" when I use it of Jones. From the fact that "Jones will die" seems assimilable to reports or predictions of a straightforward empirical sort it does not follow that "I will die," when I use it of myself, can be so assimilated. From this we also see that "I" and "death" in certain circumstances, namely, when I use them of myself, are logically extended concepts in the sense demanded by my thesis; and that attempts to assimilate them, are, as I have said, forced. Finally, this means that Flew and Schlick would not be able to make a case for "I will die" being analyzed into predictions about behavior, and nothing more; and that unless Flew is willing altogether to deny himself the privilege of thoughtfully using of himself the expression "I will die," he must involve himself in the use of what I am here calling myth. To say, "when I have died, there is nothing," is not the use of the Platonic myth nor of the Christian myth, but myth it is, nonetheless; which is to say a resort to the use of logically extended concepts. A strain is being put upon the very language within which Flew has, quite rightly, argued that the expression "I will survive my death" is a contradiction. It is this pressure that produces and legitimizes—indeed, makes inescapable—the language of myth or metaconcepts, if we are going to accord any meaning to an expression which each one of us does in fact find meaningful, namely, "I will die."

Insofar, then, as any of us thoughtfully says of himself, "I will die," he is involved in making a statement about himself which cannot be exhaustively expressed in reports or predictions about behavior, actions, or events of a straightforward sort. My dying is for me not *just* doing or ceasing to do certain reportable things, though it certainly *entails* my doing or ceasing to do these things. When I use "I" of myself, something is being named which is *for me* not just the spatiotemporal speaker or behavor from whom the noise "I" has come. If you ask me what it is that is named, hoping to have an answer given in reports of behavior alone, then of course I can't say. You are asking a question that on your terms, as I have been trying to show, is impossible to answer. If you do not ask what it is that is named *in these terms,* then my answer is quite simple: myself! Dying, therefore, (and this is true analytically) in the sense of what *I* will do, in the sense, that is to say, which is displayed by the analysis of this logically peculiar verb *to die,* is something done only by selves, only, that is, by *users* of the first-person pronoun singular. In this peculiar sense, objects don't die, only subjects die. In a world only of objects (a logical impossibility when you consider what "object" means, and one incidentally that gives us a clue to the logic of the concept "world") there is no death. This is at once why it makes sense to say, "By man came death"; and also why the Platonic tradition lacks the same anxiety over death that is characteristic of contemporary culture with its concept of a radically self-transcending subject, and with its emphasis upon subjectivity. Dying is a private affair, because being a self is. Death, then, is an eschatological concept. To say "I will die" is to say something that entails that certain empirical propositions about the experienceable world will at a certain time be true. But it is to say something *more* than and different from just this. Death in certain circumstances is a concept that applies to the experienceable world, but also extends beyond it. It is quite definitely anchored in and applies to the world of common sense, but it also stands in a different relation to that world. If my analysis will hold up, everyone believes when he says thoughtfully of himself, "I will die," that he is saying something which is true and something that is about "reality," but not just about the public world of experience. His language is being put under an unusual kind of pressure, a pressure that gives rise to a system of discourse which I am for brevity's sake calling myth. While firmly anchored in the commonsense world by the entailment of certain empirical propositions, the concept extends beyond this commonsense world. And as I have held, this is true whether one says, "When I have died, there will be nothing," "When I die my soul will become discarnate and abide eternally in a realm of forms," or "When I die, I shall have fellowship with God."

Lest you think that these three cases are not logically of the same sort, I will just observe that the man who says, "When I have died, there will be nothing," is not saying anything about the world of common sense at all like, "When I have run, I will be tired." In other words, when he asserts that death is the end, he does not exactly "know" what he is saying. Yet in another sense he and all of us know very well what he is saying. And if a dispute over alternative myths arises between ourselves and him, though we shall certainly feel that both he and we are saying something genuinely meaningful about reality, what we will be respectively saying is not about reality in the way that reports upon or predictions of observable behavior are about it. It is dubious whether we can call this a dispute, since it is not clear that there are any rules common to the disputants by reference to which a settlement might be made. But, if it is a dispute, it is not one between those who have, in my sense, an eschatology and those who do not. It is a dispute between rival eschatologies; and the apparent economy of one in which we say only, "When I have died, there will be nothing," is not as such a reason for preferring it. Indeed, one wonders whether the expression "reason for preferring" has any definite sense here.

III

I want to conclude by making a few suggestions concerning the implications of all this for our understanding of the Christian interpretation of death. To put it another way, when we allow the extended concept "death" to operate within the structure of the Christian myth, what happens?

First, I think it is important to recognize that the overwhelming majority of people in the contemporary world, Christian and non-Christian, take the essence of the Christian claim (as Flew seems to) to be a belief to the effect that "I will survive my death"; and further, that they are culturally conditioned by the same forces that induce Flew to take as his paradigm for meaningful discourse the language we use about the commonsense world; and finally that on their own premises, Flew's demonstration of the contradictoriness of "I will survive my death" must be devastating. If "death" is the kind of concept which he holds that it is, then to speak of surviving it is utter nonsense.

Secondly, earlier on I suggested that there is a profound difference between "death" as it is understood in the broadly Platonic tradition and death as it is understood in contemporary Western culture; and that this is a function of the concept of a radically self-transcending self. Now, it is in this context that we will have to interpret the doctrine of the Resurrection. That is to say, if Resurrection is the concept or system of concepts making up the Christian myth within which the logically extended concept "death" is to be operative, then "death," insofar as it is anchored in the experienceable world, while extending beyond it, will have to be anchored in what the contemporary man understands by the commonsense world, if, that is to say, Resurrection is to have any real meaning for him. In short, "death" insofar as it operates within the discourse of common sense alone will have to operate in accordance with the rules governing its use within that discourse. And this means precisely that whatever else the Christian may be claiming when tying the logically extended concept of death to the myth of the Resurrection, he or she is not claiming and could not claim that there is any *survival* after death, since, as we saw above, even this logically extended concept is so related to the empirical world that to say, "I will die," is to say something that *entails* certain empirical propositions being true at some future time, and that these propositions being true entails that we cannot believe that there *exists,* in any ordinary sense of the word, something or other, not even a ghostly something or other, after these empirical propositions will have become true. And this, for the simple reason that the condition of the possibility of something, even a ghostly something, existing is that the empirical propositions are *not yet* true. That is, either "I exist" means nothing more than that certain empirical reports about behavior, etc., are true, in which case it is logically contradictory to speak, in any sense, of my existing after my death (i.e., after the kind of behavior reported has ceased); or it means this, plus something else, which cannot be expressed in empirical existence language; in which case, I no longer exist, insofar as my existence entails certain kinds of reportable behavior, and inasmuch as the something more was precisely what cannot be assimilated to these reports. Or to put the matter differently, even though our analysis of the concept "death" demands that we give it and therefore the concept "I" as well an extension beyond ordinary empirical language, that does not mean that what is *beyond* in the concept "I" is a ghostly *thing*, for "thing" is itself a concept that can be cashed only in empirical language. If I understand "I" to mean not just the something more than what can function in straightforward empirical language, but what *can* so function *and something more*, then it is meaningless to speak of my surviving death when it is no longer possible to identify certain familiar types of behavior in the experienceable world as Poteat's animated behavior. On the basis of the Platonic account, this would not be the case, for in this account, Poteat's quite commonplace historical activity is not really thought to be any part of what it is to be Poteat. Therefore, we can meaningfully talk about Poteat surviving death even though there is no longer any animated historical behavior of Poteat. This perhaps sad state of affairs is a logical consequence of the whole body of Christian myth, which connected its logically extended concepts to propositions about the empirical world in such a way as to make it quite certain that we could no longer separate Poteat from his commonplace historical acts. One may even go so far as to say that the doctrine of the Resurrection of the body, when once it is taken seriously, makes it impossible for us any more to believe that I can survive my death in the sense that there is a *something* to which death does not write a finis.

If the Christian, then, when he uses the concept "death" uses it, as do others, in a logically extended sense; and if he understands "I" to be similarly extended; and if he insists that though "I" be extended, what it means to be Poteat cannot be separated from his historical acts and animated behavior in the experienceable world; how can he embody the logically extended concept

"I" in a myth in such a way that he can say something about the curious experience of death, say that it has been overcome, has lost its sting, etc., *while at the same time* holding both that I do not survive death and that nevertheless my historical acts are redeemed from death along with the something more which the concept "I" is thought to cover?

First, he will have to use myth. Second, the myth cannot be construed as asserting or implying that he does not die, nor that his resurrection will be a beginning all over again exactly as before, but yet in such a way as to take his historical acts into a structure of meaning *along with the something more* covered by the logically extended concept "I." It would be impossible to invent such a myth. In fact, I have posed the problem in this way because I have started with the myth of the Resurrection of the body as given.

Here we must be reminded that the myth of the Resurrection of the body has its status within the whole fabric of the concepts of biblical thought. Let us suppose that the key to this thought is the concept of a relation between man and God which is an I-thou relation. In an I-Thou relation all that makes me the person I am—both what in other circumstances can be cashed in terms of ordinary empirical reports of behavior, and the something more—is involved with another fully personal being. In the discourse in which we try to exhibit this relation, there is no place for language about body and soul, etc., but only for such notions as love, fellowship, responsibility, forgiveness, freedom, etc. And to know and be in fellowship with a person cannot be analyzed in terms of just knowing their behavior or empirical reports about their behavior or even this *and something more.* These concepts do not function in this game at all. In an I-Thou relation the distinction between me and my body disappears. Equally it is one in which the distinction between "happens" because the relation is in time and "doesn't happen" because it is in a timeless eternity does not apply. This kind of a relation does not occur because we are doing something extraordinary with reference to the world of space and time. Nor do we talk of it as though it were spaceless and timeless. Our analogy is drawn from a quite different quarter—one where we know ourselves not as "inside" our bodies, not as souls transcending them, not as dualisms of this sort at all. Here we know ourselves quite independently of these distinctions. Here we act as a unity "knowing" the difference between ourselves and our acts (i.e., knowing the difference between what could be given in empirical reports and the something more that cannot) only in that we can say of them that they are *our* acts—"I did it"—which is to say, we know ourselves as responsible.

If someone asks: "What then is eternal life? Is it living in some strange way forever? Or is it rather a quality of this life?" we reply that these questions cannot be asked in this universe of discourse. There is a more radical break with our commonsense discourse involved. We cannot say either that it is like or analogous to our present life, only it goes on forever; nor can we say that it is just a heightening of this life.

When the Christian says that he believes in the Resurrection of the body, this is one way he has of saying that he—that part of him which in other circumstances can be cashed in empirical language *and* the something more that cannot—will have fellowship with God. And if he is asked whether this takes place *in* history or at the *end* of history, he will reply "at the *end of history*," but then he will have used another eschatological concept, in some ways like that of "death." But that is another story.

The Christian myth of the Resurrection of the body, then, is legitimized in the same way that any system of discourse for embodying the logically extended concepts of "death" and "I" is. In this myth what the Christian asserts about the meaning of his own death is that he will have fellowship with God as a fully personal being. "Fellowship" is a notion that can function only in discourse about the relations between personal beings. The logically extended concept "I," which refers to the something more than just what can be cashed in straightforward empirical language, is embodied in the myth by means of person-concepts such as "love" and "fellowship." But the anchorage of this concept in the empirical world is preserved in the mythically transformed symbol of a resurrected body. What is thought to have personal fellowship with God is, in this myth, a being about which we speak in analogies drawn from our normal person-talk. Therefore, the myth is not something free-floating in an extra-existent realm, but is about the existential reality which I am, though not literally about it. None of what has been said in any way constitutes an argument for preferring the Christian myth to other possible myths. Indeed, one wonders what an argument of this sort would be. All that has been attempted here is to show that when we analyze an expression like "I will die" we discover at certain points a pressure within our ordinary language; that this pressure is felt at so commonplace a point as when we speak of our own death; that when we do, we quite naturally resort to myth; and finally, that the Christian myth is fundamentally different from alternative ones and is at least as well grounded.

WHAT IS A POEM ABOUT? _____

I want to propose a way of regarding a poem on three different levels: one that I think will enable us (1) to see what it is "about" when we examine the languages of subject-object discourse that go into its structure; (2) to appreciate the poem as a reality having an intrinsic value, independent of the semantic function of its components and of its "semantic" function as a totality; and (3) to understand what it is "about" as an intrinsically valuable reality that nevertheless has a "semantic" function.

(1) If an ordinary reader were asked what the "Ode on a Grecian Urn" is "about," he might reply that it is "about" a vase, the beauty of the relief upon it, Keats's reflections upon the "story" told by this relief. But then he would quickly add, no doubt, that it is really "about" the evanescence of time and our sense of and longing for eternity. Or he might say it is "about" our experience of these. And, finally, he might add that it is "about" how "Beauty is truth, truth beauty"—with illustrations!

Analyzed in this way, the poem yields statements about vases, statements that we take to be translations from the metaphorical thrust of the poem into straightforward metaphysical claims about time and eternity, and statements about Keats's feelings (or the reader's) concerning the vase and what the relief causes him to think and feel about time and eternity. I will call the language of these statements subject-object discourse.

The presupposition of this language is the subject-object dichotomy: a distinct experient "over against" whom there is an equally distinct something experienced. Subject-object discourse, therefore, is designed for intersubjec-

Philosophy and Phenomenological Research 17 (1956–1957): 546–50.

tive naming or referring, and therefore has three terms: the percipient, the object of perception, and the language that expresses the latter for the former. There is always some kind of behavioral test as to whether or not the language has been understood, including, of course, other verbal behavior.

Now, when we examine the poem as comprising statements of what I have called everyday subject-object discourse, we may see it to be "about" a number of different sorts of things: about vases, about time and eternity, about feelings, about beauty and truth, even about all of these things together.

When one asks, "What is this poem about?" in the everyday subject-object sense of being "about" something, the answers will be of the sort suggested above. This is the first question and answer concerning what a poem is about.

(2) But even the most pedestrian poem is not just "about" this or that, depending upon how it is regarded; or "about" this *and* that, if all of the things it can be said to be about, in this sense of "about," are taken together. It is a something in its own right. All of the things that the poem is about, in the first sense, appear as parts of a totality. The totality is a fusion of words, symbols, and images having a variety of uses upon different strata of language in subject-object discourse. And while it may sound odd to put it this way, *so regarded,* the poem is only "about" itself. But, if the "object" is itself a fusion of language into a totality, then there is no way to distinguish between expression and object expressed, i.e., one cannot determine that it has been grasped by an appeal to linguistic behavior since any linguistic behavior to which appeal might be made as a test would have to be, in principle, distinct from the expression the comprehension of which is being tested, and this would mean systematically placing the "object" within the subject-object discourse, which is to say, systematically making the "object" into something that it is not. Now, to be sure, if what I have just said were *strictly* true, it would not only have been impossible to say, but impossible to know. For, if no distinction between "object" expressed and expression were possible in any sense whatever, then the assertion of the impossibility of the distinction would be quite impossible since the presupposition of such an assertion is the possibility of the distinction, i.e., the actualization of at least one instance of this distinction. What we have to say, then, is that the poem in one sense is "about" the poem in another sense; that as having analyzable parts it is about an unanalyzable totality; and that no behavioral test—linguistic or otherwise—can be used to determine that the poem as being about itself has been grasped. Or we may put it thus: the poem in itself as a totality is an aesthetic object, and, if anyone asks to be

told what this is, nothing can be said except that it is that to which the poem in its analyzable parts refers; it is the plus that is more than the analyzable parts and about which nothing else can be said, other than that there is something which the poem is "about" concerning which nothing can be said.

For example, of what a poem is about one cannot say, "Oh, I see, what it means is this . . . ," since "what it means is this . . ." supposes that there is some "object" other than this very particular fusion of languages to which the fusion refers and to which reference can also be made with the alternative expression, "what it means is this . . . ," in order that whether we have grasped this "object" may be determined by the linguistic behavior represented by the words, "What it means is this. . . ." Thus we want to say that the fusion is "beyond" subject-object discourse in the familiar, everyday sense of that discourse. The poem as a whole is simply about itself; or rather, the only answer to the question "What is the poem about?"—on this second level of analysis—is the poem itself. Literary criticism that tells us *about* the poem and what the poem is about always falls short of presenting us with the poem itself. Yet, in this sense of "about," it is only about itself.

Something of this sort was meant, I am sure, by the late Dylan Thomas, when he said: "A good poem is a contribution to reality. The world is never the same once a poem has been added to it. A good poem helps to change the shape and significance of the universe, helps to extend everyone's knowledge of himself and the world around him."[1]

One finds a similar view taken by Mr. C. Day Lewis in his inaugural lecture:

> In the successful poem, a number of fragmentary, apparently unrelated experiences—bits of the poet's observation, thought, reading, emotional processes—have been brought together in such a way that they lose their identity, their separateness and fragmentariness, and are absorbed into a whole—a delicate complex organization which gives them meaning, and whose meaning for us is more than the sum of its parts. We say that a poem is satisfactory, we feel that it satisfies us, when we get this impression that it is a whole thing, a complete thing, to which nothing could be added and from which nothing could be taken away without impairing its value, even destroying its life.[2]

1. *Encounter* no. 14 (November 1954): 25.
2. Quoted by Charles A. Coulson, *Christianity in an Age of Science* (Oxford: Oxford University Press, 1935), 41.

The poem, then, is about itself when analyzed at this second level, when we consider it chiefly as a reality having an intrinsic value, independent of the semantic function of its components and of its "semantic" function as a totality.

(3) A poem, however, is not only about "this and that" at the level of ordinary subject-object discourse; nor only about itself as an intrinsic aesthetic whole. It is "about" in yet a third sense, in which I venture to say it has a "semantic" function—although, to be sure, "semantic" in a very odd, and certainly not in any straightforward and familiar, subject-object way. Here the poem does not tell us about or characterize something; it does not give us information or even refer to something. This would be impossible, for to refer and characterize, in the ordinary ways, we require class-terms, concepts, etc. And however many such elements may enter into the structure of a poem, it is itself not a class-term, a concept, or the member of a class of which there are other members. It is a unique and concrete reality. This was the burden of the foregoing section (2).

Nevertheless, just by being the kind of totality that it is, the poem expresses, exhibits, alludes to a kind of "fact"—albeit of a most unusual kind—and this I call its "semantic" function—with the reminder that "semantic" is being used in an odd, but, I believe, a not wholly illicit way. To bring out this third sense in which a poem is "about," I want to approach the matter obliquely. In the process, I think an affinity between poetry and metaphysics may be shown, an affinity that needs reflect no discredit on either poetry or metaphysics so long as irrelevant criteria of their meaning and value are not invoked.

If a poem, when we understand it in the way suggested in (2) above, brings us to the limits of subject-object discourse, in the familiar, everyday sense; if it goes beyond the subject-object dichotomy so that no linguistic behavioral test of its "object" is either possible or relevant—since it has no object in the familiar sense; we may still ask, "What is the significance of this impulse to reach and then go beyond subject-object discourse?" This is a fact of linguistic behavior of which some account must be taken.

One may very well reply that it springs from the desire to create an aesthetically pleasing object. This is no doubt true, but it only means that we have to raise the question all over again at a further remove: "What is the significance of this desire?" At length, we shall have to put aside all psychological, anthropological, and physiological theories about why there are poets and face the basic question: "What is the ontological root of the poetic muse?" Of course, it is perfectly possible to refuse to raise this question, or to say it is a foolish or unanswerable question. But that is only to be faced with the task of giving the credentials for all these claims.

First, let us observe that a poem as a whole transcends its parts not merely in the way, say, that a completed description transcends its parts, but also in the way a self transcends the sum of its own acts. You say: "But this isn't finished yet! Something has been left out. There—now it's finished!" In the case of the poem a different kind of unity has been achieved, a unity having a completely different logical status.

It is this characteristic of a poem that gives it its "semantic" function.

As we "participate" in the poem by the act of reading it, appropriating it, standing over against it as an intrinsic "object," in a very peculiar sense of "standing over against it," we sofarforth transcend the ordinary world of subject-object reality. It is a *totality;* it is a *verbal* totality, a wholly human and, in a sense, "created" rather than "given" totality. Unlike all ordinary subject-object experience, which is unlimited, the poem is complete and finite. It is a "world"—in the sense intended by Kant when he called "world" an idea of the transcendental reason. The poem stands as a unity "over against" and correlative to myself as a present unity of all my acts.

Insofar as the poem has the power to evoke this "experience" of "world"; to produce in myself that sense of being a present transcendent unity of all my acts through my participation in this completed verbal world; it is performing its "semantic" function. For here, by being the sort of reality that it is, it expresses, exhibits, alludes to the incompleteness of all subject-object discourse, or, in conventional philosophic language, to the contingency of the world. In this sense, it points beyond itself to another reality. The enterprise of metaphysics may be said to arise in obedience to the same impulse to fashion a "world" which is to be correlative to the unification of my several acts as a self.

Yet, it is perfectly clear that if one asks, "And this reality to which it alludes—what is it?" we can only remain silent! We can say nothing about it other than that it *is.*

The ontological root of poetry is, then, the sense of incompleteness in all-expression, or of every language-stratum, or of all taken together. A poem is therefore "about" nothing, in this third sense of "about." But for this very reason, it alludes to the mystery that our minds sense, but about which nothing can be said other than that there is "something" about which nothing can be said—which is, after all, *something* about it.

As Hölderlin has put it:

> But the serving maids of Heaven
> Are miraculous,
> Like all that's of heavenly birth.
> He who would grasp it by stealth
> Holds a dream in his hand, and him who attempts
> To grow like it by force, it punishes.
> Yet often it takes by surprise
> Him who has hardly begun to give it a thought.[3]

3. "The Journey," in *Hölderlin Poems,* trans. Michael Hamburger (New York: Pantheon Books, 1952), 189.

PART THREE

The Ambivalent
Language of Culture

THE OPEN SOCIETY AND
ITS AMBIVALENT FRIENDS

It is now only slightly less than ten years since the appearance of the first edition of Karl R. Popper's *The Open Society and Its Enemies,* a book written in a time of crisis, so passionate in its moral indignation, so substantial in its attack upon basic questions in the philosophy of the social sciences, so knowledgeable in its command of the scholarship of ancient and modern philosophies, and so trenchant in the questions that it poses, that only now have the criticisms demanded by so earnest and fundamental a work begun to appear.[1] Now that the crisis in which it was written has settled into a dull routine of anxieties on the periphery and lie detectors, loyalty boards, the "jurisprudence of security," and compulsory godliness in the center of what remains of the Open Society, and with the appearance of a second and enlarged edition of the book, it is time to assess once more the faith of Karl R. Popper, friend of the Open Society.

To say that the book in question is a tract, besides being a stringent, often brilliant, analysis of the logic of social thought, is not to speak pejoratively of it. On the contrary! Popper is assuredly one member of the class of "clerks" who will not betray the Open Society through somnolence, preoccupation, indifference, or seditiousness. Indeed, at a time when philosophers seem to account the mortal struggles of democratic society as matters indifferent to their lofty concern, it is heartening to hear from a philosopher of an older

The Christian Scholar 37.3 (September 1954): 448–59. A review of Karl R. Popper, *The Open Society and Its Enemies,* 2 vols. (Princeton: Princeton University Press, 1952).

1. See, for example, Ronald Levinson, *In Defense of Plato: John Wild, Plato's Modern Enemies, and the Theory of Natural Law* (Cambridge: Harvard University Press, 1953).

generation—and a positivist at that—a responsible and historically relevant credo.

But just because it is a tract as well as a scholarly and analytical exercise, *The Open Society* becomes of interest in and must be responsible to a public much larger than that in which, e.g., Popper's exegesis of Plato, will be debated in tome and journal.

I shall leave the latter question to those who are competent to raise it. In general, the question I wish to ask here is this: Is Popper the analyst sufficiently clear, consistent, and integrated to provide Popper the tractarian with a viable, consistent, profound, and engaging faith for the "friends of the Open Society"—who of late seem to alternate between the touching but irrelevant knight errantry of Don Quixote, defending Dulcinea del Toboso, and the eager but self-destructive baserunning of the Brooklyn Dodgers of an earlier day who frequently found themselves with three men on first!

One is reluctant to make such an undertaking. First, Popper's overall wisdom, relevance, and clarity is rare, if not unique. Secondly, one is aware that he has raised questions that it is only too easy to vex, perhaps impossible fully to clarify. Nevertheless as I read *The Open Society,* for the second time, I found myself filled with the same kind of uneasiness I had felt upon the first reading—which I then attributed to my own lack of acuity. On the one hand, I wished to applaud the moral indignation; on the other hand there was always a hesitation. Is the analysis not just slightly eccentric? And if not eccentric, then ambivalent? What follows is nothing more than an attempt to raise questions as a means to personal clarification.

It may be that in the long run the most important contribution that Popper will have made is in precipitating the question, "What is and ought to be the relation between criticism and tradition in the life of a society?" My own perplexities with his book reduce, at the end, to perplexity with this question. As a means of at least indicating what that is, I wish to analyze his understanding of "decision"; the distinction between "Natural Law" and "Normative Law"; that between "Fact-Statements" and "Norm-Statements"; and, his use of "Historicism." It is obvious, of course, that these various features of his argument are most intimately connected. I shall try, nevertheless, to keep their treatment separate. Finally, I want to consider the question raised by Popper at the very end: "Does History Have a Meaning?"; and to examine the relation of the answer to this question to the life of an Open Society.

What is the central thesis of the book? It is the conviction that (1) civilization differs from tribalism—or the Open Society from the Closed—through the application of the critical and rational methods of science to the problems of civil existence; the prizing of democratic social reconstruction—"piecemeal social engineering," instead of "utopian social engineering"; (2) historicism—the supposition that the same *logos* underlies both nature and history and that therefore man's destiny is as little subject to man's choice as that of nature—is the chief obstacle to the achievement of an Open Society; (3) historicism thus defined is the product of the failure to distinguish between "Facts" and "Decisions"; (4) when this distinction *has* been made, men see that their destiny lies in their own hands; and the living of a life where this is recognized, and where responsible decision of an appropriately pragmatic and "piecemeal" sort is practiced, is an Open Society; and (5) since Plato, Hegel, and Marx believed it to be the "task of the social sciences to furnish us with long-term historical prophecies" and that they had discovered laws of history that enabled them to prophecy the course of historical events, they are historicists and are, therefore, the chief enemies of the Open Society. "The metaphysics of history impede the application of the piecemeal methods of science to the problems of social reform."[2]

Unfortunately, as it seems to me, the basic confusion of the book is implicit in the equivocation surrounding the crucial word in this statement of the thesis, namely, *historicism*. This word, together with *utopianism* and *aestheticism* when Popper is in a more polemical tone, is forced to carry the burden of the argument. Yet it is plain that, if this has any definite meaning, it is far from simple. Popper frequently taxes the historicist with his erroneous assumption that he has grasped the laws of history and that these laws "determine" history. Nonetheless, he seems to equivocate in his own use of "law" and in his conception of the relation of laws to what we might call "the facts of history." (1) Sometimes the gravamen against historicism seems to be that it is the victim of the ambiguity in the word *law* or *rule*—e.g., law as a description and law as a prescription, also distinguished by Popper as "Fact" and "Decision." (2) At other times, the gravamen seems to be that the historicist seeks to *predict* the course of history. But not only is this harmless enough within limits—even unavoidable—and only what the positivist scientist tries to do; but Popper himself elsewhere grants that the search for

2. Popper, *The Open Society and Its Enemies* 1:3–4.

"sociological laws" is necessary and possible. (3) At still other times, the difficulty seems to be that the historicist is a metaphysician; that he imagines that he has a grasp upon a "structure of things" which does "necessitate" the future. But, is not the very denial of this "metaphysical talk"? And how does the positivist scientist claim that past sequences in nature are a clue to future sequences in nature, a presupposition of induction, save by bootlegging the metaphysical assertion, "The past is causally connected with the future"? If Popper should reply, "But the future is contingent," and were to mean by this that my knowledge of any particular future is merely probable, we would have to agree. This, however, would be a statement about my knowledge and not about the future. If on the other hand he were to mean, "I, K. R. Popper, *know* that any given future is not necessarily connected with the past"—then he would merely be exchanging metaphysical epithets with the historicist whom he thus indicts. For here he would either be saying something about his *own* knowledge and not about the future, such as, "Certain laws which have had high probabilities and which have caused me to expect a given event in the future, have proved not to be invariant." Or he would be saying something not about the limits of his *knowledge* of the future, but about the *future* itself. But this could be known to be true about the future only on the condition that what he *claimed* to know was false, since its falsity is the presupposition of this being known about the future! Yet, it may be that Popper wants to say, "While both the historicist and I assume that in a general way the past is causally linked to the future, he is guilty of supposing he can say with certainty the *specific ways* in which the past and future will be connected." In other words, he is saying, the connectedness of things is not an *essence* to be grasped, but can only be observed among actual existences. Or he may mean, in addition to all this: "I assume that the past is causally connected with the future as a general principle because it works. It is the result of a *decision*. You do not recognize that this is not a necessary assumption, i.e., not a 'Fact' but a 'Decision.'" We see, however, that this raises an interesting problem, to be deferred for the moment, of the relation of the statement "Assume that the past is causally related to the future"—which for the present we will call a policy statement or "decision"—and the various laws or "facts" that are discovered through obedience to this policy. In short, we must anticipate the question, "Is there any logical dependence 'of facts' upon 'decisions'?" (4) Finally, his specific charge seems to be that the laws which the historicist formulates are such that nothing could happen in history which would infirm these laws. This is a slightly different statement of the same problem found in (3) above. The historicist imagines he is talking about history in a manner analogous to the way in which the chemist talks about nature in Boyle's Law of Gases. What he is in fact doing is talking about it in a way analogous to the metaphysician, who says, "The past is causally connected to the future." That is, from the formulation of what we called "sociological laws"—descriptions of past recurrences in history—*taken together* with the *general* connectedness of future and past, the historicist tries to arrive at *specific necessary* connections between particular past events and particular future events.

I think at the end of all this, one has to side with Popper. But it must be said that he himself never really makes this clear and that the equivocation, however harmless it may be in a tract, vitiates the analysis—and I believe seriously confuses the friends of the Open Society. And I want further to suggest that it is this same confusion which crops up again and again.

What, then, in sum, is his charge against historicism? He is attacking its *essentialism*—that kind of rationalism which supposes it to be possible to grasp an eternal *logos* behind the contingent events of nature and the flux of history. For a science of inductive probabilities concerning contingent existents, it would substitute a deductive science of eternal essences. It aspires to grasp the *logos* of history. In supposing that it has, it causes men to abdicate their responsibility for decision in history and creates a social elite that has been initiated into the secret. This is the displacing of "Open Rationality" by "Closed Rationality."

Now, I think we must ask, en passant, "What is the presupposition of the possibility of Open Rationality?" Plato would have said: "Either the reason grasps the *logos* or the skeptics are right. There is no alternative to Closed Rationality except no rationality at all." How did it happen that out of a broken Closed Society emerged an Open Society with an Open Rationality—enabled to surrender with some equanimity the aspiration to grasp the eternal *logos,* yet still finding the world of contingent fact a worthy and possible object of science? Was it due to the Incarnation faith? The contingent fact acquired a new meaning through this. No less did hope (*elpis*) and faith (*pistis*) because of the faithfulness of God. Upon what is Open Rationality, inductive science, based but the assurance that nature and history are not mere caprice because of the *faithfulness* of God; and the modesty born of the recognition that it cannot grasp the logos because God's faithfulness is hidden, as is all faithfulness.

Therefore it cannot be fully grasped by the generalizing reason, but can only be trusted—as it is by the scientist who proposes to speak of future sequences in nature by an appeal to past sequences; and who does not cease to believe in a general causal relation between past and future because he finds his laws infirmed by negative cases in particular instances. The negative case is not proof that nature is disorderly, but only that the law is a premature presumption. The scientist repents of his idolatrous certainty, and declares of nature, "Though she slay me yet will I trust her." When God chastens Israel with the negative case of historic failure, this does not prove God's betrayal, but only Israel's presumption to be privy to God's counsel. The faith of inductive science and its relation to the recurrences of nature is the perfect correlate of the faith of Israel and its relation to God. It lives in humility before what is "given" to experience, under judgment on its probabilities from an *essentially* inscrutable course of nature, in faith and hope that something of the truth about things will be partially manifest to a "broken and contrite heart." Now this is not a mere bankrupt Closed Rationality. It is an Open Rationality. And as Popper sees, it transforms human life.

The same critical ambiguity appears in Popper's use of the word *decision*. First, it covers a range all the way from the most basic and reflectively unexamined kind of commitment such as is given in the ethos of a culture or the syntax of a language to the most self-conscious and reflective kind of intellectual activity such as opting between alternative scientific hypotheses. It is, of course, very probable that an exhaustive phenomenology of decision would yield the discovery that there is between such extremes a common feature or features. However, Popper tends to assimilate all "commitments" to "decisions." And in this is exhibited his Cartesian anthropology—his assumption throughout that thought can become radically reflexive and that the Open Society—while it depends upon tradition—is one in which tradition is not a genuine "commitment," i.e., something for which no reasons are thought necessary because never the subject of reflection, but is a "decision," i.e., something for which it is recognized no reason *can* be given. Let us notice that while the logical status of commitments and decisions may be the same, our psychological relation to each is quite different.

I would like to consider this problem as it is exhibited at two different points in Popper's argument. Implicitly, these precipitate what I have called the basic question posed by the book, namely, "What is and ought to be the relation between tradition and criticism in society?"

Popper says, "An Open Society . . . rejects the absolute authority of the merely established and the merely traditional while trying to preserve, to develop, and to establish traditions, old or new, *that measure up to their standards of freedom, of humaneness, and of rational criticism.*"[3] The question to be raised is, "What is the relation between the traditions and the standards by which the traditions are to be judged?" It appears that we are threatened by an infinite regress at this point. For even if we are unwilling to say that there is some simple commitment ultimately "given," upon which a whole society depends and from which all its decisions derive; and even if we refuse to say in advance what must be "given" in any specific case of decision; nevertheless, if there is not *something* "given," in the sense of not *now* subject to a decision of the radical reflexive sort, then either nothing can *ever* be decided, or decision is an empty caprice. For example, if we "decide" to preserve, to develop, and to establish traditions that "measure up to . . . standards of freedom, of humaneness, and rational criticism," we must have antecedently "decided" upon the "standards." But—*this* "decision" is either a purely arbitrary, momentary, and frivolous caprice that expresses no values or genuine commitments, or it *does* express basic values and commitments, but for that reason and to that extent these commitments are not *at the same time* subject to a conscious, radically reflexive act of "decision." This is to say that they are accepted on some kind of authority.

Now, I think there are times when Popper recognizes this—and this is what I mean by his ambivalence. He says, for example, "My insistence that we make the decisions and carry the responsibility must not be taken to imply that we cannot, or must not, be helped by faith, and inspired by tradition or by great examples." Yet, on the other hand, he says elsewhere, "If we analyze the term tradition into concrete personal relations, then we can get rid of that attitude which considers every tradition as sacrosanct, or as valuable in itself, replacing this by an attitude which considers traditions as valuable or pernicious according to their influence upon individuals."[4] And what of the "tradition" to consider traditions as valuable or pernicious according to their influence upon individuals? This is not a question that is easily answered. But a refusal to pose it may cause even an Open Society to destroy itself through openness by a faithlessness to what Michael Polanyi has called its "fiduciary foundations."

3. Ibid., 1:vii. Italics added.
4. Ibid., 1:66, 2:226.

The difficulties surrounding the notion of decision are obliquely made manifest in a most interesting reflection. The total impact of Popper's book leaves no doubt whatever that he has a "philosophy of history." Notwithstanding his blanket judgment that "history has no meaning"—and in the sense intended he makes good this claim by showing that there is no history to have meaning in this sense—he plainly believes that "the meaning of history is the propagation of the Open Society." He nowhere says this, of course. But when we ask, "How is Popper able to view the revolutionary and reflexive-critical impetus of the Open Society as creative—even redemptive— whereas Plato—in Popper's version of him at any rate—sees in it nothing but an unmitigated evil," we have a clue to a profound commitment upon the part of Popper. Why this difference? Popper says, "Although history has no meaning, we can give it a meaning."[5] This means then that the philosophy of history which is above attributed to Popper must have been the result of a decision on his part. But here again the difficulties with "decision" appear.

Let us take a step back. Popper is so anxious to distinguish "facts" from "decisons"—and rightly so—that he exaggerates both the "givenness" of facts and the contingency of decisions. Against this simplification I would suggest (1) that decisions enter into the discovery, utterance, acceptance, and propagation of fact-statements—a claim which Popper surely would not deny; (2) that the decision to acknowledge a fact-statement is the result of a belief that it is veridical; (3) that norm-statements or policy-statements—as when we propose a certain meaning for history—are unquestionably accepted as the result of a decision (as with fact-statements), but that they are not for this reason *only* proposals for action or the adoption of certain attitudes or expectations. Rather they are also *assertions* about what we take to be objectively the case, quite independent of our decision to act as one who has acknowledged and adopted the statement as bearing upon action. Attitudes and expectations are after all *toward* and *about* something. And I think it is manifest that Popper's real animus against historicism springs from the— I will call it—ontologic conviction that when he speaks of history, civilization, and the Open Society, using policy-proposing language, he is not merely making a proposal, but asserting what is the case. Otherwise, his indignation at Plato is simply bad manners. For example, let us ask, "When he

5. Ibid., 2:278.

says, 'History has no meaning,' what does he mean?" That there is not some *logos* of history to be grasped underneath the flux of events, deducible or inducible from these events, because any meaning in history is always relative to a decision about its meaning anterior to the events purporting to be evidential of that view. Hence, there can be no history in an objective sense. It might be stated thus, paraphrasing Berkeley: "To be an historical event is to be remembered as a part of a meaningful pattern; apart from remembered meaningful events there is no history." I think this an accurate exegesis of Popper's sense.

But, when he says, "We decide to give a meaning to history" —what is the meaning, the referent, of this word *history?* On Popper's own account, it can *only* mean "Remembered meaningful events." What then has he said? "We decide to give a meaning to remembered meaningful events"! But this is either redundant or absurd. For either our "decision" is the conscious, reflective acknowledgment that the remembered events do have for us this meaning, quite independently of this particular acknowledgment; or our "decision" is that by which something ("history") otherwise without meaning *comes* to have it. But, if I have not misread Popper, he wants to say that the word *history* used in the sense of the latter alternative has no meaning, i.e., referent. So—either our decision is an acknowledgment of *what already is the case;* or it is about a chimera!

Suppose, however, Popper replies that the statement "the meaning of history is the propagation of the Open Society" sounds like a statement of "fact"; but, when responsibly analyzed, it will be seen to be a policy proposal, e.g., "act responsibly! Do not acquiesce to fate!" What then? This will not do, since "Act responsibly!" presupposes the assertion about the meaning of history in the sense that to be responsible requires that the context of response is given. I do not know what responsible action is apart from some antecedent "decision" about the larger context of action, namely, history. But, even if I were to subscribe to the view that "the meaning of history is the propagation of the Open Society" because I have "decided" to do so, can I really "decide to" for any other reason than that I believe it to be true? And can I believe it to be true for any other reason than that it seems to assert something that really is the case about me, the context of my life and responsible action in the flux of time? In short, any statement about the meaning of history, far from being merely a proposal to "act in the midst of the chances and changes of this mortal life as if . . .," is, implicitly, at any rate, an assertion about what really and ultimately is the case with these chances and changes, with me and my responsible action. And I suggest that the moral fervor of Popper's book derives precisely from the fact that he does not for a moment believe otherwise!

What are we to conclude from this analysis of "decision"? Not merely that grave logical difficulties arise from Popper's various uses. It may cause us to ask: "Can the Open Society survive in the dry light of deracinate, critical reason and nothing more? Can, that is, the ethos of the Open Society be decided into existence by reference to a standard of evaluation which is *itself* decided into existence by individual selves which have decided themselves into existence by an infinite regress of decisons to decide? Or must it be nourished also and at the same time by a doctrine of grace, by which what is given may be received in gratitude as itself the very source of our power to choose?"

A man can decide with integrity and confidence about some things only if he does not have to decide about other things. If he tries to decide in the radical reflexive sense about everything, he becomes impotent and finally neurotic. Popper is gifted with too much common wisdom to be led to absurdity by the "logic" of his own position. It ought to be said nevertheless that, if my suggestions are correct, it would lead us to address to an infant at the age when he began to show an interest in speech the following remarks: "It's up to you to decide! What language would you like to make your native tongue? English? French? Italian? German? Or perhaps some non–Indo-European language?" But, alas, we shall have to teach him English first! And thus by the time he understands the question, he is already hopelessly committed!

The distinction which Popper thinks the historicist fails to make, thereby bringing nemesis upon us all; and the one in making which he proposes to give the lie to all forms of historicist doctrine; and hence the distinction that is the very axis of his entire argument is that between what he calls *Natural Laws* and *Normative Laws*, also called "Facts" and "Proposals of Policy." Not only is he not content to employ a single dichotomy throughout, but he uses the members of the various pairs equivocally. It is from this fact that the impression of an eccentric argument derives. Elsewhere, in making this distinction, he speaks of the logical independence of facts and decisions; or of the "autonomy of ethics." I want to turn now to a consideration of these in order.

First, he distinguishes between (1) *Laws of Nature,* statements describing regularities of nature and (2) *Laws of Nature,* norms such as prohibitions or commandments. He then suggests, in order to avoid the ambiguity surrounding the word *law*, the distinction between "Facts" and "Decisions."

Unfortunately, he does not stop there. Speaking of laws in sense (1) above he wants to say: (a) that they are "unalterable." Now, if by "law" is meant a description of the regularities of nature, then it is patently false that they are unalterable. The history of science is a history of altered or discarded laws. (b) He also says that these laws can be "neither broken nor enforced." Either he uses the word *laws* in a sense in which they *are* broken, i.e., as correlations of phenomena with other phenomena subject to constant expansion and alteration; or in a sense in which it cannot be *known* that they are *never* broken, i.e., as generalizations with no known negative cases; or in a sense in which they cannot be known *at all* on Popper's own account, i.e., as some determining *logos* of events in nature beneath the observed and described behavior of nature that can be inferred from this behavior. (c) He says that these natural laws are "beyond human control." But what does this mean? How can these be beyond human control? They are on the contrary *products* of human thought. It is rather what the laws express that is beyond human control. It would be as absurd to say, "The writer has no control over the description of the landscape he is describing"! Yet—it would be *quite* intelligible to say, "He has no control over the landscape he is describing."

In the midst of this ambiguity, what is Popper trying to say? I think he means to say either that (1) "Natural Laws are descriptions of events in nature"; or (2) "There is an objective order of things binding nature together." If he means (1), then these laws are either (a) alterable or (b) cannot be known to be unalterable. If he means, (2) then he has either (a) asserted something that cannot be known to be true or (b) uttered an imperative, i.e.: "Certain general regularities have been observed in the past. Act as though these regularities will hold for the future!" Finally, if (b), then what seems to have been asserted as a "Fact" turns out to be a "Decision."

But perhaps underneath all this lies the conviction that, on the one hand, there is *nature*, which presents man with something intractable to his will; and, on the other hand, there is *history*, which is, at any rate, not *quite* so intractable to human decisions. Who would deny this! Yet precisely what is involved in each case is far from clear.

Once again, I think Popper has a good case. But I seriously doubt he has made it.

Above it was remarked how Popper in his anxiety to make the distinction between "nature," as the sum-total of probable laws about certain events that transpire and exhibit more or less recurrent patterns, independent of human wishes and decisions, from "history," which is more precariously described in this way, since part of the subject matter is human volitions and choices, he tends to exaggerate both the "givenness" of facts and the contingency of decisions.

Since this confusion resulting from the Fact-Decision distinction is of a piece with the Natural Law-Normative Law distinction, and is equally central to the book, we must now turn to consider it.

First, I believe that however serviceable for certain limited objectives the distinction between *Fact-Statements* and *Norm-Statements* may be, if we make it absolute, we seriously vex the questions at issue; and that, in any case, their relations are very much more complex than Popper has realized or else has thought necessary to say. It is useless to hope to express this complexity here. I expect only to cast some doubt upon the simplifications that seem to me to underlie Popper's argument.

Of a Norm-Statement, Popper says, "It may be perhaps described as good or bad, right or wrong, acceptable or unacceptable; but only in a metaphorical sense can it be called 'true' or 'false', since it does not describe a fact, but lays down directions for our behavior."[6] It is supposed that this establishes the "autonomy of ethics" or the "logical independence of Facts and Decisions." I believe it does so only through what is in this context a wholly gratuitous abstraction. For notice that "directions for behavior" either "contain" implicitly or presuppose those descriptive propositions concerning the context of the behavior enjoined—or the directions for behavior are meaningless. And further, those descriptive propositions are being implicitly "asserted."

Now, I do not want here to argue that the grammar of a Norm-Statement is not distinguishable from that of a Fact-Statement; or that we cannot distinguish between the behavior enjoined *explicitly* in a Norm-Statement and the Facts asserted *implicitly* in that same statement or what it presupposes. I want only to insist that Fact-Statements and Norm-Statements are logically independent only in a special sense, to be discussed later.

On the other hand, a Fact-Statement, so far as concerns its grammatical form, is implicitly an instruction for taking heed in a certain way. It will be

6. Ibid., 1:58.

seen to be true or false, if when we have obeyed the instruction, what we heed coheres with every other relevant feature of the environment. Nor am I suggesting that there is no independently *real* world. I *am* suggesting that "the Facts" are the product of certain commitments of our attention, even if these commitments are "given" in the very syntax of our language; that they are the terminus of a certain process of taking heed in certain ways and not antecedently given; and that a person who sees "the facts" does so only because he has obeyed instructions; and that, if he does not obey them, there cannot be, for him, any such facts; and, finally, that unless *someone* obeys them, there *are* no such facts for anyone! Now, to be sure, to listen comprehendingly to one's native language is to obey these instructions, in a sense. To paraphrase Berkeley again: "To be a fact is to be the terminus of someone's interest inspired heed-taking (even if that heed-taking is induced by the syntax of the language he speaks); apart from such there are no facts; to state a fact is to issue implicit instructions for this heed-taking, using the grammatical form of a Fact-Statement."

Therefore, I dare to say that it is not the case that all Fact-Statements are logically independent of Norm-Statements; and that all Norm-Statements are independent of Fact-Statements. Norm-Statements implicitly *assert*; Fact-Statements implicitly *offer instructions* for "action."

What then is valid in the distinction that Popper draws?

Let us take two Norm-Statements (N-S) of the order "ô," i.e., $N\text{-}S_\delta$ (a) "Every event has a cause." I call this a Norm-Statement because I believe it to mean, when analyzed, "Treat every event as if it had a cause and seek that." (b) "One ought to love one's neighbors." The "logical efficacy" of these two (a and b) of order $N\text{-}S_\delta$ is the propositions of the order "1" to which they give rise, when taken in conjunction with other premises, e.g., propositions like $N\text{-}S_1$ and $F\text{-}S_1$. By this device I would like to suggest the strata of Norm-Statements and Fact-Statements; the complexity of their interrelations; the logical dependence of propositions of the form $F\text{-}S_1$ and $N\text{-}S_1$ upon propositions of the form $N\text{-}S_\delta$; and finally, the logical independence of propositions of the form $F\text{-}S_1$ and $N\text{-}S_1$ of one another.

Take (a) above. "Every event has a cause" ($N\text{-}S_\delta$). The logical efficacy of this is taken together with the premise "X is an event" ($F\text{-}S_1$) and the premise "I ought to treat X as if it had a cause" ($N\text{-}S_1$), and with appropriate investigation, it yields the statement "Y is the cause of X" ($F\text{-}S_1$). I suggest that all propositions of the order $N\text{-}S_1$ and $F\text{-}S_1$ are logically *dependent* upon

N-S_{δ}; and that they are independent of one another, in the sense demanded by Popper. Or again take (b) above. "One ought to love one's neighbors" (N-S_{δ}) plus further investigation and the premise "X is my neighbor" (F-S_1) yields "I ought to love X" (N-S_1). In short, Norm-Statements and Fact-Statements are logically independent of one another *providing they are of the same logical stratum*. This is the position that Popper seems to wish to defend. And again, I believe we must say that he has a case, but that he has not made it in the *Open Society and Its Enemies.*

Popper concludes his final volume with the enigmatic words, "Although history has no meaning, we can give it a meaning."[7] We have already noted certain logical difficulties that arise from this. I wish now, by reference to St. Paul, to suggest that Popper has not adequately distinguished between *historicist* and *nonhistoricist* interpretations of history; and that had he done so, he would have realized that we can easily go between the horn of his dilemma: Either historicism or an *as if* "decision" of policy about history.

St. Paul says, "For I am sure that neither death, nor life, nor angels, nor principalities, nor things present, nor things to come, nor powers, nor height, nor depth, nor anything else in all creation, will be able to separate us from the love of God in Christ Jesus our Lord."[8]

Now I believe this is neither an historicist claim about history nor an *as if* decision to give it a meaning. It is neither an attempt to grasp a *logos* underlying history by deduction from a first principle nor by induction from the recurrences of history; not a "decision" about history that assigns a meaning to it (which would be a statement about how St. Paul intends to act, rather than an assertion about history) independent of something "objective to" the decision *about* which the decision is made.

What, then, is the logical status of this utterance about history? (1) Clearly it is not a statement about Nature; (2) it is not a statement about social dynamics; (3) it does not pretend to arrive at goals or ends for history or in history by induction from the facts of history; (4) it is not establishing a chosen race, people, nation, or class for historic success or destiny; (5) it is not a general law of historical uniformity; (6) it is not a *prediction* on logical all fours with the statement, "The Soviet Union will not triumph," any more than the statement, "Past events are related to future events, so that from past

---

7. Ibid., 2:278
8. Rom. 8:38–39, RSV.

sequences future sequences may be predicted" is on logical all fours with "The moon will be eclipsed at 9:05 p.m. tonight." Nothing could prove either of the first of these pairs false. Something could prove both of the latter two false. Yet, it is clearly *about* history—it is *asserting* that something is ultimately the case about events, life in time, ourselves, and our decisions.

Paul's words do not suggest that he has made a decision about history (The King James version uses the words, "For I am persuaded," not, "For I have persuaded myself"). He is not telling us about a decision he has made, but rather that *about which* the decision is made. And what he asserts to be the case about events is that their meaning resides in Jesus Christ; that history is God's creature; that the chaos and contingency exhibited by these events is overcome (though he cannot say precisely how); that even if God's ways are past finding out (by a form-discerning *gnosis,*) they are faithful ways; and that man may have a responsible relation to God, not through grasping the precise relation of particular events to the full form of his intentions, but by faithful response to all his acts.

The difference between historicist and nonhistoricist interpretations of history is the difference between living according to Closed Rationality and living in hope and faith. But hope and faith are not grounded in the transparency of a radically reflexive ego, they are hope *for* and faith *in* an objective correlate, even if this cannot be grasped by form-discerning rationality, but can only be trusted!

At the end of all this the question remains, "What is the relation of tradition and criticism in the life of Society?" Is a principle of criticism, of radical skepsis—and nothing more— the possible basis of the Open Society? Does not a principle of criticism have to point beyond itself to a reality upon which it itself depends, yet cannot be simply grasped? And if so, can an Open Society long survive that points only to itself, or only to its critical principle, and not beyond itself to this reality?

For having forced us to raise these questions we are in the debt of Karl R. Popper. And we can be grateful that the Open Society has so passionate, even if slightly ambivalent, an advocate!

PSYCHOANALYTIC THEORY AND THEISTIC BELIEF

Some Comments

I

I have found Professor Alston's paper difficult to criticize in a very special way; difficult because even though while approaching this subject both critically and seriously, he is neither genuinely critical nor fully aware of the radical character of Freud's impact upon us all; difficult because, as we all know, Freud's writings are a kind of conceptual jungle where our maps are not only constantly changing, but where the compass needle does not always point North; difficult for me because I agree not only with his major conclusions, but also with many of the details of the argument by means of which he arrives at them.

But more than this, what I find to criticize in the paper has not primarily to do with this or that detailed feature of his argument. His consideration of the bearing of psychoanalytic theory upon theistic belief is not so much wrong here and there as it is wrong through and through. More exactly, his paper is really about something else.

However, even these are minor embarrassments. The one for which I have to make apology to him and to you is this: The only way I can elucidate the ways in which I regard his argument to be about something else is by

This essay was written in response to a paper by Professor William Alston, which was delivered before a symposium convened by the Princeton Theological Society in celebration of its tercentenary.

attempting to arrive at conclusions identical with his by quite another course of argument, which is to say, I have not so much to criticize what he has said as to offer an alternative to it. To do this, I shall, I am afraid, have to seem to impute to Alston beliefs which I am confident he has never held. And I shall, for purposes of emphasis, make certain exaggerations which will appear to commit *me* to beliefs I have never held.

For example, it may appear that I am representing Alston as believing that Freud's theory is some kind of quasi behaviorism, and, while vaguenesses in his paper do at times invite this curious interpretation, I have no idea at all that he in fact does hold to it.

On the other hand it may appear in my own analysis of *caused* beliefs that I want to be saying that these beliefs are really not caused at all; or it may seem that the striking analogies between the structure and affects of the Oedipal situation, on one hand, and the beliefs and feelings to be found expressed in large tracts of the literature of theistic belief, on the other, need not in my view present theistic believers with any *grave* philosophical puzzles.

These things I do not at all believe.

How then can we look at psychoanalytic theory and its bearing upon theistic belief in a more illuminating way?

II

At bottom, the limitations of Alston's analysis derive from a too great willingness to take Freud at his own word. Let's begin to suggest the difficulties.

There are, so far as concerns the present inquiry, two controlling passions of Freud's imagination: one for humanism; the other for scientific explanation. Admittedly these are vague notions. I hope that before I shall have finished they will not be quite so vague.

The first of these passions may be symbolized by the Oedipus complex—a concept, or more properly, a model, which is, let us not forget, a compact and elliptical *story* that sees human beings as *primordially* involved in a great tragic drama. Within its terms, man is regarded as unproblematically human; human in the sense in which we each think of ourselves as beings who are not machines, whose lives, however buffeted they may be by forces that we feel are alien to us, are lived-out either within or as moving toward the medium of speech, and who therefore often do act and even more often think of ourselves as acting in the light of rational choices (or at least in the light of choices that we take in some sense to be our own and for making which we hold "ourselves" and regard "ourselves" as being held in some sense responsible).[1]

The whole so-called "mechanism" of repression is inextricably bound to the concept of "guilt" and to "love/hate," which is to say to "responsibility" or at least to "proto-responsibility." Freud of course took man to be an organism, but for him he is beyond this a "proto–inter-personal" organism.

The other dominant passion of Freud's imagination may be symbolized by his never abandoned expressed hope to translate the whole of psychoanalytic theory into the conceptual framework of neurophysiology. Here he was the obedient student of his teachers in medicine and a true, if at times uneasy, subscriber to the metaphysical commitments of the nineteenth century.

As a humanist, he is the clinician, entering sympathetically even against his own rubrics, by means of speech, that characteristically human and human-making power, into the now unremembered because once forsaken past of a person until the recitation falters "at the line where long ago the accusations had begun."[2]

As a scientist, he seeks an explanation. Not just any explanation, but one

---

1. I introduce these qualifications, which will seem to common sense to be quite gratuitous, because I want to suggest that in the Freudian environment, "responsible" and "rational" have an absolutely essential and characteristic, though I believe entirely licit, role to play. Modern thought has generally gravitated toward either of two aspects of the Cartesian view of the human being: either mechanism—of which the various forms of behaviorism are sophisticated refinements; or spiritualism—of which perhaps Sartreanism is the ultimate refinement. In terms of the first model, "rationality" can only be of that sort exhibited by computers, and "responsibility" is strictly meaningless; in terms of the second model, "rationality" is such as is exhibited only by a pure, discarnate mathematical intelligence, and "responsibility" is only one radical unconnectedness of any moment of consciousness by any "antecedent" moment of consciousness.

Freud's achievement, in a sense, is that of going back to a more ancient alignment of the concepts "rationality," "responsibility," "freedom," and "fate." And it is worth observing that those who formulate their version of the problem of human fate and freedom, of rationality and responsibility in these Cartesian alternatives, tend to talk precisely the same kind of nonsense about these issues both when considering them in relation to Freud and to Greek tragedy.

2. W. H. Auden, "In Memory of Sigmund Freud," in *The Collected Poetry of W. H. Auden* (New York: Random House, 1945), 215–18.

that invokes the categories which for him will *really* count: "mechanism," "cause," "instinctual drives," "energy," etc.

The tension between these two passions and their principal categories never relaxed. It was precisely this "confusion" that was the source of his vision. Anyone who would take his Freud both critically and seriously must remember this which Freud himself forgot because he was never clearly aware of it. You cannot play one side off against the other; nor can you play one side and *then* the other.

If this tension persists throughout; if, as I have suggested, it is the source of the whole *point* of any bearing of Freud's views upon large scale philosophical questions, then to talk about this bearing in terms of "causal explanations," "reasons," "beliefs," as if it were not upon these very conceptions and their use that Freudianism chiefly bears, is greatly to relax this tension and thereby to obscure the vision.

Professor Alston has not quite gotten this matter into focus.

Before we have concluded, we shall have to examine with some care the concepts: "cause," "having and giving reasons," "explanation," "holding beliefs" or "believing," "differential readiness to accept beliefs," and perhaps others, for it is just my point that if you accord any importance to Freud's writings and sprinkle the above concepts into the new logical environment they provide then everything changes.

Let me first make a prima facie case that Alston is bewildered by the nature and extent of the conceptual shift of which I have made much by showing that he at once suspects that something of this sort has occurred, but has not yet specified what it is.

Early in his paper Professor Alston, in suggesting alternative explanatory theories of religious beliefs to those of Freud, refers to the sociological theories of Durkheim and Swanson. The view, you will remember, is that a correlation can be shown between various theological beliefs and the structures of the societies in which live those people professing these beliefs. Now, if theological beliefs of a certain sort could be adequately specified; if the cases of holding these beliefs could be determined without undue fallibility; and if the structure of the society could be defined where these beliefs were professed; and if, then, a high correlation between the beliefs and societies could be shown; this would seem to present an explanatory theory of the generation of religious beliefs having the same *logical* bearing upon the credit rating of these beliefs—though it would not be the *same* explanatory theory—

as those of Freud. It would seem, in short, to suggest that any *reasons* offered for holding these beliefs would be discredited, since a causal explanation for their being held is available—unless, of course, the act of "giving reasons" in this case is nothing more than that of saying certain words and hence logically like that construal of "holding beliefs" which interprets it, too, as nothing more than the uttering of certain words. Alston discards this sociological explanatory theory neither because it could not *in principle* explain the occurrence of certain religious beliefs on the grounds of incompleteness (though he does hold it to be so); nor yet because, even were it to be an adequate theory, it would not serve to lower the credit rating of those beliefs the holding of which it claimed to explain. Rather, he turns to the unquestionably more interesting theories of Freud because "neither he (Swanson) nor any other protagonist of this view . . . has done anything to indicate what psychological processes effect the transition between one's awareness of the structure of one's society and one's readiness to accept a certain theology." In a way, the central perplexity for Alston and for us all is foreshadowed in these words. A theory that could perform such a feat does *more* than merely establish a certain correlation between the structure of a society and that society's beliefs; it accounts also for the fact that specifiable psychological processes *cause* people who hold certain (neurotically engendered) theological beliefs, even though those beliefs could have no *reasons*, being neurotically engendered. They have "causes."

Now let us remember that Freud, in general, presumed to be giving a "causal explanation" of only *certain* sorts of belief—I have called them neurotically engendered ones—and a "causal explanation" for the need to give reasons for holding these beliefs, even when they have been "caused." Least of all did he give a "causal explanation" for holding those beliefs about the world which were Freud's alternative—expressed or implicit—to theistic belief. I am as far as possible from wishing here to score against Freud by a resort to what will appear like a rather cheap *argumentum ad hominem*. Rather I want only to indicate how, already, "cause," "reasons," "belief" are beginning to get out of hand—and to show they have a certain interesting but also dangerous new resourcefulness in the hands of Freud.

But to return to Alston's reasons for choosing for analysis Freud's explanation of the generation of theistic beliefs over that of Durkheim and Swanson. Why, in Alston's view, is Freud's theory both more complete, and more interesting, and therefore more damaging to the credit rating of theistic belief than the alternatives? Why, in other words, does psychoanalytic theory seem to strike more deeply into the human heart and its reasons than sociological or behavioral psychological theories? The answer is, I think, that Alston senses, on one hand, that the Freudian theory does not demand a violation of our own commonsensical distinction between events and occurrences for which we seek causal explanations and the holding of beliefs for which we seek justifications; and yet that, on the other hand, there is in his theory a class of beliefs of which the people who hold them seek to give justifications, while nevertheless others who do not hold them, seek to give causal explanations.

The fracture lines among concepts like "belief," "cause," "reason," and "explain" fall at new and different places in Freud's theory. In his theory, "giving reasons," "giving causal explanations," and "holding beliefs" are given an entirely novel set of logical valency bonds—so that "true" and "false," "sensible" and "nonsensical" are also given new ones.

The conceptual stresses are now such that one cannot fruitfully argue the question, "Is a causal explanation of the holding of *any* belief sufficient to render nonsensical the citation of *reasons* for holding it?"—as certain behaviorists might argue. Nor is it fruitful to take a special *class* of beliefs that are held, viz., theistic beliefs, and ask, "Is a causal explanation of the holding of this class of beliefs sufficient to render nonsensical the citation of reasons for holding them?" The new polity of concepts demands an examination of the use of words like *belief, reasons, cause, explanation,* etc., within the whole context of Freud's conceptual revisions. When this is carried out, or even just begun, we shall see that Freud is equally uncongenial—no matter, for the moment, what he *seemed* to be saying—to the simplistic behaviorist program to assimilate "giving reasons" to "adducing causal explanations," on one hand, and, on the other, to those philosophers who would argue in the face of the pressure from the whole momentum of natural science that we can preserve a sharp dichotomy between "reasons" and "justifications," "causes" and "explanations." Unless the true nature of Freud's accomplishment is set out, its bearing, in general, upon religion cannot be fruitfully assessed. In choosing Freud over Durkheim, Alston seems to sense this.

But unfortunately this is a point that he has not gotten clear. He is aware that the theory he is examining is not merely a psychological amplification of the sociological explanation of religious beliefs, but that it is a theory (or a subtheory) *of a logically different sort.* That this difference is a function of a new way of plotting the logical relations among "belief," "cause," "reason," and "explain" he fails to see. At least, he has failed to say. And while at this juncture this criticism will seem both oversubtle and captious, I want to claim that it really makes all the difference.

III

Let us attempt to sort among these crucial conceptual changes and determine whether we can get Freud somewhat more into focus.

First, under what circumstances do we more or less confidently say of Jones, "Jones believes p"? Manifestly, an analysis of this question is quite beyond the scope of this inquiry. But I think we can proceed far enough to clarify the vexed issues revolving about "belief," "cause," and "reasons."

I think we would confidently say, "Jones believes p": (1) if Jones says "I believe p" and we *believe him;* (2) if we observe Jones's behavior over a sufficient period of time to descry a certain pattern in it, from which we *infer* that he believes p; (3) if Jones is *responsible* for the belief, p. By "responsible for the belief, p," I mean not only that Jones recognizes that the behavior from which we infer that he believes p stands in a relation of his uttered words such that if the words were different, the behavior would be, in some way, different; nor do I mean only this plus Jones's recognition that such a relation between his behavior and his uttered words obtains for us also; but I mean that Jones may be said to believe p when he "owns up to" the words that he has uttered which, because he *does* "own up to" them we believe him to believe p; or else when he "owns up to" the words *we* have uttered, when contemplating his behavior, we said "Jones believes p." A machine that "utters" a recorded announcement does not "own" its own words; even less can it "own up to" them. A liar, whether it is to us or to himself—in some commonsensical as opposed to a neurotic sense—that he is lying does not "own" his words until he "owns up to" them. It is doubtless an odd, though I hope an illuminating, suggestion to make in this context, but perhaps anyone who takes possession of a form of words or who indwells a course of action as his own may be thought of as "owning up to" the beliefs which the form of words express or the course of action implies. It is not even too much perhaps to suggest that in an analogous way, a poet, as he experiments with the resources of his own language and at last takes possession of a certain form, may be imagined to "own up to" the words of which his final version is composed. Nor is the relationship between our words and deeds and our "ownings" of them a stable one, for we all know how many ways, quite different ways, we can "own up to" the very same words: when, for example, we say, "I did not realize what I was saying." It is equally true that we often come to feel very strange amid our own very familiar professions and routine acts, when it seems appropriate to speak of "disowning" these words and these acts.

I don't wish to pretend that what I have brought out here is simple, nor that it is an easy matter to decide whether and to what degree the criteria for confidently using an expression such as "Jones believes p" have been satisfied. These difficulties will simply have to be ignored here.

What I do wish to emphasize is that to claim that something is *believed* requires a universe not less complicated than one in which there are persons, using a common language in which there are personal pronouns in the first, second, and third persons, in, at least, the nominative and genitive cases, where there are acts, which bear some discernible relation to some professed intentions, and where being responsible to others, "owning" and "owning up to" words and acts is recognized to be a commonplace and unproblematic occurrence. It is, in short, a universe where we jointly indwell our native language by means of which we assent to or dissent from one another about the nature of our common world. Doing this is reasoning—giving and accepting what we take to be reasons.

On these grounds and in terms of this no doubt overextended model, I want to say that no assent, no act of "owning up to" a form of words can be *caused*. Beliefs are assents, "owning up to"; if they have what we regard as good reasons, then we take them to be true; if they do not have this qualification, we take them to be false.

I think this view could be described as a classical philosophical distinction, the distinction, namely, between adducing causes or causal explanations for events or occurrences, on one hand, and educing reasons for beliefs, on the other.

I would take it that a universe where concepts such as "belief," "person," "reason," "giving reasons," "responsible," and the like, are thought to have an autonomy and unanalyzability of their own, would provide a logical environment where, when applied to the realm of human actions, even notions like "repression," "mechanism," "regression," "infantile," "instinctual drives," "sexuality"—perhaps even "cause"—have resources, uses, meanings, come to stand in special logical valency bonds, which would not be the case were the universe *less* complicated.

But can we really hold this view, now that we have been cast out of the pre-Freudian Eden?

Suddenly, we have on our hands, beliefs of a certain class, neurotically engendered beliefs, which it seems must be construed as having been *caused*.

Let us be clear now. Freud has not said that every single belief whatever is *caused;* nor has he even said that every false belief, i.e., every belief for which its holders do not have good reasons for "owning to," is *caused*. He has said only that there are certain beliefs which are neurotically engendered, which is to say, they are in some, perhaps an importantly new, sense caused.

In this setting, let us put quite bluntly the query posed by Alston's paper: Could there ever be a case of holding beliefs which, were we to find a sufficient and necessary causal explanation for holding them, would constitute grounds for discrediting these beliefs? On the face of it, this question seems to be one about the uses of the concept "cause"; it is, it seems to me, a question as to whether there is propriety in using the notion of "cause" in the same logical environment with "belief," "assents," "ownings," "ownings-up-to," etc.

If I am right in this, then with regard to this question Alston seems to be if not of two minds, then at least not clearly of one. If we could just overlook the work of Freud, we could confidently assert that to assimilate educing *reasons* to adducing *causes* or vice versa is to make a category mistake—which would be to misuse "cause" and "belief" in relation to each other. Alston says as much: "Of course," he says, "a reason cannot be a cause, nor can a cause be a reason."

It then turns out, however, that all is not well. As we all do, Alston suddenly gets the shakes. He says that from his claim about reasons and causes it does not follow "that a statement about reasons cannot have implications concerning causes and *vice versa*." He then cites in support of this claim the following: "It seems quite clear to me that to say that A's reason for thinking that his lawn mower is in his garage is that he saw it there this morning (a cause). . . ." Surely we see displayed here the common ambiguity of the word *because*. It is true that, if asked, "Why did you, A, say your lawn mower is in the garage?" A is likely to reply, "Because I saw it there this morning." A's seeing his lawn mower in the garage in the morning may be the "cause" of certain recollections in the afternoon. But his seeing the lawn mower in the garage in the morning is not the "cause" (in the same sense of cause) of his citing his having seen it as a reason for believing it to be there. I suggest that to say this is panic, since, insofar as we can say definitely what is entailed by Freud's discovery of a class of beliefs which are caused, *this* analysis of *this* case is not required.

And yet, Alston's sound instincts do not desert him. If there are caused beliefs, then how are we to display the new, Freudian logical mapping "cause" in relation to "beliefs" and "reasons"?

Well, it seems perfectly plain to me that with regard to all beliefs which are held by men, solely excepting those that are neurotically engendered, Freud believed that they were assents that were not to be accounted for by an appeal to causes, but rather by reference to reasons. To put the matter vaguely but, I believe, accurately, Freud was very much a rationalist in this matter. He was not at all operating with a behavioristic model. There can be no doubt that in our knowledge of contingent fact, causes and causal explanations are the occasions for eliciting judgments, issuing in assents and "ownings-up-to-beliefs"; and that, in this sense, there is an interdependence of causes and reasons. It is further clear that, even on Freud's terms, the neurotic, i.e., the *caused*, components in the holding of belief of every sort whatsoever are not easy to specify. But it is also clear that Freud himself held the view of the unassimilability of "cause" and "reason" to one another: not only because had it been otherwise his theory would have been faced with a comprehensive incoherence, but also because such a view was the logical *conditio sine qua non* for Freud's breakthrough. It was precisely his *rejection* of a *causal explanation* of the beliefs of people which led him later to regard a certain class of beliefs as neurotically engendered. Only by steadfastly refusing to accept that causal explanation of neurotic beliefs which appealed to lesions in the central nervous system was it possible for Freud to devise that "causal explanation" which appealed to the Oedipus complex, the mechanism of repression, infant sexuality, the unconscious, and all the rest.

Indeed, it is no paradox to say that Freud's offense to philosophy and theology—as even to common sense—was far greater than those who were prepared to give causal explanations for all beliefs whatsoever, not only because the latter are more obviously implausible, but because by this new logical move he seems to put "cause" into the very house of reason!

Let me then emphasize that Freud was not substituting for a causal explanation of a given logical order an *alternative* causal explanation of that same order. "Cause" as used by Freud to explain neurotically engendered beliefs is not a concept on logical all fours with that use of it we find, say, in neurophysiology; which is to say, it is not the *same* concept.

How, then, does this notion function?

Curiously enough, we find ourselves wanting to say not only that there is a class of beliefs which are *caused*. We find ourselves wanting to say that these beliefs are not *exactly* caused; and that someone's *holding* a belief of this class is not just his uttering certain words that express it, followed by other words that stand to the former as reasons stand to beliefs, but is also, in a curious way, his "owning" these words: actually in one way, potentially in another, though not "owning" them in the way one "owns" the reasons for one's beliefs which are not neurotically engendered.

Now, I hope it is quite clear I am not suggesting that neurotically engendered beliefs are not after all *caused,* hence not after all what Freud thought they were, and therefore no new and peculiar kind of puzzlement for theistic belief. I am rather suggesting that in the logical environment of "repression," "instinctual drive," "sexuality," "ego," "super-ego," "unconscious," and "projection," when the logical resources of *these* concepts are in turn governed by the comprehensive model, Oedipus complex, a "caused belief" is both logically queer and remarkably resourceful. "Cause" has started keeping—perhaps often somewhat clandestine—company with "person," "assent," "own-up-to," "reason," and "responsibility."

Any argument as to the credit rating of theistic beliefs which does not have this clearly in focus contributes but little to our understanding of either Freud or these beliefs—perhaps especially so, if the conclusions at which it arrives are correct.

Holding even a neurotically engendered belief is not then merely having to issue from one's mouth certain words that express that belief, followed by yet other words that would stand to the first words as those in which we give our reasons normally stand to those in which we express our beliefs. Neither is it just setting one's body in motion in the spatiotemporal world from which motions intelligible patterns are to be read off and intentions, expectations and beliefs inferred. Even in the case of neurotically engendered belief there is an "ownership" of the words and of the acts. The person holding them is *responsible,* or at least proto-responsible, for them: *actually* responsible in one way; *potentially* so in another. He is taken by Freud the analyst as proleptically responsible. No account of neurotically engendered beliefs which lacks this built-in logical tension and complexity is Freudian; and I will say, neither is it really believable.

It is only because "believing," even "neurotic believing," is a transaction that must occur in the interpersonal universe of speech and personal identity that psychotherapy, by means of talking and a form of acting-out, can enable one who "owns" his beliefs to come to "own-up-to" them.

It is all of this that makes the Freudian use of "cause" so odd, so revolutionary, and so productive. It is a cause that can be dissolved with a word.

When this has occurred, the vindication of beliefs, whether they be theistic or the Freudian alternative, can and must proceed along the familiar, even if not always wholly satisfying and certainly rarely certain, paths we follow in all accrediting of beliefs.

IV

There still remains the more radical question. If holding beliefs—of any sort—and giving reasons for holding them are intimately involved with speech and the uses of language as I have suggested, does this not also suggest that the range of possible beliefs and of their alternatives is a function of the limits of our native linguistic or conceptual resources?

To suggest that this might be so would, I suspect, not meet with quite the same resistance as did Freudianism fifty years ago. And its implications for the credit rating of our beliefs are perhaps more far-reaching and therefore more unsettling.

But then that is, of course, another story.

NOTES ON RICOEUR ON FREUD

In reading the "Project of 1895," followed by the *Interpretation of Dreams* and the later essays of Freud on metapsychology in the order in which they are taken up by Ricoeur in book 2 of *Freud and Philosophy,* I found myself becoming aware of and, in a sense, distracted by a perplexity having to do neither with Freud's exposition and defense of his changing models; nor with Ricoeur's analysis of these and his oblique comments upon certain incoherences in them; nor yet, with the way in which Ricoeur was preparing the ground for a constructive statement about Freud in relation to hermeneutics as "the willingness to suspect, [the] willingness to listen."[1]

The puzzle being intimated can be expressed by the questions: Where is Sigmund Freud? What is he doing? How can it be done? These provoke yet another set of questions on the same "surface" level: Where am I (sitting here, as I am, reading the "Project")? What am I doing with the text, with the hardly even ghostly presence of Freud within its interstices? How can *this* be done? (I am aware, even as I rebuke myself for permitting this kind of philosophically irresponsible wool-gathering, how much it is the Enlightenment philosophic tradition in me that reprimands. This speaker in me knows that these are "surface" questions susceptible, "at least in principle," of "surface" answers; that they are "philosophically trivial" and ought therefore to be *philosophically* ignored, since should anyone bother to answer them, no one would dream of contesting the answers. *Everyone* knows, so it goes, where Freud is, where he himself is. This is not the sort of information that

---

1. Paul Ricoeur, *Freud and Philosophy: An Essay in Interpretation* (New Haven: Yale University Press, 1970), 27.

would issue from a skeptical and systematic inquiry; so, therefore, it is hardly even information. These "surface" questions and their "surface" answers are best ignored—Descartes gave us our paradigm for this in the introduction to *The Discourse on Method,* where *he* induces in himself a state of amnesia regarding who and where he is historically, culturally, mythologically, psychosomatically, conceptually, and linguistically in order that he might make haste to join the "deep," philosophically untrivial issues by means of the application of the principle of methodological doubt. Even as I read over the above words, I find myself thinking: "How can anyone find anything of the slightest philosophical importance in what you've just said about Descartes?")

Where, then, is Sigmund Freud, pen in hand, writing the "Project," choosing each German word (that I see translated in the English text) of the "Project" as it takes its integral place in a communication of its ideas to his friend Wilhelm Fliess? As he shapes each element of his argument to be comprehended by and be convincing to its recipient, does Freud fantasize *himself* as he writes and *Fliess* as he will read in images drawn from the inertial model of the human mind, which he is in the very act of constructing with his written-down words; or does his fantasy rather rely upon our mutual common sense, and does he in turn rely upon his fantasy as the very *conditio sine qua non* of his own feat of comprehendingly using his native language as the instrument for intelligible articulation of his thought to another human being? Just to ask these questions is to have them answered. That is why we so readily take them to be philosophically trivial.

For my part, as I reflect upon all this, I find myself before the internally coherent and ingenious model of the "Project," fantasizing the situation of the genius who was its author and who found it convincing. This juxtaposition of the model and my fantasy renders the model utterly incredible. For the model of the "Project" clearly cannot be integrated by a set of *explicit* rules to the terms in which I am just now aware of myself. There is no way to get from it to them without leaping a logical gap. Nor can the repertoire of quasi mechanistic concepts of which the model is comprised be translated by a set of *explicit* transformation rules into the images of my fantasy of Freud and Fliess, reading, talking, reflecting, by means of which I try to make the missing men present to this account of mind. Clearly, Freud continued to consider the "Project" and its model deserving of his attention, notwithstanding the lack of any commensurability *based upon a set of explicit rules of relation* between it and his own sense of himself. If the incommensurability is not noticed, then surely it is because there are tacit acts of intellection and imagination at work on Freud's part (and on my part), rescuing *mere* explicit thought from bankruptcy. What cannot be made to hold together as the heterogeneous features of a complete, integral, and articulated model of the human mind, *can* be held together and endowed with the potency to do its heuristic work in the living imagination of Sigmund Freud, relying upon articulate and, indeed, inarticulable powers to achieve an integration. Yet, it is just *this* Freud who is absent from Freud's own test. It is the Freud that neither he nor I may openly make present because of the a priori interdiction of "surface" questions and "surface" answers by the Enlightenment tradition.

Yet, if Freud has found the Newtonian model of the human mind plausible or heuristically powerful, it is because, in spite of all, Freud inescapably brings himself, his body, his mind, and his imagination, with all their inarticulable complexity, to the otherwise bare and putatively totally explicit text of the "Project." And if I find the model in the text plausible or useful or even just worth my attention, it is because I tacitly import the genius of Freud, as I know of it otherwise, and place the "Project" in the context of this genius—a context that also includes me and my body, mind and imagination, almost surreptitiously supplying sense tacitly where it does not and could not exist with the putatively total explicitness of the textual model, *taken by itself.*

A metapsychology is the work of man reflecting from out of his mindbody upon the nature of mind. Reflexivity is mind's ultimate power, yet it is precisely this that, as it may make all other sorts of things its objects, systematically eludes itself—in an infinite regress. So long as reflection from out of our mindbody seeks itself as an object among objects, it will fail to find itself. Yet, because it can never *lose* itself, it tacitly demands a sense even from models of itself that in its absence would be *obviously* absurd, indeed, would not even "catch our eye."

The "mystery" of our being, our unity, in apparent duality, comes to rest in the inherently equivocal status of language.

Merleau-Ponty has said, "Language becomes something mysterious, since it is neither a self nor a thing." And again: "Language is neither thing nor mind, but it is immanent and transcendent at the same time."[2]

(Here it is interesting to compare Descartes. Within the medium of

---

2. *Consciousness and the Acquisition of Language,* trans. Hugh J. Silverman (Evanston, Ill.: Northwestern University Press, 1973), 5, 6.

language (Latin and French) he articulates a program of doubt designed to call all certitudes into question. At the end we have the *Cogito, res extensa-res cogitans* as the entities that have survived the radical criticism. Yet, Latin and French, which, both before and after the *dubito,* have *some* kind of existence in the world and are crucial to Descartes's program, never themselves become subject to the radical criticism. Nor is the equivocal status of language by reason of its reflexivity addressed. Though perhaps Descartes becomes entangled in spite of himself in this inescapable reflexivity in the discovery that even an evil genius cannot seriously impeach the certitude of the existence of the *Cogito.*)

Let me propose a model in order to examine some features of the so-called mind-body problem.

The manifest commonsensical impossibility of reducing the mental phenomena of perceptual awareness, consciousness, intentionality, wakefulness, sleep, dreams, tacit judgment, articulation, explicit judgment, ratiocination, and speech to some *merely* material or physicalist substrate has given rise to the familiar distinctions between our (as it has been thought, *mere*) bodily being and "something else," e.g., extended thing-thinking thing, body-soul, soma-psyche (or soma-pneuma), matter-mind.

These distinctions, however, achieve articulation only in language. It is only from the order and hierarchy, the increasing sense of a self-other opposition, the disappearance of the "magical" connection between the self and other and the growing integration of our motility—in short, it is only from our bodily-being-in-the-world that our language derives and in which it is metaphorically rooted.

This alienation of the self from the other gives rise to language. It therefore necessarily mirrors the *lived* sense, meaning, and structure of our prelingual being-in-the-world.

Language has the sinews of our bodies, which had them first. The grammar, syntax, meaning, metaphor, and semantical intentionality of our language are preformed in that of our prelingual bodily-being-in-the-world and are their *conditiones sine quibus non.*

Mathematics is the ultimate achievement of our powers of abstraction and is also therefore the greatest medium for the alienation of our formalizing powers from their somatic roots. When we speak of our world as an object or of our own bodies as mere objects in the world, we use language derived for our *lived* being-in-the-world, still bearing traces of its primitive rootedness in this prelingual situation (though, of course, this language has long since become "literal," as we say).

When I say what I have just said about that state of affairs upon which these words bear, I am employing the most abstract *reflexive* medium within my powers *to make a second* order reflexive comment upon this power and its prereflective source.

Discourse about mental phenomena is, then, *inherently* and uniquely reflexive: it is about mind in the medium of one of mind's preeminent powers, speech, which is reflected upon itself and this power. Hence it is *naturally* opaque, i.e., the very opposite of lucid. Lucidity cuts this knot of opacity and we then become body *opposed* to mind.

Orpheus I

To sightlessness is love consigned,
And, if it love, the thinking mind
Consents no less to being blind:

So the musician at the strings,
Withdrawn from all surrounding things,
Attends to what the music sings:

Orpheus descends, as he was taught,
Towards his dear remembered thought,
But lost in seeing what he sought.

Intensity surpassing sight,
Shadows of sensing hands invite
The concentration of delight

In all whose thought and love, compact,
Feel with a long and fingering tact
For outline of an artefact:

Orpheus in minds undoes the curse
That splits us into prose and verse;
And, shaping, finds the universe.[3]

3. Elizabeth Sewell, *Poems: 1947–1961* (Chapel Hill: University of North Carolina Press, 1961).

REFLECTIONS ON WALKER
PERCY'S THEORY OF LANGUAGE

Or, It is Better to Stay with Helen Keller at the Well-House in Tuscumbia, Alabama, than to Venture to Mars and be Devoured by the Ravening Particles

I

Walker Percy's sensibility captures and holds our attention because it embodies a plexus of puzzles. One of the puzzles is this: How does it happen that a writer so absolutely right in all his philosophical instincts should, when he undertakes to give them explicit embodiment in the medium of an essay, betray his own deepest insights? In order to answer that question, I wish to undertake a serious look at Walker Percy's theory of language, set forth in *The Message in the Bottle*, in the context of his vocation as a writer and critic. I should like to avoid any appearance here of arguing ad hominem; and I wish to take "A Theory of Language" with the absolute philosophical seriousness it both requires and deserves. While however carrying out this straightforward task in familiar ways, I wish to retain as its background the image of Percy as a paradigmatic case of the dropout from the "old modern age" who has turned critic of that age. For I shall be suggesting that dropping out is the most radical philosophic feat; that only men of the most complex sensibility—more complex than that of most professional philosophers—are inclined to

Panthea Reid Broughton, ed. *The Art of Walker Percy: Stratagems for Being* (Baton Rouge: Louisiana State University Press, 1979), 192–218.

do so; and that no one can consistently succeed, since it is analogous to carrying through the Cartesian program of sundering oneself from one's roots.

At the outset the reader should know of three general premises that shape these reflections. I shall make a defense only of the second and will elaborate but not defend the third.

First, I believe that the Walker Percy phenomenon can be fruitfully examined only if we realize that the existence-sphere in which he appears is irony: he is not serious in the same way about the practice of the art of fiction as is, say, Saul Bellow; nor is he serious in the same way about doing philosophy as was Charles Sanders Peirce, or even William James, one of whom he admires, the other of whom he resembles. Academic critics neglecting Percy's ironic pose will, I suspect, find his novels at once clever and profound but aesthetically incomplete. Academic philosophers, in a generous mood, will certainly find *The Message in the Bottle* pleasant reading, provocative at points, but not really "professional." At bottom, these two sorts of criticism come to the same thing. It is as if both the novels and the essays are the works of pseudonymous authors. What does it mean to say this? It means that neither were written as ends in themselves, but were written to serve other, undisclosed ends. The works in which Percy overcomes his irony and becomes "serious" are yet to come. I myself shall feel no loss if they never do.

Second, Percy's philosophy of language, especially as embodied in "A Theory of Language," is, I want to say, at bottom, or at the crux, *profoundly* confused. I do not mean hopelessly, utterly, or trivially confused. I mean confused as the result of exigent, original, and polemically deadly thought, confused in such a way as to require a sober and concentrated effort to understand its nature; I mean that his confusion is of a kind that, when it is understood, will shed a special kind of light, for it is not just the product of the eccentricity of one man vis-à-vis his own time, singular though he be, but the embodiment of the truncated radicalism of the criticism of a whole cultural atmosphere summed up in Percy's own name for the age beyond which we now live, "the old modern age."

Third, Percy's profoundest and most original contribution to the philosophy of language and to a theory of man is to be found not in those essays in which he is being dialectically most explicit and rigorous, as in "A Theory of Language," but in those in which he is being least so, as in "The Delta Factor." As to Percy's seriousness, it appears less in his own than in another's words. The epigraph to *The Last Gentleman,* for example, is from Romano Guardini: "Loneliness in faith will be terrible. Love will disappear from the face of the public world, but the more precious will be the love which flows from one lonely person to another."

II

Percy opens *The Message in the Bottle* with "The Delta Factor," the fulcrum of which is his discovery of the clue, in three short paragraphs of Helen Keller's *The Story of My Life,* to man's "breakthrough into the daylight of language."[1] That breakthrough parallels the original emergence of *Homo symbolificus.* Presenting man as symbol-monger, Percy hints broadly about the larger purpose that a theory of language is meant to serve: it is to be the philosophic ground of a theory of man.

It is his assumption that current theories of language are untenable and that "man's theory about himself doesn't work any more" either (*MB,* 19). An investigation of the phenomena of speech may perhaps shed light upon the question as to why men "prefer bad environments to good, a hurricane on Key Largo to an ordinary Wednesday in Short Hills" (*MB,* 27). Percy knows that "A theory of man must account for the alienation of man" (*MB,* 23); but the theories of the "old modern age," obsessed by seeking ever more ingenious explanations of this alienation either in the organism alone or in the environment alone, are clearly bankrupt. Percy then wonders, "Is there any other way to understand why people feel so bad in the twentieth century and writers feel so good writing about people feeling bad than in terms of the peculiar parameters, the joys and sorrows of symbol-mongering?" (*MB,* 45).

The investigation of *Homo symbolificus,* then, is to be the source of a new theory of man, of what used to be called a "philosophical anthropology." It is to be a view of man's place in the cosmos, an answer to the question by Pascal at the beginning of the "old modern age," asked by him with the special pathos of this question in that age: "For in fact what is man in nature? A nothing in comparison with the infinite, an All in comparison with the

---

1. Percy, *Message in the Bottle* (New York: Farrar, Straus, and Giroux, 1975), 3. Subsequent references will be made parenthetically in the text with the abbreviation *MB.*

Nothing, a mean between nothing and everything . . . the end of things and their beginning are hopelessly hidden from him in an impenetrable secret."[2]

Percy, of course, entertains no pretensions that in *The Message in the Bottle* he has offered even a down payment on such a comprehensive theory. I do take him however to believe that that view of man embodied in the thought of classical antiquity, in the Jewish and Christian theological-philosophical traditions, in the Continental, English, and American Enlightenment, is derived from and developed out of premises that, as a matter of fact, we do no longer hold or are well on our way to finding suspect. For these reasons we must make a new beginning. Percy believes that the new premises may well be found in the phenomenon *Homo symbolificus* and that at least one of the virtues that an investigation of this phenomenon may disclose is its power to account for man's deep, that is, native, constitutional alienation as *Homo symbolificus*. We find that Percy seeks an explanatory theory of language to account for two different phenomena: the fact that Helen Keller, in a few hours, and most of the rest of us, in months, break through into "the daylight of language" by discovering the one-word elliptical sentence, "[this is] water," discovering, in short, that things have names; and that having made this breakthrough, we humans are forever alienated from our environment, cast out of the Eden of mere organismic life into the world to suffer the "joys and the sorrows of symbol-mongering" (*MB*, 45). Thus we feel "bad in good environments and good in bad environments" because symbols intervene between our experience and ourselves (*MB*, 3).

Let me now traverse a wide arc (to return at the end of this essay) over 253 pages from the end of "The Delta Factor" to the beginning of "A Theory of Language" in *The Message in the Bottle*, in order more explicitly to connect the aims of the developed theory to the larger philosophical goals it is designed to serve.

There is a real injustice to Percy in this procedure, since even though it follows the logic of the book and, in a sense, the logic of the argument, it reverses the actual chronology of composition. Also Percy's most compelling treatment of language is set in the philosophically ample and relaxed setting of "The Delta Factor" amid the concrete images of Helen Keller at the wellhouse, "the sadness of an ordinary Wednesday in Short Hills," and "the joys

---

2. *Pensées*, trans. W. F. Trotter, with an introduction by T. S. Eliot (London: J. M. Dent and Son, 1948), Fragment 71.

and sorrows of symbol-mongering" (*MB*, 45). Here, too, much of the argument is formulated in dialogue, that is, in the concrete representation of speech acts. Finally, in "The Delta Factor" we feel Walker Percy himself right there, in a first personal narrative passage such as this: "Would it be possible, I was wondering then in Louisiana, to use the new key to open a new door and see in a new way? See man not the less mysterious but of a piece, maybe even whole, a whole creature put together again after the three-hundred-year-old Cartesian split that sundered man from himself in the old modern age" (*MB*, 44). This pathos, this concreteness, this narrative and dialogue keep Percy close to his own incarnate reality as a speaker, himself often sad on ordinary mornings, and close therefore to the irreducible and radical truth about language that he sees.

However, if we are to take him seriously as a philosopher of language we must take him where he and we stand most to profit from what I have called his profound confusion, and for that we turn to "A Theory of Language." In this essay, we are warned in its subtitle, Percy has discovered that no explanatory theory of language exists and proposes what he calls a crude model of such a theory on the ground that something is better than nothing.

Bloomfield, Harris, and Chomsky, different though their methods are, offer no explanatory theory of language because, approaching the phenomenon "through a formal analysis of the corpora of languages," their analysis, Percy says, "abstracts both from the people who speak the language and the things they talk about" (*MB*, 299). Taking Chomsky as the example, Percy points out that "transformational grammar is not an explanatory theory of language as phenomenon but rather a formal description, an algorithm, of the competence of a person who speaks a language" (*MB*, 304). Percy then goes on to explain: "There is no evidence that this algorithm bears a necessary relation to what is happening *inside the head* of a person who speaks or understands a sentence" (*MB*, 304, italics added). I call attention to the words *inside the head* because it seems clear to me that, for Percy (though it is not clear that he appreciates this), even though the Chomskians allow for making the distinction between what is "outside the head" and what must be (logically) "somewhere else," they fail of an explanatory theory because they cannot connect what is "outside the head" with anything "inside" it. For Chomsky it would be grammar and syntax that are "outside the head" and a computerlike Language Acquisition Device or a preset restriction on the form of grammar (which would really have no logical relation to the cerebral cortex) that would be "somewhere else." For Percy and Geschwind, we learn in "A Theory of Language," the "somewhere else" would be the inferior parietal lobule "inside the head" (*MB*, 326–67).

B. F. Skinner and the learning theorists, on the other hand, do "offer a plenary model of language as a phenomenon, which meets all the specifications of explanatory theory," but it is wrong, according to Percy (*MB*, 303). My suspicion is that Skinner's proposals count for Percy as an explanatory theory, although an erroneous one, because, bad as it is, the dyadic model of S → s → r → R allows us to get "inside the head," which is a move in the right direction away from the ghostly, discarnate transformation rules of the Cartesians.

It needs to be observed here however that Skinner's model allows for the "inside the head"–"outside the head" distinction only by means of a pseudosubstitution. That is, on its face, sign and stimulus, signified and response, seem to be logically homogeneous concepts.[3] A strict application of Skinner's principles however makes it clear that either *sign* is "reduced" to *stimulus*, in which case the hierarchical distinction between "inside the head"–"outside the head" vanishes; or *sign* and *stimulus* are logically heterogeneous, and Skinner's theory is only a very clumsy and covert version of the theory Percy himself wishes to advocate. In short, Percy seems not to have noticed that the appeal to the "inside the head"–"outside the head" distinction as a ground for distinguishing between a mere descriptive theory and a false explanatory one can be applied simultaneously to his two instant cases, Skinner and Chomsky, only in a logically most *equivocal* and therefore *profoundly* (in my above sense) confusing way.

For, applied strictly in Skinner's theory, "inside the head" would refer to the "hard-nosed" empirically located excitations traveling along neural paths in the cerebral cortex; "outside the head" would refer to such S → R structures closer to the body's surface or, extending "outward" from there in the empirically located environment. In Skinner's theory as he would like it to be, logically, "inside" and "outside" are of precisely the same order. This being so, "inside" and "outside" are indistinguishable, hence without sense.

---

3. I do not argue here from Langer's distinction between "sign" and "symbol" upon which Percy relies. My premise is the more radical contention that "sign" is logically heterogeneous with "stimulus." If true, then a fortiori, "symbol" and "stimulus" are heterogeneous.

At most they refer merely to different "regions" of a homogeneous universe of S → R relations. For Percy this is an explanatory theory, but a wrong one because, though empirically grounded, it assimilates *signs* to *stimulus*.

Applied strictly in Chomsky's theory, "outside the head" would refer to "the corpora of language," which is logically irreducible to mere signs, hence to that which is logically homogeneous with events in the cerebral cortex. For Percy, this is a theory that *describes* language as irreducibly *language,* as we all understand this notion commonsensically, but it *explains* nothing because it is unable to connect these irreducibly linguistic phenomena to anything definite in our brains, except through the medium of the black-box Language Acquisition Device, which stands to Chomsky's theory as the pineal gland stands to Descartes's.

We shall have to see whether, when he advances his own "crude" explanatory theory, Percy avoids the horns of the dilemma, which he rightly deplores. But—grossly to simplify—Percy's unease with the structuralists and the behaviorists is due to the fact that the theories of both are abstracted from the irreducible phenomena, speaking-meaning, hearing-comprehending meaning: the first from the body, speech organs, and brain of the speaker situated in the world saying what he means to his hearers about their mutual world; the second from the human mind, that is, the act (as opposed to the behavior) of speaking. Chomsky analyzes "speech" as if it took place only among gods; Skinner as if it took place only among *essentially* dumb brutes. There are really no speakers in either theory.

If I understand Percy aright, he wishes in his own theory to do away with this "either an angel or a brute" dilemma and to do this in an explanatory theory that does not scant the act of speaking. However, in due course, I shall try to show that he fails to do so because he *too* has been guilty of abstraction, by a failure to keep under his feet at every moment, however usefully he might analytically elaborate upon it, that ground which is the primordial setting out of which each man's reflection upon language is generated. He fails to locate his discussion in the radical linguistic (I would say, human) reality, the admittedly precarious, conceptually elusive, and ontologically ambiguous ground upon which each one of us uniquely stands; that is, Percy too disregards our power of authoring, authorizing, standing-by, and owning-up to the words we speak in our own names.

A theory of language that is not generated out of and reintegrated to this phenomenon of speech avails us mainly confusion. Any act of reflection that does not allude to its own ontological radix antecedent to reflection will always issue in reflected dualisms that will not be healed. Thus, the study of language, wherever it may venture in the meantime, must, it begins to appear, start and finish in integration with the irreducible reality of speakers saying and meaning what they say about their ambient world and of hearers comprehending what is said and meant. And discourse on *syntax* or *verbal behavior* that does not integrate the speaking acts or writing acts of its actually existent author is an incomplete and potentially incoherent account of language.

We have seen how both Chomsky and Skinner reject, ignore, or forget this: the one as a methodological bracketing out, from which the theory in all its lucid angelism cannot recover; the other as an alleged empirical finding upon which the thoroughly incarnate theory is held to be based. Given the deepgoing intellectual currents of the "old modern age," if a theory is not incoherent at the outset, as Skinner's, but merely *incomplete,* as Chomsky's, hence only potentially incoherent, it will become *actually incoherent* when it is interpreted by the denizens of that age.

Percy's ironic relation to the "old modern age" is not enough to save him from an even subtler form of the same blunder. The Ravening Particles cast up by its residual dualisms—matter or mind, things or thought, theoretical reason or practical reason, object or subject—these devour the very substance of reflection. When the idea of the search occurs to one, as it has to Percy, he had better be prepared to take with absolute philosophic seriousness first, the irreducible equivocalness of an inquiry into language; second, the need to stake out, accredit, and dwell in a ground in his own personal ensconcement in the world; and finally the irreducible ontological hierarchy among things in the world and the logical heterogeneity of concepts.[4] The shrewd amateur's intuitive grasp of the fundamental issues, overlooked by the "serious"

---

4. The concepts of logical heterogeneity and of ontological hierarchy are complementary. Two concepts are logically heterogeneous when the repertoire of concepts with which they function is different, e.g., heart in anatomy and in contract bridge. Ontological hierarchy refers to the fact that an inventory strictly limited to the physical-chemical properties of what we antecedently know to be a machine could not include the principles of mechanics, i.e., the principles in terms of which we would understand what it is for something to be a machine. Such an inventory of the printed letters on a page equally could not include conventions of spelling, grammatical or syntactical rules. Metals and letters are ontologically—that is, as to the nature of their being—subordinate as entities to the machines and sentences that they jointly respectively make up, subject to mechanical rules and spelling conventions, grammar and syntax.

specialist who is really by definition a reductionist, even the novelist's natural eros for the concrete, will not protect him when he gets to the crux of these issues. He will have to go farther back—or down—"ontologically" before going forward.

The mystery of our human mode of being, of our lived irreducible unity in apparent duality, comes to focus, is deepened, and radicalized in the inherently equivocal status of language. Let us, then, look more closely at this, as prolegomenon to the criticism of Percy's theory.

If I were to make a list of all of the things and of all of the sorts of things that there are in the world, say rocks, Williston Bibb Barrett's funny knee, amoebas, Halley's comet, neural traces; the gross national product of Sri Lanka in 1971, the fastest one-hundred-meter footrace ever run, black holes in space, a blackwhole in space, *The Tempest,* fantasies, my postcoital depression of June 2, 1975, logical entailment, *Don Giovanni,* the square roots of all the numbers from one to ten, people writing down words as I am here writing them down, people "thinking" about words as they write them down as I am "here" "thinking" about these words—*this* very word coming out of the end of my pen—as I write it down—if, I say, I were to make such a list, I would do so by using words as I have done here.

Imagine that I hand you my list, saying, "Here are all of the things and the sorts of things there are in the world." You might properly reply: "All of the things and the sorts of things there are in the world are not on this piece of paper; only their names. And that being so, you need to add two further names of things to the list, viz., *names of things* and *names of sorts of things;* or *proper names* and *class-terms.*" Are the words I have just used to make the statement characterizing my list and your words used to take exception to that characterization of it, and to amplify it, among the things and the sorts of things on my list? If not, and I believe they are not, then what I have said to you and what you have said in reply are not among the things in the world; nor are they among the names of things in the world, not if the list is taken to be an exhaustive one, not if the limits of the list define the world. And, by the way, reader, do you notice anywhere among the words on this page, me, William H. Poteat, their author? No? Would, then, an attestation clause, signed by witnesses, help?

Here we see a few of the ways in which certain words used in certain ways with the authority of having been authored are funny sorts of things. The woman with whom I live hands me her grocery list: "Here's what we need for lunch," she says. At once a smartass and philosophically "profound," I say, "That may be what you need, but I intend to *eat* something for lunch." We are looking at the words on the list in two different, equally legitimate, equally revealing ways—though surely hers is the more ordinary way. The above words beginning with "we are looking at the words" are no part of the crossed transaction between me and the lady about what we respectively require for lunch. I want to say that *those* words, the words "We are looking at the words" are at one logical remove from *that* conversation even as what I am saying about the words being at *one* logical remove from it is at *two* logical removes. And I, William H. Poteat, who am authorizing these words, claim these words as I author them while denying that I *am* them or am exhaustively *in* them, even though I can claim what I am claiming about the incommensurability of me and my words as beings or entities only *in* words by owning them as mine. And even, if in claiming these words as mine I own them, you are not likely to take offense either at my using the words or claiming them as mine, even though they are indeed yours and you may even claim them. And if no such dispute arises between us, it is neither because our relations are unusually genial nor because we don't know how to use the words *mine* and *own,* but rather because words are these strange sorts of things that are *there,* kind of in the world, and *there* for everybody, like space and time, and yet are there at all, *as* words, only when they are, in a way, the "private" property of a speaker who knows he owns them and admits to doing so, or will do so, or will deny doing so, if asked, "Do you really mean that?"

These are only a few of the strange, fascinating, and equivocal features of the act of speaking and writing words about speaking and writing. Because of these features, and others, Maurice Merleau-Ponty has been moved to say: "Language becomes something mysterious, since it is neither a self nor a thing. . . . [It] is neither a thing nor mind, but it is immanent and transcendent at the same time."[5] Percy understands all this and writes of it with originality, wit, polemical bite, and the ingenuousness of the true amateur who allows us to share in his wonder and to be edified by his naïveté. At the same time he writes from a background of sophisticated appreciation of some of the major writings on linguistics.

---

5. *Consciousness and the Acquisition of Language,* trans. Hugh J. Silverman (Evanston, Ill.: Northwestern University Press, 1973), 5–6.

III

For all of this being so, however, between his reflections on the girl Helen Keller in an ecstasy at the well-house in Tuscumbia, Alabama, in 1887, at the discovery that things have names, through which he discovers "The Delta Factor" and his appeal in the last pages of "A Theory of Language" to the "human inferior parietal lobule" to account for this miracle, Percy acts out an intellectual drama that is as familiar as the history of the "old modern age." But Percy is a novelist who remains at once empathically close to and ironically detached from the alienated victims of abstraction, the "loss of the creature," the expertise, everydayness, and angelism that fill his novels. Yet he himself becomes a victim of that same abstraction when in his philosophical essays he loses his grip upon himself and thus upon the something that he is "onto." One of Percy's mentors, Soren Kierkegaard, might have applauded this way to "wound from behind" wherein even he who delivers the blow is himself wounded.

When we shall have examined in detail "A Theory of Language," we may come to suspect that the Martian whom Percy imagines looking pristinely at language among men on earth is in fact Walker Percy, and that Walker Percy is Williston Bibb Barrett in the Metropolitan Museum of Art where "the harder one looked, the more invisible the paintings became."[6] And so with Percy-Martian and the phenomena of speech. If only he had applied Dr. Thomas More's Qualitative Quantitative Ontological Lapsometer[7] to his own brain at the moment of wishing to view human speech from Mars, he would have immediately diagnosed that impulse as angelism!

In "A Theory of Language" Percy, obedient to Enlightenment philosophical injunctions, is looking very hard at language, but the harder one looks at the reflexivity of our relation to language, the more invisible it becomes. Language is man's singularity and therefore is a unique object of investigation; but any inquiry into speaking, hearing, and understanding is, like all inquiry, conducted in the medium of speaking, hearing, and understanding. It is therefore inherently and uniquely reflexive. That is why most readers of grocery lists think of groceries, not words, and why, as Percy says in "The Delta Factor," scientists who know a great deal about the world know less

6. Percy, *The Last Gentleman* (New York: Farrar, Straus, and Giroux, 1966), 27.
7. See Percy, *Love in the Ruins* (New York: Farrar, Straus, and Giroux, 1971), 226.

about language than about the backside of the moon. The phenomena of speech may be reflexively "observable," and speaking is certainly "observable behavior," but they are not observable as is the backside of the moon. Scientists as scientists are professionally committed to lucidity. Reflexivity is naturally opaque. The Ravening Particles—Cartesian dualism, the loss of the creature, the secret wish to "be useful to the behavioral scientist" (*MB*, 325), even while you suspect him—are "stealing the substance from [language] and viewer alike."[8]

B. F. Skinner and Noam Chomsky prize lucidity; that is why they prefer *Verbal Behavior* and *Aspects in the Theory of Syntax*, which are lucid, to accounts of speech phenomena that would make sense by coming to terms with the messy, opaque reflexivity of the speech about speech, which are not. Part of Percy's instincts, as he acknowledges in "The Delta Factor," are "on the side of the scientists in general and in particular on the side of the hardheaded empiricism of American behavioral science" (*MB*, 34); and that part of Percy is still at work insisting upon an explanatory theory of language. Thus in "A Theory of Language," he prefers the theory that refers to the "human inferior parietal lobule," because it will be more "useful to the behavioral scientist." However, Percy's own theory leaves the nature of the act of speech an utter mystery. This part of Percy harbors the same secret Promethean longings for lucidity that Skinner and Chomsky harbor; and such lucidity is the animus par excellence of the Enlightened "old modern age," of which Dr. Thomas More with his Lapsometer is the diagnostician.

IV

"A Theory of Language" proffers "a crude explanatory" theory of language on the assumption that none now exists and that something is better than nothing. Though Percy does not formulate his question as I do, I believe that I can articulate his perception of the problem. Here I am, he says, a dropout from the "old modern age," scarred by its dualisms. Commonsensically, I believe acritically in the singularity and uniqueness of my own acts of speaking and of comprehending speech. It is just as different as it could possibly be from the picture that is offered me by B. F. Skinner and his

8. Percy, *Last Gentleman*, 26.

insufferable pigeons. And yet, no doubt about it, there has just got to be an ontological connection between things like those very carnal pigeons and my carnal body and brain, so that, if I am to make integral sense of the fact that I speak, that sense will have to acknowledge my body and brain situated in the world.

On the other hand, while Chomsky reinforces my acritical belief in the unassimilability of human languages, with their literally infinite variety, to a mere limited repertoire of signs and what they signify or stimuli and the responses they produce, he shows as little interest as Skinner in my singularity as the author and owner of my own spoken words. What's more, he propagates the same sad old dualism from the other side: an "upward" or angelistic reductionism.

If I can find an explanatory theory of language (I imagine Percy thinking), one that unites in one integral comprehension the different sorts of realities of body and brain, language acquisition, the phenomenon of sentence formation, and the act of a speaker authoring and owning what he says, while even so not being contained within or exhausted by what he says, then I shall have solid philosophical grounds—and I will offer them to you—for believing what I literally cannot help believing. I shall be able to affirm that the singularity of my acts of speech and yours are not *in* the world, as acts, even when our "words" are there. I shall heal the dualisms between thinking thing and extended thing by discovering a "third" thing, namely, my personal act of authorizing my own words. I shall, in disclosing how in acts of speech I at once appear in the world, yet remain less than fully disclosed to it, thereby provide the ground for a theory of man that will account for his alienation. And, lastly, then: "Mightn't one even speak of such a thing as the Helen Keller phenomenon, which everyone experiences at the oddest and most unlikely times? Prince Andrei lying wounded on the field of Borodino and discovering clouds for the first time. Or the Larchmont commuter whose heart attack allows him to see his own hand for the first time" (*MB*, 41).

So I imagine Walker Percy thinking down there in Louisiana. Now, before taking the next step, I wish to issue, with some diffidence, since I shall not develop it at all, a necessary caveat regarding the concepts "explain" and "explanatory." They are multiply ambiguous. What counts as an explanation is not one, two, or even half a dozen sorts of things. We suffer many different sorts of mental cramp; and that will count as an explanation which relieves it. Descartes's mental cramp could not be cured by reading Aristotle. Percy's, and my, cramp about language is not much relieved by reading Skinner, Chomsky, or Rudolph Carnap. And in claiming this I am not at all suggesting that you can relieve your mental cramp by just settling for any old explanation that makes you feel good. Mental cramp is a real, objective state, and only that explanation which is specific to it will cure it.

The heart of Percy's crude model, as he calls it, both in its polemical implications for the other existing putative theories and in its constructive implications, is his distinction between a merely dyadic linear, cause-effect, stimulus-response, H_2SO_4 reacting to $NaOH$, energy exchange relation, on the one hand, while on the other hand he sets up a nonlinear, nonenergic phenomenon that is so complex that no simpler model than that of a triad will suffice to represent it—or as he has it in "The Delta Factor"—"a natural phenomenon in which energy exchanges account for some but not all of what happens" (*MB*, 39). With Helen Keller, water running over one hand while Miss Sullivan writes the word water in her other, we are confronted by a phenomenon that cannot be understood dyadically; that is, no linear stringing together of the three terms *Helen, water,* and *"water"* by a sequence of arrows, in any order, can represent the "break through into the daylight of language." The simplest formula that will not *over*simplify the reality is the figure:

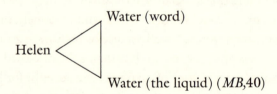

The triangle is irreducible.

This distinction between dyadic and triadic relations is the fulcrum of Percy's argument. I shall animadvert to this in due course as the source of his *profound* confusion. For the moment, let me draw attention to the diagram above in which, being two dimensional, *Helen, water,* and *"water"* are all represented as *on a single plane*—on its face a trivial deficiency, but, I think, one rich in potentiality for logical mischief. And the reason for this is that the dyad-triad distinction, *by itself,* is not sufficient to make Percy's point. The triad must be *interpreted* in a certain way, by Percy as he writes out his theory and thinks, "Does it work?" and by me when I read it, wondering the same thing. If the imagination is bewitched for an instant by the visual metaphor of the diagram, trouble is in store. If the triad must be interpreted, then it can be *mis*interpreted, which means that Percy will have to superintend the working of his metaphor with the utmost delicacy. Even dropouts from the "old modern age" are routinely bewitched by visual metaphors.

Let us, however, show schematically what it is that Percy has hoped to do with the argument from the irreducibly triadic structure of the Delta Factor. Through the application of Delta it is possible to impeach Skinner's wrong explanatory theory. By claiming, too, that it provides the ground or the model for connecting to what goes on inside the cerebral cortex the syntactical and semantical elements of the language phenomenon (which phenomenon is taken seriously in different ways and in different degrees by Chomsky and the semioticists), it is possible to articulate a true explanatory theory. Finally, the triadic model will also provide a plausible way to think of language acquisition that neither reduces the process simply to operant conditioning, as in Skinner's *Verbal Behavior*, nor capitulates in despair to a black box theory, nor makes an implausible application of Peirce's theory of abduction as a solution of the problem of the LAD as with Chomsky.

Percy, I take it, is really making the following points: a theory of language has to take seriously the facts that people speak to one another about all manner of things in their mutual world; that they are able to do this because they follow (grammatical, syntactical, and semantical) rules that they "know" and upon which they are "agreed" without ever having been taught them or ever having made a contract about them; that had anyone been initiated into a different speech community, the same sorts of requirements for speaking would obtain, and the same human powers for meeting those analogous but different requirements would be available; and finally, that these extraordinary elaborations out of our merely organismic being must somehow be seen as comportable with the bodies, brains, and speech organs of carnal men in their ambient world. All of these are equally bedrock desiderata for an explanatory theory of language.

Therefore Percy says, "The main error of a generative grammar considered as a theory of language is that its main component is syntactical with semantic and phonological components considered as 'interpretations' thereof" (*MB*, 304). The crux, then, of Percy's theory of language insofar as it is to have the desired *explanatory* power is just here. He says: "For some time I had supposed that the basic event which occurs when one utters or understands a sentence must be triadic in nature (Percy). That is to say, sentences comprise two elements which must be coupled by a coupler" (*MB*, 324). All seems quite innocent and regular, so far, even if not entirely clear. And then he continues, "This occurs in both the naming sentence, when semiological and phonological elements are coupled, and in the standard declarative NP-VP sentence which comprises what one talks about and what one says about it" (*MB*, 324).

But then suddenly I begin to suspect that Percy and I use the word *sentence* differently. I know very well what it is like to speak a grammatical sentence in English about something in our mutual world; but what is it to "couple semiological and phonological elements"? What do we gain by abstracting from the universe where speakers speak words about the world that others hear and understand? Then I remember a telling word above: the "*basic* event which occurs when one utters or understands a sentence must be triadic in nature," and I feel the ground tremble ever so slightly. If the event we are talking about is more basic (say, located in the cerebral cortex) than people talking, listening, comprehending what is being said about what it is being said, then is it conceptually comportable with concepts like "sentence" and "sentence element" used in the ordinary, old-fashioned way I had taken Percy to intend? I begin to see that Percy is taking concepts to be logically homogeneous that, it seems to me, are obviously heterogeneous; that where I would want to talk about ontological hierarchy or levels of being he, bemused, I would have a hunch, by the desire to "see man whole, a whole creature put together again after the three-hundred-year-old Cartesian split," slips in that familiar way by slow degrees toward the built-in monistic "downward" reduction of the "old modern age"—the very last thing he wants to do, and that I know. So perhaps I have him wrong.

But then the next thing I see is this diagram:

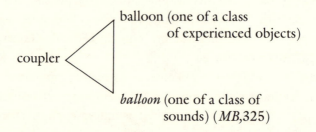

and I am told that this is a diagram of an event that occurs "inside both father and son" when a father utters the sound (why is it not a word that he utters?) *balloon* and the son looks and nods (*MB*, 324).

I stare at this diagram, cracking my head: "The coupler" (that's basic, I remember that) is inside the father. But the balloon is not inside the father; if it were, the boy would not have nodded; neither is *balloon*. The boy heard *balloon* because his father managed to get it outside. Yet the diagram, since it is drawn *on* a single plane, would suggest that the concept "coupler" means to be on the page, largely context free—and the concepts "balloon" and *"balloon,"* as they stand there on the printed page, are logically homogeneous. And yet obviously this is just not true, and, I think, "Oh, the treachery of triads!"

But, then, I say, "What an all-too-familiar mistake for us dropouts from the 'old modern age'—devoured as we are by Ravening Particles—abstraction, dualism, and reductionism." Walker didn't mean that, and he and I both know it. So absolutely right and sure of himself when, in irony, he is spoofing the behavioral sciences, he suffers an attack of reductionistic amnesia while reading with enlightened earnestness Geschwind's "Disconnection Syndromes in Animals and Man." He said it all, not quite accurately but with a fine sense for ontological hierarchy and for logical heterogeneity in his "Delta Factor." He says: "Then what can one say for sure about the three elements of the Delta phenomenon? Only this: The boy in Delta is not the organism boy. The balloon in Delta is not the balloon in the world. The *balloon* in Delta is not the sound balloon." And then he adds: "An unpromising beginning" (*MB*, 44). But then, perhaps, he asks for too much.

And I find myself wanting to say a number of other things.

First, *balloon* is not "one of a class of sounds"—sounds, that is to say, that sound like "balloon." *Balloon,* the word, does indeed have a sound, sort of like *maroon* and *poltroon,* and as having a sound, is a member of a class of soundalikes. But it is a sound that, *as word,* is a member of the class of names. "Here is conceptual hierarchy," I say to myself.

Second, a sentence, unless you are going to start doing something really funny with it, is an irreducibly linguistic entity and its elements are linguistic entities. These elements, and the sentences that comprehend the elements, exist at all *only* for speakers, that is, people who hear words with their ears rather than with their auditory cortex, even though they would be up against it when it came to hearing if they *had* no such cortex: people who comprehendingly utter, that is speak, words with their mouths and own what they have said. A conceptual universe where *speaker* and *hearer* do not appear is one in which the concept "sentence" and therefore the *concept sentence* element have no meaning. "Here is conceptual heterogeneity," I think.

It is oversight of cases of this sort that leads Percy into puzzling claims like the following. He says: "Let us say nothing about the physiological or ontological status of the 'coupler.' Suffice it for the present to say that if two elements of a sentence are coupled,"—that is balloon and *balloon* of the above diagram—"we may speak of a coupler. Indeed, the behavioral equivalent of Descartes's *Cogito, ergo sum* may be: If the two elements of a sentence are coupled, there must be a coupler. The latter dictum would seem to be more useful to the behavioral scientist, including transformational linguists, than Descartes's, because Descartes's thinking is not observable but his speech is" (*MB*, 325). There are several important philosophical contracts being negotiated in this passage, and, I believe, the ground for a good deal of litigation is being laid. I pass over in silence the questions as to the observability of Descartes's "thinking" and his "speech."

First, and in passing, it simply will not do to "say nothing about the physiological or ontological status of the 'coupler,'" for it is only by specifying this that our conceptual orientation can be established to the diagram in which it appears, to the way in which *sentence, sentence element,* and *coupled* are understood to be functioning as concepts. Without this guidance we are, where the diagram is concerned, left with very close to the complete abstraction: black triangular figure on a white ground. And if reference is made to the words about the pointing father and the nodding boy as the exegetical device for interpreting the diagram, then we are once again openly faced with the question as to how the former is overlaid on the latter, which is to raise precisely the question about the ontological status of the coupler.

It seems clear to me that Percy emphatically does want, in the interest of his own argument, at least to say that whatever may be happening in the cerebral cortex and whatever neurophysiological events may be occurring in the "human inferior parietal lobule, which includes the angular and supramarginal gyri, to a rough approximation areas 39 and 40 of Brodmann" (*MB*, 326) as the *conditio sine qua non* of speech acquisition—again, whatever happens there—the "coupler"—you, I, Helen Keller, Walker Percy, who go about naming things—has the status of a speaker, a symbol user in the absolutely irreducible sense. If this is not his point, then he has capitulated entirely; and if it is, then his argument leaves the mystery of the integration of the act of speaking with neurophysiological events—even triadic ones—in areas thirty-nine and forty of Brodmann no nearer explanation.

Percy, too, it appears, has left out the speaker! By failing to stay closely in touch with himself, the author, speaker, and writer-down of his own theory, he slips into the reductionistic amnesia of the "old modern age." This is the humiliation of dropout critics! And in "The Delta Factor," I believe Percy, with some sadness, admits that this is so.

When, therefore, Percy asks, "What else indeed is the child up to for months at a time when it goes around naming everything in sight—or asking its name—than establishing these functional intercortical connections?" (*MB*, 326), we must reply, "Why, he is naming everything in sight." And we can underline the heterogeneity of concepts that are being taken to be homogeneous by observing that in the conceptual landscape where one finds *areas of Brodmann, intercortical connection,* and *inferior parietal lobule* one will look in vain for *child* and *naming.*

Finally, a kindness to poor old Descartes from a dropout from the "old modern age": He was very careless when he promised to divest his mind of all his previous knowledge in order to begin with only the certain, since he forgot to rid it of Latin and of French. It therefore remained possible for him to say *Cogito, ergo sum* and *Je pense, donc je suis.* But when he uttered the words *Cogito, ergo sum,* I do not take it that Descartes had absconded, leaving behind only the sound of his voice on the wind. I believe he was openly and unambiguously a speaker speaking and not a coupler coupling. And confused (and *profoundly* confused, too) though Descartes often was, I think he would not have supposed as Percy would seem to have it (*MB*, 325) that the sounds (words) or the marks (words), *Cogito, ergo sum,* were really a disowned black box from which the "secret contents" in the form of a "behavioral equivalent" might one day be extracted. For, of course, there is no (merely) behavioral equivalent to the said or written down authorized words, *Cogito, ergo sum.* There is, however, a behavioral equivalent to, for example, the sworn testimony of a young constable of Amsterdam, taken in January of 1641. Geulinex de Groot, by name, a Dutchman without any classical learning, he deposed, "Renatus Cartesius, a Frenchman, otherwise known as Rene Descartes, opened his mouth and out came the hideous sounds *cogito ergo sum.*"

V

What then, in conclusion, am I saying about Percy's explanatory theory of language? Would he have been better occupied attempting other things? Not at all. The "Delta Factor" is a potent dialectical weapon against Chomsky, the transformationalists, the semioticists, and Skinner. It serves to put the language phenomenon back into the setting where it belongs, among human speakers and hearers; in doing so it clears the ground for new reflection on the human condition as Percy had hoped.

Admittedly, as he himself says, there is "very little to be sure of," but Delta does provide a better angle of vision and maybe more, yielding "a new world and maybe a new way of getting at it." And even if in the long run it were to turn out to be impossible "to arrive at an explanatory theory of language in any ordinary sense of the word" (*MB*, 323), it need not at all follow that we shall be condemned to revert to homunculus biology. The suggestion that such a reversion would be implied in this failure is but the bitter reflection of a disappointed child of the "old modern age" where total explicitness, as we were given meaninglessly and misleadingly to saying, is possible at least in principle.

Am I then saying that the integration of the "autonomous" phenomena of speech and language acquisition to what "goes on inside the brain" is impossible? I believe not; at least, I do not know that to be so. Percy, I think, has achieved an edifying and *profound* failure. This failure is especially likely to be edifying if we view him as the paradigm of the dropout from and critic of the "old modern age." He has shown us that a keen sense of ontological hierarchy and of the many valences that bind different concepts together in different ways will have to be carried into the research, along with Delta.

How, then, does all this bear upon Percy's hope that by reflecting upon man's breakthrough into the daylight of language he may come to see man of a piece, a whole creature put together again after he has been sundered from himself in the "old modern age"? How does it provide a clue for a new theory of man?

When we raise these questions on the far side of the confusions evoked by the conceptual equivocations of "A Theory of Language," they undergo a subtle change of meaning and weight. What has been perceived hitherto as Percy's philosophical naïveté suddenly can be appreciated as something intimately related to but quite different from mere naïveté, namely, the misexplication of Percy's profoundly significant intuition into the roots of our human being; Percy finds that our humanity is distinguished both by *our power to speak* and by *our alienation*.

In "A Theory of Language" Percy agonistically contends, and often unsuccessfully, with the dualism that threatens the reality of man's incarnate freedom by issuing the dilemma: either angelism or bestialism. Despite his efforts, dualism prevails in this contest. Nevertheless, in his novels, in many of the essays in *The Message in the Bottle,* and preeminently in "The Delta Factor," Percy's profoundest and most original philosophical intuition is given. Here, free of the self-set demand for a philosophical rigor that, cultivated in the "old modern age," has a built-in gravitational drift toward dualism, Percy willingly gives himself over to the power of his imagination to make an unfamiliar juxtaposition of images.

The litany of questions in "A Delta Factor" begins with "Why does man feel so sad in the twentieth century?" (*MB,* 3) and culminates with "Is there any other way to understand why people feel so bad in the twentieth century and writers feel so good writing about people feeling bad than in terms of the peculiar parameters, the joys and sorrows of symbol-mongering?" (*MB,* 45). The conclusion of these reflections, which have their own tonality and work their way with our imaginations by means of rhetorical strategies other than those of philosophical argument, juxtaposes *symbol-mongering* and *alienation,* a veritable Peircean abduction by Percy.

In *my* act of speaking (and this must always be articulated in the first-person singular), in my act of laying claim to the tokens in our mutual native language to *say* something in my own name, while relying upon my body, brain, vocal cords, and tongue *in* the world, I perform the act by which these several strata are integrated to a meaning that *transcends* the world. In this act all dualisms are healed and my incarnate freedom becomes manifest. Yet the very incommensurability of the *act* of speaking with everything upon which it relies puts me in opposition to myself; in contradiction with myself; literally, speaking against myself. In my world-transcending act of speaking there appear both my incarnate freedom and my ontological unease—in every environment that might offer ease. Because I speak and insofar as I dwell in my own words I always have the feeling of being once-removed. My existence is always threatened by being merely ironical, by being lived in the subjunctive mood. As Percy writes in *Love in the Ruins,* "Only in man does the self miss itself." *Symbol-mongering* and *feeling bad:* The model provided by this juxtaposition is, I believe, the very radix of Percy's imagination, the source of this profoundest reflection, given by him an absolutely original form, shaping everything he has written. It is singular: a more valuable contribution to the philosophy of language and philosophical anthropology than the particulars of the argument in "A Theory of Language." For it is the very stone ignored by the zealous philosophical builders. And as a model upon which to devise a new theory of man capable of expressing his finite freedom, it is heuristically more fecund and closer to our concrete being than models based upon oppositions and juxtapositions such as Buber's I-Thou versus I-It, Sartre's *en-soi* versus *pour-soi*, Marcel's problem versus mystery, or Heidegger's *Sein, das Seiendes, Dasein,* with all of which it deserves comparison.

Here, in "The Delta Factor," Walker Percy has not surrendered his sovereignty to the "experts," he has not given in to the deep-going "old modern age" longing to force all one's serious claims into a rigorous and explicit philosophic medium. Here he has retained his hold upon the creature.

GEORGE STEINER

The Extra-Territorial Critic

I

George Steiner, even were nothing else involved, would arrest our attention by the sheer grandeur of his dialectical and lexical tonus. The density of his style—the contrapuntal tension, the timbre, the nuance, the flexibility, and the resonance with the rich verbal legacy of the whole history of the literature of Western culture, whose daily recession from our literacy is an elegiac overtone to everything he writes—is itself a striking counterexample of what he has called "the retreat from the word."

With the addition of two volumes in a single year to an already impressive oeuvre, however, the Extraordinary Fellow of Churchill College, Cambridge, publishes an extra-territorial claim to being a major critic of modern culture.[1] And his announcement that he is currently engaged upon a basic work on hermeneutics, considering the sweep, the radicalism, and the flexibility of his erudition, suggests that this claim is still to be even further enlarged.

Soundings **45.4 (1972): 421–37.**
1. Steiner's *Extra-Territorial: Papers on Literature and the Language Revolution* (New York: Atheneum) and *In Bluebeard's Castle: Some Notes towards the Redefinition of Culture* (New Haven: Yale University Press) were both published in 1971. Other works in his oeuvre are *Tolstoy or Dostoevsky* (New York: Alfred A. Knopf, 1959); *The Death of Tragedy* (New York: Alfred A. Knopf, 1961); *Anno Domini* (New York: Atheneum, 1964); and *Language and Silence: Essays on Language, Literature, and the Inhuman* (New York: Atheneum, 1967).

Special credentials, to be sure, are required of a true critic of our culture, now regnant for more than three hundred years and nearly immune to criticism—even, it seems at times, to that of its own inherent contradictions.

It is in the essays in his earlier collection *Language and Silence,* which range in time of original publication from 1958 to 1966 and in subject matter from "Homer and the Scholars" to an analysis of Sylvia Plath ("Dying Is an Art"), and especially in the long piece "The Retreat from the Word"—which more than any other single utterance seems to embody the thematic center of Steiner's criticism—that we may hope to educe the themes and preoccupations of his sensibility. Only within such a biographical and moral context is it possible to diagnose the marvelously revelatory malaise of ambivalence, ambiguity, and equivocation that is at the center of *Extra-Territorial.* It is only in the light of this malaise that we may appraise Steiner's credentials as a critic of modernity.

II

What are the perceptions that define Steiner's deepest aesthetic and moral allegiances? As he explores the roots and nature of human life in this century threatened by nihilism, suicide, and totalitarian holocaust, whence does he derive the metaphors of humanity in the face of the inhumane?

Language and Silence! The echoes that resonate from this juxtaposition and opposition are heard again and again in Steiner's work. Of his book *Language and Silence* he says: "This is a book about language: about language and politics, language and the future of literature, about the pressures on language of totalitarian lies and cultural decay, about language and other codes of meaning (music, translation, mathematics), about language and silence." And more recently, in *Extra-Territorial* he says: "To speak of the generation and condition of language is to speak of that of man." And again: "Verbal reticence is the only thing that relates our publicized, exhibitionist sensibility to antique energies and sources of wonder."

What community of sensibility, whether it be primarily of historical actuality or of the imagination, has defined Steiner's sense of his own moral and aesthetic self, has formed in the radix of that identity the intuitions of man's nature that he professes with such passion, and has armed him with stratagems and a posture from which to articulate these within the polities of critical thought?

Extra-territoriality—to live in a state while enjoying amnesty from its laws—is a metaphor that Steiner uses to characterize the situation, novel in our time, of the poet who no longer dwells with unique intensity in the tissues of a native language and who therefore, like Nabokov, Borges, and Beckett, writes his works in each of several "original" languages. But extra-territoriality is in fact an even more exact metaphor of the situation one must enjoy in relation to the rubrics of a culture if one is to be its critic. One must achieve an extra-territorial vantage point. We think of Kierkegaard, insulated against modernity by his radical monotheism and by his calculated pseudonymity; of Nietzsche and Hölderlin and their incipient madness; of Wittgenstein, a prisoner of war, and of the abstractness of his early philosophy of logic, ending in silence; of Rilke in his isolation at the Castle of Duino; and of Schönberg, surrounded by the sonorities of the Western musical tradition, dwelling in his atonal world, the third act of his *Moses und Aron* unfinished.

For Steiner, the extra-territorial vantage point is his Jewishness—one wants to say his *European* Jewishness, despite all the cosmopolite wanderings. For Steiner the Jew, as also for the poets, critics, and central European intellectuals with whom he feels strong ties of identity—Walter Benjamin, Karl Kraus, Hofmannsthal, Fritz Mauthner, Ernst Bloch, and above all Kafka—and in whose personal crises of equivocation and silence at the onslaught of the Holocaust of World War II he sees embodied mankind itself in *extremis* before the inhumane, *culture is the problem*. However "wide scattered and thinned out belief comes, which is the meaning of Diaspora," Steiner has observed, culture is that to which, try though he may, the Jew, hearing ancient vocations, cannot assimilate: it is culture that is the diametric opposite of the "in-between" of Israel in the presence of Yahweh in the desert.

In a moving autobiographical essay, "A Kind of Survivor," in *Language and Silence,* Steiner has explored these deep affiliations in his life and the grounds of his own extra-territoriality vis à vis critical thought. "If I am often out of touch with my own generation," he says, "if that which haunts me and controls my habits of feeling strikes many of those I should be intimate and working with in my present world as remotely sinister and artificial, it is because the black mystery of what happened in Europe is to me indivisible from my own identity. Precisely because I was not there, because an accident of good fortune struck my name from the roll."

For all the "scatteredness and thinning out" of Steiner's belief as a Jew, and notwithstanding the strangeness to him of orthodoxy, he is unwilling to have his own Jewishness defined either by the bureaucratic identity card or a merely political obverse of that, life in Israel. Instead, unrepentently unorthodox, he nevertheless perceives the present darkness in theological terms ("When God's back parts are toward man, history is Belsen") and his own geographical placelessness is offset by a millenial rooting in time ("Six thousand years of self-awareness are a homeland"). And it is in Exodus that he finds his text.

A cosmopolite whose literacy professionally husbands the best of critical thought, he is estranged from the reformed and criticized—essentially patriated—residues of his own tradition and finds his deepest intimations of self-identity in "that which has been destroyed"—the *European* Jewry silenced by the Holocaust:

> That which has been destroyed—the large mass of life so mocked, so hounded to oblivion that even the names are gone and the prayer for the dead can have no exact foothold—embodied a particular genius, a quality of intelligence and feeling which none of the major Jewish communities now surviving has preserved or recaptured. Because I feel that specific inheritance urgent in my own reflexes, in the work I try to do, I am a kind of survivor.

To be able to anchor one's being amid the chic of contemporaneity in an allusion to precritical forms of sensibility is a boon to anyone, doubly so for one who requires extra-territoriality in order to be a critic.

His analysis of the special ethos, the unique culture of the Enlightenment among central European Jews between 1830 and 1930, bearing within itself the weighty memory of Abraham and thus so different from the older and sometimes shallow, even flippant and deracinate French, English, and American forms, again shows a sure sense for the source of his best critical instincts. In this ambience *central European humanism* (each of the three terms carrying its full charge) was born. There is in this humanism, derived from temporal density, an immunity to the worst forms of silliness and excess in the Cartesian spirit.

Memory is subversive of discarnate reflection. Therefore it is subversive of all forms of inhumanity that are born of rationalism. The "quick way with languages" of central European Jews, suddenly freed from ghetto life, is natural in a people whose being is time and memory, whose medium therefore must be the word, and these Jews, faithful to themselves, are therefore subversive of the perversities of the critical spirit. "In its golden period, from

1870 to 1914, then again in the 1920s, the Jewish leaven gave to Prague and Berlin, to Vienna and Paris a specific vitality of feeling and expression, an atmosphere both quintessentially European and 'off-center.'"

And when this world begins to sicken, it is among those in whose custody this trust is most intensely lodged that the silence is most deep. "Like certain parables of Kafka and the epistemology of the early Wittgenstein, the art of [Hermann] Broch goes near the edge of necessary silence. It asks whether speech, whether the shapes of moral judgment and imagination which the Judaic-Hellenic tradition founds on the authority of the Word, are viable in the face of the inhuman."

It is within this tradition that Steiner stands and by which his humanistic instincts are supported in the face of the immediate barbarism and also before the nihilism that has always been just below the surface of critical thought, with its deliberate acts of amnesia. Relying upon these deep-rooted instincts, his judgments are firm and his voice is always confident, eloquent and humane.

It is only when he presumes to assault the conceptual strong points of critical thought explicitly and frontally, as he does in his uncertain polemic against Noam Chomsky and "the linguistic scientists," that his gestures become forced and self-conscious. This is an irony we shall wish to examine more closely, for it is the irony par excellence of the modern imagination imprisoned in its own conceptual fly-bottle. But more of this later.

In "The Language Animal," Steiner says: "*Language* and *man* are correlate. . . . They imply and necessitate each other" (italics in the original). From this incontestable and, taken in itself, unremarkable claim, he moves on to distinguish language from the codes of higher animals, in quest of *language* in its *uniqueness* as a code, hence in quest of *man*. Many higher animals have codes of enormous sophistication that may be speedier than speech and more economical, as are indeed the many paralinguistic signals that we ourselves are continually sending and processing, even while in the act of speaking.

But then Steiner makes what should strike us as a subtle but, from the point of view of his own critical instincts and his confidence in them, a fateful shift in his angle of vision. Until this moment, or so it appears, animal codes and human speech have been perceived by him as analogous (whatever may be the many and perhaps even more important disanalogies) in the respect that they both involve the "intersubjective" exchange of tokens or signs that have the power to effect an alteration in behavior. Bees dance and their hive-mates fly to where the nectar is; I issue an order and someone obeys—or is insubordinate. Quite simply, up to this point, Steiner has spoken as if signal codes among animals and words among men serve the purpose of communication, as if, indeed, they both may be said to have a "semantic" dimension. Signal codes and words orient their "users" to one another and to their settings. It seems clear that, at this juncture in his discussion, Steiner is committed to holding that there is an analogy between codes and languages by reference to their both having, at least in this *weak* sense, a semantic dimension. "A world without words can be, and, where organic forms are present, must be, a world full of messages"—if not to their "senders" and "receivers," then to whom?

But then comes the shift. "No other signal-system is at *all comparable*, or as Noam Chomsky says, 'language appears to be a unique phenomenon, without significant analogue in the animal world'" (italics added).

At one moment, language and signal-systems *are* comparable— they both have a semantic dimension; at the next, they are not at all comparable. How does this shift occur? Steiner gives us a clue in what follows. He says:

> One cannot overstate this fundamental, all-determining point [Chomsky's "without significant analogue"]. Not at a time when it is the fashion to describe man as a "naked ape" or a biological species whose main motives of conduct are territorial in the animal sense. The Darwinism of such arguments is more naive than that of T. H. Huxley, who, toward the close of his life, noted that nothing in the theory of natural selection had accounted for the root fact of human speech.

Almost with an audible sigh of relief, Steiner embraces Chomsky's "without significant analogue" as the categorical dismissal of all reductionistic theories of human language. What Steiner *also* does at the same time, though this only begins to become clearer in "The Tongues of Men," and though Steiner nowhere in this volume shows the faintest clue that he is aware of having done so, is to embrace Chomsky's model of what a language is. Nothing could be more contrary to Steiner's instincts and overall purpose. He continues to struggle against this subtle commitment all through "The Tongues of Men" and "Linguistics and Poetics," and he is still struggling against it in the foreword to this volume in a somewhat querulous tone, perhaps because he remains deeply dissatisfied with his encounter with Chomsky.

Anyone who says that language is "without significant analogue in the animal world" clearly takes it that the capacity of language to orient its users to one another and to their settings, a capacity it has in common with animal signal systems, is *not* a significant characteristic of language. For Cartesian linguistics it is "language acquisition" and "competence," understood as the "internalization of a set of rules" and the "generation" of an infinite number of sentences in accordance with a finite set of transformation rules, that is significant—not speaking, understanding speech, exchanging information, making promises, issuing orders, giving warnings. Chomsky's interests are in an abstraction divorced from actual speakers and hearers and from speech. Steiner's real interests, however, are in language written and language read, words spoken and words heard and understood—in short, living language in the heart and at the heart of man. And the wonder is that Steiner does not recognize this fundamental difference of interest. Unraveling the philosophical confusions of Chomsky needs doing, indeed. Taxing his program for failing to do something else is no part of this task. Yet, for a moment Steiner makes an unconscious, fatal concession to the Chomskian appeal, which produces the malaise of "The Tongues of Men" and "Linguistics and Poetics." It is the appeal of clarity and distinctness, the appeal of "knock-down" reassurance that man's dignity and value, eroded by critical thought, is real.

Steiner's instincts are better, and he should have trusted them. Yet there is hardly anything surprising in his having made this subtle blunder, for we all make analogous ones daily, struggling within the conceptual options afforded by critical thought, unable to break through to a post-critical standpoint.[2] And the blunder surprises us in Steiner only because in other ways he seems so immune to it.

III

If it is the perennial temptation of critical thought to demand total explicitness in all things, to bring all background into foreground, to dissolve the

---

2. A post-critical account of human cognition would abandon the Enlightenment model of an atemporal, abstract, godlike knower whose knowledge is taken to be an accomplished fact, and would attend instead to the contingent feats of perceptual and conceptual integration in time that enter into the cognitive acts of a concrete knower achieving knowledge. Such a model resituates thought in an actual thinker, embodied in his prepersonal natural history; and it explicitly acknowledges—and reiterates—that all judgments, however routine, are acts of irreducibly personal appraisal.

tension between the focal and the subsidiary by making everything focal, to dilute the temporal and intentional thickness of perception, to dehistoricize thought—as Descartes undertakes to do as he moves through the introduction to his *Discourse* on his way to his sole initial certainty, namely, that he exists at least in the moment in which he is thinking—to lighten every shadowy place, to dig up and aerate the roots of our being, to make all interiors exterior, to unsituate all reflection from time and space, to disincarnate mind, to define knowledge as that which can be grasped by thought in an absolutely lucid "moment" without temporal extension, to flatten out all epistemic hierarchy, to homogenize all logical heterogeneity; if, in short, the temptation of enlightenment is to doubt all our previous certainties and to ground our knowledge strictly upon clarity and distinctness in the present, then Steiner, as we have said, lives instinctively in a noncritical ambience. The root metaphor out of which is generated his curiosity about language and man's nature, and to which it always seems to return, is the irreducible juxtaposition and opposition of speech and silence. It is this that lies behind such phrases as "the image one has of man's relations to the logos," "the 'pneumatological' character of human speech," "language when it is in a condition of maximal concentration, when, as Heidegger says, language is total being," and most of all when he speaks of "the 'mystery' of language, its median state between spirituality and physical articulation" and goes on, "It is in that median quality . . . that may be sought primary clues to the linguistic core of human identity."

It is Steiner's deepest perception that human speech and human silence stand in an ontological bond in the human heart. Any attenuation of it is an attack upon the human as such. As the masses of sculpture require the emptiness which is their other side, so speech requires silence to be what it is. Speech is heard only against the background of silence; silence is not a mere emptiness, for out of it speech comes forth. It is silence which gives to speech its depth; it is speech which gives to silence its weight and its dignity. Were silence lost to us, if the whole inexhaustible world of the as yet unuttered were all at once to give up its depths, we should dwell in a sonic desert. Were we to lose the power of speech, we should dwell in utter darkness.

Where language and silence impinge, where man is on the threshold of speech, surrounded by the weight and dignity of silence, there is the root of his being. There, too, is wonder, spirit, the numinous. These are there, as well, where man falls silent—at the limits of language, before the unspeakable. Only a being in whom this ontological bond of speech and silence is joined is capable of *reticence*. Max Picard has said, "Language becomes emaciated if it loses its connections with silence." *To be reticent*—given to silence, to concealment—this is a power possessed only by man. Animals cry and signal and they are exhausted in these signs. Only man withholds and equivocates.

As between language and animal signal-systems, the *humanly* important difference is *this* one—whatever powers of "creative" sentence generation a Cartesian linguistics may disclose. And this Steiner sees.

Totalitarianism and pornography both strike at the roots of reticence. In a note to the collected version of "Night Words— High Pornography and Human Privacy" in *Language and Silence*, which, when it originally appeared in *Encounter*, drew fierce commentary in the letters column for months after, Steiner observes: "What I was trying to get into focus is the notion of the 'stripping naked' of language, of the removal from private, intensely privileged or adventurous use, of the erotic vocabulary. It does seem to me that we have scarcely begun to understand the impoverishment of our imaginings, the erosion into generalized banality of our resources of individual erotic representation and expression. . . . Where everything can be said with a shout, less and less can be said in a low voice. I was also trying to raise the question of what relation there *may* be between the dehumanization of the individual in pornography and the making naked and anonymous of the individual in the totalitarian state. Both pornography and totalitarianism seem to me to set up power relations which must necessarily violate privacy."

In our sexual relations the tension, the dialectic between speech and silence reaches a special intensity and therefore the sense of the bond which is our deepest identity is disclosed. Steiner says in "Night Words," "It is in sexual experience that a human being alone, and two human beings in that attempt at total communication which is also communion, can discover the unique bent of their identity. There we may find of ourselves, through imperfect striving and repeated failure, the words, the gestures, the mental images which set the blood racing. In that dark and wonder ever renewed both the fumblings and the light must be our own. The new pornographers subvert this last, vital privacy; they do our imagining for us." In the later "The Language Animal," he says: "Verbal reticence is the only thing that relates our publicized, exhibitionist sensibility to antique energies and sources of wonder."

IV

In the introductory section of this essay it was anticipated that a diagnosis of a revelatory malaise of ambivalence, ambiguity, and equivocation at the heart of Steiner's penultimate book, *Extra-Territorial,* needed to be made. And much of the foregoing has been designed to prepare a background against which might be perceived the subtlety, ubiquity, and philosophic importance of the workings in all of us of those metaphors that, as it seems to me, issue in George Steiner's loss of nerve in his polemic against Chomsky, particularly in "The Tongues of Men" and "Linguistics and Poetics." *Extra-Territorial* is an important book because it embodies the equivocations of a shrewd, confident, eloquent, and otherwise "extra-territorial" critic of modernity. Steiner's confusion (and Chomsky's) is more interesting than other men's clarity.

It was suggested, too, that there is a special *irony* in this confusion—the irony of an intellectual with deep roots in a pre-critical sensibility, trapped in spite of this in the conceptual fly-bottle of critical thought. If this can happen to a man of Steiner's virtuosity, how much more does it happen to the rest of us?

In his foreword summary of the gravamen of his attack upon Chomsky, a summary written after—perhaps some length of time after—the particulars of his argument were formed in the collected essays, a summary that I have earlier characterized as having a somewhat querulous tone, Steiner, inter alia, says:

> The contributions of Noam Chomsky to the formalization of the theory of grammar, and to the place now held by that theory in the study of logic and psychology, are pre-eminent. . . . My differences with Chomskian linguistics . . . are more fundamental.
>
> I am persuaded that the phenomenon of language is such that a rigorously idealized and nearly mathematical account of the deep structures and generation of human speech is bound to be incomplete and, very possibly, distorting. It is the thinness, the determinism of the generative transformational case—particularly in its current dogmatic vein—that I find disturbing. . . . [There has been] a damaging failure to take just account of a good deal of the philosophic-linguistic work of Saussure . . . of Wittgenstein, and of I. A. Richards, . . . [as well as] a total indifference to the more speculative, meta-logical tradition of Dilthey and Husserl with its stress on the historicity of speech acts, on

the time boundedness and mutations of even the most elemental of semantic modes . . . the investigations by Heidegger, of Paul Ricoeur's *De l'Interpretation* . . . or . . . the school of exegesis gathered around the Austrian journal the *Brenner* . . . with its emphasis on the religious, "pneumatological" characteristics of human speech. . . .

The peremptory naïvetés of a good deal of transformational generative work make impossible any real access to language when it is in a condition of maximal concentration, when as Heidegger says, language is total being, i.e., to literature. A scientific dogmatism . . . would exclude from rational inquiry the "mystery" of language, its median state between spirituality and physical articulation.

Now, taken by itself, the foregoing strikes me as largely sound and grounded in Steiner's best critical instincts. Taken, however, as a foreword to a volume containing "The Tongues of Men" and "Linguistics and Poetics," it has to be perceived in relation to the misfocused and philosophically naive attack upon Cartesian linguistics in these two essays. To be sure, it is next to impossible to distinguish between the technical grammatical questions in Chomsky's arguments and the philosophical questions, usually peremptorily begged, that are really quite centrally involved with the former at every point. Therefore it is difficult to be either polemically on target or fair.

Even so, as foreword to these essays I find this summary querulous and unsure: querulous because surely there can be no fault in Cartesian linguistics' being and doing what it is and does, rather than something else, however trivial one may think these to be (does Steiner smart from unrequited hopes for them that his own philosophical naïveté, still unresolved, allowed him to entertain?); unsure because had Steiner perceived the profound philosophical differences, *from the point of view of his future interests,* between, say, I. A. Richards, on one hand, and Wittgenstein, Heidegger, and Merleau-Ponty (whom he quotes with approval in "The Language Animal") on the other, and because, if he had fully grasped the distance toward a *post*-critical standpoint, which the philosophical radicalism of these latter writers take on, the malaise I claim to find at the center of *Extra-Territorial* would not be there.

At a crucial point, as we have seen, Steiner makes a fateful concession to Chomsky's model of language, forgetting that whatever its structural characteristics may be, however it may be acquired, whatever account may be given of the way in which sentences may be generated by transformation rules, it is *essentially* used by actual speakers to orient themselves and one another to their settings; that therefore it *essentially* has a semantic dimension; and that even the formal systems of transformational grammar cannot coherently be imagined as having meaning, hence as functioning, without the covert presupposition of acts of participation and endorsement by persons. This last is a formidable philosophical evasion of critical thought to which, once the evasion has been explicitly made, only those are equal who have explicitly moved to *post-critical* options. The Wittgenstein of the *Investigations* is clearly moving in this direction, Merleau-Ponty in the *Phenomenology of Perception* as well; one could name others—most of all Michael Polanyi in *Personal Knowledge: Toward a Post-Critical Philosophy.*

So long as Steiner trusts his tacit good sense, his judgments are usually immune from the absurdities of critical thought. When he joins the issue explicitly, and is called upon to formulate his own explicit philosophical parameters, I fear he is over his depth. He has no developed view of "ontological" hierarchy—else he would detect immediately for what it is Chomsky's absurd proposal to argue an antideterminist position as to the "creativity" of human language-generation, while solving the mind-body dualism by an appeal to "physicalism"; nor has he grasped with philosophical explicitness the import of the Enlightenment desideratum that all knowledge should and can be made explicit.

If, in conclusion, we undertake to unravel some of the confusion in Chomsky's case, the nature and grounds of Steiner's discomfiture with it will perhaps become clearer.

Chomsky draws a distinction between an "ideal speaker/hearer" of a language and any actual speaker/hearer, subject to all the contingent factors that may enter into and, perhaps, impede his actual ability to form sentences and to comprehend them. The ideal speaker/hearer exhibits "competence" insofar as he speaks and understands according to the putatively "internalized" rules of a deep grammar. The actual speaker/hearer's "performance" reflects his "competence," but it also depends upon many other things that from the point of view of Chomskian linguistic science are unimportant. It is crucial to notice that the "ideal speaker/hearer" neither *speaks* nor *hears:* not just usually does not, but logically *could* not. It can only embody "competence" by having "internalized" deep grammatical rules from which sentences are "generated."

On this model, Chomsky then proceeds to deal with the problem of language acquisition: "The person who has acquired knowledge of language has internalized a system of rules that relate sound and meaning in a particular way."[3]

On its face, this seems to be a statement about actual feats of language acquisition by actual historically, culturally, and linguistically located actual persons, and therefore would seem always to be about instances of linguistic *performance*.

If so, one should then ask whether it makes any sense to say that a speaker acquires speech by "internalizing a system of rules" since it rather seems, on the contrary, that a speaker's language powers are "internalized" and *informal* to begin with (though they might be formalized after speech acquisition). An actual speaker's feats of language acquisition do not require the "internalization" of the formalized rules of transformation to account for their achievement, and one is hard put to it even to imagine what evidence that this occurs we might have. But if it could be coherently imagined that a human being could in some way be in possession of such a formal system of rules, antecedent to speech acquisition, it is difficult to know how possession of this system could be of any use to him. It is equally unclear what an *un*formalized or informal *rule* is.[4]

If Chomsky is not presuming to make this incoherent claim about the "performance" of an actual located speaker, then it must be of the "competence" of an "ideal speaker/hearer." If this, then we must observe that the "ideal speaker/hearer" is an abstraction with no temporal or spatial situation. His "competence"—equally unsituated—is identical with the operation of the "system of rules." "Competence" and "operation of a system of rules" are concepts that function together with others to constitute the abstraction, "ideal speaker/hearer." Therefore it is meaningless to speak of these rules having been "internalized." The "rules" are inherent to Chomsky's ideal model. An "ideal speaker/hearer" exhibiting "competence" is not an entity that could either "internalize" or fail to "internalize" a deep grammar. He (it), being an abstraction, exists only in a "logical space" and not in time at all.

---

3. *Language and Mind* (New York: Harcourt, Brace, Jovanovich, 1972), 26.

4. For example, Wittgenstein, in *Philosophical Investigations* (New York: The Macmillan Company, 1955), paragraphs 31 and 201 especially, has made some very useful distinctions bearing upon different senses of "rule" and "obeying a rule." Chomsky shows no appreciation of these different cases, and it is impossible to make sense of his "internalizing a system of rules" in these, or any other, terms.

To say of this ideal speaker/hearer that his "competence" is the function of his having "internalized" a depth grammar is to talk utter nonsense—as it is to talk of a computer "internalizing" its program. A distinction between "external/internal" in this case is plainly a category-mistake.

So again, in this case, as in its application to an actual speaker, appeal to the "internalization" of a system of rules leads to incoherence. Chomsky, it would appear, conflates the concept of a real speaker "performing" in his native language (to whom perhaps the grammarian's formalism could come to have a meaning) and to whom it makes sense to impute achievement as the result of effortful feats in time[5] with an "ideal speaker/hearer" whose "competence" is not a result of the internalization in time of a depth grammar but is rather a logical function of the very definition of a "competent ideal speaker/hearer."

But let us give Chomsky every possible advantage. It is possible, perhaps likely, that the alternative "models" mentioned above—an actual being acquiring speech, a competent ideal speaker/hearer—taken alone and in turn not only, within limits, conceptually benign, but heuristically productive. However, taken together, especially if conflated, as I have suggested they are, they conspire to eliminate all *personal* participation from the operation of formal systems. For these "models" taken together tend to lead one to think that it is *depth grammar,* rather than actual speakers, that generates the sentences of all possible languages. Whereas, on the contrary, the more descriptive account would begin and essentially remain with an actual native speaker of a language. Here in the foreground, is the speaker's reliance both upon his own deep and surface linguistic powers from which in the act of speaking *he* "generates" sentences the meaning and grammaticality of which *he* endorses and accredits.

Steiner, it seems to me, has quite overlooked this "upward" reduction of actual speech into an ideal speaker/hearer. Yet it seems clear that part of Steiner's uneasiness is associated with this conflation.

A great irony of Chomsky's "position"—and of Steiner's "antithetical" one—which categorically rejects Skinner's *Verbal Behavior* and W. V. O. Quine's *Words and Objects* because of their explanatory weakness and their "reduction" of the "creative" element of human speech acts—is that it does

---

5. "Internalization" is the Chomskian rubric that confusedly imports these notions.

not note that its wholly abstract Cartesian model of "creativity" leaves out the participation of any actual *person* exercising these powers, which is a condition of the only *humanly* meaningful concept of linguistic "creativity."

Let us now return to the question of the dependence upon the participation of a person, even in the functioning of formal systems.

Take the classically simple case of entailment, which can be symbolized $P \to Q$, meaning "if P then Q." If I were to write $P \to Q$ on a blackboard, and if you were entirely innocent of the conventions of the notational system of logicians, $P \to Q$ might evoke many different kinds of interested responses from you. But it will not symbolize the relation of entailment until and unless I gain your comprehending personal commitment to letting P stand for one sentence, Q stand for another, and $\to$ stand for the relation of entailment obtaining between a sentence to the left of the arrow and a sentence to the right of it. Under the circumstances, this is not a difficult feat. All I normally have to do is to utter the sentence with which this paragraph begins. But we must not allow the fact that this is easy, even routine, to obscure the fact that this operation with the conventional tokens of a formalism never would *and never does* get off the ground without this personal endorsement by both of us.

First, the variables P and Q must be taken every time by some person to be *variables*, that is surrogates for an indefinite number of possible sentences (they are neither entities in their own right, qua variables, nor the proper names of entities, nor the surrogates of two particular sentences—which we might judge to stand in the relation of entailment—but rather the surrogates of every member of the classes of sentences that might stand to one another in the relation of entailment).

Second, it is taken every time by some person that some of the sentences of which P and Q are possible surrogates have a bearing upon a state or possible states of affairs in the world.

Third, the relation of entailment visually symbolized by the arrow is not only as a matter of contingent fact a convention understood and tacitly (but personally) endorsed by logicians; this *endorsement* is, indeed, a *conditio sine qua non* of our being able to symbolize, visually, the relation of entailment— as also the endorsement of the above words, if *spoken*, is of our being able to express it audially. Entailment, like all relations, is necessarily for or to someone. If there were no beings in the world *for* or *to* whom such a relation could exist (and, if it did not exist for a god), then $P \to Q$ could nowhere and never express entailment. In fact, P could not even be "to the left of" Q.

Antecedent to the articulation of the visual or audial expression of the relation of entailment there must exist for some consciousness the intentional relation we now conventionally designate by entailment for the word *entailment* to express.

In every case, then, where an entity or a sign is judged to allude to, directs our attention toward, pretends or distends our consciousness in the direction of some other entity or sign, we necessarily have a triadic relation: P (which entails, means, alludes to, etc., Q), Q (which is entailed, is meant, is alluded to by, etc., P), and W. H. P. (or an abstraction from him or someone like him) whom the relations between P and Q are *for*—a consciousness in whom the intentional relation of entailment, meaning, alluding to subsists.

Therefore, be our formalisms ever so abstract, they can never be entirely abstracted from the participation of personal recognizers, endorsers, and appraisers of the formalism—even if the "persons" have become, and usefully so, abstract and cruelly truncated. A *personal act* of integrating the particulars, even in the case of the computer code, to their joint meaning, however routine this may be, is *always* involved. The suppression of this fact about human meaning-discernment is the scandal of critical thought.

This interesting, in fact paradigmatic, philosophical gaffe (if that is what it is, as I believe it is) by a critic of Steiner's vigor and eloquence should not obscure the range, originality, and excitement of his mind. I shall look forward with impatience to the appearance of his larger and more systematic study of language and silence as they are bonded in the heart of man, hoping that he will have more fully trusted his own.

MOUSTAKAS WITHIN HIS AMBIENCE

We inevitably approach a work of art from within the history of our own sensibility. This is true whether that history is only implicitly incarnate in the ways our culture has disposed us to use our eyes, embodied as they are in the unrecognizable ways in which our bodies are allowed to appear and move within the horizons of our world; or, alternatively, is more explicitly the work of literacy and reflection upon that history. It is always in fact something of both. A painting, a piece of sculpture has a being-in-the-world, over against us, as the world itself is over against us. The act of beholding it, therefore, is a transaction neither less ordinary nor less complex than the act of beholding the meanest object in our world, though a successful work of art has an extraordinary power to seduce our attention. All our sensory powers, actual and virtual, relying upon our powers of movement from within our bodies, are drawn into the ambience of this "other" that is before us, winning our submission. We do not merely "see" it. We touch it, hear it, taste it, smell it—actually or virtually—as may be appropriate to its nature. We in fact incorporate it—as it incorporates us.

As surely as our sensibility endorses certain ways of being hosts to our own bodies in the world, encouraging us to be at ease with them and to presence them with others according to an almost infinitely subtle choreography of movements, gestures, expressions, and expectations, so surely does it confirm as congenial a set of possibilities on the horizons of our being-in-the-world. Our world is indeed a range of possibilities, which we will allow to actualize themselves for us.

Faith and Art 1.4 (1973): 5–10.

Who can imagine, for example, that the humanistic sensibility of the Aegean world was not born in that very moment when the immobile and inhuman catatonia of the quadri-facially frontal Archaic Kouros of the sixth century B.C. was transformed into man, almost in a twinkling, it seems, by the tilting of the human pelvis. Man seems suddenly to become at peace with the cosmos, to be in fact its recapitulation in the harmonious form of his body.

We do not come then, to a work of art with innocent eyes. We dance toward it along the subtly choreographed path of our inherited sensibility. And if we stand transfixed by the grandeur of that Phidian horse's head in the Duveen Room of the British Museum, among the Elgin marbles, it is not at all as it is when we see its plaster model in its original place, well above eye-level, in the pediment of the Parthenon on the acropolis, in the Athenian light, imagining we can hear the processing athletes, the chariots, the horses plunging and jostling with excitement as they wind along the Pan-Athenaic way toward the shrine of Athene Parthenos.

A work of art and its maker have their own native ambience, too. Monsieur André Malraux's "museum without walls," whereby, as never in history, all the treasures of every art are accessible to our gaze—idle, curious, diffident, tumid, distraught, and acquisitive more often than humbled and made obedient by the disciplining of our expectations—is a mixed blessing that tempts us to forget this.

The imagination of Evangelos Moustakas is inhabited no less by the, to him, present reality of the Greek victory over the Persian fleet in 480 B.C. at Salamis, almost in sight from his birthplace, Piraeus, than by the railway boxcars that in 1944 passed his father the station-master's home with their cargo of Jews bound for incineration. It is filled no less with the ghosts of Mycenaeans transporting water from a spring below to the safety of the polis through a secret tunnel during the second millenium B.C. than with the dangerous urban ballet of pedestrians and Mercedes-Benz taxicabs that fills Syntagma Square, Athens, each present day between 5:00 and 9:00 P.M. For his perception there is no contradiction between these extremes, which to us are apt to seem incommensurable. For to him, the discord between man and himself, between man and the natural world, between nature and the "second nature" with which man more and more self-destructively surrounds himself are rooted in a simpler, more ordinate, less apocalyptic rhythm of birth, presumption, suffering, pain, retribution, courage, death, and regeneration.

He therefore sees without self-consciousness the June War of 1967 in a mixture of biblical and classical images; he sees life's ordinate promise and danger in figures of pregnant women, its energy and sublimity in dancing horses, its dooms in the barely audible tread of the Erinyes pursuing Orestes, its glory in the Nikes, the power of its song and dance and of the harmony between ourselves and the earth's rhythms vouchsafed to us through them in the image of Orpheos descending and ascending. It can be said of his sculpture as it has been said of his contemporary George Seferis's poetry in the collection by Edmond Keeley and Philip Sherrard:

> The Greek poet who draws on classical mythology in shaping the drama of his verse enjoys a large advantage over his similarly disposed contemporaries in England and America: he can evoke characters and settings that have mythological overtones with less danger of being merely literary in doing so, with less danger of arbitrarily imposing gods and heroes on an alien landscape—Tiresias on the Thames, or Prometheus in Pennsylvania, for example—since his own natural landscape is that to which these gods and heroes themselves once belonged and in which they still confront the mind's eye plausibly.

This then is the ambience of the sculptures of Evangelos Moustakas. If our gaze is to take in more than the stylistic range and technical virtuosity of his work, more than just the "something new" in which St. Paul accused the Athenians themselves of forever taking an inordinate interest; if we are, in short, to dwell in Moustakas's older humane perceptions as we behold his sculptures, we shall have to humble and discipline our sometimes impatient post-Enlightenment "humanistic" expectations.

Let us not pretend that this is easy.

Our history begins with Enlightenment, with the Renaissance, with Reformation. For good and for ill, we are creatures of modernity, of criticism, of revolution. Not only have we turned our backs upon the past, tradition, inherited ways, the harmonious balance between man and nature, but we have been tempted, as we have dedivinized nature, following our biblical inheritance, to divinize ourselves, and there has ensued a ripening flirtation with godhood, with infinity, restlessness, tumult, and madness.

Descartes in his *Discourse on Method* consolidated the emerging hopes of his predecessors and drafted a program for our consciousness, saying:

> By them [new principles of method] I perceived it to be possible to arrive at knowledge highly useful in life . . . *and thus render ourselves the lords*

and possessors of nature. And this is a result to be desired, not only in order to the invention of an infinity of Arts, by which we might be enabled to enjoy without trouble the fruits of the earth, and all its comforts, but also, and especially for the preservation of health.

Under the impetus of these hopes, which have become at times a "sweet dream" of the heaven on earth, we have subjugated nature. And for three centuries we have found ourselves thrown back and forth in despair between the image of ourselves as a "useless freedom" in no way commensurate with the great, inane nature that is merely our subject and the image of a mere animal whose greater complexity only renders its existence within the bosom of a nature without grandeur the more meaningless. Our "humanism" is very often the diseased offspring of this impiety. Our discarnate freedom has no place in the universe, our visible form recapitulates no cosmos, no breath of God shines in our faces. We are alternately bewildered and ashamed of our own image.

The humanism that is a child of the dark side of modernity—of Pascal, Nietzsche, and Dostoyevski—is tinged with bitterness. There is a strain of self-hatred in our Western protests against dehumanization, a bad faith that shows itself more, the more mordant and shrill the protest, as if we have to still with the sound of our own voices the deeper doubt that there is anything genuinely and intrinsically human to be defended. Who can contemplate Picasso's enraged cry of pain over the fate of innocent sufferers in Guernica without feeling, nevertheless, the hint of the human self-contempt that is also undeniably there. Our humanism keeps a mistress whose name is Nihilism.

Albert Camus explored this, our madness, in the myth of Sisyphus and sought wholeness in the Greek ideal of limits. "Greek thought," he says,

> always took refuge behind the conception of limits. It never carried anything to extremes, neither the sacred nor reason, because it negated nothing, neither the sacred nor reason. It took everything into consideration, balancing shadow with light. Our Europe, on the other hand, off in the pursuit of totality, is the child of disproportion. She negates beauty, as she negates whatever she does not glorify. And, through all her diverse ways, she glorifies one thing, which is the future rule of reason. In her madness she extends the eternal limits, and at that very moment dark Erinyes fall upon her and tear her to pieces.

This is the ambience of the sculpture of Evangelos Moustakas. To discipline our imaginations to behold it aright will tell us something about our

Cartesianism and what of both good and ill it has done to us. Greece and Byzantium have no Renaissance past, no Enlightenment past. Hence, perhaps, both the tragic sense of life and the affirmation that is given in face of it are experienced in more muted ways, expressed without either the presumption or the despair that the Cartesianism of the Europe of the West has so frantically, self-consciously, and egocentrically produced.

This Greece may have been the child of Camus's despair and his nostalgia. But George Seferis, a Greek, a poet, and, as a diplomat, a familiar of Western capitals, Western values, and Western art, can speak with authority: "You see," he says,

> we are a people who have had great Church Fathers, but we are now without great mystics; we are devoted to emotions and ideas, but we like to have even the most abstract notions presented in a familiar form, something which a Christian of the West would call idolatry. Also, we are—in the original sense of the word—very conservative. None of our traditions, Christian or pre-Christian, have really died out. Often when I attend the ritual procession on Good Friday, it is difficult for me to decide whether the god that is being buried is Christ or Adonis. Is it the climate? Is it the race? I can't tell. I believe it's really the light. There must surely be something about light that makes us what we are. In Greece one is more friendly, more at one with the universe.

The Voice of Orpheos

Why is it we feel deeply and unaccountably moved by the claim in the myth of Orpheos that his singing and playing caused rocks to move and trees to dance? Why, especially, seeing that with our conscious, reflective minds we "know" such a claim to be absurd, a merely mythical conception?

It is because as psych-somata, as mind-body unities—our history, the biography of each single one of us, is rooted (even as a tree is rooted) in a harmony of forms, structures, orders, systems (even as also are rocks and trees), which are more ancient than our conscious, reflective intelligences.

It is these forms in harmony that give to rocks their rockiness, to trees their living structure. It is these, too, that give to my body, even long before it has moved for the first time in my mother's womb (within which her beating heart rhythmically pumps the blood of life through my fetal body, forming itself toward my primal initiation into the very foundation of my first and most primitive cosmos), its growing toward wholeness destined to become a man who will discern the meaning in human speech, since even before this it will have indwelt the beating rhythm of patterned and hence meaningful sound. These forms are for me (even still for conscious, critical me) archetypically the forms of measured time: tempo, beat, strophe, pulse. There is then in my prereflective and unreflecting body itself an archaic prejudice, far older than I am, to indwell all form and order in the cosmos as kindred of the first order I have known—the order of my mother's beating heart. And this prejudice, which is older than I, is nevertheless always present, even at this very moment, as the measured beat of my own heart, the pulsing at my temples of my own blood.

Even though, therefore, these archaic forms that give me a body before I am a knowing person do not know themselves, it is only by virtue of them (unknown to themselves, yet long since resounding to the rhythm and the voice of Orpheos throughout all the cosmos) that I have a body that in time becomes the instrument of speech and hence the embodiment of intelligence.

The myth of Orpheos, then, is a representation more profound than any that reflection could give of the presence of order and of form in the cosmos; of the genesis of song and dance; and finally, of the birth of human speech and intelligence—all of which are rooted in the same ultimate ground. Far, then, from being a surprise, it is on the contrary most congenial to an imagination like mine, enfleshed as it is in a rhythmically ordered body, that dumb rocks and trees should be represented as resounding to the orphic song, even as my own dumb body itself so resounds.

A small essay for my friend "Vangeli," who, like Orpheos, makes rocks move and dumb bronze to sing.

PART FOUR

Freedom, Faith, and
the House of Intellect

ANXIETY, COURAGE, AND TRUTH

Graham Greene, whose sensibility can discern intimations of something sinister in even the quiet movement behind him of a rabbit, in the dark, on the croquet lawn of an English public school, tells in an autobiographical essay, "The Lost Childhood," of his loss of innocence forever in the discovery one summer that he could read.

There then opened before him the whole universe of literature. "All a long summer holiday I kept my secret, as I believed: I did not want anybody to know that I could read. I suppose I half consciously realized even then that this was the dangerous moment."

First there was Rider Haggard's *King Solomon's Mines* and the evil sorceress, Gagool: "Didn't she wait for me in dreams every night in the passage by the linen cupboard, near the nursery door? And she continues to wait, when the mind is sick or tired, though now she is dressed in the theological garments of despair."

Later, it was Elizabeth Bowen's *The Viper of Milan:*

> At the end, Della Scala is dead, Ferrara, Verona, Novara, Mantua have all fallen, the messengers pour in with news of fresh victories, the whole world outside is cracking up, and Visconti sits and jokes in the wine light. . . . [I learned] in Miss Bowen's novel the sense of doom that lies over success—the feeling that the pendulum is about to swing. That too made sense; one looked around and saw the doomed everywhere—the champion runner who one day would sag over the tape; the head of the school who would atone, poor devil, during forty dreary undistinguished years; the scholar . . . and when success began to touch oneself

Duke Divinity School Bulletin 31.3 (1966): 204–12.

too, however mildly, one could only pray that failure would not be held off for too long.

This reminds one of a reality too hastily suppressed in the modern climate of the mind, so much a creature of science, technology, and the optimism they breed: the radical connection between anxiety, courage, and the achievement of truth.

The modern age was ushered in by the Baconian motto, "Knowledge is power." It has been deeply underwritten in our whole sensibility by even that most theoretical of men, René Descartes, the so-called "father of modern philosophy" who wanted to start from scratch by thinking out everything clearly while sitting in a stove!

For us knowledge tends to be associated with heroism and unqualified beatitude. Everywhere in our imagination there rises up from its depths the belief that man is *saved,* not damned, by knowledge and by standing in the truth.

On hundreds of American campuses there are buildings upon which have been engraved, snatched wholly from their profounder context, the words "Ye shall know the truth and the truth shall make you free." Upon seeing them, my natural rejoinder is, "The hell it does." In the context of compulsive modern optimism these words lose all sense of paradox.

Our universities and the Great Society spend millions of man-hours, billions of dollars, in uncritical support of this belief.

Yet—it has not always been held, nor is it true.

A deeper human sensibility has known that truth is not only won at a price, but *painful* when won; that knowledge is always an ambiguous good, concealing a *threat;* that catastrophe is associated with the loss of innocence.

Recognition of this may be absent from our public myth, but in our private struggle with ourselves and our world it's there. It's always there, even when it has no name.

There are three great myths in our tradition in which the link between catastrophe and the loss of innocence is embodied. The myth of Oedipus, the myth of Adam, and the myth of Faust.

In the very name of Oedipus, the whole story is compactly told. Oedipus means "the swollen footed"—a name conferred upon the son of Laius because of the permanent scar left on his ankles by the leather straps by which his legs were bound together when he, an infant, had been left upon a hill to die. There is a profound pun in the name. *Pus* means foot and, taken with the riddle of the sphinx (what is it that *walks* on four *feet* in the morning, two *feet* at noon, and three *feet* at night), suggests that Oedipus's very heroism is bound up with the image of the being who *walks*. But this is yet another pun, for *oida*—swollen—suggests there is something basically "unnatural" in the creature who has the power to walk upright. Even more, the verb *oido,* in one of its meanings, is defined as "swollen with knowledge." And we know that Oedipus *was* swollen with knowledge, not only possessed of the power of reason by which he was enabled to answer the riddle of the sphinx, but proudly possessed of it, swollen with it—again, "unnaturally" so.

It is by the power of reason that Oedipus is able to destroy the Sphinx, that beast part bird, part lion, and part woman, which symbolized for the ancient world all the dark, irrational, nameless, and inhuman terrors that threaten man. This he does by answering the riddle into which is compactly built a profoundly disturbing image of the greatness ("what it is that walks?") and the ultimate transiency (morning, noon, and night) of human life. He answers: Man! And at a stroke he exhibits the power of human reason to plumb the secret of human life and finds that painful secret to be human mortality. Swollen with proud knowledge, he assails the riddle and discovers the tragic truth about existence. The loss of innocence leaves him with the painful, perhaps the crushing truth: I have been cast into existence and, one day, I shall be torn from it. What value can this respite have in a close prison where my life is a continual going out to the place of execution?

The Adam myth, perhaps more familiar but not better understood, exhibits, in ways appropriate to its own essence, the same motif: catastrophe and the loss of innocence, truth and danger. Eating of the fruit of the tree of the Knowledge of Good and Evil, Adam becomes—as God?—not quite. But he becomes man—now at enmity with the world, itself forever hostile to him. Cast out of Eden, naked as no animal is, vulnerable, mortal.

The Faust legend is the typical modern myth. It expresses modern man's peculiar desire for power, a desire for "guns, gold, and girls," to satisfy which no impiety is too great a risk to run. It expresses, too, the secret connections between the animus of science and that of black magic.

Karl Shapiro has seen the irony of the Faust myth symbolized in the terror of an atomic age that made a pact with the Prince of Darkness in return for the final secret of the physical world. He writes:

> Backwardly tolerant, Faustus was expelled
> From the Third Reich in nineteen thirty-nine.
> His exit caused the breaching of the Rhine,
> Except for which the frontier might have held.
> Five years unknown to enemy and friend
> He hid, appearing on the sixth to pose
> In an American desert at War's end
> Where, at his back, a dome of atoms rose.

By each of these we are reminded of what we easily forget: anxiety and courage are very much involved in our apprehensions of the truth. Knowledge, because it is always associated with a loss of innocence, is an equivocal good. Who is there who has never thought so? Who has ever thought so with untroubled conscience in face of our public modern myth?

I think certain historical confusions are in part to blame for this uneasy simplemindedness: the seventeenth century's identification of truth with the science of physical nature; the eighteenth century's identification of mind with consciousness; our contemporary identification of truth with particular contingent truths discovered by what is too uncritically thought to be a value-free, neutral "scientific" method. It is clear, is it not, that if truth is understood in terms of this model, thus construed, then it is difficult for us to concede that anxiety and courage are in any way involved. Value-free reason apprehending such truths is subject to no anxiety and hence stands in no need of courage.

The ancient and medieval imagination saw truth to be, in the last analysis, bound to *sapientia,* that is, to sapience, the endowment in virtue of which is Homo sapiens: the sole creature who grasps his total situation in the world—at once great and wretched. Plato explicitly argued that only the good man—it would not be unfaithful here to say, the courageous man—can know the truth. This is why he spoke of the radical coming into the truth as a *metanoia,* a turning round of the soul, a "thinking reversely."

But we need not go so far for a qualification of our contemporary public myth. So-called depth psychology has rehabilitated many of these ancient insights for us. It shows us quite explicitly that mind is not just consciousness, that we are neither transparent nor tractable to ourselves. Augustine's utterance could well be the motto of Sigmund Freud: "Man is a great deep. It is not possible to number the hairs of his head. Yet it is easier to number the hairs of his head than the beatings of his heart."

From this—and it is no accident that Freud's dominating concept is an elliptical story, the Oedipus complex—we learn that we are not simply available to our own conscious management; that we are in fact mysteries to ourselves. We learn too that there is painful, threatening, anxiety-producing truth about ourselves and about our human condition which we repress, concerning which we rationalize, from which we are forever in flight. And finally, we learn that none of us can face these without courage—indeed a courage that itself appears to us unbidden from our own intractable depths.

Perhaps I will not mislead you if I explicitly resort to a psychoanalytic analogy. There is a sense in which we may say that the neurotic is the creator of a world of his own "imagination" to which he then becomes subject— incarcerated as a prisoner. The job of the therapist is, as an outsider, to invade that world and to enhance his patient's wish to be free. The invasion is a kind of incarnation, for the therapist enters the neurotic world from the outside and remains, while in it, an outsider, lest he, like his patient, becomes the subject of that world, powerless against it.

Now, expand the analogy. In one sense, each of us, like the neurotic, is the prisoner of his own picture of what the world is like. This is what is meant by idolatry—the imprisonment of ourselves in any given picture of the world. It is God who invades this world, threatening us ultimately, but also setting us free.

We, each of us, have a stake in this picture. It is ours. We are defensive before every invasion of it. We are threatened by every claim that challenges it. Every new truth makes us anxious because we have made an investment of our personhood in the old "truth." If any of us ever succeeds in facing this challenge, it is because courage has come to us. We are simple idolaters— imprisoned in our imaginations—who can be set at liberty only when that imagination is ravished by reality or by God.

Pagan man could not finally face three facts: the fact of existence, the fact of freedom, the fact of death.

If it is not possible for you to adopt a positive attitude to these three radical facts, then it is impossible for you to take persons seriously—which is to say, impossible for you to take yourself seriously.

In *The Concept of Dread,* Kierkegaard characterizes *inwardness* as serious-ness, which is for him the diametric opposite of *despair.* To illustrate, he then quotes the lines written by Shakespeare for Macbeth, when, having mur-dered the king, he is in despair:

> . . . from this instant
> There's nothing serious in mortality:
> All is but toys: renown and
> grace is dead.

Pagan man could not face *existence* because it was, in its nature, *hybrid*— the very act of existing was itself a disordering of a primal order, to which all existing things would "make reparation for their injustice according to the disposition of time."

Pagan man could not face *freedom* because it introduces, in his view, an anticosmic contingency, disorder, chaos, a threat of nonbeing, and hence guilt and terror. This is the meaning of the great sigh of relief at the end of Sophocles' *Oedipus the King*:

> You that live in my ancestral Thebes,
> Behold this Oedipus,
> Him who knew the famous riddles and was a man most masterful;
> Not a citizen who did not look with envy on his lot—
> See him now and see the breakers of misfortune swallow him!
> Look upon that last day always.
> Count no mortal happy till he has passed
> The final limit of his life secure from pain.

Finally, pagan man could not take death seriously as an ultimate and genuine threat to all meaning. Therefore meaning for him had to reside finally in an immortal and hence impersonal order. If you cannot take death seriously as a genuine threat, then neither can you take our finite life with seriousness. Only when death is the last and the greatest enemy can life be cherished as worth living. D. H. Lawrence, as a novelist and pamphleteer—obsessed, perhaps, by our culture's capacity to assimilate and thereby neutralize all criticism of itself, to cerebralize and remove the sting of ultimate mystery—has Mrs. Whitt, in *St. Mawr*, say: "Now listen to me. . . . I want death to be real to me. . . . I want it to hurt me. . . . If it hurts me enough, I shall know I was alive." This puts my point very well—and points up the neopaganism of our mind against which Lawrence was here railing.

It is the very opposite of this attitude that one finds in the Greek saying, "It is best never to have been born, next best to take leave of this life."

Where existence, freedom, and death cannot be positively appropriated, *persons* can never matter.

The impact of the Judeo-Christian faith upon this pagan imagination produced Western culture.

In this faith there is no recoil from these painful truths about the human condition. In Job we read, "My days are swifter than a weaver's shuttle, and are spent without hope. Oh remember that my life is a breath."

In this view, man is made out of the dust. His life is a tale that is told.

At the same time, with seeming paradox, guilt is sin, sin is the expression of man's freedom, and his freedom is a gift of God!

The Christian declares that Jesus Christ has overcome sin and death. What, in the light of what I've said, can this mean?

It means that *now* we can accept existence as God's gift; sin as the sign of our freedom; and life as that which has been saved from meaninglessness. Now, we are able to take persons seriously. Given an ultimate courage to face the most painful truth about ourselves, there is no longer any truth we need fear.

You are all familiar, I am sure, with St. Paul's words in his Epistle to the Romans where he says, "For I am persuaded that neither life nor death, nor things present nor things to come, nor angels nor principalities nor powers, nor height nor depth, nor anything else in the whole creation, can separate us from the love of God which is in Christ Jesus."

Perhaps it has not occurred to you to remark the relevance of these words to the life of the mind.

There was no such thing as a college or a university, in our sense, in the culture that nurtured St. Paul. On the contrary, it was precisely the faith of St. Paul, expressed in these words, out of which such institutions came: the faith, namely, that Jesus Christ had overcome both sin and death; that He had deprived them of their binding power upon the human imagination. This faith nurtured the university in the Western world.

For this faith declares that the guilt that infects all existence and all freedom has been removed—if not in fact, at least in hope. The whole world of nature and of human culture is seen to be God's creature. Henceforth we can seek to discover its mystery without anxiety. The wound inflicted by our loss of innocence has been healed. Human reason is now beyond tragedy, because "Christ is God's and ye are Christ's; therefore all things are yours."

This is the regenerate mind. No student wholly lacking it, no university unleavened by it can survive.

If wisdom be grasping our total situation in the world; and if dreadful existence, anxiety-producing freedom and meaning-threatening death are facts we have to meet on the way; then only those who have a faith which takes the dread out of existence, the anxiety out of freedom, and the threat of meaninglessness out of death can have the courage of the regenerate mind. In the posture of this faith such a one will be able to say with St. Paul: "I am persuaded that neither communism nor fascism; Freudianism nor Jungianism; Einsteinianism nor the theory of an ever-expanding universe; neither historicism nor impressionism; existentialism nor logical positivism; the theory of deficit finance nor the principle of complementarity can separate me from the love of God in Christ Jesus."

Being delivered from anxiety, he then can explore, examine, criticize, or appropriate any of these, knowing that his ultimate security is not bound to the transient career of these penultimate truths.

The world of nature and human culture are therefore his to understand and love with a regenerate mind.

Whenever he is armed with such ultimate courage, he is beyond anxiety: the loss of innocence ceases to be an equivocal good.

Does anyone have this faith? Is the higher learning still the fiduciary of this legacy?

I confess I do not know. But I do believe the hour is already very late.

So now we have the new theology, paperbacks by the hundreds of thousands, upon the racks along with *Greek Tragedy, A House Is Not a Home,* and *Candy.*

"The death of God"—this is the kind of total claim from which I turn away in horror. It now seems too large a matter for my sensibilities.

I am affronted by the total claim delivered in an apocalyptic tone, especially when overnight it comes to be uttered by a thousand voices and then becomes chic. And everyone becomes Jean-Baptiste Clamence, judge-penitents, haranguing each other with wild eyes in coffeehouses, bars, and student unions, filling the air with "the death of God" and with "anguish" while silently all about them are students and colleagues dying in a quiet, humble despair for want just of hearing their own *names* called.

The great engine of higher learning is fully throttled up in the Great Society. And the whole ghastly enterprise would be a farce at which we could all laugh, if it were not in fact so dangerous.

It is not easy to know what the words of St. Paul mean; perhaps even more difficult to subscribe to them.

For myself, I must tell you that sometimes they resonate with the deepest things that are in me; at others they fall equivocally upon a tin and complacent ear.

Yet—even for me, guilty over my too modest goals, it *is* possible at least for me to pray, "Give us this day our daily bread."

May it be at least as well with you.

TRAGEDY AND FREEDOM

I

The subject of tragedy has evoked such a luxuriant literature—both dramatic and critical—that it would be absurd to suppose that its essence could be reduced to a few simple propositions. Nor is it less absurd to suppose in advance that there is something which we must call *the tragic as such* for all time—without reckoning with the shifting currents of thought and the dynamic equipoise that comprise the sociological and intellectual context for the production of literary works which we would be willing to call tragedies. I make no such pretensions here.

Nevertheless, the very fact that many different works of literature, with quite different sets of philosophical presuppositions—cosmological, anthropological, ethical—are called tragedies requires that an attempt at locating some of the essentials be made, however tentatively. Perhaps what is to follow is only slightly less simpleminded itself, but surely it can be agreed that to define the tragic situation as one in which is exhibited the greatness and wretchedness of man is altogether too general. For whatever is gained in pith is lost in silence on such matters as: What is man's greatness? What is his wretchedness? How are they related? How are they assimilated to a dramatic cosmology? What is the character of the cosmos in which these are synthesized? Or—if they are left unresolved—what sense can be made of man who is both great and wretched? But then, of course, as soon as one has begun to give specific content to the empty concept of tragedy by answering these questions,

The Carolina Quarterly 8.2 (1956): 15–27.

he is setting forth the particular intellectual commitments of a particular tragedian—and of his age—instead of dealing with the tragic as such.

However this may be, the limited objective that I entertain here has to do with a very general framework of analysis, which, it has seemed to me, has received insufficient attention: I mean the shift from ancient to Christian and from Christian to post-Christian presuppositions, and the consequences of this for the notion of the tragic.

That Sophocles, Shakespeare, Dostoyevski, and Sartre have all concerned themselves dramatically with the greatness and wretchedness of man is beyond question. That their "worlds" are profoundly different is equally so. When we fix our attention upon such differences (perforce in very broad terms in this context), how are the essential problems of tragedy and freedom illuminated?

Certainly not because it is required, independently of all commitments as to what really is the greatness and wretchedness of man, or even necessarily by an empirical generalization as to what is held to be the case, but only for the sake of the problem I wish to bring out, I should like to take Greek tragedy to be the very paradigm of the tragic as such. And so doing, I want to consider (1) the conditions of the possibility of tragedy, (2) the nature of tragedy, and (3) some differences between a literature produced on the presuppositions of classical thought and that produced within the context of Christian. To reduce the whole question to hopelessly simple terms: What difference does the Incarnation make to our understanding of tragedy and freedom?

II

Manifestly, the conditions of the possibility of the tragic situation as exhibiting the greatness and the wretchedness of man are at bottom the same as those for there being man at all. If tragedy deals with the contradictions of human existence, we must briefly consider the existential root of these contradictions. How can man be in contradiction? The short answer can be found in Pascal's "Man infinitely transcends man"—which is to say, he is forever outside himself looking in. He is a being who, as subject, stands over against the "other" as object; a self, confronted by a not-self—a victim of what Hegel called the "unhappy consciousness."

Or—to use the Sartrean metaphor—man's consciousness has a vent in it, a certain fault, a scar, a possibility, a gap, freedom, nothing; with the result that he is a being who is for-himself, i.e., stands, as subject over against himself as object, always meeting himself coming from the other direction, as it were. This being so, man "is what he is not and is not what he is." We are always spectators of ourselves: the spectator always takes up an attitude toward the self it sees, whether it be cynical, comic, pathetic, ironic, or tragic.

Kierkegaard saw this "unhappy consciousness," which is the condition of the human as such, as being rooted in dread, i.e., the *sympathetic antipathy* and *antipathetic sympathy* before the possibility of freedom.

Rilke has also expressed it in his Eighth Duino Elegy:

> We've never, no, not for a single day,
> Pure space before us, such as that which flowers
> endlessly open into: always world,
> and never nowhere without no:
> . . . .
> That's what Destiny means: being opposite,
> and nothing else, and always opposite.
> . . . .
> And we, spectators always everywhere,
> looking at, never out of, everything!
> It fills us. We arrange it. It decays.
> We re-arrange it, and decay ourselves.
> . . . .
> We live our lives, forever taking leave.[1]

I should not want to suggest by the apparent neutrality with which I employ these different analogies that it is a matter of indifference which of them we finally use, or that they all come to precisely the same thing in the end. On the contrary, it is my point that the way in which this "unhappy consciousness" is imaged is the crucial determinant of how one conceives being human and what therefore is the tragic situation, i.e., wherein consists the greatness and wretchedness of man. My present purpose, however, requires only that the conditions of the possibility of human existence be exhibited. It is precisely in the "metaphysical space" thus described that human existence as such comes into being. It is here that the contradictions of existence arise. It is because of this "space" that man transcends himself; takes himself upon

1. Trans. J. B. Leishman and Stephen Spender (W. W. Norton and Company, 1939), 67, 69.

himself; asks questions about himself and about all that is not himself, and about the relation between himself and the other. It is here that man becomes a problem for himself. Because of this man is confronted by guilt, fate, and death: guilt seems to call in question responsibility (if to act at all is to become guilty, how can I really be responsible?); fate seems to call in question the reality of self-determination; death seems to call in question the meaning of life.

What then is meant by the contradictions of existence that, it is supposed, arise within this unhappy consciousness? Clearly, these are not logical contradictions, in the familiar sense. It is rather a case of antithetic ends, a radical conflict in the values exhibited by and pursued within man's world, the appearance of axiological cross-purposes in the structures of existence.

One need not canvass the entire field to make the matter clear. Man aspires to values. He falls short. He wants what he cannot have. But is this not puzzling—that he should want what he cannot have? Man is a failure. He, in a sense, always fails. It is almost true to say that man fails by definition. Yet how can this be? What kind of a universe is this such that we fail by definition? How can we believe that these are not axiological cross-purposes: to strive absolutely and yet to fail. And is it not odd that man should suffer, not merely because he fails to achieve his goal, but chiefly because he did not meet requirements that he has placed upon himself or appropriated as his own?

Not only, however, do man's aspirations outstrip his powers, with the result that he suffers guilt; but he pursues values and frustrates himself. He pursues values and has an ambivalent will. He seeks the good and finds that to achieve it he must destroy good. He aspires to ethical ends and "loses control": his acts, even his will, fall under an alien power.

Man seems to desire the truth above all else. No man willingly and consciously lives a life of illusion. Yet we seem deliberately to deceive ourselves: we lie to others and to ourselves, not merely unconsciously but consciously. Yet this consciousness is a reproach to us, so we convince ourselves we are not lying, thus lying to ourselves on a yet deeper level.

Man is full of theories as to what the meaning of life is, feeling that it has some clear purpose for him. At the same time it all seems to be called in question by another persistent feeling: that suffering and death make it all a tale told by an idiot.

But this is of course not all. Man not only feels these particular contradictions for what they are, but he feels there is a second-order level of contradiction as well: a contradiction between this contradictory reality in which he finds himself involved and his feeling that it ought not to be so. Axiological cross-purposes of an ultimate sort are exhibited even, or especially, in the fact that man feels incensed over axiological cross-purposes. As Gabriel Marcel observes:

> My life. The fact that it can seem to me to be literally devoid of meaning is an integral part of its structure. It then appears to me as pure accident. . . . It [the I] is irresistibly driven to self-negation. . . . No doubt this thorough-going nihilism is just an extreme position, a position very difficult to hold and implying a kind of heroism. But here we are deep in contradictions, since this heroism, if it is experienced and recognized as such, immediately reestablishes the subject, and at the same time restores to existence the meaning that was denied to it; it does at least in fact exhibit one value; it serves as a springboard for the Consciousness which denies it.[2]

But again, Pascal has said the last word on this subject: "What a chimera then is man! What a novelty! What a monster, what a chaos, what a contradiction, what a prodigy! Judge of all things, imbecile worm of the earth; depository of truth, a sink of uncertainty and error; the pride and refuse of the universe!"[3]

III

All of the contradictions of human existence are not on the same level. We may—recognizing the dangers of any simple schematism—distinguish between penultimate and ultimate contradictions. Whether a contradiction is ultimate or penultimate will of course be determined by the system of thought in which it appears. It may be that what one would call a penultimate contradiction points finally to an ultimate one. It is certainly true that such a connection will be seen or not depending upon the degree of seriousness with which existence is contemplated. But all of this is eccentric to our immediate problem. The axiological cross-purposes exhibited by existence evoke different attitudes: pathos, comedy, irony, and tragedy. I want to suggest in what follows that Greek thought—even Greek metaphysics—is essentially tragic; and that by

2. *Being and Having,* trans. K. Farrer (Boston: Beacon Press, 1951), 92.
3. *Pensées,* trans. W. F. Trotter, with an introduction by T. S. Eliot (London: J. M. Dent and Son, 1948), Fragment 434.

contrast, the worldview produced by the doctrine of the Incarnate Word is ironic, i.e., the axiological cross-purposes in existence are overcome by faith!

The first basic presupposition of tragedy, as I shall be using the concept, is that the axiological cross-purposes involved are serious and ultimate. They are serious in that ironic and comic detachment are not sufficient to achieve a resolution of the conflict. They are ultimate insofar as values standing at the very top of our hierarchy are in contradiction. They are both serious and ultimate because man's highest values of personal existence or as a self—autonomy, freedom, responsibility—are in collision with something commensurate in dignity with man's freedom, which calls these into question. This is a conflict in the structure of reality as such, hence it is ultimate.

The second presupposition of tragedy is that the hero becomes involved in the axiological cross-purposes of existence, and therefore becomes guilty, e.g., the destroyer of values, or an aspirer who fails, by becoming responsible, that is by being or becoming human: an act which is not quite an act, in the ordinary sense, because it is not the product of a choice in the ordinary sense. The hero discovers that becoming responsible and being guilty are correlative facts. He takes himself upon himself. This expresses his primal freedom, his power to speak for himself. But it also is the "act" by which he becomes guilty, is caught up in the conflict of values. Nevertheless his involvement in the axiological cross-purposes through the "act" of becoming responsible, that is, human, is the occasion both of suffering and the opportunity to exhibit greatness *in* suffering.

From this it is possible to see that a typical subject matter of tragedy is a conflict within what we commonly call the ethical life: the act of choosing evil for the sake of good; of being forced to choose between evils, and so on. The hero is caught in a situation where he must consciously "speak for himself," take himself upon himself, become responsible, hence guilty because he is the agent of the destruction of values. Yet, antecedent to his act of becoming guilty as involved in some destruction of values, he is "guilty" of being human, i.e., being involved in the axiological cross-purposes of existence as man. That is, he becomes entangled in the problem of making a particular ambiguous choice in the first place, only because antecedently he has made the "choice" (which is not a choice on logical all fours with the subsequent ones) to be human.

If we take the ancestral curse in the *Oresteia* to be the symbol of a "given" guilt, we can understand the problem. The blood feud presents no conflict in values until a responsible hero appears on the scene. Orestes only becomes an *ethical*, which is to say, *tragic*, rather than *pathetic* sufferer, through his "decision" to speak for himself, to become human. To put it differently, only when he becomes aware of the ancestral curse, asks questions about it, takes it upon himself as a self-centered being, does he become, as it were, *subjectively guilty*. He "exercises" his primal freedom to become a self and thereby affirms a value; yet this very "act" precipitates him into the axiological cross-purposes of existence, throwing into question the *ultimate* value and meaning of his act of self-transcendence.

Or—to put it still another way—the ambiguity of values in the realm of the ethical, the necessity of destroying values through choice within the ethical, and the suffering that he must bear because of the guilt thus incurred is thrust upon the tragic hero because *anterior to all this he had made another "choice"—he had become a self.*

Before proceeding an important caveat must be introduced. It is precisely the absence in Greek thought of a grasp of the meaning of choice and full personal existence and responsibility as it comes later to be understood through the biblical category of the I-Thou relation that makes illicit the use of "choice" to refer to the circumstance occasioning the coming into being of the hero. The classical tragic hero is born, not made, and certainly not made by any act of personal choice. To become a self, in these terms, is the result of a "fall," in which the hero is passive. In Christian thought, one becomes a self through the responsive, responsible-making *act* of hearing God's word.

Tragedy then, as I have been using the concept, involves an affirmation and a negation—or at any rate, a doubt that is left unresolved: an affirmation of the greatness of man who takes himself upon himself; a doubt as to whether the nature of reality will succor such greatness—the greatness of personal existence. Thus we see that tragedy ends in a kind of mystification. For, if the hero becomes involved in the contradictions of existence through the "act" of becoming human; if being human is precisely being heroic; and yet, if becoming human is to become guilty and suffer the punishment that involvement in responsible existence entails; and especially if the hero is born and not made human, least of all by an act of "choice" in any satisfactory sense; then suffering and death cast doubt upon the ultimate meaningfulness of responsible existence. Even so, the plain fact is that the act of "accepting" responsible existence and exhibiting the power to bear suffering with courage are affirmations by the hero of value, and function as such for all in the audience who identify with him. Yet, it is an affirmation in the face of a serious threat, the doubt cast by suffering and death upon the meaningfulness of that personal existence which is the presupposition of responsibility and courage. If, therefore, it is to be the affirmation of a real rather than an illusory value, it will have to take place in a total frame of meaning large enough to assimilate—one might even say, synthesize—both personal existence and suffering and death: which is to say, larger than the framework of tragedy. Tragedy, therefore, points to a structure of meaning beyond itself, by putting itself under a terrible strain. But it remains silent as to what this structure is, and in so doing, resting in an ultimate *skepsis,* it affirms, paradoxically, the value of responsible human existence at a still higher level.

In other words, there seems to be an "ontological" conflict between the best and highest in human nature and the "reality" that is the "stage" upon which man's existence takes place. When man pursues his highest aspirations, he seems to be brought to ruin. Knowledge and freedom reveal to him suffering, guilt, and death.

The hero exists, i.e., he is "outstanding." Or—to put the matter in terms of the dramatic form itself—the hero breaks out of the Chorus. It is, let it be remembered, the Chorus that evaluates the situation of Oedipus at the end of the play, from the security of its life "prior to existence"—a role performed by Ishmael, saved in his coffin, at the end of *Moby-Dick,* as W. H. Auden has pointed out.

Existence as such, is the hybris of the hero. His suffering is brought upon him at the hands of the gods through the necessity of having to choose. The divine judgment upon his primal presumption of existing is having to choose! His existence is that for which he must pay—a notion appearing no less powerfully in Anaximander's judgment about the world of time and space: "The non-limited is the original material of existing things; further, the source from which existing things derive their existence is also that to which they return at their destruction, according to necessity; *for they give justice and make repara-tion to one another for their injustice, according to the arrangement of Time.*"[4]

---

4. Kathleen Freeman, *Ancilla to the Pre-Socratic Philosophers* (Oxford: Basil Blackwell, 1952), 19. Italics added. This makes us think of the line from *Oedipus the King,* spoken of Oedipus by the Chorus: "Time, who sees all has found you out" (Sophocles, *Oedipus the King,* trans. David Greene, in *The Complete Greek Tragedies* [Chicago: University of Chicago Press, 1959], line 1213).

The hero's original crime is existence itself and everything that happens from the beginning works itself out in inexorable grandeur. Everything bears home to him this necessity: the more intensely he tries to escape, the more inevitably he seems to become entangled. In trying to exercise foresight, wisdom, and responsibility for himself—e.g., Oedipus's flight when told he will kill his father and marry his mother—in seeking to extricate himself from his situation, to outwit the gods, to overcome by increase of knowledge and responsibility, he only hastens his downfall. For it is the exercise of foresight, wisdom, and responsibility for himself that produces the situation in the first place. To extend these is to exacerbate the problem still further, to compound the crime.

All of this implies, of course, that if man had never "chosen himself," he would never have had to choose at all; and that if he had never had to choose, he would never have become guilty of particular crimes. Yet, this is the greatness of man. At the same time this greatness seems somehow an anomaly in the universe. Therefore man shows his ultimate greatness in this ultimate reach of self-knowledge, which enables him to see that he is an anomaly, to acknowledge it, and to acquiesce to it. And we might then add that even for this very reason tragedy doesn't end on a note of agony, but of unrelieved mystery! So the aged Sophocles seems to say in *Oedipus at Colonus.*

IV

Let us now consider some of the differences between tragedy thus conceived and what is possible on the background of biblical presuppositions.

For the Greeks (and of course I grossly oversimplify here) the gods are either the symbols of the several *moirai* or the principle of *moira* itself—the established order. Time is the destroyer of all that is accidental. Only the time-defying is divine:

> The immortal
> Gods alone have neither age nor death!
> All other things almighty Time disquiets.[5]

A violation of this impersonal order is an act of hybris; it is impiety.

---

5. Sophocles, *Oedipus at Colonus,* trans. Robert Fitzgerald, in *The Complete Greek Tragedies* (Chicago: University of Chicago Press, 1959), lines 607ff.

For biblical thought, God is imaged as active, free, and faithful will. God's sovereignty resides not in the impersonal order that governs Him or that he governs, but in His freedom, in His power to give absolutely and freely. His divinity is His sovereign, i.e., uncoerced, will. As it is said, "I will have mercy on whom I will have mercy." A violation of this sovereign will is the attempt to "coerce" it, to identify it with this or that reality, to confine it to some anthropocentric system of meaning, to limit its freedom. This is idolatry.

For the Greeks the archcrime against the gods is impiety—the presumption to threaten their order. For the Hebrews the greatest offense against God is idolatry—the presumption to limit His freedom. A grasp of this distinction is essential to the understanding of the difference between pagan and post-Incarnation "tragic" drama and their respective treatment of human existence and freedom.

This being so, a brief, if slightly simpleminded, digression on this point may be permitted.

To ordinary common sense, experience would appear to have two principal components: the monotonous and the novel. To make sense of experience it is necessary to take account of both these elements, to establish relations between them, to seek to comprehend them both within a single framework. (I do not wish to be sidetracked at the moment by the Wittgensteinian claim that such problems arise only when "language goes on holiday." I am content here to claim that, however misguided for want of reading *Mind and Analysis,* most philosophers relevant to the present inquiry believed this to be an important part of their job.) One can take one or the other of the two classes of things to be normative: the novel—but on this basis nothing can be said, as Plato sought to show in *Theaetetus*—or the monotonous—but in this case the novel is, in some sense, not real, as appears to have been Parmenides' point. The only remaining alternative seems to be that of taking as normative a third "reality" under which these two may be subsumed, e.g., Plato's cosmos comprised of Being, Non-being, and particular things. But this is a kind of subterfuge, for it simply provides a supermonotony. In *this scheme,* we do not have to deny the *reality* of the novel; we only have to deny its *novelty*!

Biblical thought relates monotony and novelty in a quite different way, for they are both seen to be aspects of God's sovereign will, regarded from different standpoints, as it were: monotony and order are seen as the outward manifestations of God's faithfulness; yet He is "choosing to be faithful" anew, in every moment, with the result that there is real novelty both in the orderly and outside it. The contrast here is between the mythopoeic cyclicity—aesthetic rationality—underlying Greek thought and the analogy drawn from the continuity-discontinuity of human volitional life that is the root metaphor of biblical thought.

This biblical "solution" to the problem of course means that the *apparently* novel may be *really* novel in the way every one of my acts, in so far as it is this act, is novel; but at the same time it need not be meaningless because irrational, i.e., form-defying. For however erratic may seem the act of a person, however defiant of our power to place it into a finite and hence comprehendible context of interpretation, it may nevertheless be meaningful to the infinite context of interpretation open to faith—biblically understood—(e.g., Job's absolute trust of God). The novel, erratic, unpredicted act of will cannot always be rationally known to be related to the stable purposes of that person. But it need not be the case for that reason that it has no relation whatever when we grasp the act as proceeding from a person whom we trust and hence for whose acts we are committed in advance to finding a wider frame of interpretation, and whom we shall not cease to trust even if we fail to find one!

All this further means that biblically speaking, the world is neither rational nor irrational—in the Greek senses of these words. The world is a creature, i.e., an act of God. Therefore it is, like any act, both continuous and discontinuous with the other acts of an agent—even though a given act may appear to be so radically discontinuous (e.g., God's "mistreatment" of Job) as to require the context of absolute trust to retain any continuity whatever.

The point, however, is that within this scheme the world can still exhibit a certain monotony—the faithfulness of God—at the same time that novelty—the unsearchableness of God's faithfulness—is expected and accepted; and that, therefore, freedom, God's gift to man, is meaningful, indeed, is itself the *Imago Dei,* but only in a context larger than that provided by pagan tragedy; in short, only in the context of absolute trust.

This means of course that *existence* and *freedom*—responsible, human selfhood—are not as such hybris. Rather it is egocentric existence and perverted freedom that are pride and sin and, therefore, produce suffering. Sin is thus not *impiety*—the violation of an *established* order. It is the *idolatrous* act of seeking to enclose the other "self" in relation to whom we stand in our own ego-centered world. This is the violation of the personal relation by which, biblically speaking, our existence as selves, created to stand freely in relation, is constituted.

By way of summary we may then say (putting the matter far too simply) that for Greek thought the ultimate ground of Being is an impersonal cosmic order or law derived from the cycles of nature and the movements of the planets. From this it follows that order is imaged primarily in terms of measure, limit, the finite, the monotonous, *logos*. The circle or sphere becomes the perfect symbol of finiteness, since they can be grasped by an aesthetic reason that remains in complete stasis and repose, and do not in any way "point" beyond themselves. Existence (whether it be of "things" as for Anaximander or heroes as for the dramatists), "freedom," being outstanding, i.e., heroic, are *measure-defying*, hence are impiety. "Character"—since it is for the Greek an essentially aesthetic notion, one might almost say, an "architectural" notion—is a structure that is an externalized and "visible" ordering of stresses and strains; is therefore strong or weak; and *hamartia* is a structural "fault" that causes the structure to be destroyed. The "fault" is thus an immitigable ontological "blemish" without positive meaning. The gods, as personifications of the several orders or *moirai* that are more primitive than they, are *jealous* of man's impiety. Thus being heroic is itself hybris. Therefore, the value of the hero's self-knowledge and power to bear suffering with courage—in short, the value of freedom and responsible existence—remains ambiguous and subject to doubt until the end. Necessity underlies this worldview. Its final word upon human existence tends to be:

> Look upon that last day always.
> Count no mortal happy till
> he has passed the final limit
> of his life secure from pain.[6]

By contrast, for the background provided by post-Incarnation thought, the ultimate ground of Being is a personal, purposing, and providential will, derived from an analogy of personal existence, volition, and identity. Order is imaged after the analogy of the consistency of a faithful will. Law, or as Kant would say, "the maxim of one's acts," is the "shape" of the will—the perfect symbol of faithfulness. Yet this faithfulness can never be grasped by an aesthetic rationality since neither an act nor a sequence of acts can reveal the

6. Sophocles, *Oedipus the King*, lines 1528ff.

innermost purpose or will of their agent; and this inner dimension is the essential feature of the faithfulness of a personal being. "Character," rather than being an aesthetic conception, is an ethical and, ultimately, religious conception. It is internalized to the very center of the person, and is not weak or strong, but faithful or faithless. But this means that *hamartia* is not a structural fault. It is *freedom*—the element that remains "irrational," i.e., form-defying, for aesthetic rationality. But this is the very *conditio sine qua non* of the meaning of both faithfulness and faithlessness; and as sin it is but the misuse of the *Imago Dei* through the breaking of that relation the standing within which constitutes true personal existence. Therefore, even sin testifies to a positive value. It is the sign not of man's aesthetic incompleteness or imperfection, but that man, as being man, "ontologically" and "essentially" truly *exists* in a personal relation to God (albeit this sign is one that testifies to the present perversion of that relation).

It follows that existence, freedom, and assuming responsibility for oneself before God are not guilty as such. These reflect the image of God in man. Existence and freedom are gifts. Hybris—or, properly, sin—is instead egocentric existence; it is *perverted* freedom. Therefore, possibility underlies this worldview. With Greek drama we always say: What a pity it had to be thus; in post-Incarnation "tragedy" we say: What a pity it was thus, when it might have been otherwise.[7] "Hybris" is then the act of turning the gift of freedom into a theft; the act of claiming existence, which is essentially a gift, as though it were one's own to scrutinize, judge, take or leave, and justify for oneself, rather than something to be received.

In terms of these categories, the "jealousy" of God becomes different also. God is not "jealous" of man's freedom—as with the Greeks; he is, after all, its author. He is jealous that man should fulfill rather than frustrate his freedom. The jealous God is none other than the loving God when he is apprehended by the guilty conscience. The wrath of God is misapprehended love; it is the appearance that God's love has when we confront it in egocentric infidelity to that relation which constitutes our existence.

This finally means that post-Incarnation "tragic" drama is the "tragedy" of defiance. It is truly "tragic" in that, within the limits of the literary work in which it is presented, there is no resolution of the defiance. Ahab, Iago,

---

7. I am indebted to W. H. Auden for this distinction.

Macbeth, Claggart, Ivan Karamazov, Kirilov—all are overwhelmed by the wrath of God and variously respond with defiance. They willfully destroy themselves or others. God does not damn them, they damn themselves by their own defiant choice, thus showing the greatness of man's freedom.

Even so, the "cosmos" in which these acts of defiance occur is not a closed but open one. We feel: It might have been otherwise. These heroes are damned by God's refusal to deny to them this ultimate extension of His gift of freedom. God does not—nor ought the author—save them with a deus ex machina. Yet even the damned are not ultimately damned—or at any rate—are not *known* to be ultimately damned. The *eschaton* and the Last Judgment are symbols within Christian thought of the tentativeness of the ultimate situation of the damned vis à vis God. In these we have a much more explicit indication of the extra-tragic frame of meaning to which, I have said, pagan tragedy points but upon which it remains finally silent, since it was committed at the outset to the limits of aesthetic rationality. Purgatory is a symbol of the belief that even for the damned hope is not exhausted. We feel of these "tragic" heroes that at any moment— during or after the drama is over—they *may* be saved through repentance.

Thus, the flaw is not in the "fundamental structure of reality" (if this slightly question-begging phrase may be permitted), but in the self that destroys its freedom through its eccentric exercise. For the pagan tragedians salvation comes through acquiescence to fate: the foreswearing of existence and freedom as a gift!

At the outset, I held that the tragic was one of several attitudes that we may adopt to the contradictions of human existence, it being the one that we most naturally adopt when these contradictions are thought to be both serious and ultimate. I want now to conclude by saying that in view of the extra-tragic frame of meaning given in post-Incarnation thought, the drama dominated by this worldview is serious irony rather than tragedy. The cosmos of the Christian faith is an open cosmos. It cannot, therefore, be comprehended by aesthetic rationality. Hence, where the Greeks "know too much" concerning the ultimate cosmic destiny of the hero, the Christian is not sure; and where the Greeks "know" nothing at all, the Christian is quite certain—though certain by faith (trust) alone—that a providential, purposing, creating, and freedom-giving God has the final word in all things.

Therefore, even if the contradictions in human existence are serious, they are not *known* to be ultimate; for God has the final word; that word has not yet been spoken; and a meaningful freedom still has all possibility before it.

NOTES TOWARD THE
DEFINITION OF FREEDOM

I

Fyodor Dostoyevski, in his powerful novel *The Possessed,* is concerned to portray, among other things, the world as it appears to a group of young nihilists. Having declared God to be dead, they live the life of absolute and pathological self-assertion, which in a passionate nature is the honest, perhaps inevitable, conclusion of such a declaration. In Stavrogin we encounter the apotheosis of the egocentric self, the man so withdrawn into himself by his own refusal that he is incapable of any relationship with other men. He is a "windowless monad," possessed of no human sentiment or passion, no longer a man because no longer capable of participation in community, one to whom adjectives like *cruel* or *kind* would be applied with equal inappropriateness. He is neither demon nor wild beast, but a once human being from whom transcendence has been emptied; which is to say, something infinitely horrible.

When men cease to recognize that which transcends them, they become incapable of any kind of mutuality. Any relationship that requires the giving of the self is not only unintelligible—a fact which alone might not be serious—but the deepest springs of personal existence are dried up. A man will say: "If God is dead, then I must make myself God. Anything is permitted." Saying this, he becomes capable of that militant kind of self-affirmation that we see in Kirilov, Stavrogin's companion. These men spiral inward toward their own hard core. They end in self-destruction as the ultimate

motive 13 (1953): 4–9.

expression of egocentricity and the last act of self-exploitation. As Kirilov says, "Every one who wants the supreme freedom must dare to kill himself."

But why such an introduction to a discussion of freedom? Let us hear once more from Kirilov. He says: "There will be full freedom when it will be just the same to live or not to live. That's the goal for all." And then he adds, "He who dares to kill himself is God."

Here Dostoyevski exhibits that clairvoyance into the soul of modern man for which he is celebrated. Observe what Kirilov has said in this dramatic utterance. There will be full freedom when living or dying is a matter of *indifference*. In other words, full freedom is indifference; not a relative or tentative indifference—we might say, hesitation—such as is involved in that "suspension" of the will just prior to the act of choosing, but an absolute indifference concerning the ultimate alternatives—life or death. Freedom thus becomes not opting this in preference to that because this more fully evokes our love and thus more deeply completes our acknowledged incompleteness. It is rather the absolute assertion of ourselves as complete; our freedom is this fact and this assertion. To be free is to be able to deny, to refuse, to withdraw into the self, to achieve detachment and independence, to be indifferent. To be absolutely—or to use Kirilov's word, fully—free is *fully* to deny, refuse, withdraw into the self; to achieve detachment, independence, and indifference *absolutely*. To succeed in these, and to testify to it in the sacrament of suicide is to perform a godlike act; *indeed* to become God. "Everyone who wants the supreme freedom must dare to kill himself."

Thus, a world no longer capable of being thought of in terms of providence and grace affords no alternative to man but ultimately to affirm himself against the "eternal silence of the infinite spaces" by an absolute denial of everything except his power of refusal, which he affirms in the act of refusing.

Do I exaggerate when I suggest that Dostoyevski perfectly expresses the logic of modern man's conception of himself and his freedom? It is certainly true that modern philosophers before Dostoyevski would have recoiled from Kirilov's view of freedom with the same horror as we may presume that Dostoyevski did. Neither can it be denied that Kirilov is prophetic, as the reading of a Nietzsche or an atheist existentialist such as Jean-Paul Sartre will confirm. But what of modern tendencies as a whole? Are there clear, even if unconscious and inadvertent, anticipations in the thinkers of the seventeenth and eighteenth centuries? Has the fact that the modern world came into existence through the effort of a middle class to liberate itself *from* an old, feudal, and aristocratic society produced in its thought an analysis of the self and its freedom that has emphasized individualism, autonomy, and detachment *from* institutions and other men? Does this cause us to overlook the possibility that freedom may be *for* something other than itself? Have others suggested that freedom is indifference?

Descartes, the so-called father of modern philosophy, says in his Fourth Meditation, "For the power of will consists only in this, that we are able to do or not do the same thing . . ." Now, I don't think Descartes was being very careful here, or he wouldn't have put the matter just so. Nevertheless, in this unguarded moment he betrays a significant attitude found elsewhere in his writing. A philosopher's oversights—often gladly corrected when called to his attention—are unquestionably the result of his dominant interests and motives. When we discover his characteristic slips we should be grateful for what they reveal about these. Two things are important here: (1) Perhaps inadvertently, Descartes's analysis of the will is highly abstract; (2) Therefore he tends to identify freedom with indifference.

He calls the power of the will the ability *to do or not do the same thing*. I call this an abstract analysis for two reasons. First, because it deals with the will only in the moment when it performs the act of election—the abstract point at which it—to use an unhappy metaphor—flips the switch this way or that. Secondly, because we get the idea that it is saying "yes" or "no" to X, rather than "yes" to X or "yes" to Y. This may not appear to be important. All I have said is that instead of "doing or not doing the same thing," as Descartes has suggested, we actually *do* this or *do* that. In volition, in short, we *never* really withhold. To will is to *affirm*, not to deny.

This kind of abstract analysis leads to his identifying freedom of will with indifference. Why? If you see the nature and functioning of the will primarily in terms of the abstract point at which it "elects"—says "yes" or "no"; if you recognize that a moment of suspension—a relative indifference to or "distance" from alternatives—is a condition of this election; and if you equate the will's freedom with its capacity to perform this feat; then you assume that its freedom is this very indifference.

I don't want to put too fine a point on this. But I suggest that Descartes's view, even if he fell into it while looking for something else, is consistent with a modern prejudice concerning the nature of the "self," which is conceived to have a right to freedom; and that it is not a mere Cartesian eccentricity.

For the moment let us call this the *egocentric prejudice*. By this, I mean the assumption, quite legitimate for certain limited purposes, so far as I can see, that we can start with something called "my consciousness," which is "something there" for my investigation before anything else and quite capable of being explored as this discrete "something" without any reference to anything *of* which it is a consciousness. This is a highly sophisticated, abstract, and, in certain instances, valuable way of lifting my "self" out of the concrete world in which it exists. Being related to the world constitutes my individual selfhood.

In fact, it is precisely this procedure that enables us to see at the moment of "suspension" just before the will elects, that there is a kind of "indifference"—a pause before the act of choice, a certain setting at a distance of the alternatives, a detachment, a brief instant of "refusal." But it leads us to think of selves as if lying about in a room like loose marbles, into the interior of each of which we may look to know what is inside, and the freedom of which is held to be the radical "irrelevance" to each of all the other marbles. A more common-sense, and, in this case, relevant view of the matter reveals that selves are "concerned" with other selves and with things; that whatever "freedom" they really have is one which is had *in relation* to *what concerns them;* and that to think of an unconcerned self is to think of a chimera.

This same prejudice is the standpoint of Immanuel Kant. He says: "What else then can freedom of the will be but autonomy, that is the property of the will to be a law to itself? But the proposition: The will is in every action a law of itself, only expresses the principle, to act on no other maxim than that which can also have as an object itself as a universal law." Now, Kant assuredly does not mean that a free will "does as it pleases." Quite the contrary. It legislates its own maxim of action in terms of its universal applicability and then acts in accordance with this maxim. Its autonomy lies in this self-legislation of the maxim.

But what is important to us is this: The autonomous will of which he speaks is a high abstraction. To will is on one hand to legislate a maxim for action, and on the other to act in accordance with it *because it has been legislated by the will,* and because it might be universally followed. The only way that the will is brought into relation with objects, states of affairs, or other selves is by means only of a maxim universally applicable. This all takes place in a realm where there is only my will, my maxim, and my action in accord with this maxim. It all happens in grand isolation from the world of things and of other selves who concern us. Indeed, for Kant this detachment is the *condition* of a good will. The will wills the principle of its willing.

However much we may prize this analysis for its austerity and high serious-ness, the same difficulty is found here as with Descartes.

Descartes starts with his own private consciousness, initially independent of all that is not his consciousness, and ends by equating freedom with an option that takes place within that consciousness and is in no wise dependent for its fulfillment upon that toward which the option is directed. In Kant, the analysis is different, but the prejudice is the same. We must ask whether a description of freedom that defines it completely without reference to the world in which we as selves live in relation to others is adequate, whether freedom treated in terms of an "unconcerned self" does not overlook impor-tant elements of our actual experience.

One could, if necessary, extend the analysis to Thomas Hobbes and John Locke, as well as others, to show the persistent modern tendency to define freedom in relation to a self that is radically, and by its very nature, indepen-dent and autonomous. I am far from suggesting that these thinkers were willfully pursuing a course that would end in the utterance of Kirilov. Profound philosophical differences may derive at length from what were initially the subtlest differences of emphasis.

But the world today is joined in a terrible struggle concerning ultimate questions of human life and destiny. Both sides declare themselves to be the advocates of full freedom. We have no a priori reason to dismiss the claims of the Marxist as cynical or meretricious. Yet—either there is nothing to fight about, or we understand the meaning of freedom in profoundly different ways. A post-Cartesian analysis of freedom is therefore essential.

II

What follows must in this limited context be nothing more than some very fragmentary suggestions. Rather than thinking of it as an analysis, let us conceive of it as "notes on elements to be considered."

What is the substance of the argument having to do with freedom which has interested so many college bull sessions? Let us begin by saying what it is not or what it ought not to be.

I don't believe it is over the question of determinism-indeterminism. This is an interesting question having to do with whether there are events in nature that we cannot predict. But this is not one likely to evoke strong partisan enthusiasm such as is excited by the problem of freedom. It is equally not the still interesting but more general philosophical question of necessity and contingency—or of what has to be and of what either may or may not be. Nor finally does the discussion revolve about whether we can discover events that are the antecedents of my acts—that is, whether there is open to inspection a sequence of events one of which is *what I do*. These are all important and must be faced in any ultimate statement of our problem.

The real animus of the argument, however, is something very much more important to the participants. It is the question: "Do I have the power to will; is there a something called 'I' which enters a sequence of events as elector, chooser, decider, initiator of acts?"

I am not going to argue this question. I shall answer it by saying that we do have the power to will in this sense. What concerns me here is this: Is this all we mean by freedom? If we could answer the above question with an unqualified "yes," would this satisfy us that we are free? Let us consider this further.

If we take "initiator of acts" to connote the efficacy of the will in the causal world of events where tables and chairs move when I push them, then presumably we have said not only that the will "decides," "elects," etc., but that it is efficacious in an objective sense—something happens as the result of my choice that is not identical with the choice itself. Notice, I am not suggesting that we do not frequently choose without realizing the objective chosen; nor that when we elect this or that but fail of attainment that the act of election is meaningless. I am rather asking whether, when trying to define what it means to be free, we can pretend that fulfillment is not an element in it that must be reckoned with.

Let us go back a moment. Suppose we define freedom as election of one among alternatives, plus causal efficacy—in the sense that something happens in the objective world as a result of our volition. Would this satisfy us? Here is a perfectly terrible illustration. At a dinner party I am offered coffee or tea by the hostess. After due reflection, I decide in favor of tea. But when I have instructed my hostess of my wishes and have received the tea, I find, inexplicably, that I can put the cream and sugar in, lift the cup to my lips, etc., but cannot drink. Am I free?

You might possibly reply: "Well, this was merely a case of bungling, or neurosis or what not. It doesn't decide anything at all concerning the general question, 'Is man a free being?'"

But suppose this happens every time I choose. Remember now, I really do elect among possibilities; my will is efficacious in the objective world of events—so that when I reach with my arm, I can grasp the object. But I never am able to drink the tea. I can will efficaciously all the acts leading to a fulfillment of my wishes except the one act which actually fulfills them. I can will all of those acts that by being conducive to the end which I desire are its means; but I can never will the last act, which would bring me the end. Am I free?

I suggest that I would not be. And this is our whole point. Freedom involves both *option* and *fulfillment;* the power both of electing and of relating ourselves to that which satisfies us. The will's freedom must be understood in terms of at least these two components: the "withdrawal" from things that enables it to "suspend" desire by which election is accomplished, and the return to things in which desire is satisfied. The liberty of the self is not only in its denial or refusal; not merely in the act of setting at a distance the world in which it lives in order that its options may be objectively inspected; not in an indefinite protraction of that "indifference" which we observe in the instant before choice. It is these, balanced with a return to the very things which satisfy it, that is, which possess a capacity fully to evoke our ability to respond; and apart from which it is incomplete, empty, truncated—not a self at all.

Let me repeat. This does not mean that in this world we get what we want; or that what we want we ought to have. All of us want things that we don't, and that, in the nature of things, we cannot get. A colloquial distinction is helpful here: either have what you want, or want what you have. This clearly recognizes, first, that there are at least two ways of having a satisfied will; second, that the will is not satisfied merely by the exercise of its own power to choose, but requires the actual possession of an object.

Therefore, for man to be free it is not necessary that any given choice results in fulfillment. It is necessary that his will do more than merely exercise a capacity for option. It must be satisfied by that "other" toward which it is directed.

Now, I don't believe there is anything the least surprising about this. I think you will recognize that this is exactly what really matters to us. And yet this is just the factor that Descartes, Kant, and others overlook in their analysis. Further, I believe that even if this is not a surprising discovery, it is nevertheless an important one through which we may be able to discover something very significant not only about freedom, but about the nature of man as well.

But before going forward, we must digress a moment. Let us take another brief look at *option* and *fulfillment*. What is involved here?

In order to choose there must be some *objectivity*. To opt would seem to involve the setting of alternatives before my attention for comparison. I compare A with B. To do this I no doubt have to find them both relevant to my interest, I have to objectify "my interest"—what is this interest? I have to know, before knowing exactly *what* A and B are in relation to my interest, that they are in some sense competitors for my present attention. Hungry, I may have been almost unconsciously drawn toward the cafeteria from which came a mingling of delectable food odors. I may have found myself in line at the steaming counters before I realized it. Or I may even "come to" after having actually eaten a meal, in which case we would agree that very little choice entered the process, however much organic satisfaction I may have received.

The point is this: in order for real option to take place, *objectivity* has to be achieved. At some place in this process, there must be a suspension of the will that has moved me from the sidewalk into the cafeteria. I have to *withdraw from, pause in, interrupt* my more or less unconscious course of action in order to choose. I must become "indifferent" to the difference between steak and chicken—that is, weigh them on equal terms—*so far as my appetite is concerned*, and consider them *as they are in themselves* in relation not to my now very hungry self, but *in relation to a person like myself* who has certain tastes such as I have.

This withdrawal from the immediacy, where steak and chicken are primarily a confused and as yet undefined mixture of delectable odors present to the sense of smell, enables me to choose. The meats are no longer merely "objects of my interest"; they become in some kind of objective sense (and this admits of various degrees) something in their own right. Choice therefore involves objectification through detachment and the *acknowledgment* of the *otherness* of that which is the subject of my interest. There then follows upon this the act of *decision*. Literally, there is a cutting loose. One option is accepted, the others are rejected. This is one phase or element of the will's act—the phase of *option*.

But let us remember what has gone before and not make an abrupt separation between this and the next phase. We are not here concerned with the various crises that enter the life of volition. We are interested in what we mean by its freedom.

Having detached myself in order to choose, it is now necessary, if I am to enjoy that which I have chosen, to commence a movement in an opposite direction. If I am to complete the movement that makes me free, I must return to the object of my choice with an interest—not to say surrender—that admits of no tentativeness. This is a familiar experience for all of us. When we have been deeply torn between two attractive alternatives but at length succeed in making a decision, if we persist in an attitude of tentativeness, if we incline to return, intellectually, to the point of the original option, we never succeed in giving ourselves to that which we want. To be in this state is anything but freedom. It breeds the very worst kind of anxiety, and in such a situation one would appear quite reasonable in defining freedom as the condition of being able to give oneself without stint. Indeed, certain modern irrationalists, reacting unqualifiedly against the tentativeness and bloodless irresolution of their contemporaries, made a *cult* of surrender.

A much better illustration can be found in a situation in which the object of my choice is the woman whom I wish to marry. The same elements are present here as above—with perhaps minor changes. The difference lies in the greater importance and vividness of the latter.

The point I have been trying to make is this: A single rhythm of selfhood is involved in my example from my initial response to the smell of the food to the savoring of the steak and the satisfaction of my whole being by it; and any attempt to define freedom as a quality of selfhood that limits it to any part of this rhythm is in error. *Option* requires *detachment; fulfillment* requires *participation.*

This means something very important: *Freedom is not independence any more than it is dependence. It is a participation by the self in that which is other than the self through a conscious act of detachment and return.* What I am trying to say is that freedom is an experience of the self. The self wills, the self is satisfied *by that which is other than it,* the self is free. This experience has two poles: the choosing "I" and the chosen "other." The latter is quite as important to the full experience as the former. The object upon which it depends as its desire, and the satisfaction of it by the object, are conditions of the self's freedom. Therefore we can no longer think of freedom as the absolute independence of a self-centered being such as we encounter in the Cartesian and Kantian analyses. The self's freedom is conditional upon the possession of an "object"; it involves its dependence upon what is not itself.

To what does all this bring us? I think we may summarize as follows: Man forfeits something of his humanity if, losing his power of rational detachment, objectivity, and hence his capacity to choose, he becomes subordinated to immediacy. Nature, other men, his own impulse, have him at their mercy. On the other hand, he destroys something equally essential to his humanity if, withdrawing from nature, other men, and his own impulse absolutely, he loses the power to give himself to that which is other than himself, to fulfill himself in participation. He becomes a Kirilov of absolute indifference. He may lose authentic selfhood in either direction. In purely political terms this means that we must be "detached" from each other through *rights;* and enabled to "participate" in one another through *duties.*

Let us say then that truly to be a self is to be *independent-dependent;* and let us call by the name *liberty* the negative and positive conditions for being selves (which, be it noted, include infinitely *more* than the rather exterioristic safeguards such as civil liberties—in fact, include all we mean by *culture*).

Now, one may ask why the conclusions of this analysis are important. Here is a partial answer.

In defining liberty as independence, modern man has been led—as Kirilov—to equate egocentricity, withdrawal, denial, refusal, and rejection with the very essence of his being as man. He is therefore not an atheist—this is too dispassionate a term. He is a militant atheist, a passionate denier—*and this as a matter of principle.* Men in other ages have denied or rebelled against God. Only modern man has made this into a principle and a program that permeate a whole civilization. God—believe it or not—has become the Devil. If God really is sovereign, then man is not autonomous; which is to say that man is not what the modern world passionately believes him to be. His declaration of independence—in the bad sense that I have defined—has provided him with both a creed and cultus for worship, and a guide to action.

This exaggerated emphasis upon the individual and autonomous self has contributed to the increasing emptiness or dementia of personal existence, and to the consequent bankruptcy of community. With the loss of community, reason is destroyed, and man is caught up in what Max Picard has called "the world of flight." Pascal says, "It is natural for the mind to believe, and for the heart to love, so that for want of true objects they must attach themselves to false." Man naturally needs the "other"—that which is not himself. Modern man, in trying to declare his independence, has not succeeded in rejecting the object upon which he depends. He has only attached himself to false ones.

Furthermore, we shall have to admit that however perversely the Marxist has tried to do so, insofar as he has (while forgetting the other half of the truth) insisted that freedom is not *option* but the *fulfillment* of the individual's life by relating him to an end other than himself, he has provided in his own dangerous half-truth an important corrective to the one-sided individualism of our own tradition. The Marxist is too sure that he knows what fulfillment for everyone is. His vision of fulfillment is so grand and his certainty of it is so great that he is willing to subordinate everything, even choice, to its achievement. Freedom for him is *participation*. He exalts a half-truth into a noxious lie. However, we would be foolish indeed not to correct our own half-truth in the light of his. For freedom is not choice alone either.

III

Alas, from the standpoint of the Christian faith, this endless alternation of *detachment* and *participation* is life under what St. Paul called the Law. The freedom of the Christian man of which he speaks, the deliverance from "this body of death" for which he cries, is rescue from that very bondage which the world calls liberty.

To be a self is to possess liberty. But when we plumb the depths of the self, we discover—often to our horror—that this is the very imprisonment from which we cannot escape because we are no longer taking action against this limitation or that, but against the very self which is the agent of all our action.

The rhythm of *detachment* and *participation* is in its very nature egocentric. It is concerned ultimately with the self: either as it seeks its own identity through *detachment* or its own satisfaction through *participation*. From this we cannot deliver ourselves, for it is from ourselves that we seek deliverance. To be sure, without liberty we would not be selves. These are the limits of natural man. But as selves we are very much at war, and it is from this internal conflict that we seek deliverance. This is what religion means by redemption. It is what Christianity means by grace.

I would like to conclude these reflections by asking a final question. The "Collect for Peace" for morning prayer in the Book of Common Prayer contains these words, speaking of God: "In knowledge of whom standeth our eternal life, *whose service is perfect freedom*" (italics added). In what sense can the service of another be my perfect freedom—and I am using the word to refer to the deliverance from the war that goes on in myself? Let us be very brief.

The service of God is loving response to him because in Jesus Christ he first loved us and enabled us through his son to know and love him; and loving response to our neighbor because he stands in the same relation as we to God's love, and because we desire to reflect upon him the love God has shed upon us. Why is it that this service results in *perfect freedom*? I believe it is because the relation—if it is authentic—between myself and God, the "object" upon whom above all else I depend, and apart from whom I am incomplete, anxious, and threatened by meaninglessness, is not a relation determined by the rhythm of *detachment* and *participation* with its egocentric concern for the self.

Here we have to take an analogy from the relationship of authentic love— between men and women, parents and children. It is wholly unintelligible to discuss such a relationship in terms of *my freedom,* which is over against my *obligations* to my wife or children. The situation has changed. *Detachment* and *participation* are replaced by *giving* and *receiving.* I do not have to make an "object" of the person to whom I am thus related to know and acknowledge her and to know myself as in relation to her. She gives herself to me, she addresses herself to me, and I receive her. But I also receive from her myself, as I stand in relation to her. On the other hand, I give myself to her in the same way, and she receives herself from me. We can no longer speak of *choosing* or *having.* Each self in this relation finds itself by losing itself; for each declares to the other the other's being and his or her acceptance of that being as a gift, and thus establishes the self of the other anew. Such a liberation is all too rare—painfully so. But when we experience it, we know it to be the bestowal of grace.

It is easy for us to become complacent about the freedom that is a gift— since we know that it is the only perfect freedom. But in fact we recognize that one way in which we respond to the giver of this gift is to struggle within the realm of history and nature to procure for all the sons of God that *liberty* apart from which they cannot receive their true inheritance. Nevertheless we labor as those who know that though men may win in history proximate victories for *liberty, perfect freedom* is a gift that cannot be seized, but can only be received; and that it is to this that we bear witness as Christians in the world.

CHRISTIANITY AND
THE INTELLECTUAL

I

The first problem posed by the title "Christianity and the Intellectual" is: What point-of-view does one adopt toward it? And as soon as one asks this, one begins to wonder: How is one to define, in the present cultural situation, a point-of-view? Except for those for whom everything is dogmatically settled in advance, the problem is precisely that of formulating a point-of-view which can both carry personal conviction and maintain some vital relation to the culture as a whole. A notion as to what it is to be a Christian, an intellectual, and, above all, a Christian intellectual are not premises with which it is possible to begin. At best they are matters that we may hope to clarify—although not even *this* within the scope of the present paper. As little can we assume to begin with the premise that fidelity to the church's Lord may not demand that we explicitly denounce the church and renounce the "Lord" who is at once both her creator and her creature.

My task is made further difficult by the fact that in an embattled America there is hardly a man who dares publicly to say that he regards Christianity as an unqualified fraud—which, after all, it may be—and a dangerous one, at that; although I should not want to be commissioned to show it to be very dangerous, fraudulent, or otherwise. Nor yet is it easy to find one who identifies himself frankly as an intellectual. If Christianity, no matter how vague in content or how absurdly propagated, is as little subject to public

J. Coburn and N. Pittinger, eds. *Viewpoint: Some Aspects of Anglican Theology* (Greenwich: Seabury Press, 1959), 144–61.

314

pillorying as is, say, virginity (and, least of all, explicitly so by one who names himself an intellectual), it is difficult to arrive at any clear conclusions—except perhaps the one that Christianity has become a part of "manners," a rather indefinite species of the yet more indefinite genus "faith," so widely hymned in our culture from the furrowed brow of Edward R. Murrow to the bland countenance of Perry Como.

II

Why, indeed, do we even ask about the Christian faith and the intellectual? In a culture that has almost always taken its Christianity neat as simple interpersonal decency, and has wanted its theology "helpful," "practical," "down-to-earth," rather than over-laden with theory, where is the intellectual likely to meet it at any important point, except, being himself essentially a mild and generally decent person, to find himself following doggedly along in the general decency? And in a culture so aggressively egalitarian, where is there the man who will be presumptuous enough to come forward as a thinker by calling—not just one who thinks about his "field." Our universities are full of these last who, outside their special competence, are capable of a naïveté, dogmatism, unreflectiveness, and lack of imagination that would more than justify their less educated neighbors' jibes at the "egg-heads" and the "professors," were it not for the important exceptions. It is an irony of a culture which is so dependent upon intelligence and which officially takes pride in untrammeled thought that it should make anyone professing to be a thinker feel arrogant or silly. In this light "Christianity and the Intellectual" seems like something "made-up" by the Professor of Apologetics to ensure himself something to do.

The very notion of the intellectual has become equivocal. Is not "intellectual" without logical context? Does it not carry a whole worldview on its back? Is it used by Christian and non-Christian in the same way? By thirteenth-century and twentieth-century Christians identically? Has not "mind" (however understood) and its place in "nature" (whatever this has meant) been the most disputed of all questions?

Surely, even for us, the intellectual is not just a man who earns his bread by the power of the word or symbol rather than by the sweat of his brow. Even the scribes of Madison Avenue do as much. He is a man who by vocation feels responsible to thought; whose life is, at least in principle, ordered by reflection; who seeks to overwhelm the chaos of experience by interpenetrating *every level of it* with radical questions that may unify it; who *aspires* to "see" things—above all, his own life—as a whole. And yet, to be forced by experience to concede that none of us ever succeeds in this, may be more than a merely embarrassing shortcoming. It may be precisely the threat to our human meaning that perennially tempts us to idolatry—the idolatry, namely, of believing we really *are* able to see our life as a whole. Nevertheless, is there a man who has asked of himself any radical questions who does not find Christianity hopelessly shabby and shallow? But, even if we were sure about the role of the intellectual, it is no longer as easy to perform that role in our culture as it was thought to be in the nineteenth century. Specialization has worked out its own inner logic. Increasingly, there is an almost unremembered loss of joy in the whole range of human experience within which intellectual curiosity *as such* has self-justifying prerogatives, at whatever level of sophistication it may be exhibited. For a man to think about his "field"—*this* we all understand. To think about one's life—for this a man must apologize!

Then, too, any analysis is faced with the further complication that being religious has become intimately associated with one's being a healthy and public-spirited American at the very moment when the criticism of religion once afforded by the radical Left, groping its way to a new, more positive evaluation of American culture, is no longer available. All discussion is curiously conformist, or at least silent on this topic. If culture and religion are not to become identical, however, criticism is absolutely necessary. The ex-radical intellectuals have little, that is new or relevant, to say. Isolated, even if significant, voices are heard from the church. And it is chiefly from what Morton White has called "Atheists for Niebuhr" that there comes a genuinely new kind of criticism of religion by non-Christian intellectuals. If there has been a betrayal by the church, there is also a treason of the clerks.

"Middle-class" has almost ceased to be an economic or social concept. It has become a system of values, a goal of life. Our griefs are national, political or social, never personal. We are a "lonely crowd," who interpret our triumphs and failures in purely social images. Therefore, in the American way of life there is little of the tragic sense, for tragedy is always personal. There is no place in our official consciousness for guilt because, in our official consciousness, we are, as a people, innocent. There is no growing old, no incurable disease, no death—except in the brutal anonymity of the statistics of journalism.

All these take place behind the scenes. They are literally obscene. In America you go bankrupt or suffer political humiliation in public. Dying is a private affair.

Anglicanism in America, whatever else it is, has by and large become the community of those who have realized for themselves this middle-class dream of Eden. And to all this is added what is an extra bonus gift for an otherwise deracinate, restless, and highly mobile people: Anglicanism is old, very old—older than America, older than the modern world. Withal, it is said, it is always right up with the latest thing. We suffer from neither the gaucheries of the sects, nor from the nostalgia of the Romans. Anglicanism, it is widely believed among Anglicans, has built into an institution a solution to the problem of how to be both in the world and not of it!

If one were to believe this official myth, however, he would be seriously misled. Beneath our surface optimism and even beneath our surface anxieties there lies a hidden and profound anxiety. And whenever this is addressed, it produces shock. But it also produces relief, as the purging of deep emotions and the facing of the truth always do. This rarely happens in church. The church rather seems as if designed to *frustrate* its happening.

In spite of their contrived sound, there they are in the title, clearly juxta-posed—"Christianity" and "the intellectual." Why is this putative special class singled out for attention? Is it because we hope now to find among intellectuals a tolerance for the Christian faith, which has been so profoundly involved in the production of the modern world and is now so deeply im-bedded in it as to have lost its identity? If so, we might be far better occu-pied elsewhere, since such tolerance we already have a hundredfold and, indeed, bid fair to be smothered to death in it. Is it because we hope that out of the desperation of the modern mind at wit's end, we hope to hear of many conversions? Let William Faulkner, whose imagination has journeyed to the end of night, create a character named Joe Christmas and there will be psalms sung, if not in heaven, then at least all over Christendom by all the good grey Christians whose imaginations have never so much as strayed from the Nicene Creed. Or could it *really* be that we wish to journey ourselves to the innermost precincts of the modern experience in order to stand under the judgment of our own irrelevance? If this last were so, we might genuinely hope for repentance. And there may be some of us, and I am among them, who feel that baptism into the church in our culture may be the first act in an increasingly well-plotted program for betraying God; that the faithful prophets of our age are Nietzsche's Superman, Dostoyevski's Ivan Kara-mazov and Kirilov, and Sartre's Orestes, who have dared to say that God has disappeared.

But in fact none of it is as simple as I have made it out. There is a disturbing and characteristic nostalgia evident in our question of Christianity and the intellectual. It reminds us of that spate of books produced in the nineteenth century in which it always appeared that the Christian intellectual knew what he was defending and against whom, while his antagonist was equally clear about all this. In fact, it is frequently a polite family argument in which points are scored and points conceded because everyone vaguely senses that none of it matters terribly! In the twentieth century we have lost this innocence, though characteristically we try to return to it. The very minds who were laying an explosive charge at the foundations of nineteenth-century compla-cency are our real twentieth-century intellectuals: Kierkegaard, Nietzsche, Dostoyevski, Marx, Freud, Ernst Mach, Einstein. We are children of an ironical time when argument has become dead serious and at the same time well-nigh impossible. The sober among us grapple with each other not as in a game, but as those seeking to grab hold in shipwreck.

We are reluctant to admit it, but the crisis in the culture in which we live is very deep. Indeed the crisis *is* precisely that we don't know how to formulate the question about what is happening to us. There is, to be sure, no want of complacency on hand. Eighteenth-century intellectuals believed credulity to be required of the Christian; in our terrible century they have come to feel only superficiality is. But genuinely sober men, be they "Christian" or "anti-Christian," know, in some more or less tentative sense, that there are no longer any clear lines of argument drawn up between them, for they are both victims of an anguish to which complacent, or even chastened and importu-nate, argument is inappropriate: the anguish, that is, of not knowing who they are. Either the Christian or the non-Christian intellectual who is quite sure he knows how to articulate and defend the deepest things that are in him is living in a fool's paradise. The problem for all of us, in a phrase of Michael Polanyi, is that of "learning how to hold our beliefs." The Anglican commu-nity is fond of mistaking its own ease in Sion for sobriety, even as the secular critic of Christianity frequently takes his dogmatism for deep thought. Kierkegaard once said: "It happened that a fire broke out backstage in a theater. The clown came out to inform the public. They thought it was a jest and applauded. He repeated his warning, they shouted even louder. So I think the world will come to an end amid general applause from all the wits, who believe it is a joke."[1]

The rightly prized virtue of Anglicanism (and perhaps every day it is prized by more) is its profound sense of continuity. Ironically, this very virtue may be the ultimate source of its blindness—if that it be—to the radical and growing discontinuity between our own and the Renaissance culture out of which Anglicanism came to self-consciousness. Modernity has long been under attack, and with it all that has helped to make it and is woven into its fabric. Can we really go on believing that the world which produced Kierkegaard and Nietzsche, Sartre and Camus, Heidegger and Bultmann, A. J. Ayer and Wittgenstein, Cézanne and Monet, Picasso and De Chirico, Klee and Jackson Pollock, has suffered a purely transitory disorientation and may be expected to right itself in due course? That there will always be an England, always be a Prayer Book? We do indeed seem to think so!

III

I do not labor these points merely out of bitterness or frustration. I believe nothing of any great value concerning the Christian faith and the intellectual can be said—at any rate said by me—until it is established that the question posed by the title now has a new and very different range and meaning from any it might have had when Christian and non-Christian occupied opposite corners of a commons room, itself essentially secure. I rather do so to call attention to novel elements or characteristics in the Christian's encounter with the intellectual, especially when they are one and the same man— which, I believe, go unnoticed.

If one reads books on theology—whether dogmatic or apologetic—or if one reads that form of theological literature in which Anglicanism seems to specialize, which may be called "Adult Confirmation Instruction," and in which we all of course are represented as knowing quite well what the gospel is (or at least what the church teaches, which may be quite another matter) and also what the non-Christian is likely to say against it, and in which problems are neatly resolved because none have been seriously raised—and if

1. *Either/Or*, trans. David F. and Lillian M. Swenson, vol. 1 (Princeton: Princeton University Press, 1944), 24.

one goes at this with proper piety, there are times when he is apt to feel rather like Alice in Wonderland when she fell down the rabbit-hole, or perhaps even oftener like Kafka's Gregor Samsa, who awoke one morning from a troubled dream to discover he had turned into a giant cockroach! To be sure, it's all done quite literally: urbane references to T. S. Eliot or even Tennessee Williams; a knowing allusion to Freud or Toynbee; then—back to the Nicene Creed. But there is a troubling sense of unreality about it, as though somehow Eliot and Williams, Toynbee and Freud had exposed a raw nerve to the contemporary world, were speaking to real experiences which we are getting in this "instruction," if at all, only secondhand; and in any case, which have nothing to do with the Creed or, more properly, with which the Creed has nothing to do.

It is more difficult to find the apologetic literature of the anti-Christian—at least in explicit form—though it is to be had. Occasionally, as in the recent republication of Bertrand Russell's *Why I Am Not a Christian,* something appears, and when we read it, it seems like some prehistoric species of fish caught while carelessly swimming up out of the Philippine Deep. There is one document that is of great interest: *Religion and the Intellectuals,* a symposium of some thirty philosophers, writers, critics, and artists, built around questions set by the editors of *Partisan Review*.[2] These short utterances range from the dogmatically and aggressively antireligious through the ruefully, sensitively, even grievingly, "unreligious" to the heterodoxly religious and the more or less orthodox (as though that meant something!).

My reasons for calling attention to this book, however, are two: (1) One is profoundly struck by the fact that, with several notable exceptions, these gifted and articulate people do not have a very clear idea either of what religion in general is (whatever that *is*) or of what Christianity in particular is. There is a deep uncongeniality of their sensibilities to that dimension of experience of which they write. Men who write sensitively and with great insight about the human situation in other connections, when writing about religion, turn pedantic or oratorical. There is something secondhand about what most of them say, which reminds one of nothing so much as of Anglican Adult Confirmation Instruction! (2) Therefore when, as they do, some take an aggressively antireligious stand, the same atmosphere of unreality appears.

2. *Partisan Review,* 3d series, 1950.

The debate seems not to be about anything that matters or, if so, only mattered the day before yesterday.

What does this mean? I shall try in due course to answer at length. But let me tentatively offer a suggestion. Just as much Christian apologetic takes its departure from the assumption that we all know quite well what the gospel is, what are its principal intellectual pitfalls, and who are its most dangerous opponents (other than ourselves), so also much anti-Christian apologetic assumes that its *own* critical standpoint is fixed and secure and the lines against which it hurls itself are well-defined and the positions worth taking.

These assumptions do not seem to me to have any bearing whatever on the present situation. The problem of the Christian faith and thought in our time is far deeper than this. If it were not, I should want to abandon them both and take up something really serious such as murder, say, or suicide, as Albert Camus has put it. It is not the question, "Can the man of intellectual integrity (where we assume we have an undisputed concept of what he is) be a Christian (and we assume we have acceptable clarity as to what this is)?" Sober intellectuals have to confess that their own anguish arises precisely from their wondering what intellectual integrity really is. And contrite Christians have to confess that it is very difficult to *understand* what it is to be a Christian. Men in such a condition are hardly prepared to *state* their positions, even less to dispute over them. They cannot even be sure whether and how they are at enmity. Above all, they need desperately to *listen*. There are no previously prepared positions.

Now, lest the foregoing be dismissed as mere melodrama, let me hasten to try to bring conviction to it through some elaboration.

IV

In the above I have assumed that when we speak of the Christian faith and the intellectual, we are wondering about their relations *at the level of reflection*. And this means, of course, that we are speaking of the relation of the Christian intellectual, *as an intellectual*, to his non-Christian counterpart. I have tried until now to suggest certain hazards in encounter that are not so much the function of their being Christian and non-Christian, as of their being creatures of our distressful time. In the course of doing this, I made the paradoxical remark that when argument becomes dead serious, as it has for us, suddenly it seems to become well-nigh impossible. I want now to clarify what this remark means, and why I believe it is so, by approaching the Christian and the non-Christian primarily as *reflective* men; and, therefore, to view their encounter not chiefly in the light of their common historical and cultural situation, but rather in terms of *argument*—the instinctive resort of all reflective men. To do this I want to enlarge somewhat upon the *notion* of argument. Even this discussion, however, must keep in view at every stage the present cultural situation of the reflective man. As different arguments are appropriate to different sorts of dispute, so the kinds of reflective encounter that will occur in times of deep cultural confusion must differ from those that occur in periods of relative stability. It has been part of my thesis that failure to accept this distinction has given an atmosphere of unreality to the encounters between the intellectual and Christianity.

The great temptation of the reflective man—be he Christian or non-Christian—(particularly as "reflection" is understood in our excessively verbal and literal-minded culture) is an inordinate faith in the word. Or better, the reflective man in our culture, which aspires to transact its serious thinking in a language modeled on the ideal accepted by modern science, is likely to overlook the well-concealed traps set for him in *all* language, except in a completely univocal one such as mathematics. His occupational hazard as a verbalizer, therefore, is that of being taken-in by words. As an adept and familiar of words, he is not always aware of the momentous commitments harbored by certain familiar words when they appear in slightly unusual contexts—or for that matter in usual ones. He may forget that some of the most axial concepts we all use as a matter of course cause us to take hold of the world in one way rather than in another. A concept appearing on the surface is rooted in a sometimes very complex metaphor, so deeply buried in our language that not only is it not noticed, but it actually requires a great feat of reflection to discover its hold upon the mind. He may forget that certain gross images or models preside over and regulate the behavior of our most familiar and indispensable concepts: concepts like "real," "know," "true," "believable," "faith," "person," "nature," "reason."

The other side of this excessive confidence in words, when he is dealing with the world in terms of theory, is the reflective man's suspicion of what I will call the syntax of each man's nonconceptual relation to the world. In saying this, I perfectly illustrate, as a verbalizer, the perils to which I call attention. For in speaking of "syntax," I have employed a concept that is used about the use of words. I have, in other words, "talked" about the nonverbal in a "wordly" way. Furthermore, "communication," a word I was forced to use, functions in our culture for the most part in accordance with an essentially verbal, indeed an increasingly electronic, model. And "world," I fear, is governed by a no less definite model, with all of its submerged commitments.

The fact of importance here is that the "shape" of the world in which we live is not given only, perhaps not even primarily, in concepts. It certainly can only be *talked* about with concepts (where "talked about" operates in the environment where dictionaries are a standard tool). But it is *lived* in through our bodies, our choices as they are manifested in our actions, our movements, our routines, gestures, rituals; through our expectations as they are manifested in what surprises or disappoints us; through the way our affections are related to, evoked, and structured by, shapes, colors, and sounds that have undergone a symbolic transformation and that, therefore, constitute for us an "atmosphere." When we feel joy or depression and anxiety, features of the world in which we live have a special *coloration* or meaning; the brightness of light, the weight of the overcast sky, the threat of night. These symbolic associations—and, of course, words that ordinarily name concepts become parts of a symbol when incorporated into a poem—are elements in the structure or shape of each one's own way of living in the world. Our way of feeling *in* the world, the rhythms of our being at home here have some kind of order, and therefore may be thought of as having a kind of syntax.[3] As such, though not conceptual, these structures cause each of us to take hold of our world in one way rather than in another. Each man's own existence is essentially the enactment of a drama, having for its stage both the conceptual and the nonconceptual. If it were not so, deep personal disorientations of the sort with which psychoanalysis has to deal—and, one might add, with which theology deals—could quite simply be cured by a bracing verbal clarification, an attempted translation of the symbolic into the verbal. There is a very strong hint of this in Freud's theory (in contradistinction to his practice, of which he was a bad observer). There is also the recurrent return to this belief in Ludwig Wittgenstein's remark that what appears to be deep philosophical perplexity is not *solved* but *dissolved* by linguistic clarification—as though

---

3. See Erich Fromm, *The Forgotten Language* (New York: Grove Press, 1951), where a psychoanalyst unhesitatingly speaks of the nonconceptual ordering of our world after the analogy of language.

one's world, and therefore one's perplexities about it, are definitely and exhaustively conceptual.

The child who knows what it is to be securely and lovingly held lives, moves, deploys his body, and expresses himself in action in a *very* different world from that of one who has never known this.

The *official theory* is such that the intellectual in our culture, in his theoretical posture toward our common world, is tempted by that theory to accord small place to this nonconceptual shaping of each man's own life.[4]

Even so great a genius as Freud, the contemporary articulator of the profound importance of the nonconceptual world and of what we have rather simplemindedly called the irrational, betrays the power of rationalism over his own imagination by repeatedly implying that the norm for *human* existence is the power which man has to *conceive,* that the *rational* or conceptual grasp of the etiology of one's own past is that by which man becomes human; rather than the far richer notion that man becomes human through the capacity for assuming responsibility, for taking his own past upon himself, for speaking in his own name, for saying "I."

The intellectual may, therefore, suppose that all our significant differences can be resolved at the conceptual level. He then fails to notice the built-in nonconceptual syntax of his own culture or subculture. The nonconceptual for which I have no special "feeling" may be analogous for me to the world unknown to the anxious child. The nonconceptual culture of the Western world, the shaping of our deepest sensibilities, is so pluralistic that we have to admit it to be both Christian and many other things as well—even now.

What does this mean for an assessment of the encounter between the "Christian" intellectual and his "non-Christian" counterpart, especially at a time of profound upheaval? At least this: We cannot, whoever we are, meet one another's worlds in purely *conceptual* terms because the world is for each one of us more than we can simply say. Beyond speech and the use of symbol, each of us can only *enact* his world—though even this enactment has to be "read," not only by others, but also by myself. And if it can be "read," then it

---

4. I am not for a moment arguing that every nonconceptual component of one's world is radically private, and that therefore there can be no nonconceptual "public" world. Indeed the very opposite is the case. It is only that we cannot have a nonconceptual world that is "public" in the same way in which we may have a "public" conceptual world; and that a conceptual test of publicity for a nonconceptual world is rather like having bridge rules for refereeing a poker game!

can also be *mis*read—as much by oneself as by another! A relentless obedience to the merely conceptual (as this is construed in our culture) and to argument (understood in terms primarily of a conceptual model) will make us blind rather than make us to see.

Of course, I am not suggesting that one should or could abandon words; or even that speaking and hearing are not normatively human actions.[5] I am rather making the obvious point that we not only understand ourselves and one another by the use of words, but we also *mis*understand ourselves and one another by means of them. Launching a word into the world is always the *action of a person* and is as liable to misrepresent the agent to a strange interpreter as is a gesture. In a time such as this, I believe we all feel acutely the shock of discovering that sometimes the stranger who has misinterpreted our own action of speaking is ourselves! It is well to be aware of how this happens and that this perennial difficulty is seriously exacerbated in a period of deep historical crisis (and these are *always* crises in communication), *especially when this crisis is in large part the product of an excessive confidence in an oversimple model of communication!*

When the church and its critics carry on their conversation in a fashion more or less reckless of this fact, confusion is confounded.

I have been suggesting in all this that the hazard to the reflective man is his inordinate trust in argument. He is tempted, therefore, to suppose that all *genuinely* intellectual encounters—that is, encounters where agreements are achieved or frustrated—are essentially *arguments* and that all arguments *are of one sort.* To take an extreme example, with a formalistic model of argument in mind, he may hope for knockdown proof and overpowering conviction where such an expectation is "unreasonable." He may become impatient when, as I believe is now the case, we reach that point where disagreement becomes so profound that, even with good faith on all sides, we no longer know quite how to formulate our disagreement. Discussion at this depth, the groping, the attempts to find a path, are I believe, *genuine intellectual activities,* and in fact may, with complete propriety, be called *argument.* It is

5. Although a whole career of conceptual analysis and exegesis would be required to make this quite clear. For example, what is it really to speak and to hear? We might naturally say of an electronic brain that it can "speak" and "hear." It becomes odd, however, for me to remark of such a machine, "It is not really listening to me," or "It is not paying proper attention." Yet, to say such things of another person is not at all odd. To this extent "speak" and "hear" are different in the two cases.

very different, however, from an argument where the problem is clearly defined, assumptions clear and shared, and rules of inference given. It is just where we begin to be puzzled in this most radical way that argument becomes at once both dead serious and well-nigh impossible. The fact that the context and use of many of the key concepts of all discussion can be imagined as being what they are only on the assumption that the culture that has borne and propagates them has been deeply infected by the belief that the Word became flesh, far from providing a bridge, actually produces a stumbling block.

Clearly, it is possible for people to be said to have different "attitudes" when they can be thought to share a common universe of meaning. In a universe where "right" and "wrong" are meaningful concepts, it is a familiar fact that people are in dispute as to what kinds of action are correctly called "right" and what called "wrong." We can be puzzled about different things, find meaningless, or meaningful, different subjects of concern within a world that is, in gross terms, a common one. Different classes in a society may hold variant attitudes on, for example, divorce, petty larceny, or lying. But imagine a fictitious people for whom "right" and "wrong" are empty concepts. They could not, *in the same sense,* be said to have different attitudes from those for whom they are not *empty.* The former may be said not even to have noticed the sorts of things toward which the latter have attitudes—and even a wide variety of attitudes.

The reflective man, when he discovers this kind of deep disagreement, is tempted to despair. His confidence in argument, understood as just one sort of intellectual transaction, has been shaken. Having been inordinately trustful of words and of argument, fitted to a simple model, he feels betrayed. From the edge of truly profound disagreement, which at times borders on a kind of schizophrenia, this man either retires to the private world of his own "field" where all is once again secure because all others in it are the familiars of a clearly defined and commonly shared, even if spiritually truncated, universe, or else—and this is not as different a response as it appears—he loses all hope in the power of the human person to participate in a reality other than itself. Holding to a particular model of "reason," he becomes distrustful of human reason as such, and this because, as a reflective man in our verbal culture, he has forgotten that the condition of any conceptual culture whatever is an antecedent nonconceptual openness and responsibility of persons to one another.

V

In view of all this it is perhaps now possible to say the following without seeming to indulge in willful paradox-making.

First: Aside from the much celebrated exceptions, as a profound influence upon the sensibilities, as a maker of attitudes and shaper of the imagination (beyond what occurs simply in the general culture into the making of which it entered), *Christianity is as if it were not* for intellectuals. It would be quite impossible, to be sure, to understand, say, the plays of Jean-Paul Sartre or the paintings of Picasso without seeing them as having a milieu in which Christianity has been and is even now an ingredient. What reassurance is to be drawn from this fact, I am sure I do not know! Yet it would be equally absurd to argue that Christianity has been or is likely to become for either of these men an explicit problem for debate or argument or that it will manifest itself in an explicit iconographic way. And when it does become such for their like, the discussion takes on that air of unreality I have tried to describe and which I believe shows that it is not very real for them—real, let us say, as it was for Kierkegaard, for Nietzsche, for Dostoyevski, and even for the young Karl Marx.

Not only so. This quality of secondhandedness also pervades and deadens much of the reflective Christian's thought about Christianity. Nowhere, I believe, is this more profoundly so than it is in Anglicanism, for Anglicanism, which is very old, insulates one against the sharp bite of our contemporary experience, the precise factor that gives rise to really *serious* thought. Even so radical, so mercurial, so witty, so essentially sober an intelligence as is manifest in the works of W. H. Auden's frankly Christian imagination, is capable, in the context of discussion of Anglicanism with fellow Anglicans, of sounding like a nineteenth-century English vicar!

Secondly: I believe it is far easier for one to take with radical seriousness, in secular intellectual circles, the question, "What is it for me to be a Christian?" When a "Christian" asks this of his fellow "Christians," he may be applauded as a devilishly clever Socratic sort of fellow, but he will not be believed to be quite serious! It is here that I think it possible to see why the profoundest attack upon Christianity in the modern world has come from a Christian—Kierkegaard—and that its greatest defense has come from a so-called atheist existentialist—Nietzsche! For both of these men one's human existence is not to be redeemed simply by one's being born, for Kierkegaard, into the church, or for Nietzsche, into Western middle-class "Christian" society. It is worth noticing, too, that neither of these men "argued" in any ordinary sense, nor considered himself to be engaged in argument. A major import of the work of both of them was a disagreement with their own time over what it is to disagree and, therefore, over what it is to agree. Yet they have both confronted us in our humanity more profoundly than either Christian or anti-Christian apologists of the obvious sort have done or are now doing.

Finally: One has to say, I think, that the irrelevance to the intellectuals of Christianity as it is formally ordered and propagated may become the occasion of repentance. As our sterile, word-imprisoned, meaning-blind debates come to impress us as more and more futile; and as the "non-Christian" intellectual comes to listen with less and less patience to us, we may fall silent and begin to listen. In our time, really sober men, whatever their *conceptual* picture of themselves, seem able to touch something of their own and one another's deepest human reality, when they meet in the non-conceptual world given by poetry, painting, the novel, drama, music. If we are not too quick to see our own conceptual image reflected in all of this, to look for the familiar Christian situation, the recognizable Christian icon, it may be possible, coming with broken and contrite hearts, for us to begin to see what it is to be a Christian at this moment of history. Idols not only contain and limit the God who reveals himself by being present, but also veil from us the God who manifests himself no less by becoming absent. Now is a time when we have to feel God's distance from us. If we remember this humbly, it may be that when we ask our question, we shall be heard; when we grope for an answer, we shall be understood.

CAN AND SHOULD A
COLLEGE BE CHRISTIAN?

Defining Some Central Issues

I

I take it to be the function of this paper to ask, first, "Is it meaningful to use the adjective *Christian* before the noun *College*?" Second, "If it is meaningful, how do we know when it is properly used; what, that is, would a Christian College be?"

In addressing myself to these questions, I do not pretend to be concerned with the current usage of these words. Nor am I supposing they cannot be used in other ways than I propose to use them here. This is an essay in definition. I am suggesting that we talk in the following way!

For my present purposes I find it convenient to use the word *college* to refer to a community of persons united in the rational pursuit of truth. A "community" I shall understand to be an aggregate of individual and relatively autonomous persons who in some sense and in varying degrees have a "private" existence, a sphere of private decisions and an inassimilable personal depth; who are nevertheless bound together respecting certain goals and evaluations; who live a corporate life through the means of certain symbols or propositions expressing the general attitudes and evaluations that bind them together; into whose *identity as individuals* these symbols and evaluations of corporate life really enter; and, finally, whose life together is expressed in *particular* evaluations, decisions, and acts from day to day.

The Christian Scholar 37 (1954): 12–18.

I will call the ultimate evaluations (and the symbols in which they are expressed, which constitute the foci of communal existence), First Order Decisions. The word *decision* is somewhat misleading in this case. One does not really *decide* upon his worldview in any detached sense. But the use of *decision* does serve to indicate what is the case, namely, that we are related to these symbols fundamentally through *sentiment*. Among First Order Decisions are not merely the explicit ground of *this* corporate life, but implicit evaluations concerning the nature of man, the meaning of history, the meaning of the "created" world, the role of *this* community in the life of the individual who is its communicant, and its place in the process of history and culture as a whole, etc. These "decisions" are what are at times called "metaphysical presuppositions."

The particular day-to-day evaluations, decisions, and acts of the community, a community that has its existence through this relatively stable set of First Order Decisions, I shall call Second Order Decisions. In a highly complex and heterogeneous community, the relation among the several First Order Decisions is not neatly logical; and the relation between Second Order and First Order Decisions is not simply deductive. But, there is a tolerable order among the First and a real logical and psychological relation between the Second and the First; else the community is destroyed. The ultimate decisions express the identity of the community. The penultimate ones exhibit its fidelity to itself.

Now, if a college is a community, then like every community, it is an aggregate of persons united by certain corporate First Order Decisions which have some logical and psychological bearing upon their private and corporate Second Order Decisions. These First Order Decisions express not only the corporate intention of pursuing the truth rationally, but implicitly express also decisions concerning the ultimate nature and value of reason and truth, as well as attitudes, evaluations and judgments concerning the nature of the world, of man, the meaning of history, etc.—in short, an implicit "metaphysic." I take it that no one would dispute the claim that in this broad sense of the word, there are distinguishable Christian, Marxian, and Liberal Democratic "metaphysics." Hence, it *is* meaningful to use adjectives such as *Christian, Marxian, Liberal Democratic* before the noun *College*.

So much for the first question! I have deliberately resorted to a somewhat dogmatic tone in order to get the issue clearly before us. I hasten now to introduce the qualifications that seem to be crucial, if the second question is to be relevantly considered.

II

The task of seeking the most general attitudes, evaluations, and affirmations of a given individual or historic community or society is always perilous in the extreme. The spectator achieves a kind of detachment that makes possible and at times fruitful generality, but at the price of an abstractness that is at best partial, at worst a falsification, and of a selectivity that may have no more than a personal relevance for him. The participant, on the other hand, is able to grasp the *affective* relations between ideas not so readily available to those more interested in their logical relations, but at the cost of an immediacy in which the image of the life of the community loses all shape. One has to resort to both of these in turn with a full sense of the limits peculiar to each standpoint.

This task is complicated by at least two further facts: First, one has to seek these general attitudes, evaluations and affirmations not only in the symbols and general propositions through which a community expresses these to itself and to others, but also in the more specific decisions, actions, and evaluations of day-to-day existence. The relation between the latter and the former is a highly complicated one, and it is almost certainly not a simple deductive one. This seems to be the case both because every decision, at the time that it is made, is based upon contingencies that may render it foolish from the point of view of hindsight, which, not being involved in the decision, fails to see the problem in its concreteness, the objective toward which it was directed, and the basis upon which probabilities were calculated; and because concrete decisions always bear both more and less than a merely deductive logical relation to general evaluations on the one hand and to probabilities on the other. Every concrete act, in other words, expresses not merely a general set of attitudes—e.g., Christian, Liberal Rationalist, Marxist—but the concrete attitudes of a community *at a given moment of decision, in all its particularity.* These may actually be a betrayal of values of a more general sort. In short, men and communities frequently act irrationally. It is dangerous, therefore, to move from particular attitudes and decisions to the general affirmations of a community. Communities do not always act rationally; their specific decisions do not bear a necessary and *deductive* relation to their general beliefs since the former, *at the time they are made,* are based upon contingencies. The best we can say is something like, "Given our belief (B) concerning the nature of the world in the situation (S) with characteristics a, b, c, d, and possibilities 1, 2, 3, 4, we very probably ought to do X." However, even if the relation is not deductive and men are not even as logical in their actual behavior as they could be in principle, it would be absurd to suppose that there is *no* connection— either logical or psychological—between their general attitudes toward the world and their specific behavior in it. If the latter were the case, there would be nothing to which the words *community* and *society* could possibly refer, and therefore, a fortiori, no way of contrasting one with another.

The task is complicated in the second place, because in the nature of the subject investigated, whether one at the moment takes the standpoint of spectator or participant, one is taking up an attitude toward the general evaluations of a community from the standpoint of either the same or different evaluations, and this predisposes him to attach significance to some things and not to others. In short, the investigator is himself axiologically involved.

I introduce these elaborate and apparently gratuitous disclaimers not to disarm criticism of what I am saying, but rather in the hope that some of the, I believe, entirely irrelevant arguments between interpreters of the Christian College and between the former and advocates of some form of so-called "secular" education in a democratic society may be removed. I would not suggest that there is no issue here. On the contrary, the argument seems to me to have very great theoretical and practical import. At the same time, much confusion seems to me to derive from a failure to clear the ground of certain misunderstandings and equivocations. For example, if what I have said above does in fact hold, and there is some logical and psychological connection between specific decisions, evaluations, and judgments in the life of a community and certain general attitudes and affirmations which give to that community its identity, then we must exclude entirely the limiting case of a "presuppositionless" college, a university that is "just a university," to which the qualification Christian, Marxist, or Liberal Rationalist is irrelevant. This means that in the discussion, in which educators compare the relative virtues, etc., of "Christian" and "Secular Democratic" colleges, they must have in mind something to which their terms refer. They clearly do not intend, in this context, to compare the architectural style of buildings, but a certain community of people, bound together by certain common objectives, living a corporate life more or less based upon certain ultimate evaluations, in terms of which daily decisions of policy are made and attitudes toward the world taken up with more or less logical consistency and fidelity. I wish to emphasize the qualification, "more or less."

Therefore, I do not believe there is really such a thing as a *college-or-university-as-such,* in any other than the trivial sense that despite different ultimate evaluations and affirmations, "Christian" and "Liberal Rational" universities have certain characteristics in common.

At the same time, those who recoil from the imagined implications of such a view are not unqualifiedly mistaken. Indeed, it is in the attempt to make the legitimacy of their protest plain, and thus their partial truth once again available to the discussion that I have sought to clear the ground. Doctrinaire analyses on both sides have introduced needless contentiousness into a debate in which there really are two sides.

Those who say a *college-as-such* is a pure and meaningless abstraction because every human community decides, acts, evaluates, and lives its corporate life in terms of certain ultimate affirmations about the world, usually go on, in too rationalistic a fashion, to relate every element of that corporate life to these affirmations. They want to show, e.g., that Liberal Rationalist presuppositions enter into the discipline of economics and chemistry, and into the mind of the teacher of economics and chemistry—or so they appear to be suggesting. The suggestion that there is "Liberal Rationalist Economics" and "Liberal Rationalist Chemistry" naturally offends the man who is quite sure his study is "objective"—i.e., free of the gratuitous intrusion of affirmations concerning the nature of the world, etc. Now, this is an extremely complicated epistemological and methodological question—one into which we must forbear to enter here. I am quite sure that the presuppositions of economics are related to a set of ultimate affirmations in a different way and to a different degree than are the presuppositions of chemistry. In this context, however, I will limit myself to saying that both those who would try to say there is something called "Liberal Rationalist Chemistry" and those who would insist that "Chemistry is chemistry" and is in no way related either logically or psychologically to affirmations of a more general metaphysical order are oversimplifying.

What is very much to the point here is that the means used by those who have wished to indicate the implicit faith underlying the "Christian" college or the "secular" college have tended to overstate their case, thus at once arousing the just suspicion of their opponents and obscuring the truth in the protest of their opponents. I think we must say that every human enterprise and the existence of every human community involves either implicit or explicit "metaphysical assumptions"—that ultimate attitudes concerning the nature of the world and man enter logically and psychologically into the penultimate judgments, evaluations, decisions, and actions of men and communities. If this were not so, there would be no rhyme or reason in human existence. What then, in face of this, is the truth in the protest of those who want to remove from before the word *college* or *university* the qualifying adjectives *Marxist* or *Christian*—as the case may be?

Many Christian critics—and let me observe en passant that most of their criticism is epistemological and hence in no peculiar sense "Christian"—adopt the traditional Faith-Reason dichotomy and argue that "faith precedes reason"—hence there are no presuppositionless philosophies and weltanschauungen—and therefore no historical communities whose rationality is not ultimately dependent upon a certain commitment of the community's affections. Now, I believe it to be true that faith, understood as the response of a community to reality, does precede reason, understood as bringing to consciousness this faith and the explication of all of its implications. But this view opens itself to attack when it supposes that the relation between faith and reason in the actual life of an individual or community is a simple deductive one from which all contingent elements can or ought to be removed. Consequently they actually argue or—more frequently—are misunderstood as arguing that the actual rational activity of a community has the same deductive relation to its own "postulates" as the conclusions of a deductive argument to its premises. This goes entirely too far, as I try to argue in my opening qualifications.

Others speak in terms of absolute presuppositions and relative presuppositions. Again the relation between the latter and the former is certainly not *merely* psychological. But neither is it neatly logical. In the concrete life of a community these relations are much more confused, the logical and psychological interpenetrate much more complexly than any simple epistemological inquiry is able to discover or express. This is particularly true of highly advanced and heterogeneous societies such as our own.

This element of contingency enters into the volitional and evaluative life of communities in two ways. A particular act of judgment and decision is based not merely upon a commitment of greater generality, but also upon circumstances that cannot in principle be known at the time of decision. We therefore cannot *know* that X is the "right" thing to do in the same deductive fashion as we know that a given conclusion to a syllogism is the "right" one. Contingency enters here. At the same time contingency enters in the very fact of man's freedom.

This contingency is one of the factors which keeps a community humane. Only a Marxian-Communist society that eliminates all contingency in the concept of the dialectic of history imagines radical consistency to be possible and defines inconsistency—whether conscious or unconscious—as treason. All societies not illusioned by a rationalistic prejudice expect and can assimilate, even encourage, within limits, both inconsistency and dissent. At the same time, there are always limits to this tolerance that cannot be transgressed without the society ceasing to be, even if these limits are both difficult and dangerous to define too precisely in advance and in too abstract terms. We can never say precisely how much strain can be put with impunity upon the basic principles of a society at a given moment. It is always dangerous to sound the alarm prematurely. Yet the tragic fact of human societies seems to be that when we are quite sure it is not too soon to sound the alarm, it is already, in fact, too late.

III

In full recognition of these reservations, we may now turn to the second question before us, namely, "What would a Christian College be?" I wish to make it quite clear that this is *not* the question, "How do we create a Christian College?" I seriously doubt that anyone can "create a Christian College," and I believe it is reckless from the point of view of culture and idolatrous from the point of view of God's sovereignty to try! We are as incompetent to "build" a Christian College as we are to "build" the Kingdom of God. We can only make specific decisions and act in a given historical context, with all the limits that it imposes upon us—including our own finiteness and sin—as men who have made certain Christian First Order Decisions—recognizing the contingency, relativism, ideology, anxiety, egocentrism, infidelity, pride, and fear of death that infect all our Second Order Decisions.

Even so. I think it not impossible to formulate a limiting concept that will express in part the "logical" structure of a community whose First Order Decisions are generally Christian. Therefore, I would suggest that a Christian College is a community of persons united in the rational pursuit of truth in which the dominant and effective First Order Decisions ultimately express the affirmation that Jesus Christ is Lord; where therefore Second Order Decisions and evaluations ultimately express a response to Him. To rescue this definition from a completely empty generality, we might say that a Christian College is a community where men understand themselves, the world, and their own corporate life in terms of the First Order symbols of Incarnation, Creation, Fall, and Eschatology.

Jesus Christ as bearer of *Grace* and *Truth* is the ultimate concern of the Christian College. The college is a community in which men as unitary beings encounter one another in a multiplicity of ways. Here the whole human drama unfolds. Here is evidenced the shadow of man's *Justitia Originalis;* the fragmented but still partly viable community. Here is exhibited man's dependent-independent nature; his sinfulness; his existential anxieties; his fear of death and meaninglessness. Here is dramatized man's vanity, egocentrism, pride of reason, etc. Here, in short, is man's greatness and wretchedness. Jesus Christ as the bearer of *Grace* brings illumination and healing—after he has brought judgment to this community.

But the college is a community in which men and women encounter one another uniquely, consciously, and systematically as minds, directed toward the truth. Here, Jesus Christ as the bearer of *truth* must be related *as the bearer of the Truth* to the conflict among *truths*. Here, the gospel opposes itself as *thought about the world* premised upon the event of Incarnation to other thought about the world.

A final word concerning cultural pluralism. Pluralism is not merely a contemporary reality in American culture that we have to face. It is not merely a sociological fact of life with which we find ourselves forced to compromise. It is a theological fact also—a fact of creation. The world is full of a number of different things. To acknowledge the creator is to take up a *positive* attitude toward the fact of pluralism. At the same time we do not subscribe to pluralism as an end in itself, because of any tentativeness concerning the ultimacy of Jesus Christ. On the contrary, we affirm pluralism *because* we affirm the ultimacy of Jesus Christ. We subscribe to it because we are not wise enough or good enough to say with finality exactly who Jesus Christ is and what is meant by His ultimacy, and certainly not what this means in any given situation; and even *this* we know only because we confess Jesus Christ as Lord. We know, for example, that the virtues of the non-Christians are always a judgment upon Christians and frequently mitigate the concrete evils of which Christians are the agents.

When we view our situation from the standpoint of Creation, Fall, Incarnation, and Eschatalogy we know above all else that there is no neat correlation between our intentions and our historic successes, nor between our historic successes and the providence of God.

INDEX

Abraham: call of, 41

Absence: of God, 15, 101, 131–41 passim; of presence, 15–16

Act(s): agent of, 45n2, 69, 300; and identity, 107, 121–22; and the concept "I," 172; and will, 119–21, 299–300; as enacted designs, 150; assumption grounding, 82; Austin's view of speech, 56n10; difference between potentiality and, 106; difference between self and, 191; distinction from behavior, 182; entered into with lucidity, 47n4; God is, 107; human, 67, 149; in relation to faith, 120–24, 149; integration of motor, 85; involvement with existence and guilt, 284, 291–94; mindbodily, 81; myths as intimations of, 66; novelty of, 298; of absolute evil, 134; of coming to know, 80; of electronic machines, 70; of God, 151, 157, 176, 298; of movement into speech, 59; of persons, 69, 171–76, 298; of rebellion, 157; of reflection, 86, 239–40; of speaking and writing, 79, 88, 239–45, 253, 259, 268; of suicide, 158, 161–65, 177; of using "I," 165; personal backing behind, 55, 64; policy statements and, 61; second-order, 83; sovereignty over some, 35; tacit component of, 84; unable to reveal will of agent, 299–300; Wisdom's view of novels as, 51

Action(s), 43–73; Braithwaithe's policy assertion for, 59; Christ points to, 111; concept of, 68–71; decisions and responsible, 209; Fact-Statements and, 213; hero's in presence of death, 178; history and, 71–72, 209; in relation to myth and stories, 61–62; mindbodily being-in-the-world as condition for, 82; moral, 40; personal I and, 110–11; related to grace, 127, 129; related to place, status, and room, 39; respecting the future, 120; space as field of, 23; speech as, 56, 56n10; ultimate attitudes enter into, 333; view of Ryle, 182n8, 187

Adam: myth of, 39, 157, 280–81

Agent: and cause, 88; of actions, 69–71; of intentions, 119; of particular acts, 45n2, 64; of the destruction of values, 293; radical, 162–63; transcends acts, 149

Alienation, 100, 132, 140; Percy's view of, 235–36, 245

Anxiety, 279–87; of Pascal, 40; over being awake, 126; over death, 187

Argument: a post–*Polanyian Meditations*, 19; as both serious and impossible, 318, 321; Augustine's concerning God's foreknowledge and freedom, 143; connection with assumptions in Polanyi, 79, 81; eschatological myths in theological, 73; notion of, 322–26; of *Personal Knowledge*, 75, 91; understanding personhood issues in forms of the ontological, 45n2

Aristotle, 144, 147

Assumption(s), 45, 85, 74, 91, 126; implicit of second-order accounts, 74;